ORGANIZATIONAL BEHAVIOUR
AN INTRODUCTORY TEXT

ORGANIZATIONAL BEHAVIOUR
AN INTRODUCTORY TEXT

David A. Buchanan   Andrzej A. Huczynski
University of Glasgow

Prentice/Hall PHI International

ENGLEWOOD CLIFFS, NEW JERSEY   LONDON   MEXICO   NEW DELHI
RIO DE JANEIRO   SINGAPORE   SYDNEY   TOKYO   TORONTO

To our parents

British Library Cataloguing in Publication Data

Buchanan, David A.
  Organizational behaviour: an introductory text.
  1. Organizational behaviour
  I. Title   II. Huczynski, Andrzej
  302. 3'5   HD 58.7

  ISBN 0-13-641069-3

Prentice-Hall Inc., *Englewood Cliffs, New Jersey*
Prentice-Hall International (UK) Ltd., *London*
Prentice-Hall of Australia Pty Ltd., *Sydney*
Prentice-Hall Canada Inc., *Toronto*
Prentice-Hall Hispanoamericana S.A., *Mexico*
Prentice-Hall of India Private Ltd., *New Delhi*
Prentice Hall of Japan Inc., *Tokyo*
Prentice-Hall of Southeast Asia Pte Ltd., *Singapore*
Editora Prentice-Hall do Brasil Ltda., *Rio de Janeiro*

Printed and bound in Great Britain for
Prentice-Hall International (UK) Ltd.,
66 Wood Lane End, Hemel Hempstead, Hertfordshire, HP2 4RG
by A. Wheaton & Co. Ltd., Exeter

8   90 89 88

Contents *

* Each chapter starts with a list of key concepts and objectives, and ends with a list of sources.

FOREWORD

Individuals learn about organizational behaviour mostly from their personal experience of organizations. They cannot avoid joining organizations. Having done so they must cope as best they may with sometimes capricious demands of bosses and adjust to what their peers say and do. The pursuit of valued personal aims in organizational settings and fulfilling obligations to respected others also play their part in the coping process. Given space to make choices and the courage to make them, the individual will also learn by experiencing the consequences of choosing. All these experiences provide raw material for generalizing about cause and effect; all individuals develop their own home made organization theories. We are all do-it-yourself social scientists. Even University social scientists behave in the University setting much as lay persons do. It is only as professional observers of organizations that they deploy to the full their tool-kit of methods of observation and theory building. We are all theorists of organizational behaviour because our mental and emotional balance depends on our making sense of and coping with our surroundings. We are also applied social "scientists" because our own organizational behaviour is driven to some extent by the theories we espouse, although it has been observed that some of us have "public theories" which we stress in conversation and argument, which are different from the, presumably, less reputable "private theories" that govern our actions. We sometimes change our theories when we see that they do not explain or predict events very well. More commonly, we derive personal comfort by attributing the unexpected to the moral, political or mental shortcomings of others. In this way our theories deteriorate into unsupported prejudices, less-than-wise 'saws' and dogmatic opinions.

Patently our organizations are far from being perfect instruments to accomplish the purposes for which they were intended. Since the theories of those who design and run them are learned by coping, one might expect that the attempts of professional social scientists to apply scientific rigour to the study of organizational behaviour would be welcomed universally. That is certainly not the case. The reasons are not hard to find. To the extent that the "discoveries" of social scientific enquiry resemble the learned prejudices and opinions of the practitioner, the latter may well judge that social science applied to organizations is the expensive and painstaking pursuit of the blindingly obvious. If the discoveries do not so correspond then they could be dismissed variously as "contrary to common sense", "impractical", "subverting of cherished values" or "political propaganda" - "pure jargon" or even as an incomprehensible joke. My own experience is that the prejudices of many senior businessmen and Trade Unionists against academic social science still run very deep. The idea that social science findings should influence practice runs deeper still. We encounter the odd circumstance, or so it seems, that the systematic search for new knowledge about organizational behaviour, which is manifestly needed badly, is much less than warmly welcomed by those who could apply it with the prospect of improvement in the human condition, or whatever other valued ends they have in mind. The systematic collection of facts and opinions, social surveys as "raw material" for policy makers and as information for the interested citizen, is of course now commonplace. This is, however, far from accepting the construction which tested theoretical know-ledge might put on such facts and opinions.

The authors of this book are not alone in remarking that the same scepticism does not arise in the case of the experimental sciences (such as physics) or in the case of science-based arts such as engineering, medicine and weather forecasting. The "wonders" of science as reflected in modern electronic information processing machines, manufacturing robots, deep sea oil exploitation and new healing drugs and treatments are readily judged as "good"; as further evidence of the acceleration and consolidation of mankind's conquest of nature and as creating wealth for further investment and consumption, actually and potentially adding to the material quality of life, to greater leisure and improved health. Examples of the disastrous economic and social concomitants of some scientific and technological advances, as in Concorde and some aspects of space exploration, are readily accepted as the inevitable price of progress.

Our social arrangements on the other hand, and especially those for the smooth absorption of technological change are full of conflict and inefficiency, as even a cursory glance at the media shows. We never speak of the "wonders" of social science. Management, which should surely be one of the arts based on social science is far from being so anywhere. There are of course exceptional managers who use social science findings and methods. Most managers are trained initially to be technologists, engineers, accountants and financiers. Such training as they might receive in psychology, social psychology and sociology is usually too short, too late and too dangerously superficial. Those managers whose professional bias is apparently to social science, eg personnel specialists, tend to be regarded not as expert advisors on the diagnosis and prognosis of organizational ills, but rather as dissolvers of organizational impediments to the pursuit of economic and technical goals, or tidiers of the human mess left by ill considered organizational decisions on economic, structural and procedural matters.

There are several plausible explanations for the pretty dismal failure of the social science of organizations to establish itself as a legitimate scientific endeavour, an acceptable basis for the art of management in whatever sphere (business, hospitals, trade unions, political parties, the Civil Service) and as part of the tool-kit of the well informed citizen.

In the first place the social sciences, like the experimental and applied sciences, have in their development spawned many specialisms and sub-specialisms, experimental psychology (which is more like the physical sciences), social psychology (where experiment is difficult), occupational psychology, cognitive psychology, psycho-analysis, macro-sociology, urban sociology, industrial/organizational sociology, social anthropology, cultural anthropology and so on. Each discipline develops its own academic networks, its own journals and jargon and insofar as its members are interested in behaviour in organizations, they look at those aspects of it which would enable them to make fresh discoveries within the boundaries of their sub-discipline, focussing on problems defined as central to it, and using and developing ideas, models and methods of investigation designed to advance knowledge of such problems. The audience for the reports of these discoveries and methods are mostly other researchers and eventually the students who will be taught from monographs, articles and textbooks containing knowledge which has been 'received' by the discipline. To the lay student (eg manager, or a Trade Union official; or the man in the street) the task of fitting the pieces together to arrive at a composite perspective on organizational behaviour, is almost impossible. It is difficult even for a specialist to keep up with what is going on in other specialisms whose field of study is behaviour in organizations. Small wonder they stick to their own DIY theories.

Secondly, the research has for the most part addressed itself to the empirical study of theoretical puzzles without much thought as to whether the solutions to the puzzles would cast light on difficulties and issues as experienced by practitioners. The social scientist should not I think attach himself to any one organizational group, managers for example, and take their problems (as they define them) as the sole object of investigation. Rather, he should define his own problems (puzzles) but try to ensure that as far as possible that they are recognizable as likely to throw light on the difficulties of practitioners, that the methods used to collect and process data are understandable and accessible and that the language in which the results are published is easily translated into practitioner parlance.

For example, one of the puzzles sociologists, social anthropologists and social psychologists, myself amongst them, have addressed is "why and in what circumstances do working groups tend to establish output norms regarded by others as restrictive?", and much is known now about this phenomenon. An associated problem/issue for managers, trade unionists, work group members could be "what would be the consequences of a unilateral attempt by management or unions where such norms exist and are considered restrictive to try to diminish worker control? What would happen if this were attempted by reorganizing the work, the technical layout, the procedures for allocating work and recording performance, and the pay system? Would these consequences be worth avoiding?" Faced with such an issue a knowledge of the research findings would enable focussed diagnostic questions to be asked and a course of action planned.

Another puzzle relates to technical innovation; "in what circumstances and for what reasons are technical innovations likely to be impeded in implementation by whom and at what cost to whom?". The associated issue/problem is "what would be the most effective way, given the circumstances, to organize the introduction of new technology in a way that minimizes the costs and maximizes the benefits to everyone involved?". In this case the seekers of solutions to the puzzle have also evolved systematic ways to resolve the issue -some of which have been tested in action. Reference is made to these in parts 4 and 5 of this book.

Thirdly, organizations themselves divide into specialisms and sub-specialisms, R & D, marketing and Sales, Purchasing, Finance and Accounting, Management services, Personnel, Manufacturing for example and within them, sub-specialisms like Production Planning and Control, home sales, overseas sales, project management and training and career planning, to name just a few that might exist in a medium to large manufacturing concern. Each of these professional activities is based on a body of knowledge useful in its application to the organization, each having its own procedures for advancing it and each having within it assumptions and theories about organization behaviour.

A production planner for example confronted with the perfectly reasonable idea that up-to-date knowledge of social psychology could be an essential part of his mental tool-kit might be puzzled to know why, since the out-of-date knowledge of social psychology that might be implicit in his professional behaviour seems to serve him very well and no-one that he respects is pressing him to change it. He might also have a view of organization which inclines him to the view that 'people problems' are of no concern to him but are the province of the senior management and the personnel specialist. To spread through and across the specialisms a common knowledge-based and continually updated approach to organizational behaviour is a different task and a lengthy and expensive one in which the calculable short-term costs are more sharply in focus than the possible long-term benefits.

For all these reasons it is best to introduce those who will work in organizations early in their professional training as engineers, accountants, scientists or whatever to the fields of knowledge which contribute to our understanding of organization with especial emphasis on the methods used to observe behaviour and to analyse it and to arrive at a conclusion. These can be the basis on which diagnostic questions can later be framed. Particular research findings are important but less so since these will be under greater challenge subsequently than the methods.

There are those to be found particularly amongst the designers of the professional curricula, who argue that the course time tables are already too crowded to admit more than a short superficial treatment of what 'after all is somebody else's professional stuff', and who also prefer to place such studies at the very end of a professional course as an add-on on the grounds that it is not easy to understand about organizational behaviour until one has reached some level of professional maturity: and that the methods of the professional discipline must come first as well as the induction into the profession, its mysteries and its preservation.

That, to my mind is a mistaken view (I might add that I also believe that social science professionals should be introduced early to science and technology). It signals to the student what is important and what isn't and leads to the tendency mentioned in the text of this volume for scientists and engineers to regard the psychological and social sciences as less exact and less intellectually exacting. Any reader coming fresh to them via this book will find that this is very far from the truth.

Buchanan and Huczynski have done valuable service in giving teachers in higher education a text on which to base an introduction to organizational behaviour. They accurately report the research methods and findings of those social and psychological sciences which study organizational behaviour from every aspect and level - individual, group, organization - and match them to the issues that could well be of concern to the practitioner. The matter in this book should I think be presented in parallel with and not before or after professional studies and as far as possible integrated with them. The 'maturity' argument is spurious because even schoolboys "know" about organizations in the sense of having experience in some of them and so having something to start with.

One day the necessary task of developing a new comprehensive discipline of organizational behaviour which integrates the methods and findings of those disciplines which have something significant to say about it will be completed. It is encouraging that so many steps are now being taken in that direction. This book is one of them. It tackles the three obstacles to the acceptance of the social science of organization discussed above and unlike so many others, it has a special British, even Scottish, flavour both in its examples and in its encouragement of the participation of students in the process of learning, in itself a valuable skill for future work in organizations.

Tom Lupton
Manchester Business School
January 1985

Acknowledgements

We would like to thank Dr E. A. Johns of Slough College of Higher Education and Giles Wright of Prentice-Hall for their consistently helpful and valuable comments and advice. We would also like to thank the other anonymous reviewers whose suggestions have enabled us to improve the text.

Guide to the book

This book has three objectives:

1. To provide a basic introduction to the study of human behaviour in organizations for students with little or no previous social science education. This book is intended to serve as a starting point for further study in the area. We hope to stimulate interest in the subject and an enthusiasm for more knowledge.
2. To make the subject matter of social science applied to the study of organizations intelligible to students from various different backgrounds.
3. To confront and overcome the prejudice that some natural science, engineering and other professional groups of students hold regarding the importance and value of social science to their own spheres of activity.

This text is aimed primarily at readers new to organizational behaviour and to social science. Organizational behaviour is currently taught at various levels and on courses where the main subjects are not social sciences. Accountants, lawyers, engineers, teachers, architects, data processing specialists, personnel managers, bankers, hoteliers, surveyors and nurses, for example, often have no background in social science, but find themselves studying organizational behaviour as part of professional examination schemes.

We have written this book mainly for British students, but have tried to stimulate awareness of the cultural and political factors that affect the applicability of social science research findings across cultures. Most texts in this field are American, and the American contribution to the field has been great. But American experience does not always travel well to other parts of the world. Social science theories can be culture bound in ways that natural science cannot be, as laws and traditions vary from country to country.

We have written this book from a multidisciplinary social science perspective. Our understanding of organizations is derived from several social science disciplines. Most organizational behaviour texts adopt either a managerial or a sociological perspective. Our readers are not all going to be managers or sociologists, and many people beyond these two occupations need an understanding of organizational behaviour. If one is going to work for, work with, resist or subvert organizations, then one needs to know why and how they exist and function.

We have used a format and style more structured than commonly found in applied social science texts. Each chapter begins with a list of the key concepts to be covered, and a set of objectives for readers to achieve. The aim of these features is to encourage an active approach to the text. We have attempted to make the book interesting by using novel, varied and unusual material. Examples, illustrations, exercises and cases are used to break up the pace, rhythm and appearance of the text and make it more digestible. We hope to challenge readers by inviting them to confront real, practical and theoretical problems and issues for themselves. Readers are invited at several points throughout the text to stop reading and to consider controversial points, individually or in group discussion.

The style and content of the book reflect the teaching approaches that we use in our own courses in organizational behaviour. We would not teach *to* a text like this, but teach *from* it. We expect that this text will be used:

1. To introduce basic concepts and theories to students beginning their study of social science and organizational behaviour, to enable them to turn more quickly to specialized and advanced texts in the field.
2. As a basis for discussion. Many of the issues covered are controversial, and we have in general avoided presenting personal or popular resolutions. There are no "right answers" to organizational behaviour questions. We have throughout the text presented contrasting perspectives and ways of thinking about the issues involved.

We have attempted to avoid jargon, and to explain terms clearly where appropriate. Ideas and theories build systematically through the text, from individual psychology, through group social psychology, to organizational sociology and politics. Each chapter attempts to cover practical as well as theoretical ground, to demonstrate the practical relevance and use of social science ideas. Theories and concepts are not simply presented here in an academic vacuum.

Each chapter is self contained. The understanding of one is not dependent on a prior reading of others, although in practice the topics are closely interrelated. The book can be used as the basis of a one year course which covers two parts of the book a term for the first two terms and one part in the third (summer) term. The material does not however have to be covered in the sequence in which it appears in the text, and individual lecturers may wish not to cover some of the material that is introduced here.

We have listed at the end of each chapter the main sources that we have found useful in understanding the topic covered and in writing the chapter. The needs and interests of the teachers and students who will use this book are likely to be wide. We leave to them the responsibilities for selecting and consulting further works.

David A. Buchanan
Andrzej A. Huczynski
Glasgow, 1985

Chapter 1

Introduction

The study of organizations

The organizational dilemma

Key concepts:

Once you have understood this chapter, you should be able to define the following concepts in your own words:

> Organizational behaviour
> Organization
> Controlled performance

Objectives:

On completing this chapter, you should be able:

1. To appreciate the importance and value of the study of organizational behaviour.
2. To summarize the major dilemma of organizational design.

THE STUDY OF ORGANIZATIONS

Groups of people can achieve much more than individuals acting alone. The quality and standard of life that we experience can be improved by tackling human needs and problems collectively. Human beings, like many of the other creatures on this planet, are social animals. We enjoy the company of other people. We thus get psychological satisfaction and material gain from organized activity.

Our society is heavily dependent on collective, organized activity. Organizations have a strong claim to the title of dominant institution in contemporary industrial societies. The ultimate limitation on human goals is not human intelligence or technology, but our ability to work together effectively in organizations. If we eventually destroy this planet, the main cause will not be nuclear weapons. We will have destroyed it with ineffective forms of organization. The study of human behaviour in organizations is thus recognized as an important area in its own right.

Definition

The study of *organizational behaviour* is: "the study of the structure, functioning and performance of organizations, and the behaviour of groups and individuals within them."

From D. S. Pugh (ed), *Organization Theory: Selected Readings*, Penguin Books, Harmondsworth, 1971, page 9.

Organizations of course do not "behave". Only people can be said to behave. The term organizational behaviour is a verbal shorthand which refers to the activities and interactions of people in organizational settings like factories, schools, hospitals and banks.

Organizations pervade our social, cultural, political, economic and physical environment. We tend to take organizations for granted because they affect everything that we do, but this familiarity can lead to an underestimation of their impact. It is not possible to live in our society and claim that you are not influenced by organizations.

The study of organizations is multidisciplinary, drawing mainly from sociology, social psychology, psychology and economics, and to a lesser extent from history, politics, geography and anthropology. The study of organizational behaviour is a separate discipline, but is an area in which the contributions of the different social sciences can be integrated. The extent of that integration, however, is still weak.

STOP!

Organizations are difficult to define. Before you read on, consider the

following list. Decide which of these you would call organizations and
which not.

- A chemicals processing company
- The Jones family
- The University of Glasgow
- A general hospital
- Rangers football club
- The MacKenzie clan

- The local squash club
- A baby sitting circle
- A mountaineering society
- A biscuit manufacturer
- The Azande tribe
- The local school

Organizations affect everything you do

This advertisement appeared in *The Sunday Times*, June 8, 1980.

**If you don't wash
or use deodorant, shave
or wear make-up,
eat, feed your dog,
work on a farm or wear wellies,
drive a car,
play records, go on holidays,
or stay at home,
sleep on a mattress
or take pills, comb your hair
or wear a hat,
brush your teeth or wear
false ones, go to the movies,
watch television,
listen to the radio,
buy books or read newspapers,
then BP
doesn't affect your life.**

Almost every minute of every day you're within reach of something
in which BP products play a part.
   One of the reasons, perhaps, why we're one of the most successful
companies in the world.
   Come to that, without chemicals like ours, printers couldn't print
the newspaper you're reading now. **BP Britain at its best.**

Reproduced by permission of BP.

So what makes organizations different? Why did you feel uncomfortable
about calling some of the items on that list organizations? Perhaps you

considered size? Some of these are places where people are employed for money, and maybe you thought that was an important distinguishing feature? Difficult, is it not?

Now consider the following definition:

Definition

Organizations are social arrangements for the controlled performance of collective goals.

This definition should explain why you found it awkward to label a family or a baby sitting circle as an organization, but not a chemicals company, a university or a hospital. Let us examine it more closely.

Social arrangements

Organizations are collections of people who interact with each other in a particular way because of their common membership of a particular group. But all of the items in our list are social arrangements, and this feature is therefore not unique to organizations.

Collective goals

Organizations exist where individuals acting alone cannot achieve goals that are considered worthwhile pursuing. But again, all of the phenomena in the list are social arrangements for the pursuit of collective goals, and this feature is therefore not unique to organizations either.

Controlled performance

Organizations are concerned with performance in the pursuit of their goals. The performance of an organization as a whole determines its survival. The performance of a department determines its survival within the organization and the amounts of resources allocated to it. The performance of individuals determines their pay and promotion prospects.

Not any level of performance will do, however. We live in a world in which the resources available to us are not sufficient to meet all of our conceivable needs. We have to make the most efficient use of those scarce resources. Levels of performance of individuals, departments, and organizations, are therefore tied to standards which determine what counts as inadequate, satisfactory, or good.

It is necessary to control performance, to ensure that it is either good enough, or that something is being done to improve it. Control involves setting standards, measuring performance against standards, taking decisions about the extent to which performance is satisfactory, and taking appropriate action to correct deviations from standards.

Organization members have to perform these control functions as well as the operating tasks required to fulfil the collective purpose of the organization. The need for controlled performance leads to a deliberate and ordered allocation of functions, or division of labour, between organization members. The activities and interactions of members are also intentionally programmed and structured.

Admission to membership of organizations is controlled. The price of failure to perform to standard is usually loss of membership. The need for controlled performance leads to the establishment of authority relationships between members. The controls work only where members comply with the orders of those responsible for performing the control functions.

The Jones family, the MacKenzie clan, the baby sitting circle and the Azande tribe are not preoccupied with performance. Their continued existence does not depend on satisfactory performance. They do not allocate control functions to monitor performance, do not order and programme their activities, and do not control their relationships and membership. That is why we are reluctant to call them "organizations".

The *preoccupation with performance* and the *need for control* distinguish organizations from other forms of social arrangements.

STOP!

What about the squash club? What features would you use to decide whether or not it is an organization?

In what ways could a family be said to be concerned with performance and control?

Are organizations different from other forms of social arrangements in degree only, rather than different in kind?

THE ORGANIZATIONAL DILEMMA

Organizations do not have goals. Only people have goals. Collectively, the members of an organization may be making biscuits, building houses, curing patients, educating students and so on, but individual members pursue a variety of goals of their own. Senior managers may decide on objectives and attempt to get others to agree with them by calling them "organizational goals"; but they are still the goals of the people who determined them in the first place.

Efficiency versus human values.

This cartoon appeared in *Punch* on September 18, 1974.

Reproduced by permission of Punch

Organizations are efficient ways of producing the goods and services that we consider useful and essential to our way of life. But organizations mean different things to the different people who use them and who work in them. Organizations are also sources of:

- money, physical resources
- meaning, relevance, purpose
- order, stability
- security, support, protection
- status, prestige, self esteem, self confidence
- power, authority, control

The goals that individual members of an organization seek to achieve are quite different from the collective purpose of their organized activity. This creates a central practical and theoretical problem in the design and study of organizations. Individual goals may be inconsistent with the collective purpose of the organization.

STOP!

What are the stated objectives of the organization to which you currently belong?

What are your own reasons for being a member of this organization?

Can you identify the points at which these organizational and personal objectives overlap and diverge?

The need for control over the use of resources creates opportunities for some human beings to control others. Organizations are social arrangements in which people strive to achieve control over the use of resources to produce goods and services efficiently. Some individual members therefore hold positions from which they control and coordinate the activities of others in the interests of the organization as a whole. But organizations are also political systems in which people strive to achieve control over each other to gain status, wealth and power.

The power to define the collective purposes or goals of organizations is not evenly distributed among their members. One of the main mechanisms of control in organizations is hierarchy of authority. Managers at the top of the hierarchy wear business suits and sit in comfortable offices. They take decisions on behalf of workers at the bottom of the hierarchy on shop floors, who wear boiler suits and operate machine tools. Members who have little or no such influence usually have to comply, or leave. Organizations attract the complaint that they dominate the liberty of the individual.

The concern with performance leads to work that is simple and monotonous and to strict rules and procedures which employees are expected to follow. These features may contribute to the efficiency with which collective activity can be carried out because they simplify the tasks of planning, organizing, coordinating and controlling the efforts of large numbers of people. The need for efficiency, however, conflicts with human values such as individual freedom, creativity and development. It is difficult to design organizations that are efficient both in using resources and in developing human potential.

Many of the "human" problems of organizations can be identified as conflicts between individual human needs, and the constraints imposed on individuals in the interests of the collective purpose of the organization. Attempts to coordinate and control human behaviour are thus often self-defeating.

But that is a pessimistic view. Organizations are social arrangements, constructed by people who can also change them. Organizations can be designed to provide opportunities for self-fulfilment and individual expression. The point is that the human consequences of organizations are not automatic. They depend on how organizations are designed and run.

SOURCES

Pugh, D. S. (ed.), 1971, *Organization Theory: Selected Readings*, Penguin Books, Harmondsworth.

Chapter 2

Natural and social science

The social sciences are different

Social science research methods and designs

Key concepts:

Once you have understood this chapter, you should be able to define the following concepts in your own words:

Behaviour	Phenomenology
Behaviourism	Research method
Positivism	Research design
Action	Internal validity
Cognitive psychology	External validity

Objectives:

On completing this chapter, you should be able:

1.   To identify the features that differentiate the natural and social sciences.
2.   To understand the research implications of the fact that people attach meanings and purposes to what they do.
3.   To describe the various research methods and designs that social scientists use.
4.   To explain the criteria on which the findings of social science research can be evaluated.

THE SOCIAL SCIENCES ARE DIFFERENT

Are the social sciences really "sciences"? Can we study human behaviour in the same way that we study the behaviour of chemicals or metals? The study of organizational behaviour involves the use of what are called social sciences. Many natural scientists argue that it is not possible to submit people to any study that can be called scientific. If the standards of investigation applied by the natural sciences cannot be applied to the study of people, then that study cannot be recognized as scientific. Some social scientists also deny that they are "scientists" in the way that biologists, chemists and astronomers are scientists. This book is based on the findings of social science research. If there are doubts about that research, we must examine them before we begin.

The contribution of the social sciences to human knowledge is often regarded with scepticism and suspicion. It is easy to demonstrate the practical value of the natural sciences. The published output of the social sciences is vast, but does not appear to help to put people on the moon, build transport and telecommunication networks, or find cures for heart disease and cancer. Textbooks in electrical engineering, naval architecture and quantum mechanics tell the reader how the world works and how to do things. Students from such disciplines find sociology texts disappointing because they do not appear to contain useful messages of that kind. Social science texts often pose questions rather than answer them.

Human beings and their organizations are not beyond the reach of scientific study. The aim of this section is to give readers a chance to assess this claim for themselves. We wish to overcome prejudice that is based on misunderstanding of social science methods and what they can achieve. We wish to encourage critical assessment of social science, based on an understanding of the problems that face all students of human beings.

The natural sciences are able to rely on:

- Direct observation;
- Consistent relationships between variables through time and space;
- Experimental methods to test hypotheses;
- Mathematical reasoning.

Natural science works. We can put people on the moon, and one day will no doubt be able to prevent or cure cancers. Can the study of people ever achieve this degree of practical value?

STOP!

Here are some typical comments about the problems of social science.

These statements are taken from a questionnaire given to Scottish managers, mainly engineers and accountants, studying organizational behaviour.

Do you agree with them?

Give reasons for your answers.

_____

_____

Social science is not science because . . .

There are problems with observing and measuring:
- "Social science deals with the intangible. You cannot see motives or perceptions so you cannot measure them."
- "There are just too many variables."
- "Natural science problems are easy to express clearly and unambiguously in terms of fixed laws and precise definitions."
- "Social and human problems cannot be quantified, expressed in numbers."
- "Social science is forced to rely on the judgement of the researcher rather than on measuring instruments. It is based on intuition and guesswork."

There are problems with establishing cause and effect:
- "You cannot observe cause and effect."
- "People cannot be studied like chemicals and metals. They do not behave in consistent ways."
- "People change, so you cannot repeat experiments under the same conditions."
- "You cannot conduct controlled experiments on individuals and groups of people, so you cannot test hypotheses."
- "The presence of the researcher influences the activity studied."

There are problems with generalizing findings and making predictions:
- "People have attitudes, ideologies, philosophies and per-spectives that change over time, and differ from culture to culture, so we cannot make generalizations."
- "Nature is well ordered, but people act irrationally and are subject to group pressures."

Therefore:
- "The social sciences have no practical, material, tangible, economic benefit."

_____

These statements (except the last one) are broadly accurate reflections of the problems facing social science. In a fuller treatment we would qualify these statements, and add some more. The goals of science are description, explanation, prediction and control of events. These represent increasing levels of sophistication in the scientific endeavour. Some natural and social science work is content to stop at description of what is going on. The problems of social science can therefore be summarized as follows:

goals of science	practical implications	social science problems
Description	Measurement	Invisible variables People change Ambiguous variables
Explanation	Identify the time order of events	Timing of events not always clear
	Establish causal links between variables	Cannot always see interactions
Prediction	Generalization from one setting to another	Uniqueness, complexity and lack of comparability between human phenomena
Control	Manipulation	Moral and legal constraints

These problems become criticisms only if we expect social science to conform to natural science practices. If the study of people is a different kind of enterprise from the study of metals and chemicals, then we need different procedures to advance our understanding. Social science may be a different kind of science from the natural sciences. Social scientists are divided on the nature of their work.

Some social scientists argue that there is a "unity of method" in the study of natural and human phenomena. The theoretical basis of this argument is that human behaviour is governed by general, universal laws of the same kind that govern the behaviour of natural phenomena. One practical implication of this perspective is a concern with refining social science techniques. Greater care is taken to define terms unambiguously, to measure and quantify, to conduct controlled experiments, and to overcome the potential bias created by the researcher's presence. Social scientists may just have to work harder to achieve rigour in their work. A second practical implication of this perspective is a concern with producing a "social technology" that can be used to control human beings as effectively as we use conventional technology to control the natural world.

Our argument is that social and natural sciences are fundamentally different. The study of people cannot become more scientific by simply following more closely the procedures of the natural scientist. The main differences and their practical implications can be examined under the four objectives of description, explanation, prediction and control.

Description

There are three methods by which social scientists produce descriptions of the phenomena they study. These are observation, asking questions, and studying written documents. These three basic methods can be used in various ways. The people studied may or may not know that they are the subjects of research. Questions can be asked in person by the researcher, or through a questionnaire. Written documents may be diaries, letters, company reports, or published works. Natural scientists use only observation. Metals and chemicals cannot respond to interrogation and do not write their memoirs.

Some of the interesting variables in social science, like motives and learning, cannot be observed. Where observation is possible, it can be difficult to give unambiguous definitions that can be used to provide reliable measurements. Consider, for example, how you might define aggression to measure its occurrence at student dances. We must use terms like this consistently.

This need not create difficulties. Consider the process of learning, for example. As you read through this book, we would like you to think that you are indeed learning something. But if someone could open your skull as you read, they would find nothing much going on inside to which they could point and call "the learning process". Some changes must take place inside your head if learning is to occur, but neuro-physiological techniques are not yet sophisticated enough to track down the physical and biochemical events involved (although we do know something about the general nature of these events). This has not stopped psychologists from using the concept of "learning", and we now have a good knowledge of the process and how to make it more effective.

We could, for example, test your knowledge of organizational behaviour before you read this book, and repeat the test afterwards. We would of course expect the second set of test results to be much higher than the first. So we can *infer* that learning has occurred. Your ability to carry out a particular task has changed, and we can use that change to lead us to the factors that caused it. We can study the inputs to the learning process in terms of teachers, learners, abilities, time and resources. We can study the teaching process in terms of methods and materials. We can study the outputs from the process in terms of changes in learner behaviour. The relationships between the variables involved can be identified. Our understanding of the learning process can thus develop systematically and we can suggest ways of improving it.

Difficulties arise when we have to rely on individuals' accounts of what they are doing. Observation is limited. What could you say about a man's motives by merely observing his behaviour in a bar ? He could be there for a large number of different reasons, which we could not guess by watching him. Eventually we would have to ask him. The answers that we get are our research data. The validity of those data, as an accurate reflection of the truth of the situation, may be dubious for three reasons.

First, the person may deliberately lie. He may be waiting for the colleague with whom he is about to rob the bank next door. He may be enjoying his solitude and resent the intrusion of a social scientist. People hide their motives from others for a variety of reasons. There are ways in which we can check the accuracy of what people tell us, but this is not always possible and is often inconvenient.

Second, the person may tell us what he thinks we want to hear. People rarely lie to researchers. They create problems by being helpful. The man in the bar may simplify his answer rather than spend time relating a complex tale of intrigue, heartbreak and family strife. The acceptable answer is preferable to no answer at all, especially where the person feels that he should have an answer. People may tell us that their attitude to a particular piece of current government legislation is favourable, although they have never studied its content and effects.

Third, the person may not know. Human beings possess minds, and social sciences study what goes on in them. The mental processes behind human motivation operate without our conscious effort. Few of us take the effort to dig these processes out from our unconscious and examine them critically. Most of us get through life quite happily without teasing our minds with questions like "why am I here?", and "what am I doing?". The researcher gets the answers that the person is consciously aware of. The lack of self-critical examination can lead to self-deception. The man in the bar may be an ageing academic who wants to be seen in the company of the younger clients of that establishment because that suits his personal image. He is not likely to tell a researcher this. He is more likely to give a rational answer that he believes is more acceptable.

Explanation

It is usually possible to infer that one event has caused another (or to infer causality) where the variables or phenomena are not visible. If your organizational behaviour test score is higher after reading this book than before, and if you have not been studying other relevant material at the same time, then we infer that reading this book has caused you to improve your performance. The relative timing of events is sometimes hard to establish. Causes must happen before the effects they are said to explain. Many managers believe that being a woman causes you to be able to tolerate repetitive and boring work better than men. But if women are brought up in our society to believe and expect that the work available to them will be repetitive, the causal arrow may point the other way. The existence of such work may in fact predate the development of female acceptance of it.

The "laws" that govern human behaviour are different from the laws that govern the behaviour of natural phenomena. The way in which we understand causality in human affairs thus has to be different.

Consider the meteorological law that "clouds mean rain". That holds invariably around the planet. A cloud cannot break that law, either deliberately or by accident. The behaviour of the cloud is determined by natural forces, and the cloud does not have to be told about raining. It has no choice. Compare this with the human law that "red means stop" to motor car drivers. We can choose, because some people are red–green colour blind, to change to a system in which blue means stop. The human driver can get it wrong, by deliberately jumping the light, or by not concentrating and going through it accidentally. We learn the rules of our society from the actions of others. We can choose to disobey them.

The social scientist cannot expect to discover rules that govern human behaviour and that are consistent across time and place. The cloud comes into existence with an inbuilt set of guidelines on how to behave. Human beings are not born with such a guide to behaviour. We have to learn the rules that apply in our society. The rules differ from society to society, from culture to culture, and differ within societies and through time.

Human beings are self-interpreting. We attach meanings to what we do. We can ask car assembly workers why they strike. We cannot ask a car body why it rusts. Natural science has to stop at discovering how things happen. The social scientist has to go further, to ask why — to explore the reasons that people have for their behaviour.

People behave in accordance with their own theories and understanding of how the world works. These are not rigorously and systematically formulated. We do not subject them to critical scrutiny and evaluation. We share this understanding with others in our society, and we act competently without being objective and scientific about what we do. We know what behaviour is appropriate in particular situations, and what is not. We take our theories of how the world works for granted. We regard our knowledge of how society works as common sense.

We behave in accordance with our own theories of the world . . .

"Every act of a manager rests on assumptions about what has happened and conjectures about what will happen; that is to say it rests on theory. Theory and practice are inseparable. As a cynic once put it: when someone says he is a practical man, what he means is that he is using old fashioned theories."

From D. S. Pugh (ed), *Organization Theory: Selected Readings*, Penguin Books, Harmondsworth, 1971, pp. 9-10.

We live in a social and organizational world in which "reality" means different things to different people. We live in a world of multiple realities. The natural scientist does not have to work with this complication. Our view of reality depends on our social position, and is influenced in particular by our organizational position. Managers and manufacturing operators for example tend to have different views of the role and value of trade unions.

Social science uses common words in unusual and special ways. The medical profession on the other hand uses special terms. Your sore throat, for example, is laryngitis to the doctor. This special use of language is necessary to ensure rigour and consistency in our thinking. The problem is that the "technical" terms of the social scientist are often words that most people use all the time, and this can lead to confusion if we are not careful. To clarify our argument up to this point, it is necessary to introduce two such terms:

Definition

Behaviour is the term given to the things that human beings do that can be directly detected by the senses of others.

We see you walk, hear you talk, smell your perfume, touch your hair and taste your cooking. There is a school of psychology called *behaviourism* that confines its studies to human phenomena that can be detected in these ways. This view of human beings seems to be incomplete and restrictive. People have thought processes and images of the world around them. These processes and images are part of our daily conscious experience, they influence our behaviour, and thus deserve to be objects of study in the same way as observable behaviour. There is a school of sociology called *positivism* that restricts its investigations to phenomena that can be directly observed and measured.

Definition

Action is the term given to the things that people do and the reasons that they have for doing them. Action is meaningful behaviour.

Cognitive psychology regards the internal, invisible workings of the human mind as a legitimate object of investigation. Sociologists have also adopted an action perspective, and several approaches have developed with esoteric names like phenomenology, hermeneutics, ethnomethodology, ethnography and symbolic interactionism.

We promised to avoid jargon, so we will use these rather awkward terms as little as possible. The main issue is that there are two broad standpoints from which human beings can be studied. We believe that the second of these, the action or phenomenological perspective, is more interesting and useful. The title of this book does not indicate an allegiance to behaviourism. We could have called it organizational action, but we choose to obey the rules currently in force in our academic subculture. This is an introductory text, and research from both perspectives is therefore included.

STOP !

We would like you to consider the implications of the distinction that we have just made for yourself.

What features have to be added to descriptions to produce adequate explanations of human phenomena ?

In what main ways do explanations of human behaviour differ from explanations of natural phenomena if we adopt an action or a phenomenological perspective ?

Can you identify the rules that govern:

- The way you dress for lectures ?
- Conversation topics in the student refectory ?

Prediction

Social science predictions are usually probabilistic, rather than determinate. We may be able to predict the rate of suicide in a given society or the incidence of mental illness in a particular occupational group, or the likelihood of strikes in particular types and sizes of factory. We can rarely predict whether or not specific individuals will try to kill themselves or develop schizophrenia, or forecast when a particular factory will suffer industrial action. This is not a serious limitation. We are often more interested in the behaviour of groups of people than in what individual members do. It is interesting to note that a similar restriction on predictive power also applies in quantum physics.

Social science communicates findings about people to people. Suppose that you have never thought very much about the question of the ultimate reality of human nature. One day you read a book by an American psychologist called Abraham Maslow, who tells you that human beings have a fundamental need to develop their capabilities to their full potential. He calls this the need for self-actualization. If this sounds like a good idea, and you believe it, and act accordingly, then what he has said has become true. His prediction fulfils itself. Many social science predictions are like this.

Many social science predictions are intentionally self-defeating. We can change the social arrangements that we construct. Social science research can point to the options, and show how those options may be evaluated. The social scientist is therefore in a position to tell, say, a manager, that if he treats his workforce in a particular way, they are likely to respond in a manner that the manager considers undesirable. The prediction is made in the expectation that the manager will alter his treatment of the workforce. The kinds of predictions that natural scientists make cannot have this effect on the natural phenomena that are studied.

We can discover regularities and pattern in human behaviour and action that enable us to make predictions about what people may do in given circumstances. But it is important to remember that these regularities are not fixed and universal laws of nature. They are social products, based on individuals' own interpretations of their circumstances, which are generally shared with and influenced by others in their society.

Control

Social science findings induce social change. The natural scientist does not study the natural order of things to be critical of and change that order. It does not make sense to ask whether nature could be better organized. It would not be appropriate to evaluate as good or bad the observation that gases expand in volume when heated. But social scientists are generally motivated by desires to change society, and organizations. An understanding of how things currently work is essential for that purpose. Such understanding is not necessarily an end in itself. Social science can be deliberately critical of the social and organizational order that it discovers, because that order is only one of many that human beings are capable of constructing.

This is different from controlling or manipulating human behaviour, which most people in our society would regard as immoral or unethical. We do not in fact have a social technology, comparable to "hard" technology, that enables us to do this anyway, and for this we should perhaps be grateful.

Our judgements are based on evidence, and on our values. Social science is often criticized as ideology in disguise. If you accept our argument you should see that that position is inescapable. We can evaluate the jobs that we find on a motor car assembly line. The work may be repetitive, and the workers on the line may be bored and unhappy. But management may show that regardless of the feelings of the men on the line, that system is the cheapest and fastest way of making the cars that consumers want to buy. What one says about a social or organizational arrangement thus depends on one's values. Social science text books often confuse students from other disciplines by admitting this attachment to value judgements.

We have presented two broad perspectives from which human beings are studied. Here is a brief summary of the distinctions between these two perspectives:

	perspective	
	behaviourist or positivist	*cognitive or action or phenomenological*
Description	*Studies observable behaviour*	*Studies meaningful action and the unobservable*

Explanation	Seeks fixed and universal laws that govern behaviour	Seeks individual's own understanding and interpretation of the world as basis for behaviour
Prediction	Based on knowledge of relationships between variables	Based on shared understanding and awareness of different human, social, and organizational realities
Control	Aims to shape behaviour by manipulating appropriate variables	Aims at social change by stimulating critical awareness

We have tried to convince you in this section that social science is a fundamentally different kind of enterprise from natural science. Many of the issues raised here still generate debate and are far from resolution. We hope that you will debate these issues with colleagues and teachers, whose positions may be quite different from ours. It has been our intention to present the main problems in a way that will stimulate you to think them through for yourself, rather than simply to agree with the arguments presented.

SOCIAL SCIENCE RESEARCH METHODS AND DESIGNS

This book is based on the findings of research about human behaviour in organizations. It is helpful if you know how these research findings have been produced and that you understand the issues involved in drawing conclusions and deriving theories from them.

Definition

A *research method* is a technique for collecting information or data.

As we have already mentioned, social science uses three research methods:

1. Observation;
2. Analysing documents;
3. Asking questions.

Observation

This simply means using one's senses to see, smell, touch, occasionally taste, and to listen to what is going on in a given social setting. This can be done in three ways.

First, through the use of *unobtrusive measures* the researcher can identify patterns of social activity without actually coming into direct contact with those being studied. Examples of unobtrusive measures include:

- Wear on floor coverings which identifies popular and unpopular routes through buildings;
- Seasonal variations in coffee and cigarette sales in student refectories and shops which identify the incidence of pre-examination stress.

Unobtrusive measures such as these can provide valuable insights and this research method could be used more frequently than it is at present.

Second, through *non-participant observation* the researcher is physically present but only as a spectator who does not become directly involved in the activities of the people who are being studied. The researcher's presence allows a wide range of observations to be made. But people sometimes behave abnormally in the presence of a scientific observer.

Third, through *participant observation* the researcher takes part in the activities under investigation. The researcher could for example become an assistant storekeeper in a factory, or join a group of trainee nurses. By becoming a member of the group to be studied the researcher can achieve a high level of understanding of their behaviour, feelings, values and beliefs. People being studied in this way are more likely to behave naturally, especially when they have become accustomed to the observer's presence. Non-participant observers can clearly be identified as researchers or as "outsiders" by those being studied. Participant observation is however sometimes used without the knowledge of the subjects of the research and this raises moral and ethical issues.

STOP!

Do you think that it is morally justifiable in the interests of science to study people without telling them that they are the subjects of research?

Analysing documents

Written materials, diagrams, tables and pictures are produced in a wide variety of forms which are never published in journals or books. Organizations are potentially rich sources of documentary evidence of this kind. Examples of potentially valuable documents include:

Diaries	Letters
Memoranda	Committee minutes
Equipment operating manuals	Customer or client records
Productivity analyses	Company accounts
Company policy statements	Autobiographies by key figures

There are various ways in which this kind of data can be analysed. Quantitative records can be analysed with a variety of statistical techniques. Qualitative or textual data are normally analysed by a procedure called content analysis in which the data are systematically classified into themes and subthemes.

Asking questions

This is undoubtedly the most popular social science research method and can be used in two main ways.

First, respondents can be interviewed in person by the researcher. In a structured interview, respondents are taken through a predetermined sequence of questions. In an unstructured interview, respondents are asked to talk about general themes with no determined question sequence.

Second, respondents can be asked to complete a questionnaire, sometimes called a self-report questionnaire. Questionnaires can be posted to people whom the researcher cannot meet personally, and can be completed by large numbers of people in a short period. Every respondent answers the same questions in the same sequence. Answers are in a uniform format which can be more suitable for computer analysis than the "conversational" data collected in interviews. But if a question is ambiguous and misinterpreted the researcher is not always there in person to correct the error.

The choice of method depends on the type of data required — the rich and varied data about feelings and values that an interview can produce, or the systematic and uniform coverage from a questionnaire.

STOP!

You have been asked to evaluate the opinions of your colleagues to your organizational behaviour course.

What are the advantages and disadvantages of using interviews and questionnaires to do this ?

Definition

A *research design* is a strategy or overall approach to tackling a research question or problem.

There are three broad types of research design:

1.   Experiments;
2.   Case studies;
3.   Surveys.

Experiments

Social science uses experimental research to study social phenomena in much the same way as natural science. The advantages of *laboratory experiments* lie with the control that the researcher has over the variables that are to be studied. The real world tends to vary in ways which make it difficult to establish cause and effect relationships clearly. The disadvantages of laboratory experiments lie in their artificiality. People may not behave normally in a scientific laboratory setting.

Experiments are used to measure the effects of one variable on another. Suppose we want to study the effect of Scotch whisky consumption on student examination performance. Whisky consumption is called our *independent variable*. Examination performance is called our *dependent variable* because we believe that it will depend on how much whisky students have drunk. (Note that if we were studying alcoholism among students we would want to explain why students drank alcohol and whisky consumption would be the dependent variable in such a study. You might like to consider what the independent variables could be in such research.)

The laboratory setting allows us to measure these variables very accurately. We control how much each student is given to drink and assess how well they do in our examination. Everybody works under the same conditions and the only factor that could cause variations in behaviour is the amount of whisky drunk. In the real world, all kinds of factors also vary and interfere with our ability to draw conclusions about the effects of the whisky.

Researchers are sometimes able to manipulate events in the real world and conduct *field experiments*. The work methods of one group in an organization can be changed and the effects on job satisfaction and performance compared with those in another group whose work methods have not been changed. This is less rigorous than a laboratory experiment as there are lots of factors which the researcher cannot control but which could affect the outcomes. These factors may include other organizational changes and events outside the organization in the private, domestic lives of those being studied. The main advantage however is that the experiment is conducted in a real setting. The main problem is that organizations rarely want social scientists to experiment with their members.

The *naturally occurring experiment* is the answer to that last problem. Organizations often change slowly, a section or a group at a time. This can create opportunities for researchers to simulate field experiments.

Case studies

Case studies are detailed investigations of single individuals, single groups or departments in an organization, or a whole organization. No attempt is made at experimental control although it is important to identify accurately the time order of events. Case study data can be extremely rich and varied and detailed. The sequence of events can help to establish cause and effect relationships. Case study data can be collected over an extended time series to produce what are called *longitudinal studies.*

Case study work is normally used to study new fields and to generate insights for more rigorous and systematic investigation and more carefully controlled research. This is a flexible research design which can produce interesting and valuable results in its own right. Psychoanalysis for example is based on a handful of case studies which Sigmund Freud carried out on neurotic Viennese women in the nineteenth century. Our understanding of the effects of contemporary technical change on behaviour in organizations is largely based on case studies of a number of organizations in Britain in the early 1980s.

Surveys

Surveys are perhaps the most popular social science research method and tend to be equated in the public mind with social research. They can be based on interview, questionnaire, observation or document collection and analysis methods. Surveys are *cross sectional* as they study a range, or variety, or cross section of people, occupations or organizations. This approach enables the researcher to establish a form of control over independent variables at the data analysis stage. For example, in a survey of people's voting behaviour, all respondents can be asked to reveal their age and sex as well as their voting preferences. The results for each sex and age can then be computed separately and compared to see if there are systematic differences. This is not however a true experimental approach but it is useful as the coverage can be extremely wide and the setting real rather than artificial.

Within any one research study, methods and designs can be varied and mixed according to the requirements of the topic in hand. The research design does not always dictate the methods that have to be used and vice versa. A combination of methods and designs can be used to approach the same issue from different angles — to see whether the same answers appear.

STOP!

You have to design a research project to evaluate the effectiveness of different types of study techniques for passing organizational behaviour examinations.

Which research design or designs would you use to tackle this problem?

Justify your choice.

Research findings can be evaluated on two principal criteria:

Definition

The degree of *internal validity* is the degree of confidence with which it can be claimed that the independent variable really did cause the observed changes in the dependent variable.

Internal validity is assessed by considering factors other than the independent variable which could have caused the changes in the dependent variable. In our whisky drinking student group, we may have to consider the amount of sleep, food and perhaps other alcohol each student may have had before attending the experiment.

Definition

The degree of *external validity* is the extent to which the findings from the research setting can be generalized to other social settings.

This again is a matter of judgement. Our results may only apply to Scottish students (who may be accustomed to drinking whisky) and not to students from other nationalities. The results may only apply to students of a particular age group (who may prefer beer) than to mature students. The research findings are more or less generalizable depending on the nature and representativeness of the original research subjects.

Research designs that are strong on internal validity tend to have poor external validity and the reverse also applies. The ability to control variables in experiments helps internal validity but the artificiality potentially limits external validity. The reality of case study research strengthens external validity but the lack of control over variables weakens the internal validity of such findings. The position of surveys is more complex and depends on the nature of the research subjects and the type of analysis to which the data are subjected. But although surveys appear to lie in some middle ground between the respective strengths and weaknesses of the other designs, they are not necessarily best.

SOURCES

Berger, P. and Luckmann, T., 1966, *The Social Construction of Reality*, Penguin Books, Harmondsworth.
Oppenheim, A. N., 1976, *Questionnaire Design and Attitude Measurement*, Heinemann, London.
Pugh, D. S. (ed.), 1971, *Organization Theory: Selected Readings*, Penguin Books, Harmondsworth.

Ryan, A., 1970, *The Philosophy of the Social Sciences*, The Macmillan Press, London.

Ryan, A., 1981, "Is the study of society a science?", in David Potter (ed.), *Society and the Social Sciences*, Routledge and Kegan Paul/The Open University Press, London, pp. 8-33.

Selltiz, C., Wrightsman, L. S. and Cook, S. W., 1976, *Research Methods in Social Relations*, Holt, Reinhart and Winston, New York.

Shipman, M., 1981, *The Limitations of Social Research*, Longman, London.

PART 1

THE INDIVIDUAL IN THE
ORGANIZATION

Overview

Definitions

Psychology is the science of mental life. It is concerned with the interaction between individual and environment.

Organizational psychology is concerned with the interaction between the individual and the organizational environment.

The study of human behaviour in organizations is a multidisciplinary endeavour, and it seems logical to begin this study with the smallest practical unit of analysis — the individual. Part 1 describes the nature of three basic psychological processes, *perception*, *motivation* and *learning*, and their relationships with the structure and development of human *personality*. Part 1 is a short introduction to selected topics from psychology, concentrating on the contribution that psychology can make to our understanding of human behaviour in organizations.

The psychological processes examined here are dealt with one at a time, but their influence on human behaviour is simultaneous and interactive. What a person does in a given set of circumstances is a product of the combined effects of these processes. An adequate explanation of human behaviour must take this into account.

Psychologists study things that go on inside people's heads (or at least cognitive psychologists do). Perception, motivation and learning, and the mental aspects of personality, are "intangible". These labels cannot be attached to anything that the psychologist can see directly, have direct contact with, dissect, or spin in a centrifuge. But as explained in Chapter 1, this does not stop us from studying these processes. We can infer from changes in behaviour that these processes are going on inside people's heads, and use the understanding of these processes derived in this way in our explanations of behaviour.

Source

Miller, G., 1962, *Psychology: The Science of Mental Life,* Penguin Books, Harmondsworth.

Chapter 3

Perception

It all depends on how you see it . . .

A lady ordered a salad in a restaurant.

When the waiter brought it, she looked at the plate and asked,

"Excuse me, but what meat is that, please?"

"Tongue, madam", replied the waiter.

"Oh dear", exclaimed the lady, "I could not eat something that had been inside a cow's mouth. I'll just have an egg instead."

Key concepts:

Once you have understood this chapter, you should be able to define the following concepts in your own words:

The perceptual process	Perceptual set
Habituation	Perceptual world
Perceptual selectivity	Stereotyping
Perceptual organization	Halo effect

Objectives:

On completing this chapter, you should be able:

1. To list the main characteristics of the process of perception.
2. To give examples of how behaviour is influenced by the ways in which individuals perceive themselves and the world around them.
3. To explain how we perceive ourselves and our environment.
4. To explain how we perceive other people.
5. To identify and explain common kinds of perceptual error and ways of improving accuracy of perception.

INTRODUCTION

Of all the topics covered in this text, perception is perhaps the one that most explicitly sets social science apart from natural science. The phenomena studied by social scientists — human beings — attach meanings, values and objectives to their actions. What we do in the world depends on how we understand our place in it, depends on how we see ourselves and our environment, depends on how we *perceive* our circumstances. We describe and explain what we and others do using terms such as "reason", "motive", "intention", "purpose", "desire", and so on. Physicists, chemists and engineers do not face this complication in coming to grips with their subject matter.

Different people see things differently; management and unions, teachers and students, the businessman and the tax inspector, the car driver and the traffic warden. This chapter examines this phenomenon by asking, "Why do people perceive things differently?"

We humans do not just passively register sense impressions picked up from the world around us. The raw incoming data is interpreted in the light of our past experiences, and in terms of our current needs and interests. Although we all have similar nervous systems, and although in general terms the basic features of the perceptual process are common to us all, we each have different social and physical backgrounds, different expectations of what happens to us and around us, and therefore different perceptions. Human beings do not behave in, and in response to, the world "as it really is". In fact this chapter sets out to demonstrate that this idea of "the real world" is somewhat arbitrary and not a useful starting point for developing an understanding of human behaviour. Human beings behave in, and in response to, the world as they *perceive* it. We each possess our own "perceptual world" that is often different from what is "really the case", and is invariably different from the perceptual worlds of other people. In trying to discover why we behave as we do, and why others behave as they do, this concept of perceptual world is a useful point of departure.

The psychology of perception is fundamental to an understanding of human behaviour in organizations because the theories of motivation, learning and personality that are covered in later chapters are based on concepts introduced under the heading of perception.

THE PROCESS OF PERCEPTION

Definition

Perception is the active psychological process in which stimuli are selected and organized into meaningful patterns.

We normally carry out this process instantaneously and without conscious deliberation. We often in fact have no real control over this process, and such control is not generally needed. As an active process of interpretation, perception modifies the raw data that the senses collect. The ways in which perception modifies sensory information are systematic and involve the characteristics of selectivity and organization.

Mental activity as information processing

As we get on with day-to-day living, our senses are bombarded with vast amounts of information. Some of this information comes from inside our own bodies, such as sensations of hunger, lust, pain, and muscular tension. Some of this information comes from people, objects and events around us. The human body is equipped with sensory apparatus that can detect this variety of information for processing by the human brain. This is a useful way of thinking about human mental activity — as information processing.

In general, we all possess the same kind of sensory apparatus, although some people are better at sensing some kinds of information than others. The design of the apparatus is basically the same, but the "manufacturing quality" varies from person to person. This apparatus displays several regular character-istics which apply to everyone.

The difference between sensation and perception

A distinction must be made, in both theory and practice, between sensation and perception. The senses — sight, hearing, touch, taste and smell — each consist of specialist nerves that respond to specific forms of energy, such as light, sound, pressure and so on. There are some forms of energy that our senses cannot detect; we cannot hear radio waves and very high or very low pitched sounds; we cannot see infra-red radiation and can in fact see only a portion of the electromagnetic spectrum. Some birds, such as owls, have much better eyesight than we do, and bats, dogs and porpoises all have better hearing than us. Although our sensory apparatus is pretty good for most of our purposes, it does have built in limitations that we cannot overcome without the aid of special equipment. There is therefore a lot of information, which psychologists term "stimuli", that is not received. Stimuli that are not sensed cannot directly influence our behaviour.

The constraints imposed upon us by our sensory apparatus can be modified in certain ways by experience. The term given to the limits of our senses, the boundary between what we can pick up and what we cannot, is *threshold*. Noises that are too high or too low in pitch or in volume to be heard are said to be outside the upper and lower auditory thresholds. It is a straightforward process to investigate systematically individual differences in these thresholds across the various senses. But how can these thresholds be altered by experience?

If there is a clock in the room where you are reading, you have almost certainly not been aware of its ticking. If you are in a library, close your eyes for a few seconds and listen carefully; you will be astounded at the level of background noise in the library that you had not previously heard. But surely you must have heard it, as you must have heard the clock ticking, if your ears are working properly? The nerves that make up our senses respond not simply to energy, as suggested earlier, but rather to changes in energy levels. Having detected a stimuli, such as the clock, the nerves concerned seem to become tired of transmitting the same information indefinitely and eventually give up, until the stimuli changes (like when the alarm goes off). One can often be surprised as a noise, say from a piece of machinery, stops suddenly. Once stimuli become familiar, therefore, they stop being sensed. This familiarization process is called *habituation*, and its usual effect is to raise the perceptual threshold, stopping detection of stimuli of comparatively low intensity.

The active interpretation of sensory information

Our knowledge and understanding of the world about us thus depends upon sensory stimulation. But our brains are not passive recorders of "what is out there", in the way that a computer passively records the information that it is given. The mis-spelled control statement or omitted comma that would stop the computer does not normally interfere with the comprehension of the human reader. Only gross typographical blunders interfere with our reading, and words out of place or spelled wrongly are not usually difficult to understand. The human brain can therefore interpret incoming information in a way that computers cannot do, or at least find very difficult. It is this active interpretation that makes the process of perception different from, and also more than, mere sensation.

HOW THE PERCEPTUAL PROCESS SELECTS INCOMING STIMULI

Our sensory apparatus has finite limitations that lead to a screening out or filtering of much of the information around us like x-rays and dog whistles. The process of perception, however, acts as a secondary filter, preventing stimuli that are sensed from entering our consciousness. Information that is familiar, non-threatening and unnecessary to the task in hand is screened out and is prevented from entering our awareness. If you are tempted to argue otherwise, try the following experiment.

Stand on the pavement of a busy street for a few minutes and try to pay attention to as many different stimuli as you can: the volume and speed of traffic; the colour and condition of the cars; the smell of rubber, fuel and exhaust gases; the pressure of the pavement on the soles of your feet; the feeling of the breeze across your face; the smell of the perfume of a passing woman; the clothes of the man across the road and the type of dog he has with him ... and so on. When you think that you are taking it all in, start to cross the road. If you get across safely, you will find that your heightened awareness has lapsed, dramatically. In fact you would be mown down fairly quickly if this were not the case because you would inevitably not see or take appropriate action to avoid the fatal vehicle.

Definition

Perceptual selectivity is the process through which we filter or screen out information that we do not need.

There are just too many environmental stimuli around at any one time for us to pay adequate attention to all of them. What actually gets inside our heads has therefore been through two screening stages, sensation and perception, and is at best only a partial representation of what is "really there". This finding leads us to the conclusion that human beings do not behave in accordance with reality as such, but in accordance with how they perceive that reality to be.

The major factors that affect perceptual selectivity are illustrated in Figure 3.1. These factors, taken together, determine what information gets through the selection process and what is kept out. The external factors are those outside the individual while the internal factors refer to characteristics of the individual.

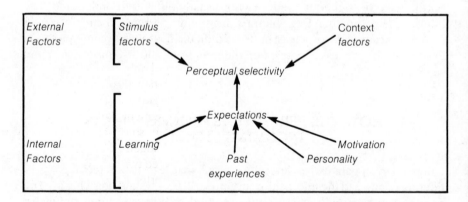

Figure 3.1: The factors that affect perpectual selectivity.

There are just too many stimuli for us to pay attention to all of them.

"All the time we are aware of millions of things around us — these changing shapes, these burning hills, the sound of the engine, the feel of the throttle, each rock and weed and fence post and piece of debris beside the road — aware of these things but not really conscious of them unless there is something unusual or unless they reflect something we are predisposed to see. We could not possibly be conscious of these things and remember all of them because our mind would be so full of useless details we would be unable to think. From all this awareness we must select, and what we select and call consciousness is never the same as the awareness because the process of selection mutates it. We take a handful of sand from the endless landscape of awareness around us and call that handful of sand the world."

From Robert M. Pirsig, *Zen and the Art of Motorcycle Maintenance: An Inquiry into Values*, 1974, Corgi Edition, New York, p. 75.

Reproduced by permission of The Bodley Head and W. Morrow & Co. Inc.

The external factors include stimulus and context factors. As a general rule, our attention tends to be drawn to stimuli that are

large	rather than	small
bright		dull
loud		quiet
strong		weak
unfamiliar		familiar
standing out from their surroundings		merged with their surroundings
moving		stationary
repeated (but not repetitive)		one off

Designers of advertisements and road signs use this knowledge of stimulus factors to attract and hold people's attention. Some road hazard warning signs tend to be flashing and bright rather than dull and static to attract the attention of motorists. Advertisers sometimes try to place their products into unusual surroundings to attract the attention of consumers.

STOP!

Can you identify examples of how different advertisements in newspapers, magazines, billboards and on television use these stimulus factors?

All other things being equal, the large will attract more attention than the small, the bright more than the dull, and so on. But this general rule is frequently broken because these features do not occur on their own. A given stimulus will possess a *pattern* of features; it may be small, bright, familiar and repeated, or small, dull, strong and moving. It is to this pattern that our sensory apparatus responds, and not always to single, specific features. A familiar sound that is normally heard once only at a time may attract more attention if it is repeated.

The way in which something is perceived also depends on the context in which it appears. For example, the naval commander on the bridge of his ship and the housewife in the kitchen may both have occasion to shout "fire". But to those within earshot, these identical utterances will mean quite different things, and will lead to quite different forms of behaviour, one to take human life, and the other to save it. The people who have to respond to these utterances need no special information to interpret them, given the context in which they are spoken.

The effects of motivation, learning, and personality on perception are covered in the following chapters. The most powerful influences are learning and past experience.

Most of our perceiving can be described as categorization or classification. We categorize people as male or female, energetic or lazy, extravert or shy. It has been claimed that there are two types of people in the world, those who like dichotomies and those who do not. Our classification schemes are normally more complex than these examples suggest. We classify objects as cars, buildings, desks, coffee cups, and so on, and we further refine our classification under each of these headings. How many ways, for example can you classify cars? We classify animals as cats, weasels, giraffes, and so on. Most of the work of perception is of this kind. But we are not born with a neat classification scheme "wired in" with the brain. These categories are learned. To the British, snow is just snow is just snow, but Eskimos have several names for different kinds of snow. Europeans and Americans, on the other hand, have a large number of terms for alcohol.

These categories or classifications are called *concepts*. You have never seen our neighbours' cat Ben, but if you did, you would know that it was a cat without having to be told. Why? Because you have a mental image of what constitutes a cat and this image, or concept, enables you to distinguish effortlessly between all those objects in the world that are cats and those that are not. A good deal of human learning is thus concerned with learning concepts. Concepts like perception, motivation, learning and personality are just harder to define clearly.

Read the box on the right quickly, if you have not already done so, then take a closer look at it. Few people spot the mistake here first time. What we learn is culture bound. The language that we speak certainly is but so are most of the values, motives

> PARIS
> IN THE
> THE
> SPRING

and practices that our culture transmits to us. An Indonesian visitor to Glasgow pointed out that "In your country, you feed the pigeons. In my country, the pigeons feed us." Our revulsion at the thought of eating dog meat, and the Hindu's revulsion at the thought of eating beef, are culturally transmitted emotions based on learned values. Problems arise when we believe and act as if our culture has a monopoly of "right thinking" on issues like this, other cultures with other beliefs being perceived as strange and wrong. Different people within the same culture clearly have different experiences and develop different expectations from each other.

RIDDLES

These riddles stump most people from western cultures.

Can you solve them?

Why do you think many people find them difficult?

1:     A man and his son are involved in a car crash. The man is killed,
       and the boy, seriously injured, is rushed to the hospital for surgery.
       But the surgeon takes one look him and says: "I cannot operate
       on this boy. He is my son." The boy's father is dead, and the
       surgeon is telling the truth.

How can this be?

2:     Man: "How many animals are there in your zoo?"

       Zookeeper: "Well, in my zoo there are 64 heads, and 186 legs.
                  You can work it out for yourself from that."

       The man could not work it out. Can you?

The internal factors contribute to the creation within us of expectations
about the world around us, what we want from it, and what will happen in it. We
thus often tend to select information that fits our expectations and ignore
information that does not. Most people expect to find the phrase PARIS IN THE
SPRING, and that is what is read because the extra word is not expected. You
should be able to find a number of everyday examples of the influence of
expectations on perception.

HOW THE PERCEPTUAL PROCESS ORGANIZES
INCOMING STIMULI

Even though the retina of the human eye receives light on a two dimensional
surface, we do not simply see mosaics of light and colour. For those of us with
normal eyesight, the world that enters our eyes is a sensible three dimensional
place and we do not have to perform any conscious visual tricks to see it that
way. The two dimensional mosaic is organized into meaningful patterns for us
by the mental wiring in our heads.

Definition

Perceptual organization is the process through which incoming stimuli
are organized or patterned in systematic and meaningful ways.

The principles by which the process of perceptual organization works were first identified by Max Wertheimer in 1923. The eye for example tends to group together or to classify stimuli that are close to each other. This is called the proximity principle and can be simply illustrated as follows:

a b   c d   e f
• •   • •   • •

Here we perceive three pairs of dots rather than just six dots; dots a and b are seen as "belonging" to each other in a way that dots d and e do not, because they are closer to each other.

The eye also tends to group together or classify stimuli that are similar in appearance to each other. This is called the similarity principle:

■ ■ • • ■ ■ • •

Here we perceive four pairs of symbols — two pairs of dots, two pairs of squares and not just eight symbols.

We are also able to fill gaps in incomplete or ambiguous patterns of stimuli in ways that make them meaningful. This is called the closure principle; we "close" partial and confusing information to make it intelligible and useful to us.

These principles of perceptual organization apply to the perceptual process in general, and not just to visual stimuli. You should be able think up some examples of your own of how these principles apply to the other senses, particularly hearing.

Of more direct interest here, however, is the way in which these principles apply to our perceptions of other people. How often do we group people together in our perceptions because they live in the same area, work in the same office or factory (proximity) or because they wear the same clothes or have the same skin colour (similarity)? This raises the problem of stereotyping people, which is dealt with later. How often do we take pieces of information and draw inferences from them (closure) that turn out to be incorrect? This can cause the spread of false rumours in organizations through what is sometimes known as the "grapevine".

THE INDIVIDUAL'S PERCEPTUAL SET

We have seen how the process of perception is responsible for selecting stimuli and arranging them into meaningful patterns. We have also seen how this process is influenced by the internal factors of learning, motivation and personality. These internal factors give rise to expectations which make the individual more ready to respond to certain stimuli in certain ways and less ready to respond to other stimuli. This readiness to respond is called the individual's *perceptual set*.

The figure on p.41 was first published in 1915 by the cartoonist W. E. Hill and there are two ways of perceiving this figure. Discuss what you see with colleagues; some will have one interpretation, some another, some will be able to offer both. It is interesting to reflect on the perceptual sets of those who see something here that perhaps you do not see, or did not see until someone pointed it out. (If you can make no sense of this figure at all, your perceptual set may need tuning.)

It makes no sense to argue over which interpretation of Hill's drawing is the correct one. Such an argument would be fruitless; we have to accept that different people can look at the same thing and perceive it in different ways. Failure to appreciate this feature of the perceptual process creates many organizational problems. For example, managers may perceive that employees and union officials are unreasonable and disruptive over trivial issues while employees perceive that they have a genuine grievance and that management cares nothing for them. Again, it makes little sense to ask whose perception is the correct one here.

DeWitt Dearborn and Herbert Simon once asked 23 American executives to identify the most serious problem facing a company from a case study report. The sales executives said that the company's biggest problem was a sales problem. The industrial relations and personnel executives said that the biggest problem was with human relations. Organization managers looking at the same information are thus likely to select and emphasize those aspects of a problem that relate to their own activities and goals.

THE INDIVIDUAL'S PERCEPTUAL WORLD

The world out there "as it really is", is not a good starting point for developing an understanding of human behaviour. Each of us has a personal and unique version of what is "out there" and of our own place in it. We each have, therefore, our own *perceptual world*, i.e., an image, a map or a picture of our environment.

We each have a perceptual world that is selective and partial, concentrating on features of interest and importance to us. From the formation of perceptual set (through learning, motivation and personality), we each have different expectations and different degrees of readiness to respond to objects, people and events in different ways. Through perceptual organization we each strive to impose meaning on received patterns of information. The meanings that we attach to objects, people and events are not intrinsic to these things but are learned through experience and are coloured by our current needs and objectives.

To understand an individual's behaviour, therefore, we must begin by attempting to discover the elements in that person's perceptual world and the pattern of influences that have shaped it. Developing an understanding of one's own perceptual world is quite difficult because there are many influences of which we are not directly or indirectly fully aware. Information about the perceptual world of someone else can be hard to come by, and although this is by no means impossible, it poses a barrier to our understanding of others. We are prone to forget that our own perceptual world is not the only possible or correct one.

The factors that influence the way we see ourselves and our environment are summarized in Figure 3.2, and clearly there is much scope here for the development of individual differences. But fortunately there are broad similarities between us in the form of:

- similar sensory apparatus;
- similar basic needs;
- common experiences and problems;

that make the task of mutual understanding possible.

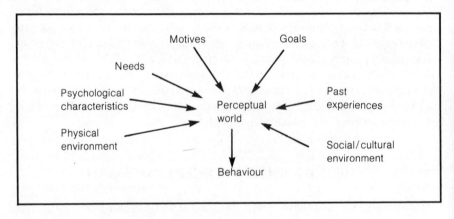

Figure 3.2   The factors that influence the individual's perceptual world

PERCEIVING OTHER PEOPLE

The ways in which we perceive the dots, lines, and ambiguous figures presented earlier are reflected in the ways in which we perceive people. An understanding of these basic psychological phenomena is therefore useful in understanding human behaviour in organizations, and in raising awareness of the sources and nature of many organizational problems. There are two prominent features of the process of *person perception*:

The halo effect

Perceptual selectivity operates when we are perceiving other people. When we make judgements about others, we are often influenced by striking character-istics such as dress, speech or posture. This can colour our judgement of other features that we discover later on. This is is called the halo effect (a term first used by the psychologist Edward Thorndike in 1920), and it can operate in either a positive or a negative direction.

In the selection interview for a job, the applicant who is clean, well dressed and friendly may often have a better chance of being given the job than the applicant who is scruffy and aggressive. Tall men get more job offers than short ones and tend to get higher starting salaries. Men tend to discriminate against attractive women in employment, believing that they do not have the qualities required of management. But since when did the cut of someone's suit or the breadth of their smile correlate with, say, ability to design bridges or manage a sales department?

The halo effect acts as a screen that filters out information that is not in agreement with an assessment based on quickly and easily recognized information. The problem is that what we notice first about a person is often irrelevant to the assessment that we want to make. A confounding factor is that we give more favourable judgements to people who have characteristics in common with us, these being the characteristics that we look for and recognize without difficulty in others.

Stereotyping

Perceptual organization operates when we are perceiving other people. "Stereotyping" is a term given by typographers to previously made up blocks of type, and the term was first applied to bias in person perception in 1922 by Walter Lippman. We group together people who have similar characteristics and allocate traits to them on the basis of this grouping:

- Scots are mean
- Students are lazy
- Italians are emotional
- Blondes are more fun
- Accountants are boring
- Trade unionists are Communists

We can thus attribute a variety of qualities to an individual on the basis of apparent group membership.

Stereotypes are over-generalizations and are bound to be radically inaccurate on occasion. But they may sometimes be convenient, because by adopting a stereotyped point of view, we may be able to shortcut the evaluation process, and make fast predictions of behaviour. We have problems, however, with the individual who falls into several categories that have conflicting stereotypes.

Most managers are men, although the number of women in the labour force in Britain has grown rapidly in the past 20 years. Why? Are male managers afraid of the competition that the "weaker sex" might give them if allowed into their ranks? Are female careers simply cut short by child rearing?

Madeline Heilman and Lois Saruwatari designed an experiment to discover how errors in the person perception process could lead to discrimination against women.

The researchers asked 45 male and female subjects to take part in a study of decision making in selecting people for jobs. Half of the subjects were asked to assess four applications for a non-managerial, clerical record keeping job. The others were asked to assess four applications for a managerial, problem solving, decision making job.

Some of the fictitious applicants were male, others female; some were attractive, some not. The subjects were asked to rate the suitability of each applicant for the job, suggest a starting salary, and rate the applicants on their masculinity and femininity.

There were no differences between the male and female subjects in the way in which they assessed the applicants.

Attractive applicants of both sexes were more likely to be hired for the non-managerial job than unattractive applicants.

Attractive males were more likely to be hired for the managerial job. But attractive females were not thought to be suitable for the management position. Unattractive females were more likely to get the managerial job, and even get a higher starting salary.

Why is discrimination strongest against attractive women with management aspirations?

Heilman and Saruwatari argue that when we assess attractive people, we make the perceptual error of assuming that they conform to the stereotype of their gender. Attractive males are thus thought to have masculine personalities, and to be:

- ambitious;
- unemotional;
- decisive.

Attractive females are thought to be more feminine, and therefore not to have the personality characteristics considered necessary to management. Unattractive females got higher ratings on those masculine features. The implication of this research is that good looking women should appear plain and masculine to make their way in the world.

From: Madeline Heilman and Lois Saruwatari, "When beauty is beastly: the effects of appearance and sex on evaluations of job applicants for managerial and nonmanagerial jobs", *Organizational Behaviour and Human Performance*, 1979, vol. 23, no. 1, pp. 360-72.

PERCEPTUAL ERRORS: PROBLEMS AND SOLUTIONS

The sources of error in person perception are thus:

1.   Not collecting enough information;
2.   Using irrelevant information;
3.   Seeing only what we want and expect to see;
4.   Allowing early information to affect perception of later information;
5.   Allowing one's own characteristics to affect the way we perceive others.

The remedies are:

1.   Take time; avoid making hasty judgements about people;
2.   Collect and consciously use more information about people;
3.   Develop self awareness and an understanding of personal biases.

Paradoxically, in order to understand others, we must first have a knowledge of ourselves. We often do not have this self-knowledge, or the opportunity to develop it. In organizations, status and power barriers prevent people from expressing their true feelings about each other. There are also cultural constraints which inhibit the public expression of emotions. Even when information about our attitudes, values and behaviour is available in some form, psychological defence mechanisms may interfere with our ability to use it effectively.

As a result, the popularity of training courses to help individuals to overcome these problems has grown. Courses in "social skills", "self-awareness", and "personal growth" are widely available. These courses typically emphasize openness in personal relationships, and the giving of non-evaluative feedback on how people on such courses perceive each other.

SOURCES

Dearborn, D. C. and Simon, H. A., 1958, "Selective perception: a note on the departmental identification of executives", *Sociometry*, vol. 21, pp. 140-4.

Heilman, M. and Saruwatari, L., 1979, "When beauty can be beastly: the effects of appearance and sex on evaluations of job applicants for managerial and nonmanagerial jobs", *Organizational Behaviour and Human Performance*, vol. 23, no. 1, pp. 360-72.

Pirsig, R., 1974, *Zen and the Art of Motorcycle Maintenance: An Inquiry into Values*, Corgi Books, London.

Zalkind, S. S. and Costello, T. W., 1962, "Perception: some recent research and implications for administration", *Administrative Science Quarterly*, vol. 7, pp. 218-35.

Chapter 4

Motivation

Introduction

Motives: the goals of human behaviour

Motivation: the mental process of decision making

Motivation: the social process of influencing others

Why do people behave the way they do?

Throughout the 1960s, the American Telephone and Telegraph company suffered high labour turnover. One of the top managers made the following comment when shown the figures:

"We are going to have to make some changes in our thinking about the attitudes of young people today.

"We are told our potential employees are not motivated by fear of job security, for instance. We are going to have to appeal to them through having a reputation for providing jobs that allow a young person to make meaningful contributions in challenging work. Something is wrong, and we are going to have to look closely at our work, our measurements, our style of supervision . . ."

From Robert N. Ford, *Motivation Through the Work Itself,* American Management Association, New York, 1969, p. 15.

Key concepts:

Once you have understood this chapter, you should be able to define the following concepts in your own words:

Drives	Expectancy theory
Motives	Subjective probability
Self actualization	Valence
Motivation	Job enrichment

Objectives:

On completing this chapter, you should be able:

1. To understand the different ways in which the term motivation is used.
2. To understand the nature of motives and motivation processes as influences on human behaviour.
3. To use the components of expectancy theory of motivation to analyse human and organizational problems and to develop solutions and recommendations for change.
4. To assess the strengths and limitations of the technique of job enrichment as a way of motivating people to work harder.

INTRODUCTION

What motivates people? The organization's concern with controlled performance puts a high premium on the correct answer to this question. Our ability to design organizations that motivate their members to adequate and superlative levels of performance is still poor. We know that fear and money are not the only ways, and that they are not particularly good ways, to motivate people to work — or indeed to do anything.

Human beings have reasons for the things that they do. Our behaviour is *purposive*. The importance of this is indicated by the large number of different words that we use in our language to express purpose in our affairs, such as:

purpose	need	want	plan
aim	desire	drive	objective
intent	goal	demand	resolve

You should be able to add other similar words to this list yourself.

We behave as we do because we choose to do so. We do not simply react passively to influences in our physical and social environments. We process the information picked up by our senses, impose meaning on that information, and make decisions about what we are going to do next. Human beings are *proactive*, rather than reactive. A lot of our day-to-day decision making is habitual and unconscious, but we have access to it if we are prepared to stop and reflect.

Our needs, purposes and motives are part of our experience. We naturally think of our behaviour as related in meaningful ways to these experienced motives. The need to make sense of our own behaviour is a particularly strong human motive in its own right. To make sense of the behaviour of others, we ascribe motives to them. To claim that someone's behaviour is senseless, thoughtless, mindless, or without reason, is to admit our own ignorance of their motives. We discussed in Chapter 2 how human beings attach meanings to their behaviour; we said that humans are *self-interpreting*. Our motives are a central part of that self-interpretation.

The terms "motive" and "motivation" are used in everyday language in three distinct ways. They are used to mean:

1. The *goals* that people have. Achievement, status, power, friends and money are commonly regarded as important human motives. They constitute reasons for doing things, reasons that lead to behaviour. These are some of the more important *outcomes* of particular types of human behaviour.

2. The *mental processes* that lead people to pursue particular goals. People have or develop desires for, say, achievement and friends, and develop expectations about the relationships between their behaviour and these outcomes. In other words, we acquire an understanding of what we have to do to achieve these goals. These mental processes involve the individual in taking *decisions* about what to aim for and how to go about it.

3.   The *social processes* through which some individuals try to change the
     behaviour of others. Managers are constantly trying to find ways to get
     their subordinates to work harder. Our society tries to teach us to value
     wealth and status acquired through hard work and monogamous family
     life. Most of us indeed learn about and direct our desires for money,
     achievement and sex in these conventional ways. These social processes,
     therefore, involve attempts to *influence* the things that other people do.

When we discuss motives and motivation, we must be clear about the sense in
which we use the terms. This chapter looks at each of these three uses.

MOTIVES: THE GOALS OF HUMAN BEHAVIOUR

Are the goals that we pursue part of our genetic inheritance, or part of the
knowledge that our society transmits to each new generation? This is a
controversial issue, and its resolution has profound practical implications. If our
motives are *innate*, then we may be able to do little to change them, and may
simply have to live tolerantly with the ones we do not like. There is, for example,
a long running and unresolved debate concerning whether or not human
beings are innately aggressive. But if our motives are *learned*, the position is
quite different.

Human behaviour is clearly influenced by the biological equipment with
which we are born. We have a strong need for survival which appears to be
innate. When deprived of essentials, our needs for oxygen, water, food, shelter,
warmth and sex are overpowering. But some religious orders inflict celibacy on
willing members. Altruism can overcome the individual's personal desire to
survive in extraordinary circumstances such as war and other disasters. The best
that we may claim is that these biological forces are basic determinants of the
behaviour of most of us most of the time. These biological forces are called
needs or *drives.*

Definition

Drives are innate, biological determinants of human behaviour that are
activated by deprivation.

These drives come with the body. We cannot wish them away. We do not
have to learn to be hungry, cold or thirsty. These drives get us behaving when we
do not have food, warmth or water. It is important to note, however, that there
are circumstances in which other goals can displace these drives. The reason
that we can override them is that they satisfy the physical needs of the body, not
the intellectual and emotional needs of the mind. It is the mind that ultimately
takes the decisions about behaviour.

Drives do not influence behaviour in direct, specific and predictable ways. When birds build nests, and squirrels collect nuts, they do so in quite specific and repeated ways. Their behaviour patterns are triggered by events in their environment and are dictated by instinct as a computer's operations are programmed. Birds and squirrels cannot override their programming, but remain fixed in their niche in nature. Human beings are not locked into their environment and their inheritance in that way. The ways in which we seek to satisfy our drives are innumerable. The best illustration of this comes from the vast range of things that people do to satisfy their sex drives. Our behaviour patterns are flexible or *plastic*.

Drives do not determine everything that we do. We do lots of things that do not contribute in direct and obvious ways to the physical needs of our bodies, or to our survival as individuals or as a species. Play and exploration, for example, and all the different behaviours described by these two terms, appear to be unnecessary for biological and physical reasons. Much of human behaviour, therefore, cannot be explained by pointing to innate drives.

Definition

Motives are learned influences on human behaviour that lead us to pursue particular goals because they are socially valued.

Much of what we do is clearly influenced by the ways of thinking and behaving typical of the society into which we have been born. Our society or our culture influences our motives through the values, ideals, standards and modes of behaviour of other people. We seek status because that is the appropriate and accepted thing to do in our society. We seek work for the same reason. Those behaviours that are typical and conventional tend to become socially necessary, as those who do not conform may be shunned, or even imprisoned. Polygamy is a crime to us, but a social norm and a sign of male achievement, wealth and status in parts of the Arab world.

There is a further distinguishing feature between drives and motives. If we have just eaten, hunger ceases to motivate our behaviour. But if we have made friends and money, or learned something new, for example, we tend not to regard ourselves as having had enough for the time being. We tend to try for more. The drives lead us to *avoid* particular experiences. We are on the other hand motivated actively to seek certain other experiences, sensations and forms of excitement.

The distinction between drives and motives is summarized as follows:

Drives	*Motives*
are innate	are learned
have a physiological basis	have a social basis

are activated by deprivation	are activated by social environment
are aimed at satiation and	are aimed at stimulation
avoidance	

We noted earlier that human beings are proactive. We are active sensation seekers as well as passive responders in our environment. This proactive component in our natures, that leads to playful and exploratory behaviour, has led psychologists to suggest that we have innate desires for:

Self understanding: to know better who and what we are.
Competence: to develop understanding, and ability to control our environment.
Order and meaning: to have certainty, equity, justice, consistency, reliability, and predictability in the world

We must now point out that the distinction between innate physical drives and socially transmitted motives is not as clear as we have suggested. We satisfy our innate needs in ways acceptable to our society. The socially accepted ways in which we behave satisfy what may be innate sensation- and information seeking motives. We get pleasure from eating, drinking and breathing, but that is not enough. We also get satisfaction from exploring, learning about and influencing the world around us. It has even been suggested that these knowledge seeking motives are the driving force behind science, natural and social. It can be argued that stimulation- and information seeking do have survival value in physical terms. The more we know about the world around us, the more able we become to survive in it by adapting to it or manipulating it to make it more amenable to us.

The motivation theory of the American psychologist, Abraham Maslow, integrates the points raised so far in this chapter, and helps to resolve the confusion. Maslow argues that we have seven innate needs. These are:

1.   Physiological needs: for sunlight, sex, food, water, and similar outcomes basic to human survival.
2.   Safety needs: for freedom from threat from the environment, animals and other people, for shelter, security, order, predictability, for an organized world.
3.   Love needs: for relationships, affection, giving and receiving love, for feelings of belongingness.
4.   Esteem needs: for strength, achievement, adequacy, confidence, independence, *and* for reputation, prestige, recognition, attention, importance, appreciation, for a stable, high self-evaluation based on capability and respect from others.
5.   Self-actualization needs: for development of capability to the fullest potential.
6.   Freedom of inquiry and expression needs: for social conditions that permit free speech, and encourage justice, fairness, and honesty.
7.   The need to know and to understand: to gain and to systematize

knowledge of the environment, the need for curiosity, learning, philosophizing, experimenting and exploring.

Self actualization needs.

Maslow did not coin the term, but defined it in the following way:

"A musician must make music, an artist must paint, a poet must write, if he is to be ultimately happy. What a man *can* be, he *must* be. This need we may call self actualization. . . It refers to the desire for self fulfillment, namely, to the tendency for him to become actualized in what he is potentially. . . the desire to become more and more what one is, to become everything that one is capable of becoming." (p. 382)

From Abraham Maslow, 'A theory of human motivation', *Psychological Review*, 1943, vol. 50. no. 4, pp. 370-96.

The first two sets of needs, physiological and safety, are essential to human existence. If they are not satisfied, we die.

Love and esteem needs concern our relationships with others. If these needs are satisfied, we feel self-confident, capable and adequate — we feel that we are useful and necessary in the world. If these needs are not satisfied, they lead to feelings of inferiority, helplessness, discouragement, and can give rise to mental disorders.

Self actualization, Maslow argued, is the ultimate human goal. He felt, however, that fully satisfied and self-actualizing people were in the minority. He also felt that establishing the conditions appropriate for enabling people to develop their capabilities was a challenging problem.

Maslow regarded the last two needs on that list, for freedom of inquiry and expression, and for knowing and understanding, as essential prerequisites for the satisfaction of the other five sets of needs. They are the channels through which we find ways of improving our needs satisfaction.

Maslow's theory is that the first five sets of needs are organized in a loose hierarchy, with the following properties:

1. A need is not effective as a motivator until those before it in the hierarchy are more or less satisfied. You are not likely to worry about the sharks if you are drowning, for example.
2. A satisfied need is not a motivator. If you are well fed and safe, you cease to be preoccupied with food and shelter and turn your thoughts elsewhere. Once you are deprived of these they become dominant again.
3. Dissatisfaction of these needs adversely affects mental health.
4. We have an innate desire to work our way up the hierarchy.
5. The experience of self actualization stimulates the desire for more. This need cannot be satisfied in the way that the others can.

STOP!

Can you recognize the needs in Maslow's theory in your own behaviour?

Can you identify the things that you do to satisfy each of the seven
needs?

At what points in the hierarchy are you currently concentrating?

In what ways does society influence the ways in which you satisfy these
needs?

In what ways does society influence the extent to which you can satisfy
these needs?

Maslow did not mean this hierarchy to be regarded as a rigid description of
the development of human motivation, but as a typical picture of what might
happen under ideal (and therefore rarely attained) conditions. Different
individuals regard these five needs in different ways. A lot depends on your past
success and failure in trying to satisfy these needs. Some people seek self-
actualization at the expense of love. Some pursue creativity at the cost of their
personal safety and survival. Traumatic and depressing experiences can so affect
an individual's thinking that they become blocked at one level in the hierarchy.
Lengthy deprivation of a particular need may lead the individual to over-
emphasize that need, to concentrate on satisfying it so that they are not deprived
again. The emphasis placed on each need by an individual may change with
time, with age and the accumulation of experience. An individual may pursue
several needs at the same time.

There are two main problems with Maslow's theory.

First, it is difficult to see how it can predict behaviour. The amount of
satisfaction that has to be achieved before one may progress from one step to the
next in the hierarchy is difficult to define and measure. If we could take
measurements, the extent to which different people emphasize different needs
would make our predictions shaky. The theory is vague.

Second, Maslow's theory is more like a social philosophy than a
psychological theory. We can find enough evidence to show that some, if not
many, individuals in our society indeed pursue these needs. Some of us even
pursue them more or less in the order that Maslow suggested. It is still not clear,
however, whether the "higher order" needs (beyond physiology and safety) are
innate or learned. It is a "good" theory, in that it makes you feel warm inside:
would the world not be a much better place if what Maslow proposed was true?
Maslow may simply have reflected American middle class values and the pursuit
of the good life, and may not have hit on fundamental universal truths about
human psychology.

But Maslow's work has been extremely influential and has stimulated a lot of thinking and research. It has also led some organizations to change their practices for motivating employees. It is a pleasant theory, and if it is a prescriptive social philosophy, we can at least evaluate it and consider how far we are from the ideal that it specifies, and what we might have to do to get there should we wish to do so.

More important, Maslow is clearly correct to draw attention to the fact that human behaviour is influenced by a number of different motives. He also showed that people behave in ways that they believe to be intrinsically valuable. It is important for our study of organizational behaviour that the potential motivating power of money is examined in this context.

STOP!

Money is regarded as an important factor in motivating people to work.

Which of Maslow's needs does money satisfy?

Maslow may have described American middle class values . . .

Different cultures have different beliefs about the ways of living that are desirable and preferable. Societies, and groups within societies, are distinguished by the values that their members share.

Donald Clare and Donald Sanford studied the values of 132 American managers to find out what their values were.

The managers were asked to rank nine values concerning their *goals* in life, and nine values concerning acceptable *means* for achieving these goals. They were also asked how they thought the average American and their immediate subordinates would rank these values.

Their rankings were as follows:

Their valued goals:		To be achieved by being:
Sense of accomplishment	Rated high	Ambitious
Self respect	↑	Capable
Comfortable life		Logical
Freedom		Independent
Wisdom		Broad minded
Exciting life		Self controlled
Social recognition		Imaginative
World at peace	↓	Helpful
Pleasure	Rated low	Cheerful

These managers were characterized by their personal, achievement orientated goals and means for achieving them. These findings confirm the stereotype of the tough minded individualist American manager.

They also felt, however, that the pleasure seeking, social goals that they rated low, would be ranked more highly by their subordinates and by average Americans.

How would you rate these goals and means ?

From Donald A. Clare and Donald G. Sanford, "Mapping personal value space: a study of managers in four organizations", *Human Relations*, 1979, vol. 32, no. 8, pp. 659-66.

MOTIVATION: THE MENTAL PROCESS OF HUMAN DECISION MAKING

We do not come into the world with a mental package labelled "motives" that contains the goals that we are predestined to pursue. Different people are motivated by different outcomes. Different cultures encourage different patterns of motivation in their members. We thus appear to have some choice of motives, and means of achieving them, although social conditions push us in some directions and inhibit others.

Maslow's theory is called a *content* theory because it adopts a package approach to human motivation. It is possible to suggest other sets of contents for this package, and many other commentators have done so. Content theories are all open to the criticism, however, that they do not recognize individual choice and social influence. Maslow's theory is also called a *universal* theory because he argued that it applied to everyone. Universal theories of human behaviour attract the criticism that they cannot explain differences between individuals or between cultures.

Definition

Motivation is a decision making process through which the individual chooses desired outcomes and sets in motion the behaviours appropriate to acquiring them.

A motive is an outcome that has become desirable for a given individual. The process through which outcomes become desirable and are pursued is explained by the *expectancy theory* of motivation. This is a *process* theory because it does not assume that individuals come complete with a package of motives to pursue.

Motivation theories are divided into two opposing groups, each dominated by a different philosophical perspective on human nature. Behaviourist, or "stimulus-response", theories consider human behaviour to be reflexive and instinctive, driven by unconscious and inherited drives. Cognitive theories assume that individuals are aware of their goals and their behaviour, and consider humans to be purposive and rational.

Expectancy theory is cognitive. It was originally formulated by the American psychologist Edward C. Tolman in the 1930s as a challenge to the behaviourist theories of his contemporaries. Tolman argued that human behaviour is directed by the conscious *expectations* that people have about their behaviour leading to the achievement of desired goals. That is why it is called expectancy theory.

Expectancy theory is a general theory of human motivation which has been developed as an approach to work motivation by several American organizational psychologists. It was first used by Georgopoulos, Mahoney and Jones in 1957 in a study of the work performance of over 600 workers in a household appliances company. They called their theory a "path–goal approach to productivity", because they assumed that motivation to work productively depended on the individual's:

- specific needs, and
- expectation of fulfilling those needs through productive behaviour.

In other words, productivity has to be seen as a path to valued goals. Behaviour depends on the outcomes that an individual values, and the expectation that a particular type of behaviour will lead to those outcomes. If an individual needs more money, and expects to be given more money for working hard, then we can predict that the individual will decide to work hard. If the individual expects that hard work will win only smiles from the boss and not bring more money, then we can predict that the individual will decide not to work hard. Individuals behave in ways that are *instrumental* to the achievement of their valued goals.

Georgopoulos, Mahoney and Jones found that workers who expected high productivity to lead to valued goals tended to produce at a higher level than workers who felt that low productivity led to valued goals. Suppose the individual values the friendship of workmates, and expects that superlative work performance will annoy those friends. We can explain and predict the individual's low productivity in terms of particular valued goals and expectations of achieving or frustrating those goals. The goals which were most important to the household appliance assemblers were:

- Making more money in the long run;
- Getting along well with the work group;
- Promotion to a higher wage rate.

Another American psychologist, Victor H. Vroom, produced the first systematic formulation of an expectancy theory of work motivation in 1964. His approach provides a way of measuring human motivation. He called the preference that the individual has for a particular outcome its *valence*. As one may seek or avoid certain outcomes, or be ambivalent about them, valence may be positive, negative or neutral. Vroom used the term *subjective probability* for the individual's expectation that behaviour would lead to a particular outcome. This is subjective because individuals differ in their estimations of the relationships between their behaviour and outcomes. As a probability, it may vary between 0 and 1, from no chance at all to absolute certainty. The strength of motivation, or force, to perform an act thus depends on both the valence of the outcome and the subjective probability of achieving it.

Definition

Expectancy theory states that the strength or "force" of the individual's motivation to behave in a particular way is

$$F = E \times V$$

where   F =   motivation to behave
        E =   the expectation (the subjective probability) that the behaviour will be followed by a particular outcome
        V =   the valence of the outcome

This is called the *expectancy equation*.

In most circumstances, however, a number of different outcomes will result from a particular behaviour. The expectancy equation thus has to be summed across all of these outcomes, and the complete equation is therefore:

$$F = \sum (E \times V)$$

The sign $\sum$ is the Greek letter sigma, which here means "add up all the values of the calculation in the brackets".

Expectancy and valence are multiplied because when either E or V is zero, motivation is also zero, and this is what we would expect. If we add expectancy and valence, we get unrealistic results. If you believe that a particular behaviour will certainly lead to a particular outcome, but place no value on that outcome, then you will not be motivated to behave in that way. On the other hand, if you place a high value on a goal, but expect that the probability of attaining it is zero, your motivation will again be zero. Only when both of the terms are positive will motivation exist.

The individual may expect that hard work will lead to more money, smiles from the boss, and loss of friends. The calculation thus has to take into account the values, positive, neutral or negative, that the individual places on these outcomes. Money may be valued highly, smiles from the boss may count for nothing, and friendships lost may cause slight discomfort. The calculation also has to take into account the different probabilities or levels of expectations that the individual has of achieving these outcomes. The individual may expect that hard work will certainly not lead to more money, will definitely lead to smiles from the boss, and will almost certainly cost friends.

We can do this simple calculation for the individual's motivation to work hard, and then do the same calculation for the motivation to take it easy at work. The higher F value tells us which behaviour the individual will adopt. The absolute value of the F number itself tells us very little. It is useful when compared with the results of calculations for other behaviours that the individual may adopt, and for comparison with similar calculations for other individuals.

This process theory of motivation, expectancy theory, is more difficult to understand than the simpler content theory of Maslow. We have introduced a lot of new and unusual terms in a short space. Let us sum up what we have covered so far:

1.   Expectancy theory states that human behaviour results from a conscious decision making process that is based on the individual's *subjective probability* — the *perceptions* that the individual has about the results of alternative behaviours.
2.   Expectancy theory, as it is based on individual perceptions, helps to explain *individual differences* in motivation and behaviour, unlike Maslow's universal content theory of motivation.
3.   Expectancy theory attempts to *measure* the strength of the individual's motivation to behave in particular ways.
4.   Expectancy theory is based on the assumption that human behaviour is to some extent rational and that individuals are conscious of their goals or motives. As people take into account the probable outcomes of their behaviour, and place values on these outcomes, expectancy theory attempts to *predict* individual behaviour.

STOP!

Behaviour depends on the outcomes that an individual values, and the expectation that a particular type of behaviour will lead to those outcomes.

Will you work hard for your organizational behaviour course?
We can use expectancy theory to predict the answer to this.

First: List the outcomes that you expect will result from working hard for your organizational behaviour course, such as:

1.   High exam marks
2.   Bare pass
3.   Sleepless nights
4.   No social life
•   ?
•   ?

Second: Rate the value that you place on each of these outcomes, giving those you like +1, those you dislike -1, and those for which you are neutral 0. These are your "V" values.

Third: Estimate the probability of attaining each of these outcomes, giving those that are certain the value 1, those that are most unlikely the value 0, and those for which there is an even chance the value 0.5. Estimate other probabilities as you perceive them at other values between 0 and 1. These are your "E" values.

Fourth: Now put your E and V values into the expectancy equation,

$$F = \sum (E \times V)$$

and add up the result.

Fifth: Compare your F score with the scores of your colleagues.

            We predict that:

            • those with higher scores are the course "swots";

            • those with higher scores will get higher exam marks.

Expectancy theory is complex. Do we really carry out the analysis implied by the theory before behaving in a given way? Are we indeed capable of carrying out such a calculation? Lawler emphasizes that, although human beings are rational, our rationality is limited. Human behaviour is based on perceptions that are simplified by taking into acount only a limited number of factors and alternatives. Our behaviour is "satisficing" rather than "maximizing", and Lawler argues that the theory is capable of illustrating and analysing this.

Expectancy theory suggests how some goals, through experience, may come to be desirable for the individual and sought. This does not mean that we have to drop Maslow's approach altogether. Many of the outcomes that we pursue are contained in Maslow's list.

Whether we are born with these, or whether we adopt them as the current values of our society, we can still feed them into the expectancy equation as potentially valued outcomes. The process expectancy theory and the content theory of motivation are not necessarily mutually exclusive approaches to explaining human motivation. They each have something to contribute to our understanding of why people do the things they do.

Expectancy theory has been influential, both in stimulating research, and in providing a tool for diagnosing and helping to resolve organizational problems. The main set of influences on the individual's perceptions, on how the individual works out the expectancy equation, is experience in the organization. People come to recognize what is valued in a particular organization, and learn what they can achieve and what is not possible. It is therefore possible to identify features of organizational life that influence people's expectations and valences. If these features lead to dissatisfaction and poor performance, then it should be possible to identify and change them. One of the main ways in which this theory has contributed to organization practice in this respect is through the technique of job enrichment which is examined in the following section.

STOP!

Consider the following questions in discussion with colleagues.

1. Are we human beings really as rational in our thinking as expectancy theory requires?
2. Is the attempt to measure and quantify the strength of human motivation realistic?
3. How can work experience affect individuals' subjective probabilities and the outcomes that they value?

Expectancy theory can be used to diagnose and resolve organizational problems . . .

One of the answers to the organizational dilemma outlined in Chapter 1 is to let employees take part, with management, in making decisions that affect the organization and their workroles in it. This is called "participative management".

Linda Neider studied whether or not participative management increased employee work performance.

Neider studied attempts to increase the sales of 110 clerks in four retail shops. The chain that owned the shops had a history of employee dissatisfaction with pay and company policies. Managers were not participative.

One store set up discussion groups to examine and to resolve grievances about work methods and conditions. A second store introduced a "cafeteria" incentive scheme where employees could choose from a range of rewards, as well as basic pay, for good sales records. The rewards included cinema tickets, days off with pay, and being assistant manager for a week. A third store had both the discussion groups and the incentive scheme. A fourth store was not changed and had neither.

> The store with the discussion groups and the cafeteria incentive scheme had the sharpest rise in sales.

> The fourth store then went through the same full treatment, with the same results.

> The participation and incentive schemes, on their own, had no significant effects in the other two stores.

Neider, using expectancy theory, argues that people only work well when:

- They expect their efforts to produce good performance;
- They expect rewards for good performance; and
- They value these rewards.

The cafeteria incentive scheme gives employees a choice of rewards and covers the third of these conditions. Employees who are not sure what to do to perform well, and who perhaps do not know what level of performance is considered to be "good", need participative managers to tell them. In other words, management behaviour influences the expectations of subordinates about the consequences of their efforts.

From Linda Neider, "An experimental field investigation utilizing an expectancy theory view of participation", *Organizational Behaviour and Human Performance*, 1980, vol. 26, no. 3, pp. 425-42.

MOTIVATION: THE SOCIAL PROCESS OF INFLUENCING OTHERS

We have looked at motivation from three perspectives. First, we considered motivation in terms of the goals towards which human behaviour is directed. Second, we considered motivation as the process through which those goals are selected and pursued. The third and final perspective that we will consider is motivation as a social process.

Motivation in an organizational context is a social process in which some people try to influence others to work harder and more effectively. Organizations as social arrangements are dependent on being able to motivate their members to join, to stay, and to perform at acceptable levels. Organization managers are thus very interested in theories of motivation in the hope that they will discover techniques for motivating people to work harder, and be loyal, committed and innovative.

Most manual jobs on factory shopfloors and clerical jobs in offices are designed using an approach advocated by an American engineer called Frederick Taylor (whose influential work is examined in more detail in Chapter 12). Taylor's technique for designing jobs was as follows:

1. Decide on the optimum degree of *task fragmentation*. This means breaking down a complex job into its simple component parts. The job of assembling a table lamp for example can be broken into its components of fixing the base to the stem, fitting the bulb holder, mounting the shade, fixing the flex, wiring the plug, and inserting the bulb.
2. Decide the most efficient way of performing each part of the work. Studies should be carried out to find out the best method for doing each of the fragmented tasks that have been identified, and for designing the layout of the workplace and the design of any tools that are to be used.

3.   Train employees to carry out the fragmented tasks in precisely the manner determined as best.

The advantages of task fragmentation are that:

- Individuals do not need expensive and time consuming training;
- Specialization in one small task makes people very proficient;
- Lower pay can be given for unskilled work;
- It simplifies the problem of achieving controlled performance.

The disadvantages are that:

- The work is repetitive and boring;
- The individual's part in the organization is small and meaningless;
- Monotony creates apathy, dissatisfaction and carelessness;
- The individual develops no skills that might lead to promotion.

Taylor's approach to job design appears to create efficient ways of working. But it creates fragmented jobs that do not stimulate human motivation and which are dissatisfying to those who do them. There are thus both economic and human reasons for rejecting Taylor's approach.

The most widely used technique which motivation theories have generated, largely as an antidote to Taylor, is the technique of *job enrichment.*

Definition

Job enrichment is a technique for changing the design and experience of work to enhance employee need satisfaction and to improve work motivation and performance.

Expectancy theory can be used to aid understanding of a range of human behaviours, but Lawler and his colleagues have been concerned mainly with its relevance to questions of work motivation and performance. The experience of work can affect the individual's perception of the terms of the expectancy equation. By changing the design of a job, it is possible to change individuals' perceptions and create a different expectancy calculation, which preferably (for employees) increases need satisfaction and preferably (for management) increases performance.

The design of an individual's job determines both the kinds of rewards that are available and what the individual has to do to get those rewards. *Intrinsic rewards* are valued outcomes within the control of the individual, such as feelings of satisfaction and accomplishment. *Extrinsic rewards* are valued outcomes that are controlled by others, such as promotion and pay. The relationships between performance and intrinsic rewards are more immediate and direct than those between performance and extrinsic rewards. Lawler argues that intrinsic rewards are therefore more important influences on motivation to work.

Job design can influence the outcomes that the individual values. The individual discovers through experience in different jobs what kinds of outcomes to expect. It is possible that changes in work experiences can change the outcomes valued by a particular individual.

The design of jobs can thus have a significant effect on the experience of work and on the terms of the expectancy equation. The *job characteristics model* is the basis of the expectancy theorists' job enrichment strategy:

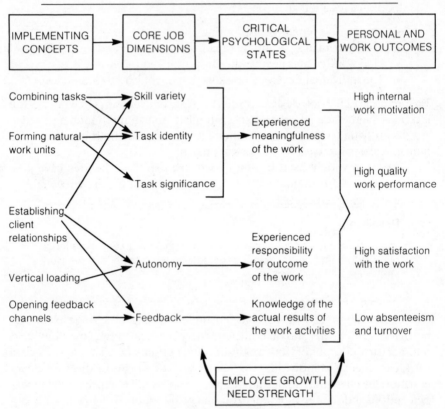

From J. R. Hackman, G. Oldham, R. Janson and K. Purdy, 1975; © 1975 by the Regents of the University of California. Reprinted from the *California Management Review*, 1975, vol. 17, no. 4, p. 62, by permission of the Regents.

The job characteristics model sets out systematically the links between characteristics of jobs, the individual's experience of those job characteristics, and the resultant outcomes in terms of motivation, satisfaction and performance. The model also takes into account individual differences in the desire for personal growth and development, or what Maslow called self-actualization. The strength of the links in the causal chain set out in the model are determined by the strength of the individual's personal growth need, so the model does not apply to everyone.

The heart of the model is the proposition that jobs can be analysed in terms of five *core dimensions*, which are defined as follows:

1. *Skill variety* is the extent to which a job makes use of different skills and abilities.
2. *Task identity* is the extent to which a job involves a "whole" and meaningful piece of work.
3. *Task significance* is the extent to which a job affects the work of other organization members or others in society.
4. *Autonomy* is the extent to which a job gives the individual freedom, independence and discretion in carrying it out.
5. *Feedback* is the extent to which information about the level of performance attained is related back to the individual.

The content of a job can be assessed on these five core dimensions, by asking employees to fill in questionnaires about their experience of the work. A *motivating potential score* can then be calculated for each job, using the equation:

$$\text{MPS} = \left[\frac{\text{skill variety} \ + \ \text{task identity} \ + \ \text{task significance}}{3} \right] \times (\text{autonomy}) \times (\text{feedback}).$$

If one of the three main components in this equation is low, then the motivating potential is low. Autonomy and feedback are considered to be more important in their motivating influence, and the equation is designed to reflect this. A near zero rating on either autonomy or feedback, for example, would greatly reduce the motivating potential score. A near zero rating on one of the other dimensions would not have such an effect.

These five core dimensions induce the three psychological states critical to high work motivation, job satisfaction and performance. These three states are defined as follows:

1. *Experienced meaningfulness* is the extent to which the individual considers the work to be meaningful, valuable and worthwhile.
2. *Experienced responsibility* is the extent to which the individual feels accountable for the work output.
3. *Knowledge of results* is the extent to which individuals know and understand how well they are performing.

Jobs that have high motivating potential scores are more likely to lead their incumbents to the experience of these critical psychological states than jobs that have low scores. Expectancy theorists argue that all three critical psychological states must be experienced if the personal and work outcomes on the right hand side of the model are to be fully achieved. One or two out of the three is not good enough. It is important to recall that individuals who do not value personal growth and development — whose growth need strength is low — will not respond in the way suggested by the model.

The model also shows how the motivating potential of jobs can be improved by applying five *implementing concepts*. These are:

1.   *Combining tasks*
      Give employees more than one part of the work to do. This increases the variety of the job, and increases the contribution that the individual makes to the product or service. For example, all typists could handle short memos, letters and major reports, instead of having separate groups of typists each of which specializes in one of these tasks.

2.   *Forming natural work units*
      Give employees a meaningful sequence of work to perform, rather than a fragmented part of what is required. This increases the contribution that the individual makes to the work, and increases the significance of the job. For example, each typist could type all the work for an author or group of authors, and follow every job through from start to finish, rather than divide work between a number of typists, and have different typists involved at different stages.

3.   *Establishing client relationships*
      Give employees responsibility for making personal contact with others within and outside the organization for whom and with whom they work. This increases variety, gives the person freedom in performing the work, and also increases the opportunities for receiving feedback. For example, typists could be allowed to deal directly with the authors whose work they type, rather than contacting them through a supervisor.

4.   *Vertical loading*
      Give employees responsibilities normally allocated to supervisors. These include granting discretion for:

      | Work scheduling | Work methods | Problem solving |
      | Quality checks | Training others | Cost control |
      | Work times and breaks | Deciding priorities | Recruitment decisions |

      This gives individuals autonomy in their work, and can be achieved by removing the supervisory role, or redesigning it to involve other tasks.

5:    *Opening feedback channels*
      Give employees direct relationships with "clients" and direct perform-ance summaries. This is aimed at improving the opportunities for feedback of performance results. For example, typists could be given

written accounts, analyses and summaries of their performance as individuals and as groups, to let them know exactly how well they are seen to be doing, and to provide a basis for performance improvement.

The technique of job enrichment was first "invented" by American psychologist Frederick Herzberg in the 1950s.

To find out what characteristics of work influenced job satisfaction and dissatisfaction, 203 Pittsburg engineers and accountants were interviewed and asked two "critical incident" questions. They were asked to recall events which had made them feel good about their work and events which had made them feel bad about it.

Content analysis of the critical incidents suggested that factors which led to satisfaction were different from those which led to dissatisfaction at work. Herzberg called this a "two factor theory of motivation".

The events which led to satisfaction were called "motivators" or "content factors" and were:

Achievement	Recognition	Responsibility
Advancement	Growth	The work itself

The events which led to dissatisfaction were called "hygiene factors" or "context factors" and were:

Salary	Company policy	Supervision
Status	Security	Working conditions

Improvement in the hygiene factors, Herzberg argued, might remove dissatisfaction, but would not increase satisfaction and motivation. The redesign of jobs to increase motivation and performance should thus focus on the motivator factors, and Herzberg suggested the application of seven *vertical job loading factors* to achieve job enrichment:

- Remove controls
- Increase accountability
- Create natural work units
- Provide direct feedback
- Introduce new tasks
- Allocate special assignments

STOP!

What similarities and differences can you identify between the theories of Maslow, the expectancy theorists, and Herzberg?

Answer Herzberg's critical incident questions in relation to your own work experiences and analyse your replies along with those of your colleagues. Do you get the same answers as Herzberg?

How would you assess the internal and external validity of this research design and method?

The first application of the expectancy approach to job enrichment was reported by Edward Lawler, J. Richard Hackman and S. Kaufman in 1973. They redesigned the jobs of female telephone operators in an American company, whose work was originally organized in the following way:

Job title	*Numbers*
Chief operator	1
Group Chief Operators (GCOs)	7
Service Assistants (SAs)	14
Operators	39

There were two types of operator job. The "directory assistance" job involved what in Britain is called "directory inquiries". The "toll" job involved placing, timing and charging long distance telephone calls. All of the employees filled in a questionnaire about their attitudes to their job two weeks before their jobs were changed, and they filled in the same questionnaire six months after the change. Due to labour turnover and work scheduling problems, only 17 operators completed the two questionnaires. All the GCOs, five of the SAs and eight Operators were also interviewed.

The job enrichment process was given the title "Initiative and Judgement Programme" by the company. It was conducted by company employees. The Operators and the SAs were not involved in any decisions about what the changes were to be. The following changes were made to their jobs:

1. They were allowed to choose the phrases in which they replied to customer requests. Previously, they worked with set phrases.
2. They were allowed to omit citing their number at the start of each call.
3. They were allowed to leave their workplaces to check records and look up numbers without getting the supervisor's permission.
4. Directory assistance operators were free to help the toll operators at their own discretion if the latter appeared to be overloaded.
5. They were free to deal with customers with large numbers of requests as they felt best, perhaps by calling them back when the work load fell.
6. They were free to visit the toilet without the supervisor's permission, and without signing out on a blackboard.
7. They reported the number of calls they handled themselves.

STOP!

Can you identify the core dimension affected by each of these changes?

These changes reduced the training time for the directory assistance job from five days to two. The Service Assistants, however, spent much more time on training and less on routine office management. The changes did not have the expected effects on satisfaction and motivation. The questionnaire replies showed that the jobs had not been markedly changed on the core dimensions. The operators were not low on growth need strength, so there was still something wrong with the job design.

STOP!

Why do you think this project was not successful?

One set of reasons for the lack of success of the project concerned the changes that were made to the job of the Service Assistants. Operators were given tasks previously carried out by the Service Assistants, and this upset relationships between the two groups. The Service Assistants were worried about their job security because they no longer made decisions for the operators, and the operators no longer relied on them to solve work problems. The researchers admitted that they paid too little attention to how the Service Assistants' job would be affected.

The management thought that the whole project had been successful because:

- The reduced training time had reduced costs;
- They could reduce the number of supervisors;
- Absenteeism and turnover fell during the study;
- Productivity and work quality were not affected.

Job enrichment was a popular management technique throughout the 1970s and contributed to the development of a "quality of working life movement" in Britain, Europe, Scandinavia and America. The world economic recession prevailing since the turn of the decade has diverted attention away from these issues and led to a preoccupation with curing unemployment and inflation. The quality of working life is less important when there is little work to be had. There are a number of organizations still in existence whose aim is to promote improvements in the experience of work, however, and the influence of this movement is likely to resurface.

SOURCES

Buchanan, D. A., 1979, *The Development of Job Design Theories and Techniques*, Saxon House, Farnborough.

Clare, D. A. and Sanford, D. G., 1979, "Mapping personal value space: a study of managers in four organizations", *Human Relations*, vol. 32, no. 8, pp. 659-66.

Ford, R. N., 1969, *Motivation Through the Work Itself*, American Management Association, New York.

Georgopoulos, B. S., Mahoney, G. M. and Jones, N. W., 1957, "A path — goal approach to productivity", *Journal of Applied Psychology*, vol. 41, no. 6, pp. 345-53.

Hackman, J. R., Oldham, G., Janson, R. and Purdy, K., 1975, "A new strategy for job enrichment", *California Management Review*, vol. 17, no. 4, pp. 57-71.

Herzberg, F., 1966, *Work and the Nature of Man*, Staples Press, New York.

Herzberg, F., 1968, "One more time: how do you motivate employees?", *Harvard Business Review*, vol. 46, no. 1, pp. 53-62.

Lawler, E. E., 1971, *Pay and Organizational Effectiveness: A Psychological View*, McGraw-Hill, New York.

Lawler, E. E., 1973, *Motivation in Work Organizations*, Brooks-Cole Publishing, New York.

Lawler, E. E., Hackman, J. R. and Kaufman, S., 1973, "Effects of job redesign: a field experiment," *Journal of Applied Social Psychology*, vol. 3, pp. 49-62.

Maslow, A. H., 1943, "A theory of human motivation", *Psychological Review*, vol. 50, no. 4, pp. 370-96.

Maslow, A. H., 1970, *Motivation and Personality*, Harper and Row, New York (second edition).

Neider, L., 1980, "An experimental field investigation utilizing an expectancy theory view of participation", *Organizational Behaviour and Human Performance*, vol. 26, no. 3, pp. 425-42.

Vroom, V. H., 1964, *Work and Motivation*, John Wiley, New York.

Chapter 5

Learning

Key concepts:

Once you have fully understood this chapter, you should be able to define the following concepts in your own words:

Learning

Behaviourist psychology
Stimulus-response psychology
Empiricism

Pavlovian (classical or respondent) conditioning
Skinnerian (instrumental or operant) conditioning
Conditioned and unconditioned stimulus
Conditioned and unconditioned response
Respondent
Operant
Shaping
Intermittent reinforcement

Cognitive psychology
Information processing theory
Rationalism

Cybernetic analogy
Feedback (intrinsic, extrinsic, concurrent and delayed)
Plan
TOTE unit

Objectives:

On completing this chapter, you should be able:

1. To explain the main components of the behaviourist and cognitive approaches to learning.
2. To identify the main arguments for and against each of these approaches.
3. To apply theories of learning to training and performance evaluation practices in organizations.

INTRODUCTION

How do animals learn?

"Next comes the vexed question as to what one should do when a puppy makes a puddle on the floor. Some people advise rubbing his nose in it. What a wicked idea. Should the puppy make a puddle, catch him, show him what he has done, and scold him resoundingly by your tone of voice, then immediately take him out to his usual spot. This usual spot is another vital link in the training chain. The puppy quickly gets to connect that spot with his 'jobs' and associations are quickly made. If, after puddling the floor, you put him out and he does it again outside, praise him fervently, and with great love in your voice."

From *Dog Training My Way and Difficult Dogs*, Barbara Woodhouse, Rickmansworth, 1973, p. 23.
Reproduced by permission of Barbara Woodhouse.

How do we learn? How do we come to know what we know, and to do what we are able to do? These questions have puzzled philosophers and teachers for centuries, and continue to generate controversy. These problems lie at the heart of human psychology and our knowledge of them is in a constant state of development. It is therefore not surprising that the student of learning is confronted with a variety of different approaches to the topic. This variety helps to maintain controversy, excitement and interest in the subject, which in turn help to generate new ideas, new theories, and new methods. The student of learning should welcome controversies and contradictions, and not be confused by them.

This chapter explains two approaches to learning which are current and influential, based on behaviourist psychology and cognitive psychology. These perspectives are in many respects contradictory, but they may also be viewed as complementary.

Psychology is associated by many people with the study of rats in mazes. Rats, and other animals, have indeed contributed much to our knowledge of human behaviour, and have been widely used by psychologists concerned with the development of theories of learning. Rat biochemistry is in fact similar to ours. We have to face the fact that we humans are animals in many (if not all) respects and that we can learn something of ourselves through studying the behaviour of the other creatures on this planet.

The ability to learn is not unique to human beings. Animals can and do learn, as dog owners and circus fans are well aware. A feature that seems to distinguish us from animals is our ability to learn about, adapt to and manipulate our environment for purposes that we ourselves define. Animals can adapt to changes in their circumstances, but their ability to manipulate their environment is restricted, and they appear to have no choice over the goals of their behaviour. So although animals can learn, they have developed no science or technology comparable with our own.

The study of rats and pigeons has given us insights into human abilities and so has the attempt to give machines "intelligence", or what we might recognize as intelligence. When students of "artificial intelligence" try to build a machine to do something that humans do easily, naturally and effortlessly, they quickly discover how complex human skills are.

The ability of humans to learn is important to organizations preoccupied with controlled performance. The members of an organization have to know what they are to do, how they are to do it, and how well they are expected to do it. Learning theories have thus influenced a range of organizational practices, such as:

- The introduction of new recruits to the organization;
- The conduct of job training;
- Supervisors' evaluations of subordinate performance.

The theories set out in this chapter thus have far reaching implications for skills training and development in organizations, and for indoctrination in the ways of particular occupations and professions.

The terms skill and training are used here in a sense broader than that normally implied in common usage. Skill to a psychologist covers a wide range of human behaviours, from the specially acquired ability to play tennis, to the routine ability to walk down the street. When the latter is analysed in detail, it turns out to be an extremely complex and sophisticated performance, and quite an achievement for the individual doing it. It is therefore entitled to be called a skill. Training in organizations covers not just the acquisition of manual skills, but also the learning of the "right" attitudes, values, beliefs and expectations.

THE LEARNING PROCESS

We hope that when you have finished reading this book you will be able to say that you have learned something. The test is whether or not you will be able to do things that you could not do before you read the book. You should, for example, know what the study of organizational behaviour is concerned with and you should be able to tell others what you know and think about it. You should be able to write essays and examination answers that you could not previously tackle. If you can do none of these things, then you will have learned nothing.

We are concerned here with two related aspects of learning:

1. How we come to know things at all, through the *process* of learning.
2. The organization in our minds of our ideas, thoughts and knowledge, which constitutes the *content of memory*.

We refer to the process as *learning*, and to the result as *knowledge*.

Definition

Learning is the process of acquiring knowledge through experience which leads to a change in behaviour.

Learning is defined as changes in behaviour through experience. It is important to note this restriction. Behaviour can be changed by many other factors and in ways which we would not wish to call learning. These factors include growing up or "maturation" (in children), ageing (in adults), drugs, alcohol (a particularly popular and socially accepted drug), and fatigue.

We cannot see what goes on inside your head as you learn. We can only infer that learning has taken place by examining changes in behaviour. If we assume that human behaviour does not alter spontaneously for no reason, then we can look for experiences that may be causes of change. These experiences may be derived from inside the body, or they may be sensory, arising outside.

Changes in behaviour, and in particular those which happen at work, can be quantified using a "learning curve". This might represent the learning curve for a trainee word processor operator:

Number of weeks on the job

The learning curve can be plotted for an individual or for a group of trainees. This (fictitious) learning curve shows that:

1. It takes about 6 months for operators to become proficient.
2. Top output is around 30 pages a day.
3. The trainee's ability develops slowly at first, rises sharply during the third month, and hits a "plateau" during the fourth month of training. Most training curves for manual skills show such a plateau, but of course not always in the position shown here.

The shape of a learning curve depends on the characteristics of the task being learned and the individual learner. It is however often possible to measure learning, to compare individuals with each other, and to establish what constitutes good performance.

STOP!

How could your learning of organizational behaviour be measured throughout your course of study?

What is the shape of your learning curve for this course?

Why is it that shape?

Should it be that shape?

What could you do to change the shape of your learning curve?

The experiences that lead to changes in human behaviour have a number of important features.

First, the human mind is not a passive recorder of information picked up through the senses. We can usually recount the plot of a novel that we have read, for example, but remember very few of the author's words, beyond those that refer to key actors and events, and none of the author's sentences, apart from those that we have deliberately committed to memory. So we do not record our experiences in any simple, straightforward way.

Second, we are usually able to recall events in which we have participated as if we were in fact some other actor in the drama. We are able to see ourselves "from outside", as objects in our experience. Now at the time when we experienced those events, those cannot have been the sense impressions that we picked up. This feature of our thought processes is the product of reflection which takes place after the events concerned.

Third, new experiences do not inevitably lead to changes in behaviour. These experiences must be processed in some way to become influential in determining future behaviours.

Fourth, the way in which we express our innate drives depends partly on our experiences. We raised the question of whether motives are innate or learned in Chapter 3. This distinction, as we saw, is too simple and artificial. Humans do have innate drives, but these are expressed in behaviour in many different ways. How they are expressed depends on many factors, including past experiences. This is also true for animal learning. Our innate makeup biases our behaviour in certain directions, but these biases can be overridden or modified by variations in experience.

We will explore in this chapter two contrasting perspectives on the psychology of learning.

Behaviourist, or *stimulus-response*, theory argues that what we learn are chains of muscle movements. As brain or mental processes are not observable, they are not considered important aspects for study.

Cognitive, or *information processing*, theory argues that what we learn are mental structures, and that mental processes are both important and amenable to study.

These approaches are based on the same empirical data but their interpretations of that data are radically different. The stance that one adopts has implications for practice, both in teaching and in organizations. These approaches are explained in more detail below and are summarized in the following table for convenience and reference:

Behaviourist; stimulus-response	Cognitive; Information processing
Studies only observable behaviour	*Also studies mental processes*
Behaviour is determined by learned sequences of muscle movements	*Behaviour is determined by memory, mental processes and expectations*
We learn habits	*We learn cognitive structures (and alternative ways to achieve goals)*
Problem solving is by trial and error	*Problem solving also involves Insight and understanding*
Dull, boring, but amenable to research (?)	*Rich, interesting, but complex, vague and unresearchable (?)*

We should not of course refer only to difficulty and complexity as criteria for accepting or rejecting a particular perspective. Note how the cognitive position contradicts the behaviourist position on some counts, but adds to it on others. We suggested earlier that these approaches may be considered complementary in some respects.

THE BEHAVIOURIST APPROACH TO LEARNING

The oldest theory of learning states that ideas that are experienced together tend to be associated with each other. Today, behaviourist psychologists speak of the association between stimulus and response.

The behaviourist approach to human learning is based on a theory of how people come to know things — an epistemology — called *empiricism* or *associationism*. This theory of knowledge is different from that which lies behind the cognitive approach to learning. Empiricists and associationists argue that the human mind is dependent on the experiences of the senses. There can be no thought without sensory input. The mind deals with that input by *abstraction*, that is by concentrating on its main features and paying less attention to the detail. Relationships and associations in the incoming sensory information are revealed as the information is ordered, arranged and compared. The process of abstraction is thus a kind of information sorting process, and the output is the recognition of pattern and the formation of concepts. This is how we infer (or "induce") the properties of objects and events, and regularities in their relationships. We store these abstractions in memory, and can learn also by making logical deductions from the stored information through reflection.

Learning is the result of experience. We use the knowledge of the results of past behaviour to change, modify and improve our behaviour in future. You learn to write better assignments and get higher examination grades by finding out how well or how badly you did last time and why. Human beings cannot learn without *appropriate feedback*. Behaviourist and cognitive psychologists agree that experience influences behaviour, but disagree over how this happens.

Feedback may be either rewarding or punishing. Common sense seems to suggest that if a particular behaviour is rewarded, then it is more likely to be repeated. If it is punished, it is more likely to be avoided. Rats are thus trained to run through mazes at the whim of the psychologist using judicious applications of electric shocks and food pellets. In the language of behaviourist psychology:

Rewards are positive reinforcement

Punishments are negative reinforcement

The American psychologist John B. Watson introduced the term "behaviourism" in 1913. He was critical of the technique of *introspection*, a popular research method at that time, which was used to find out what went on inside people's minds. Subjects were simply asked to talk about their sensory experiences and thought processes as clearly as possible. They were asked to look inside their own minds, to introspect, and to tell the psychologist what they found there. Watson wanted objective, "scientific" handles on human behaviour, its causes and its consequences. He could see no way in which introspection could ever produce this. This took him, and many other psychologists, away from the intangible and invisible contents of the mind to the study of the relationships between:

visible stimuli and *visible responses*

That is why behaviourist psychology is sometimes referred to as "stimulus–response" psychology.

Reward or punish . . . ?

One well established principle of behaviourist psychology is that reward is more effective than punishment in changing behaviour. This principle has been derived from extensive work with rodents, and has also influenced practice with humans. The problem with punishment is that it creates fear, resentment and hostility in the punished person. Rewards for good behaviour are thus more likely to ensure compliance.

Charles O'Reilly and Barton Weitz studied how 141 supervisors in an American retail chain store used punishments to control the behaviour of their subordinates at work. Four sanctions were in common use:

- Informal spoken warnings
- Suspension from work
- Loss of pay
- Dismissal

Supervisors used these sanctions against "incorrect" subordinate behaviours such as:

- Slack timekeeping
- Sloppy appearance at work
- Low sales records
- Discourtesy to customers

Supervisors dealt with these incorrect behaviours in different ways.

Some supervisors preferred to confront such problems directly and quickly, gave subordinates frequent warnings, and were quite prepared to fire subordinates who did not behave as required. One supervisor described his readiness to sack subordinates as "an acquired taste".

But other supervisors had difficulty in dealing with these problems, tried to avoid them, and got depressed when they had to fire someone. They described their dealings with poor performers as "traumatic". These "employee oriented" supervisors were more sensitive to their subordinates' needs and liked to give them time to put problems right.

The research showed that the departments run by the employee oriented supervisors had poorer performance ratings than the departments run by the hard line supervisors.

Does this contradict the behaviourist position that punishment is not an effective way to influence behaviour?

Individuals at work learn from others the behaviours and attitudes that are appropriate in particular circumstances. The employee who comes late to work regularly, or who does not work as hard as colleagues, violates the *socially* established and accepted standards.

The punishments used by supervisors may thus be effective where:

- They are perceived as maintaining the accepted social order; and
- They are perceived as legitimate by the victim.

From Charles O'Reilly and Barton A. Weitz, "Managing marginal employees: the use of warnings and dismissals", *Administrative Science Quarterly*, 1980, vol. 25, no. 3, pp. 467-84.

This approach assumes that what lies between the stimulus and the response is some simple mechanism that will eventually be revealed as our knowledge of the biochemistry and neurophysiology of the brain improves. This is a mechanism that relates stimuli to responses in a way that governs behaviour. We can therefore continue to study how stimuli and responses are related without a detailed understanding of the nature of that mechanism. In other words, behaviourists argue that nothing of psychological importance lies between the stimulus and the response.

The central task of behaviourist psychology is to discover how new connections between stimuli and responses are formed. Learning is thus the development of associations between stimuli and responses through experience. This happens in two different ways, known as *Pavlovian conditioning* and *Skinnerian conditioning*

Pavlovian conditioning

This is also known as classical and as respondent conditioning. It is the discovery of the Russian physiologist Ivan Petrovich Pavlov (1849–1931). Classical conditioning demonstrates how a behaviour or response that is already established can become associated with a new stimulus. Pavlov's work with dogs is well known and his name has become a household word.

If you show meat to a dog, the dog will produce saliva. The meat is the stimulus, the saliva is the response. The meat is thus called an *unconditioned stimulus* because we do not have to do anything to the dog to get it to salivate, which it does naturally. Similarly, the saliva is an *unconditioned response*. Unconditioned responses are also called *reflexes*. Your lower leg jerks when you are struck just below the kneecap; your pupils contract when light is shone into your eyes. These are typical of many human reflexes. Humans also salivate at the sight and smell of food.

Suppose we now ring a bell when we show the meat to the dog. Do this often enough, and the dog will associate the bell with the meat. Eventually the dog will salivate at the sound of the bell. The bell is a *conditioned stimulus*, and the saliva is now a *conditioned response*. The dog was able to salivate before the conditioning process began. It has now learned, as a result of that experience, to salivate at the sound of a bell as well as at the sight of food. It does not of course have to be a bell. All kinds of stimuli can be conditioned in this way.

Suppose we now stop giving the meat to the dog after the bell. The dog will continue to salivate at the sound of the bell alone. But if we continue to do this, the amount of saliva produced falls and the association between the conditioned stimulus and conditioned response suffers *extinction*. The dog learns that the bell no longer means food and stops salivating at the sound of the bell.

The conditioned response may also be invoked by stimuli that are similar to the original conditioned stimulus, such as another bell with a different tone. This phenomenon is called *stimulus generalization*. A complementary phenomenon, *stimulus discrimination*, can also be learned in the same way. The dog can be conditioned to salivate at a bell of one pitch, but not at another.

The conditioned response in animals is an observable, consistent and reliable phenomenon. Pavlov studied it in great detail, changing the stimulus, manipulating the timing of the conditioned and unconditioned stimuli, and measuring the quantities of saliva produced by his dogs under varying conditions. He extended this work to other animals and to other responses. We are not going to look at this work in more detail here, because it is the central concepts with which we are concerned.

The argument from this work, therefore, is that human behaviour is the result of conditioning. Changes in our behaviour, or learning, are the result of further conditioning. The basic unit of learning in animals and humans is the conditioned response.

Skinnerian conditioning

This is also commonly known as instrumental and as operant conditioning. It is the discovery of the American psychologist Burrhus Frederic Skinner (b. 1904). Instrumental conditioning demonstrates how new behaviours or responses become established through association with particular stimuli.

Any behaviour, in a particular setting or context, that is rewarded or reinforced in some way will tend to be repeated in that context. Skinner put a rat into a specially designed box with a lever inside which, when pressed, gave the animal food. The rat was not taught in any systematic way to press the lever for its meals. However, in the process of wandering around the box at random, the rat eventually pressed the lever. It may sit on it, knock it with its head, or push it with a paw. That random behaviour is rewarded with food, the behaviour is reinforced and is likely to happen again.

Classical conditioning has that name because it is the older of the two conditioning phenomena described here. Skinnerian conditioning is also called instrumental conditioning because it is related to behaviours that are instrumental in getting some material reward, in this example food. Skinner's rat has thus to be under the influence of some drive before it can be conditioned in this way. His rats were of course hungry when they went into his box and their behaviour led to the appropriate reward.

Where do the terms respondent and operant conditioning come from? Watson's stimulus — response psychology stated that there was no behaviour, or no response, without a stimulus to set it in motion. One could therefore condition a known response to a given stimulus, that is, one could attach that response to another stimulus. Such responses are called *respondents.* Knee jerks, pupil contractions and salivation are well known and clearly identified responses that are amenable to conditioning.

Skinner argued that this was too simple and inconsistent with known facts. Animals and humans *do* behave in the absence of specific stimuli. In fact, he argued, most human behaviour is of this kind. Behaviours that are emitted in the absence of identifiable stimuli are called *operants.*

Operant conditioning explains how new behaviours and new patterns of behaviour can become established. Respondent conditioning does not alter the animal's behaviour, only the timing of that behaviour. Skinner introduced the concept of *shaping* behaviour by selectively reinforcing the desired bits of behaviour. In this way he was able to get pigeons to play ping pong and to walk in figures of eight — a famous demonstration of how random or spontaneous behaviour can be shaped by operant conditioning.

Apart from this distinction between respondent and operant conditioning, Pavlov's other concepts apply to operant conditioning also, including extinction, generalization and discrimination.

Like Pavlov, Skinner studied numerous variations on the operant conditioning theme. One important variation is to not reward the required behaviour every time, by varying the intervals between responses, or by varying the proportion of correct responses that are rewarded. Why do gamblers keep playing when they lose so often? Why do anglers continue to fish when they are catching nothing? Life is full of examples that demonstrate the power of what Skinner called *intermittent reinforcement.*

STOP!

In what ways is your own behaviour conditioned by intermittent reinforcement?

How important a determinant of your behaviour do you think operant conditioning is ?

Skinner claimed to be able to explain the development of complex patterns of human behaviour with the theory of operant conditioning. This shows how our behaviour is conditioned or shaped by our environment, by our experiences in that environment, and by the selective rewards and punishments that we receive. Thinking, problem solving and the acquisition of language, he argued, are dependent on these simple conditioning processes. Skinner completely rejected the use of "mentalistic" or cognitive explanations and "inner psychic forces" in explanations of human behaviour. These he argued, following Watson, were not observable, not researchable, and not necessary to the science of human psychology.

Skinner's objective was to predict and to control human behaviour. Mental, invisible, intangible constructs are not useful because they do not tell us which variables to manipulate to control that behaviour. If behaviour is determined by environment and experience, we need to be able to identify the factors in that environment that affect behaviour, and to discover the laws that relate behaviour to these variables.

Skinner's ambitious project and its output have been enormously influential. His experimental work has been extended to animals and humans of all types and ages. They have led to the widespread use of programmed learning, a technique of instruction designed to reinforce correct responses in the learner and to let people learn at their own pace. The development of microcomputers in the late 1970s reinforced the popularity of this technique. Skinner has also developed "behaviour modification" therapies for mental and some criminal disorders. This usually means that undesirable behaviours cease to be rewarded, and praise and rewards follow those behaviours that are considered acceptable. The behaviour of a conditioned animal is consistent and predictable, and this knowledge can be used to test the effects of drugs for eventual human consumption.

STOP!

Is Barbara Woodhouse's technique of puppy training, explained at the beginning of this chapter, an example of respondent or of operant conditioning?

THE COGNITIVE APPROACH TO LEARNING

It is possible to study the internal workings of the mind in indirect ways, by inference. Why should we look only at observable stimuli and responses in the study of human psychology? Behaviourism seems to be unnecessarily restrictive. It also seems to push out of psychology those features that make us interesting, different, and above all, human.

The cognitive approach to human learning is based on a theory of how people come to know things — an epistemology — called *rationalism*. This theory of knowledge is different from the empiricist or associationist epistemology that lies behind behaviourism. Rationalists argue that the human mind relies on *reasoning* as a basis for understanding, and is not wholly dependent on the senses. We have in our heads a more complex and elaborate representation or image of the world than empiricists allow. Our minds do not accept any and all associations. We are able to distinguish those associations that make sense from those that do not. We know what belongs together and what does not. Sensory information is incomplete and unstructured. It presents itself to the mind in a chaotic state and is the raw material for a process of interpretation. That process organizes the data and imposes meaning on it. This is not a sorting and abstracting task as empiricism argues. We do not hear sounds, we hear music; we do not see multicoloured mosaics, we see buildings, people, cars, and streets.

How do we select from all the stimuli that bombard our senses those to which we are going to respond? Why are some outcomes seen as rewarding and others as punishments? This may appear obvious where the reward is survival or food and the punishment is pain or death. But with intrinsic or symbolic rewards this is not clear.

To answer these questions we have to consider states of mind concerning perception and motivation. Cognitive psychologists admit that things happen inside the mind that the psychologist should and can study.

The rewards and punishments that the behaviourists call "reinforcement" work in more complex ways than conditioning theories suggest. Reinforcement is always knowledge about the results of past behaviour. It is *feedback* on how successful our behaviour has been. That knowledge or feedback is *information* that can be used to modify or maintain previous behaviours. This information of course has to be perceived, interpreted, given meaning, and used in making decisions about future behaviours. The knowledge of results, the feedback, the information, has to be processed. Cognitive theories of learning are thus also called *information processing* theories.

This approach draws concepts from the field of cybernetics which was established as a separate field by the American mathematician Norbert Weiner. He defined cybernetics in 1947 as "the science of communication in the animal and in the machine". One central idea of cybernetics is the notion of control of system performance through feedback. Information processing theories of learning are based on what is called the "cybernetic analogy". The elements of a cybernetic feedback control system are:

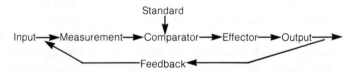

Consider a domestic heating control system. The temperature standard is set by the householder. When the system is switched on, a heater (effector) starts to warm up the room. The output of the system is heated air. Changes in temperature are detected (measured) by a thermometer. The temperature of the room is continually compared with the standard. When the room reaches the required temperature, the effector is switched off.

The cybernetic analogy claims that this feedback control loop is a simplified model of what goes on inside the human mind. For standard, we should read motive, purpose, intent, goal. The output is behaviour. The senses are our measuring devices. The comparator is the perceptual process which organizes and imposes meaning on sensory data which controls behaviour in pursuit of given objectives, and which learns from experience.

We have in our minds some kind of "internal representation" or "schema" of ourselves and the environment in which we function. This internal representation is used in a purposive way to determine our behaviour. This internal representation is also called the *image* — what in Chapter 3 we called the individual's perceptual world.

How does the image influence behaviour? Our behaviour is purposive, and we formulate *plans* for achieving those purposes. The plan is a set of mental instructions, similar to a computer program, for guiding and controlling the required behaviour. Within the master plan (get an educational qualification) there are likely to be a number of subplans (submit assignment on time; pass the organizational behaviour examination). The organization of our behaviour is hierarchical — a concept which can again be illustrated by comparison with a computer program in which instructional routines and subroutines can be "nested" within each other.

The basic component of behaviour is the TOTE unit. TOTE is an acronym for Test, Operate, Test, Exit. The TOTE unit is another way of applying the feedback control model to human behaviour, like this:

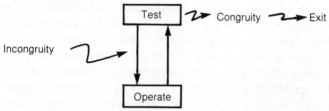

Complex behaviours can be explained by "nesting" TOTE units within each other. Behaviour can be described as a series of attempts to carry out plans which comprise a number of subplans which themselves each comprise a number of sub-subplans, and so on. Consider a man hammering a nail into a piece of wood. He tests the nail after each blow to see if the head is flush with the surface of the wood. Until it is flush, he continues to operate, or to hammer. This action may be part of another plan that concerns joining two pieces of wood together; this plan may in turn be nested inside the plan of making a chair; this plan may be nested inside the plan of selling chairs to make a living; and so on.

The feedback that we get comes in different forms.

Intrinsic feedback comes from within our bodies, from the muscles, joints, skin, and other internal mechanisms such as that concerned with maintaining balance when walking.

Extrinsic feedback we get from our environment, such as the visual and aural information needed to drive a car.

Concurrent feedback arrives during the act and can be used to control it as it proceeds. This is of course also necessary in driving.

Delayed feedback comes after the task is completed, and can be used to affect future performances. Feedback on student examination performance is usually delayed.

It is hard and often impossible for humans to behave at all without appropriate feedback. Consider walking down the street blindfold. It is also hard and often impossible for humans to learn without appropriate feedback. Consider the student who consistently fails examinations but is never told why. The saying, "practice makes perfect" is only partially correct. It should read "practice with appropriate feedback . . . ".

The plans that we choose to pursue depend on our needs, motives, values and beliefs about ourselves and the world in which we live. The conduct of these plans depends on our ability to draw on acquired knowledge, skills, procedures, and on our ability to learn from the successes and failures of previous plans. Feedback is therefore vital to learning. Information on how things went in the past is required to control future actions. We learn to adapt to changes in our circumstances, and we learn to improve the effectiveness of our behaviour, by switching plans and subplans.

Cognitive psychology is therefore not concerned with the relationships between stimuli and responses, but with the plans that people choose and the means they adopt for pursuing them, and how these plans and subplans are modified and improved by experience.

Feedback, rewards and punishments, knowledge of results, have a motivating effect on behaviour, rather than simply a reinforcing effect. Several writers on human motivation have argued that opportunities to learn new skills and knowledge, to understand more, to develop more effective ways of living and coping with our environment, are intrinsically motivating. The theory of psychological growth of Frederick Herzberg, for example, claims that we have innate needs to know more, and to be creative. Another American psychologist, White, has suggested that we have a need to develop "competence" in dealing with our environment and that this gives us satisfaction. Abraham Maslow also examined the motivating role of curiosity, learning and experimenting. One of the most optimistic advocates of this argument is Gardner Murphy who wrote:

> "This urge towards discovery, this living curiosity, beginning with a sort of 'freeing of intelligence' from cultural clamps and moving forward in a positive way activated by thirst for contact with the world and for understanding and making sense of it, will begin to develop a society in which the will to understand is the dominant new component."

> From Gardner Murphy, *Human Potentialities*, George Allen & Unwin, London, 1958, p. 19.

LEARNING IN THE ORGANIZATION

When individuals join an organization, of any kind, they give up some personal freedom of action. That is part of the price of membership. The individual member thus agrees that the organization may make demands on their time and effort, as long as these demands are seen to be legitimate.

The problem for the other members of the organization is to teach new members what is expected of them, what is customary, what is accepted. Different organizations have different standards concerning, for example:

- What counts as adequate and good work performance;
- Familiarity in everyday social interactions at work;
- The appropriate amount of deference to show to superiors;
- Timekeeping;
- Dress and appearance;
- Social activities off the job;
- Attitudes to work, workers, managers, unions, customers, and so on.

The newcomer has to learn these standards and the ways of behaving that they involve, to be a successful and accepted member of the organization. It is not enough just to learn the knowledge and skills required to perform work duties and responsibilities. The individual does not have to believe that the organization's standards are appropriate. What matters is that individuals behave as if they believed in them. Individuals arrive in a new organization with values, attitudes, beliefs and expectations that they have acquired elsewhere. These may have to change or be pushed aside.

The process through which new members "learn the ropes" is usually an informal one, rather than a planned programme of instruction. Some organizations do have "induction programmes" for new recruits, but these are generally short and superficial. The individual learns about the organization by just being there. This is achieved by giving rewards such as praise, encouragement, privilege and promotion for "correct" behaviour. It is achieved by punishments such as being ignored, ridiculed or fined for behaviour that is out of line.

STOP!

Most organizations plan the punishments and material (financial) rewards that their members will get, but leave their symbolic rewards to chance.

From your knowledge of motivation and learning theory, what would you predict to be the consequences of such a policy ?

The process through which individuals learn the skills and knowledge required to carry out specific jobs is on the other hand usually a formal one. Learning theories can offer advice for ensuring that such job training is effective:

1.   The trainee must be motivated to learn. The trainer should establish what these motives are, and point out advantages of training that the trainees may not have considered. These motives may include money, a prestigious job title, career opportunities or the acquisition of a valued skill.
2.   The task to be learned should be divided into meaningful segments for which performance standards can be established. The more meaningful the task, the stronger the motivation to learn. It may be possible to break the whole task down into a hierarchy of goals and subgoals, with specific objectives for each. If the trainee is asked to learn too little at a time, the learning will be too easy and meaningless. If on the other hand trainees are confronted with too much at a time, they may become frustrated, lose confidence, and learning is less effective.
3.   Trainees should be given clear, frequent and appropriate feedback on their performance and progress. Intrinsic feedback is usually inadequate in learning job skills, and the trainer has to provide the relevant extrinsic feedback. Recognition and praise for good work is more effective than

We need appropriate feedback at work . . .

Appropriate feedback on work performance is necessary to ensure the learning and development of job skills. But do supervisors always tell their subordinates the truth? Daniel Ilgen and William Knowlton designed an experiment to answer this question.

The researchers asked 40 students each to supervise a group of three workers doing a routine clerical job for two hours. The supervisors were first shown the results of a "personnel test" which was supposed to have measured the abilities of their subordinates for such a task.

But each group had one worker, a confederate of the researchers, who performed much better or much worse than the others, behaving either very enthusiastically or apathetically. The supervisors were led in this way to believe that the level of performance of this exceptional group member was due to either high or low ability or motivation.

After the work session, the supervisors rated the ability and motivation of all their subordinates on scales ranging from "unsatisfactory" to "outstanding". They then completed a separate "feedback report form", believing that they would have to discuss it with the exceptional worker in person.

For the feedback, the supervisors were asked to choose from 12 statements the one which best described their evaluation of that worker, such as:

- "You have done very well. I believe I would try to do even better next time if I were you."
- "Your performance is not good at all. You really need to put much more into it."

They also had to recommend further action for the subordinate, to change either ability or motivation, such as:

- Attend a special training session;
- Concentrate more on the task;
- Try harder.

The supervisors were then told about the deception. There was no feedback session. The researchers wanted to find out how truthful the supervisors were with their feedback to their subordinates.

As expected, ratings of the ability and motivation of subordinates were higher when supervisors believed that they would have to tell the subordinates this in person. Where low performance was attributed to low motivation, the feedback did reflect this accurately. But where low performance was blamed on poor ability, supervisors recommended an inappropriate mix of feedback, directed at both effort and skill.

The researchers conclude that supervisors may systematically distort their assessments of subordinates and inhibit their learning.

From Daniel R. Ilgen and William A. Knowlton, "Performance attributional effects on feedback from superiors", *Organizational Behaviour and Human Performance*, 1980, vol. 25, no. 3, pp. 441-56.

hostile criticism. The reasons for poor performance should be explained and the trainee shown the correct procedures.

4. Punishment does not tell trainees what they are doing wrong or what they have to do to improve. Punishment for bad work is more likely to instil dislike, distrust and hostility in trainees and remove their motivation for learning. The effects of punishment are thus likely to be less predictable that those of reward. Encouragement and recognition creates feelings of confidence, competence, development and progress that enhance the motivation to learn.

5. Delayed feedback is less effective than concurrent or rapid feedback. Research into the effectiveness of employee performance appraisal systems shows that this is usually done casually and annually — in other words, too little is done too late to be of any use in developing job knowledge, skills and performance. Supervisors need to give frequent feedback in a helpful and considerate manner. People may react positively to helpful, encouraging, and motivating criticism.

SOURCES

Annett, J., 1969, *Feedback and Human Behaviour*, Penguin Books, Harmondsworth.

Hilgard, E. R. and Bower, G. H., 1975 *Theories of Learning*, Prentice-Hall, New Jersey (fourth edition).

Ilgen, D. R. and Knowlton, W. A., 1980, "Performance attributional effects on feedback from superiors", *Organizational Behaviour and Human Performance*, vol. 25, no. 3, pp. 441-56.

Miller, G. A., Galanter, E. and Pribram, K. H., 1960, *Plans and the Structure of Behaviour*, Henry Holt, New York.

White, R., 1959, "Motivation reconsidered: the concept of competence", *Psychological Review*, vol. 66, pp. 297-333.

Chapter 6

Personality

Introduction
The problems of definition
Personality types and traits
The development of the self
The study of the self
Nomothetic versus idiographic?

Key concepts:

Once you have fully understood this chapter, you should be able to define the following concepts in your own words:

Personality   Idiographic
Implicit personality theory   Self
                                           I
Nomothetic   Me
Type   Generalized other
Trait
Emotionality   Thematic apperception test
Neuroticism   Projective test
                                           Need for achievement

Objectives:

On completing this chapter, you should be able:

1. Realistically to assess the main characteristics of your own personality.
2. To distinguish between type, trait and self theories of personality.
3. To identify the strengths and limitations of both formal and informal approaches to personality assessment.
4. To explain the use and limitations of objective questionnaires and projective tests as measures of personality.

INTRODUCTION

Useful Latin words and phrases:

per sonare	to speak through
persona	an actor's mask; a character in a play
persona grata	an acceptable person
persona non grata	an unacceptable person

We are each unique individuals who deal with the world in our unique ways. What makes us different from each other? How can we identify and describe these differences and compare individuals with each other? Psychologists have tried to answer these questions using the concept *personality*.

Personality is a comprehensive, all embracing concept. The way in which you understand the world and your place in it, the things that motivate you, and the way in which you learn, are all aspects of your personality. The concept of personality thus integrates the processes of perception, motivation and learning.

Definition:

The individual's *personality* is "the total pattern of characteristic ways of thinking, feeling and behaving that constitute the individual's distinctive method of relating to the environment".

From J. Kagan and E. Havemann, *Psychology: An Introduction*, Harcourt Brace Jovanovich, New York, 1976, third edition, p. 376.

The term personality is usually used to describe features, characteristics or *properties* of the individual. These characteristics or properties concern the individual's way of coping with living. Perception, motivation and learning are *processes*. Personality defined in this way is not a process. But we must distinguish between an individual's current personality on the one hand, and how it arrived at that state on the other. The latter concerns personality development, which clearly is a process.

Personality is a broad, integrating concept, but we are not interested in all properties of the individual. Most of us have two legs, talk, dislike pain and get drunk at least once in our lives. These properties are not remarkable and do not set us apart from others. A one legged, dumb, alcoholic masochist is however exceptional and therefore interesting. Our definition of personality is thus restricted to those properties that are:

Stable

We are interested in properties that appear in different contexts and that endure through time. We are not interested in properties that are occasional, random and transient.

People who are not punctual tend to be late for all occasions. People who are hardworking, cheerful and optimistic tend always to be like that.

Distinctive

We are interested in the pattern of dispositions that are unique to the individual. We are not interested in properties that all or most people possess.

You may be aggressive with waiters, shy with women and terrified of mice. You may share the first two of these dispositions with a friend who breeds mice as pets.

Some personality dispositions may be strong and appear frequently. One may always be happy, optimistic and telling jokes. Other dispositions may be weak and aroused infrequently or only in specific contexts. One may only be aggressive in restaurants and with waiters. In these ways, there can be endless variations in personality differences between people.

If the concept of personality is to be useful in understanding human behaviour, we have to accept two propositions.

First, we have to accept that human behaviour does indeed have stable, lasting characteristics. Most of us can recognize consistency in our own thoughts, emotions and behaviour. We do have established, routine ways of relating to others, of meeting our needs, of solving problems, of coping with frustration and stress, and so on. Our behaviour is not random, inconsistent and irrational. There are regularities in the ways that we think and in what we do that can be identified and studied.

Second, we have to accept that the distinctive properties of an individual's personality can be measured in some way and compared with others. Measurement does not necessarily imply numbers or quantities, although one of the personality theories that is explained later in the chapter is based on sophisticated techniques of statistical analysis. One can always attach numbers to human phenomena, like aspects of personality, but whether or not the outcome is meaningful is open to debate.

THE PROBLEMS OF DEFINITION

There are some peculiar problems associated with the definition and use of the word personality. We must therefore look at these before we proceed. The word personality is common in everyday speech as well as in psychological research. The popular uses of the term usually refer to:

"Key characteristics"
We say that one person has an aggressive personality, that another has a shy
personality, and so on. We often describe the personalities of others by using
only one prominent feature or property of their behaviour.

"Quantity"
We say that one individual has lots of personality, that another has little or no
personality. What we usually refer to in this context is an individual's physical
attractiveness or social success, such as with "personality girls" used in some
forms of advertising, and "television personalities".

These are not incorrect uses of the term. They are accurate and fully
understood in the contexts in which they are normally used. But the
psychologist regards these uses as oversimplified and imprecise. They are not
adequate for the purposes of understanding human behaviour in a rigorous,
comprehensive, scientific way. So we must here avoid using the term
personality with these popular meanings.

We are in fact all "informal" personality theorists. We are continually
assessing the personalities of others, and we normally do this unconsciously.
We categorize or *stereotype* people according to immediately noticeable
characteristics of their behaviour, appearance, dress and speech. We build up
pictures of their personalities on the basis of that limited information:

"Attractive individuals are intelligent, honest and reliable."

"Women are too emotional to make good managers."

"Fat people are always jolly."

"The Chinese are inscrutable."

"Small, thin, dark haired Scots are mean."

Stereotypes serve a number of useful purposes. They give us simple explanations for human behaviour. They help us to make predictions about what
others are likely to do next. They give us a basis from which to guide our own
behaviour in relating to and reacting to others.

Stereotypes therefore are *implicit personality theories.* They are implicit
because they are not stated in any formally or carefully defined sense, and they
are not supported by empirical research evidence. They are theories because we
use them to explain and to predict the conduct of others and to control our own
personal conduct in their presence. Implicit personality theories do not
conform to the psychologist's standards either. But again they have a use in the
context in which they are popularly used.

Our ability to assess the personalities of others rapidly and accurately is an
essential aspect of coping with our social world. We are not normally
consciously aware of this achievement, and we do not have to be aware of it to
do it effectively. We interact competently with members of our families, with

people at work, with friends, with restaurant staff and so on. We ask them questions, tell them things, give them instructions, and each time know precisely how they will respond. If we were not able to make reasonably accurate judgements, decisions and predictions about other people, we would lead extremely embarrassing and difficult social lives.

But research has consistently shown that we are very poor judges of each other's personalities. Those stereotypes must be incorrect. There may be a small, thin, dark haired, mean Scot somewhere in the world, but few people have met him. There are many successful female managers; women usually do not get managerial jobs due to discrimination by male managers, not due to female personality defects. Chinese physiognomy may appear mysterious and impenetrable to western eyes, but most Chinese people are warm, open and friendly. When we make personality assessments, we tend to use little information, make our decisions rapidly, oversimplify, and we make mistakes.

How can we display such a high degree of competence in our interactions with others if we are such poor judges of personality? We must surely be able to judge others with enough accuracy to continue our interaction with them successfully. We do this well and without much effort because we interact with most other individuals in contexts in which only a limited range of behaviours is possible and important.

We usually interact with other people in specific *roles*. Roles are social positions defined by the set of expectations which someone in the role must fulfil. Consider one individual in the role of bank customer interacting with another in the role of teller. The range of physical actions that each may perform, and the content of their conversation, are limited by their shared expectations of what people in their positions in banks do. The customer may be more or less impatient. The teller may be more or less helpful. But both know what the other is likely to say and do and the opportunities for either of them to display other facets of their personalities are tightly constrained. The teller who at parties tells lots of jokes would be considered strange if he offered to relate them to a customer whose money he was counting. Similarly, bank customers know that bank tellers are not the best sources of advice on where to hire video tapes, and do not ask such questions.

Only in extraordinary circumstances will either or both of the individuals in this example break the rules and move out of their respective roles into the limitless field of other acts and utterances that they are each quite capable of performing.

STOP!

Think of another common, everyday interaction in which you are involved.

Identify the role expectations that govern this interaction.

What would be the consequences of breaking these expectations ?

Try breaking some of these expectations and note the results.

Our respective behaviours are bounded by social rules that tell each of us what is expected and what is allowed in our interactions. It is therefore comparatively easy to appear competent in social interaction, as long as everyone knows the rules and is prepared to play by them. We rarely interact with "the whole person". That is comparatively difficult as there may be few rules to guide our behaviour.

So when we interact with other people we are usually confronted with only a small number of facets of their personalities. This makes the task of assessing personality a fairly straightforward one. We do not have to cope with the whole person and the whole personality. This explains how we can get through the day with ease, without too many social mistakes or embarrassment. So it is not inconsistent to claim that we are socially competent and that we are poor judges of the whole personality.

In this chapter, we deal with the task of assessing the stable and distinctive properties of the whole personality of an individual. Psychologists disagree, however, on just what that should include. We have already said that personality incorporates human perception, motivation and learning. It can also include how we think, how we solve problems, how we relate to others, and how we understand ourselves. So although we have said that we are interested in the properties of the individual that are stable and distinctive, we are still left with a problem of what to include and what to leave out.

Psychologists use the term in more or less broad and in more or less narrow senses. Broad definitions include all the qualities and features of a person and emphasize the wholeness and uniqueness of the individual. Narrow definitions exclude intellectual and observable physical qualities.

One important controversy concerns whether or not intelligence should be regarded as a facet of personality, or as a separate psychological characteristic. Here intelligence is regarded as separate and as outside the scope of this book. (Intelligence testing has a specialized function that is not directly useful to organization theory.) But this is a convenient position for us to adopt and is not a generally accepted one.

Different psychologists have developed different approaches to the study of personality. The previous chapter examined two approaches to understanding learning, based on behaviourist and on cognitive theories respectively. The two approaches to personality examined in this chapter differ on another dimension.

Some psychologists argue that an individual's personality is inherited. This means that our thoughts, feelings and behaviour are determined by the genes that we inherit from our parents, by our physical appearance and abilities, and by the biochemistry of our brains. This relationship is of course "one way". Your genetic endowment determines your personality and the reverse cannot happen. From this perspective, the individual's personality is fixed at birth, if not before, and life's experiences do little or nothing to alter that position.

Other psychologists argue that an individual's personality is determined by environmental, cultural and social factors. This means that personality is influenced by the individual's experiences of living and interacting with other people. We learn how to behave from other people. Every culture has its own accepted ways of doing things. We cannot possibly be born with this detailed local knowledge. We have to learn how to become a *persona grata* in our society, or in any society in which we find ourselves. This relationship is "two way". Other people influence us, and we in turn influence others. From this perspective, the individual's personality is flexible and can change with experience. It may be that psychological well being depends in part on an individual's ability to adjust to changing circumstances in this way — by altering facets of personality.

The controversy over the effects of heredity and environment on personality (and on intelligence) is also known as the "nature - nurture" debate. It is clear that both sets of factors do have some influence on human psychology. But theorists disagree over the respective strengths of their influences and over the nature and extent of the interaction between them. An additional complexity is that some personality dispositions may only appear in the "right" environment, as a particular allergy may only be evident in the presence of, say, cats or dust.

There are in fact more approaches to this topic than we can cover here. So we have chosen to present two current, influential perspectives. The preferred perspective will depend of course on the reader's personality.

PERSONALITY TYPES AND TRAITS

A Scottish manager describes his personality . . .

"I am relatively introverted. I am aggressive with those who report to me, but not towards my superiors. I am fastidious and a perfectionist when it comes to other people's work, but not my own. I am relatively tolerant of other people, but intolerant of what I perceive as stupidity. I am reasonably hard working intellectually, but lazy when it comes to physical tasks. I find it difficult to concentrate on the task in hand. I am not scrupulously honest in all situations. I am quiet and prefer to work on my own rather than as a member of a team. I am trustworthy and conscientious in the work situation. I am insecure and have a need for recognition.

"I am responsive to the needs of others and can put myself into the other person's shoes relatively easily. I like an intellectual challenge but have a dislike of change. I thrive in a stable environment. I am mean where money is concerned though I try to overcome this trait. Other people seem to think that I am irresponsible, irreverent, good fun, and aggressive. My wife thinks I am a romantic."

The first approach to the study of personality that we examine here is called a *nomothetic* one. This is contrasted in the section that follows with the *idiographic* approach.

Nomothetic means "law setting or giving". Psychologists who adopt a nomothetic approach to the study of personality are thus looking for regularities or for laws that govern human behaviour.

The nomothetic approach adopts the following procedures and assumptions.

First, the main dimensions on which human personality can vary are identified. The manager's description above indicates several of these dimensions — one of which is introversion — and we will examine others shortly. This procedure assumes that one person's introversion is the same as another's — that our personalities do indeed vary on the same dimensions.

Second, the personalities of groups of people are tested by questionnaire. Some magazines occasionally use short versions of these types of tests. The questionnaires collect information at one point in time, although retests can be conducted, and they are usually completed by the individuals themselves. The questions usually ask individuals to choose between a fixed number of answers and are called "forced choice" questions. The way in which individuals answer these questions determines their scores on each of the personality dimensions measured. This procedure assumes that individual questionnaire answers reflect actual behaviour.

Third, an individual's personality profile is constructed across all the dimensions measured. Individual scores on each dimension are compared with the average score and distribution of scores for the group as a whole. This enables the tester to identify individuals with average personalities and those with pronounced characteristics that deviate from the norm. Most individuals get scores around the average. The overall approach is a rather impersonal one and it is difficult to use the results to predict the behaviour of individuals, even those with extreme scores.

Fourth, the total group may be split into subgroups, say by age, sex, or occupation. This produces other references or averages against which individual scores can be compared, and permits comparisons between subgroup scores. Patterns of similarities and differences among and between groups enable general laws about human personality and behaviour to be identified. One may find, for example, that successful Scottish male managers tend to be introverted. It may therefore be possible to make probabilistic predictions about the behaviour of groups of people.

The nomothetic approach rests on the assumption that personality is primarily inherited and that environmental factors and experience have little or limited effect on personality; we are stuck with the personality that we are born with. If human personality was continually influenced by environmental factors and was more flexible, the identification of such laws might not be possible. But note how nomothetic assumptions determine the way in which the approach proceeds, and the nature of the results that are obtained. The assumptions, the methods, and the findings come as a complete "package", not just as separate stages of argument and evidence.

Personality is whatever makes you, the individual, different from other people. It may appear odd that one major approach to the study of personality relies on investigations that cover large groups of people at a time. But in assessing the personalities of groups of people, one discovers what is "normal" or average in those groups and compares individuals with that. Note that the terms norm and average are used in this context in the statistical sense. Individuals who "deviate from the norm" are not to be branded as abnormal social outcasts or criminals.

One of the first personality theorists was Hippocrates, the Greek known also as "The father of medicine" who lived around 400 BC. He suggested that differences in personality or "temperament" were caused by different quantities of body "humours" in the individual. His theory suggested the following relationships:

body humour	temperament	behaviour
blood	sanguine	hopeful, confident, optimistic
black bile	melancholic	depressed, prone to ill founded fears
bile	choleric	active, aggressive, irritable
phlegm	phlegmatic	sluggish, apathetic

These terms are of course still in use in the English language with approximately those meanings when applied to behaviour. Hippocrates' theory, however, is unsound for two reasons. First, what we now know about the relationships between body chemistry and behaviour fails to confirm the theory. Second, our own personal experience should tell us, intuitively, that there are more that four types of people in the world.

Attempts to describe the components and structure of personality have focused on the concepts of *type* and *trait*. Type approaches attempt to fit people into predetermined categories possessing common patterns of behaviour, like cholerics and phlegmatics.

A personality trait on the other hand is any enduring or habitual behaviour pattern that occurs in a variety of circumstances. Punctuality is a personality trait on which individuals can be compared. A trait can also be regarded as a disposition to behave in a particular way. Some individuals seem to be disposed always to arrive late for meetings.

STOP!

There are over 17,000 adjectives in the English language which are used to describe individual behaviour. Examples include reserved, outgoing, emotional, stable, trusting, suspicious, conservative, experimenting, relaxed and tense.

How many others can you identify — and can you identify contrasting
pairs like those in the examples which we have just given ?

How could you design a personality test around these adjectives ?

Trait approaches assume that there is a common set of traits on which we can all
be measured and compared. The adjectives that you have just listed are labels
for personality traits. Individuals can have different traits and have different
strengths of the same traits. This does appear to do more justice to the
uniqueness and complexity of the individual personality than type approaches.
Another way to look at this distinction is to consider that traits belong to
individuals, but individuals belong to type categories. You can *have* a trait, you
fit a type.

Hippocrates' theory is therefore a *type* theory of personality. But when
people are divided into categories or types of this kind, artificial boundaries are
created and the richness and complexity of the individual are disguised. Type
theories of personality work on too high a level of abstraction and generalization to be of much use. This ancient type theory is interesting but too simple.

One of the most powerful and influential current theories of personality is
that developed by Hans Jurgen Eysenck who was born in Germany in 1916 but
now lives and works in Britain. His research has identified two major
dimensions on which personality can vary: the extraversion — introversion or
"E" dimension, and the neuroticism — stability or "N" dimension.

Eysenck's approach is a nomothetic one. He has sympathy with those
behaviourist psychologists who seek a scientific, objective, experimental,
mathematical psychology. His explanations of personality and of personality
differences between people, however, are based on genetics. Behaviourists
claim that behaviour is shaped by environmental influences. As usual, the
differences between psychological approaches and theories can be traced back
to different underlying assumptions about "human nature".

Eysenck argues that personality structure is hierarchical. Each individual
possesses more or less of a number of identifiable traits — trait 1, trait 2, trait 3,
and so on. Individuals who have a particular trait, say trait 1, are more likely to
possess another, say trait 3, than people who do not have trait 1 or who have it
weakly. In other words traits tend to "cluster" in systematic patterns. These
clusters identify a "higher order" of personality description, in terms of what
Eysenck calls personality types. This can be shown simply in the following
diagram:

This does not mean that every individual who has trait 1 is a type A personality. It
means that questionnaire analysis has shown that individuals with high scores

on trait 1 are more likely to have scores on other traits that put them into the type A category.

Eysenck argues that there is statistical evidence from personality test questionnaire results to support the existence of personality traits, trait clusters and types of this kind. Individuals can vary in a continuous distribution on trait scores and this takes into account what was said earlier about the dangers of oversimplification with type theories.

The E dimension of Eysenck's theory divides the human world into two broad categories of people — extraverts and introverts. These terms have passed into popular use and were first coined by another German psychologist, Carl Gustav Jung. The American popular use of these terms tends to refer to sociability and unsociability. European use emphasizes spontaneity and inhibition. Eysenck's account combines these notions.

Extraverts are tough minded individuals who need strong and varied external stimulation. They are sociable, like parties, are good at telling stories, enjoy practical jokes, have many friends, need people to talk to, do not enjoy studying and reading on their own, crave excitement, take risks, act impulsively, prefer change, are optimistic, carefree, active, aggressive, quick tempered, display their emotions and are unreliable.

Eysenck argues that seven personality traits cluster to generate the personality type extraversion. These traits are:

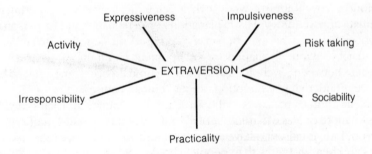

Individual "profiles" on personality test scores tend to "hang together" in this way, but this does not always happen.

Introverts on the other hand are tender minded people who experience strong emotions and who do not need the same intensity of external stimuli as extraverts. They are quiet, introspective, retiring, prefer books to people, are withdrawn, reserved, plan ahead, distrust impulse, appreciate order, lead careful sober lives, have little excitement, control and suppress their emotions, are pessimistic, worry about moral standards, and are reliable.

The seven personality traits that cluster to form this personality type are:

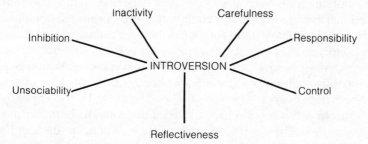

Most of us fall somewhere between these two extremes. These are not totally exclusive categories. They lie on a continuum from one extreme to the other with most people around the centre and a few out at the extremes.

The N dimension of Eysenck's theory attempts to measure personality on a continuum between neuroticism and stability. Neurotics are also sometimes labelled emotional, unstable and anxious. Stable individuals are also described as adjusted.

STOP!

Complete this personality test — a short example of the type of test developed by Eysenck to give you a feel for the procedure.

1 Do you sometimes feel happy, sometimes depressed, without any apparent reason?   Yes   No

2 Do you have frequent ups and downs in mood either with or without apparent cause?   Yes   No

3 Are you inclined to be moody?   Yes   No

4 Does your mind often wander while you are trying to concentrate?   Yes   No

5 Are you frequently 'lost in thought' even when supposed to be taking part in a conversation?   Yes   No

6 Are you sometimes bubbling over with energy and sometimes very sluggish?   Yes   No

7 Do you prefer action to planning for action?   Yes   No

8 Are you happiest when you get involved in some project that calls for rapid action?   Yes   No

9 Do you usually take the initiative in making new friends?   Yes   No

10 Are you inclined to be quick and sure in your action?   Yes   No

11 Would you rate yourself as a lively individual?   Yes   No

12 Would you be very unhappy if you were prevented from making numerous social contacts?   Yes   No

Now for the scoring. A 'Yes' answer in any of the first six questions scores one point towards emotionality, while a 'No' answer does not score at all. Similarly, a 'Yes' answer to any of the last six items scores one point towards extraversion. You can therefore end up with two scores, either of which may run from 0 (very stable, very introverted) to 6 (very unstable emotionally, very extraverted). The majority of people will have scores of 2, 3 or 4; these indicate middling degrees of emotionality or extraversion.

From H. J. Eysenck and G. Wilson, *Know Your Own Personality*, Maurice Temple Smith, London, 1975.

If you got a high N score, then you may describe yourself as neurotic or as emotionally unstable. Neurotics tend to have rather low opinions of themselves and feel that they are unattractive failures. Neurotics are also disappointed with life, the world and everything. They are pessimistic and depressed. They worry unnecessarily about things that may never happen and are easily upset when things go wrong. Neurotics are also obsessive, conscientious, finicky people who are highly disciplined, staid and get annoyed by lack of tidyness, cleanliness and disorder.

Neurotics are not self-reliant and tend to submit to institutional power without question. They feel they are controlled by events, by others and by fate. They often imagine that they are ill and demand sympathy. They blame themselves excessively and are troubled by attacks of conscience.

The seven traits that cluster to form the personality type emotional instability are:

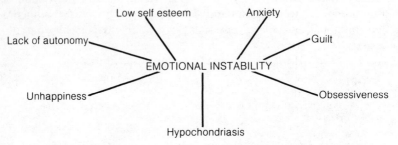

Stable individuals are self-confident, optimistic, resist irrational fears, are easy going, realistic, solve their own problems, have few health worries, and have few regrets about what they have done in the past.

The seven traits that form the emotionally stable type are:

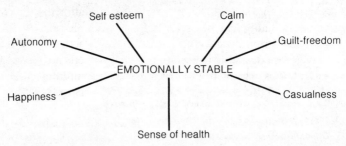

The questionnaire that Eysenck normally uses to measure the E and N dimensions of personality has 96 questions, 40 for each dimension, and 16 lie scale questions to assess the subjects' honesty in answering the other questions. The questions are mainly in the "yes/no" format. The E and N dimensions are not themselves correlated. So if you are extraverted, you could be either stable or neurotic. The individual's score on one of these dimensions does not appear to influence the score on the other.

The questionnaires are constructed in the following way.

First, questions are worded in ways that appear, on face value, to measure the trait under consideration. The question, "Are you inclined to be moody?", appears intuitively to concern emotional instability, so it is included. The question, "Are you inclined to be quick and sure in your actions?", appears intuitively to measure extraversion. Several questions are chosen that appear all to measure the same trait.

Second, a "pilot" or trial questionnaire is constructed and given to a number of subjects to complete. The subjects may be chosen at random, they may be representative of a particular group, or they may be chosen for their already known personality biases.

Third, the pilot results are used:

- To screen out the questions that everyone answers in the same way, and which therefore do not discriminate between those who have a trait and those who do not;
- To identify the questions which systematically get the same responses, or the questions on which responses cluster as explained earlier; this provides an internal check on the questions, confirming that the different questions do indeed appear to measure the same thing;
- To label the answer clusters in terms of what they appear on face value to be assessing or measuring;
- To compare the results with the results of other tests on the same people, and with the results of the same test on other people with known trait patterns; this provides a check on the questions, confirming that the test does identify the trait under consideration;
- To construct the main questionnaire.

It is not possible to argue that one personality type is good or superior to another. In organizational employment, it has been difficult to show that one personality type is more successful in a particular occupation than another type. The extravert personality may be thought more desirable because those who have it are sociable, friendly, good company, cheerful, active, lively and funny. These are all socially desirable things to be. But extraverts are also unreliable, fickle in friendships, easily bored and are bad at uninteresting or time consuming tasks. So there are positive and negative aspects of the extravert personality.

But surely a stable personality on the N dimension is much more desirable than a neurotic one? Probably not. An open display of emotion is desirable in some contexts, although embarrassing in others. Emotions are a major source of motivation to sustain activity, and an inability to display or share emotional feelings can be a serious drawback.

It is more important for us as individuals to be aware of our own personality features, and to be aware of the characteristics that might be seen by others as our strengths and our weaknesses. To understand other people, one must begin with an understanding of one's own personality and of the effect that one has on other people.

So on the neuroticism — stability dimension, it probably does not matter where your personality lies. Neurotics are usually aware of the mental states that lead them to be described in this way and do not generally resent the classification. Neurotics also usually operate with complete competence in everyday life and could not be described as "ill" in any way. It is unfortunate that the label neurotic tends to be wrongly associated with "sickness". Neurotics may however have personality traits that render them prone to some more serious physical disorders.

Extraverts need higher levels of stimulation . . .

Some students always sit in the busiest and noisiest sections of the library, seem to spend their time socializing instead of studying, and disappoint the swots by passing their exams anyway. John Campbell and Charles Hawley have produced evidence which suggests that some people need these kinds of distractions to study effectively.

According to Hans Eysenck, *extraverts* need and enjoy the presence of others while *introverts* prefer the peace and quiet of solitude.

John Campbell and Charles Hawley interviewed 102 students in the library at Colgate University in New York and gave them Eysenck's personality test questionnaire. The first and third floors in the library contained individual desks separated by eight foot high bookshelves. The second floor was an open reading area with soft chairs and large tables.

The researchers expected to find the introverts on the first and third floors and the extraverts on the second. The results confirmed their expectations.

The researchers argued that the extravert students were probably working as hard as their introverted classmates. Eysenck's personality theory is based on knowledge of the biochemistry of the brain. Extraverts need higher levels of stimulation to get their grey matter going and need frequent changes in stimulation to maintain their interest. Introverts need less stimulation to arouse them and can sustain their concentration without interruption.

So the crowded areas of the library give extravert students more opportunities for short study breaks which prevent them from getting bored.

Introverts should clearly try to find areas of the library where they will not be interrupted by extraverts.

From John W. Campbell and Charles W. Hawley, "Study habits and Eysenck's theory of extraversion - introversion", *Journal of Research in Personality*, 1982, vol. 16, no. 2, pp. 139-46.

Eysenck's theory of personality has a physiological basis. Neuroticism, for example, appears to be associated with aspects of the human nervous system that control heartbeat, body temperature, sweating and digestion. Extraverts have a brain neurophysiology that is different from introverts. They need higher levels of stimulation to attract and maintain their interest. This supports the argument that personality is determined by genetic and biological factors rather than by environment and culture.

Eysenck argues that personality is an inherited, genetic endowment and that consequently the individual can do very little to change it in any fundamental way. The influence of the individual's environment is therefore regarded as limited. Extraordinary and traumatic circumstances may however have an effect on personality. This argument does not imply that we are all simply copies of our parents. We certainly inherit their chromosomes and genes, but these may not even give us the same colour of hair or eyes as either of our parents. Hereditary mechanisms are more complex than that. This however is a controversial area and a detailed discussion is outside the scope of this book.

The identification of personality types and traits is based on statistical analysis of the answers to questionnaires. Questionnaire development relies on statistical criteria. Questions that discriminate and correlate are retained while those that do neither are dropped. The results from the final questionnaires are analysed with sophisticated statistical routines.

Statistical operations merely reorganize information. They provide another way of describing the quantity of data collected. The statistical results may therefore not be directly related to human psychological processes. Despite the statistics, a lot of human, subjective judgement goes into the wording and screening of the questions that are used, and into interpreting the output of the statistical analysis. It is therefore possible that the results are a product of the way in which the tests are constructed.

The interesting question for those who work in organizations is — what personality types and traits are needed to make one a successful banker, machine tool operator, typist, lecturer, pilot, policeman or nurse? But that question is naïve. Personality is only one influence on an individual's role in life. Ability, opportunity and luck all have a significant influence on an individual's job performance.

It has not been possible satisfactorily to correlate individuals' personality test scores with job performances. The quality of an individual's work depends on many factors, including motivation, the organization of the work, training, the payment system, supervisory style, company policy and so on. The individual's sex, age and general intelligence are also important, although these factors have not been considered here under the heading of personality. It is therefore hazardous to make predictions about someone's performance on a job on the basis of personality test results.

Eysenck's questionnaire data are not designed to make predictions about specific individuals. An individual score is only meaningful in comparison with the scores of others. It is therefore important always to identify the group being used for comparison and its main characteristics (such as age, sex, occupation, culture). The results are more useful for predicting general tendencies in large groups of people.

The tests may be used in a clinical context to identify individuals with extreme scores which may (but not necessarily) indicate psychological problems in need of further treatment. People with extremely high or low scores have what Eysenck calls an "ambiguous gift". This may be a sign of an unbalanced personality, but if individuals are aware of such features, they may be able to act in ways to control and exploit them to their advantage. Problems arise mainly when one does not have this awareness.

In clinical and research settings, most people co-operate willingly with doctors and researchers and give honest and accurate responses to questions. Most of us are interested enough in ourselves to be curious about our scores and their interpretation.

Personality test data are fairly easy to falsify. They may not therefore be considered reliable for job selection and promotion purposes where the individual's future career may be at stake. The "lie detecting" questions are themselves fairly easy to detect and to answer in the "correct" way.

Some individuals have fixed or set reactions to completing questionnaires of this kind. They may:

- Be hostile to fixed choice questions and want a "maybe" or "sometimes" option instead of always having to say yes or no;
- Always agree to statements made by "experts";
- Always give the middle, or most neutral response possible;
- Always give the most extreme or radical response;
- Always give what they believe to be the desirable or expected response;

These are called "response sets", because they describe how the individual is set to respond to questions in a predetermined way. Response sets can thus bias systematically the results of personality tests.

Which response set should you adopt . . . ?

How to cheat on personality tests, by W. H. Whyte:

". . . you should try to answer as if you were like everyone else is supposed to be. This is not always too easy to figure out, of course, and this is one of the reasons why I will go into some detail. . . "

Whyte's general rule is:

"To settle on the most beneficial answer to any question, repeat to yourself:

(a)   I loved my father and my mother, but my father a little bit more
(b)   I like things pretty well the way they are
(c)   I never worry much about anything
(d)   I don't care for books or music much

(e)   I love my wife and children
(f)   I don't let them get in the way of company work."

From William H. Whyte, *The Organization Man*, Simon and Schuster, New York, 1956, p. 373.

One final criticism of Eysenck's approach is that limited answers to simple and hypothetical yes/no questions do not appear to tap the depth, richness and complexity of an individual's thought processes. These questions do not allow the individual freedom of expression and are in fact designed specially to prevent this. Many people dislike these tests because they feel that they give a false impression of themselves. These tests are perhaps not magic and scientific keys with which to unlock the secrets of the psyche. They must be handled with care.

THE DEVELOPMENT OF THE SELF

The second approach to the study of personality that we examine here is called an *idiographic* one. This is contrasted with the *nomothetic* approach set out in the previous section.

Idiographic means "writing about individuals". Psychologists who adopt an idiographic approach to the study of personality begin by constructing a detailed picture of one individual. This approach aims to do justice to the uniqueness, richness and complexity of the individual personality. It is therefore a valuable way of deepening our understanding, but does not readily lead to the generation of laws of human behaviour which is the aim of the nomothetic approach.

The idiographic approach adopts the following procedures and assumptions.

First, each individual possesses unique traits that are not directly comparable with the traits of other individuals. My sensitivity and my aggression may be similar to yours but they work in different ways and are not directly comparable with your sensitivity and aggression. Idiographic research produces in depth studies of both normal and abnormal individuals, collecting information from interviews, letters, diaries, and biographies. The data includes what people say and write about themselves.

Second, we are not merely biological organisms driven by the machinery of heredity. This is only part of our nature. Each of us is also a socially self-conscious individual. Our behaviour patterns are influenced by experience and conscious reasoning, not just instinct and habit.

Third, we behave in accordance with the image that we each have of ourselves — our *self*, or "self-image", or "self-concept". We derive our self-image from the ways in which other people treat us. Our self-image is not something that we construct internally and personally. We learn about ourselves through interactions with others. We take the attitudes and behaviours of others towards us and use them consciously to adjust our self-image and our behaviour. This ability to modify our actions through experience is called *reflexiveness.*

Fourth, as the development of the self image is a social process, it follows that personality is open to change through new social interactions and experiences. The development of the individual's personality is therefore not the inevitable result of biological and genetic inheritance. It is only through interaction with other people that we as individuals can learn to see and to understand ourselves as individuals. We cannot develop our self-understanding without the (tacit) help of others. There is no such thing as "human nature". We derive our nature through social interactions and relationships.

It is our self-understanding that determines our behaviour. For example, confidence in one's ability to do something is strongly related to the successful demonstration of that ability. Ability combined with lack of confidence usually leads to failure or poor performance.

The ability to consider and reflect on its functioning is an important and interesting feature of the human mind. We experience a world "out there" and contrast that with the world inside our heads. But we are capable also of experiencing ourselves in that outer world, as objects that live and behave in it.

We observe, evaluate, and criticize ourselves in the same conscious, objective and impersonal way that we observe, evaluate and criticize other people and objects, and we experience shame, anxiety or pride at our own behaviour. Our capacity for reflective thought enables us to evaluate both past and alternative future actions and their consequences.

The American psychologist Charles Horton Cooley introduced the idea of the "looking glass self". The mirror that we use is other people in our society with whom we interact. We observe and evaluate the actions and reactions of others towards us and our behaviour. We are able to complete the statement, "other people see me . . .". If others respond warmly and favourably towards us, we develop a "positive" self-image, one with which we are content. If others respond to us with criticism, ridicule and aggression, we are more likely to develop a "negative" self-image.

The personality of the individual is thus the result of a process in which the individual learns to be the person they are. Most of us learn, accept and use most of the attitudes, values, beliefs and expectations of those around us — of the society or part of society in which we are brought up.

In other words, we learn the stock of knowledge available in and peculiar to our society. Red means stop. Cars drive on the left hand side of the road. An extended hand is a symbol of respect and friendship, not of hostility or aggression. Considered singly, these examples may sound trivial. But taken together they comprise a knowledge of how our society works that we take for granted. The "rules" that govern our behaviour are created, recreated and reinforced through our continuing interactions with others based on these shared definitions of our reality. We interact with each other comfortably and competently because we share this broad understanding of what is going on.

How could we develop such a shared understanding on our own in isolation from society? What we inherit from our parents cannot possible tell us how to behave in a specific culture. We have to learn how to become *personae grata* through living in society and interacting with others.

Clearly rules such as "red means stop" are not laws of human behaviour of the same type as the physical law that says "clouds mean rain". We can change these human laws, and we can break them. Change may be difficult, and infringement may carry unwelcome penalties, but these options are there. Clouds cannot alter or repeal the laws that apply to them.

If we all share the same ideas and behaviours, we have a recipe for a society of conformists. This is of course not consistent with the available evidence. The theory however does not imply this. George Herbert Mead argued that the self has two components, the:

"I": The unique, individual, conscious and impulsive aspects of the individual; and the

"Me": The norms and values of society that the individual learns and accepts, or "internalizes".

Mead used the term *generalized other* to refer to the total set of expectations one believes others in one's society have of one. The "Me" is the aspect of the self where all these generalized attitudes are organized. The "Me" is not a physically identifiable location in the brain. It refers rather to the mental process that enables us to reflect objectively on our own conduct. The "Me" is the self as an object to itself.

The "I" is the active, impulsive component of the self. Other people place social pressures on us to accept and conform to current values and beliefs. But reflective individuals regulate their part in the social process and adjust it. We can initiate social change by introducing new social values. Patterns of socially acceptable conduct are specified in more or less broad and general ways. There is therefore plenty of scope for flexibility, modification, originality, creativity, individuality, variety and significant change.

This sounds like a recipe for conformity, but . . .

"We can reform the order of things; we can insist on making the community standards better standards. We are not simply bound by the community. We are engaged in a conversation in which what we say is listened to by the community and its response is one which is affected by what we have to say. . . . We are continually changing our social system in some respects and we are able to do that intelligently because we can think."

From George Herbert Mead, *Mind, Self and Society*, University of Chicago Press, Chicago, 1934, p. 168.

Carl Rogers illustrated this two sided self in the following way:

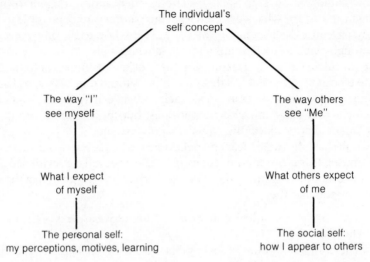

The self-concept gives the individual a sense of meaning and consistency. But as the individual's perceptions and motives change through new experiences and learning, the self-concept changes and behaviour changes. Personality is therefore not stable as the self-concept can be reorganized.

We have perceptions of our qualities, abilities, attitudes, impulses and so on. If these perceptions are accurate, conscious, organized and accepted, then we can regard our self-concept as successful in that it will lead to feelings of comfort, freedom from tension, and of psychological adjustment. Well adjusted individuals thus have flexible self-images that are consistent with what they think, feel and do, and that are open to change through new experiences.

Personality disorders can be caused by failure to bring together experiences, motives and feelings into a coherent and consistent self-image. We usually behave in ways that we feel are consistent with our self-images, and when we have new experiences or feelings that are inconsistent we either:

- Recognize the inconsistency and try to integrate the two sets of understanding — this is the healthy response; or

- Deny or distort one of the experiences, perhaps by putting the blame on some one or something else — this is an unhealthy defence mechanism.

"Maladjusted" individuals are those who perceive as threatening those experiences and feelings that are not consistent with their self-images. They deny and distort their experiences in such a way that their self-image does not match their real feelings or the nature of their experience. This leads to a build up of psychological tension as more defence mechanisms are required to keep the truth at a distance.

Rogers also argued that the core of human personality is the desire to realize fully one's potential. To achieve this, however, the right social environment is required. Rogers argued that this is an environment in which one is treated with "unconditional positive regard". This means a social setting in which one is accepted for whatever one is; in which one is valued, trusted, accepted and respected, even in the face of characteristics which others dislike. In this kind of environment, the individual is likely to become trusting, spontaneous, flexible, leading a rich and meaningful life with a harmonious self-concept.

This is far from the type of social environment typical of most organizations in our society today. Most people at work, at all levels, face highly conditional positive regard, in which only a narrow range of thoughts and behaviours is approved and accepted.

Personality and the job: which determines which?

Does an individual's personality influence their choice of job? Or does the job influence an individual's personality?

John Jermier and Leslie Berkes argue that these questions are important to police forces accused of brutality, corruption, inefficiency and insensitivity to public opinion. Their research indicates that police behaviour is influenced by organization structure and the style of police leaders.

The researchers first examined two myths of police work. The first myth is that effective crime fighting must be organized in a bureaucratic, military manner. The second myth is that police work attracts people with authoritarian personalities who like working in bureaucracies.

The bureaucratic myth has some basis in organizational theory which recognizes that different tasks require different organizational arrangements. The police task is to fight crime and to deal swiftly with emergencies. Is a bureaucratic structure appropriate here, with a rigid hierarchy of ranks, closely defined duties and responsibilities and impersonal decision making? Jermier and Berkes argue that police have little regular contact with their superiors and must use judgement and discretion in their work. Police work often resembles social work and their community services extend far beyond crime fighting.

The authoritarian myth is based on attitude surveys which suggest that American police value rigid social control, routine, order and conformity and prefer directive leadership. But basic training procedures indoctrinate recruits who soon learn that obedience plus adherence to the rules equals promotion. People subjected to this type of control are likely to adopt similar strategies to control the behaviour of others.

Jermier and Berkes surveyed 158 American policemen with a questionnaire which assessed their job satisfaction, commitment to police work, job characteristics and their supervisors' behaviour.

Contrary to the authoritarian myth, these policemen did not want simple routine jobs with superiors always telling them what to do. High job satisfaction and commitment were associated with supportive, participative leadership. These findings confirm the general belief that democratic leadership is more likely to foster morale and loyalty than autocratic leadership.

So the next time you meet a cold hearted cop, ask him how he gets on with his boss. Jermier and Berkes claim that police behaviour in public could be improved by changing organization structures and management styles inside police forces.

From John M. Jermier and Leslie J. Berkes, "Leader behaviour in a police command bureaucracy; a closer look at the quasi-military model", *Administrative Science Quarterly*, 1980, vol. 24, no. 1, pp. 1-23.

THE STUDY OF THE SELF

Compared with the nomothetic approach, the idiographic appears to be a rather complex, untidy view of human personality and its development. It has however been particularly influential in phenomenological approaches to understanding individuals and society.

How can the individual's self-understanding be studied? It should be clear that Eysenck's questionnaires are not a good instrument for this because both the questions and the answers are determined in advance by a researcher. An individual may reject both the questions and the suggested answers as inappropriate to his or her personal self-concept.

We need therefore to find a route into the individual's head that does not reflect the understanding and biases of the researcher. We can ask individuals to write about themselves. We can record individuals speaking about themselves and transcribe the tapes. These and other techniques of the clinical psychologist are in popular use, including free association, interpretation of dreams, and the analysis of imagination and fantasies.

These various approaches give the individual complete freedom of expression and do not tie responses down to predetermined categories. The researcher's job is then to find the *themes* in what people write and say that indicate their preoccupations and interests.

These techniques appear to be rather unstructured, and therefore unscientific. Here is one systematic technique for getting access to the content of someone's mind. We would like you now to work through the technique for yourself, before the rationale behind it is explained.

STOP!

Read these instructions carefully before you proceed.

On the next page, there is a picture that we would like you to look at then write an *imaginative* story about. Read these instructions first, turn over and look at the picture for around 20 seconds, then cover the picture and write an imaginative story that is suggested to you by the picture. Do not spend more than 5 minutes writing this story.

To help you think about the possible elements of a story in the time allowed, try answering these questions:

1. What is happening? Who are the people?
2. What has led up to this situation? What has happened in the past?
3. What is being thought? What is wanted? By whom?
4. What will happen? What will be done?

These questions are only guides for your thinking and need not be answered specifically. Your story should be continuous and not just be specific answers to these questions.

Do not worry about whether there are right or wrong stories to write. The most important thing is to make up a *vivid, imaginative* story. The picture is designed to give you an idea of what to write about, but don't be concerned about describing the picture perfectly. Use the picture and the questions as a guide to telling a creative, dramatic story. Write your story now.

Photograph: Trevor Graham

The story that you have now written is in fact a means of testing the strength of your *need for achievement*. It is not a test of your imaginative story writing ability. You can assess your story as follows.

Determine whether any of the characters in your story has an achievement goal. That is, does he *want to perform better,* or does he *care* about performing better? Performing better is indicated by a character in your story doing one or more of the following four things:

- Doing something better than someone else;
- Meeting or excelling some self imposed standard of excellence or performance;
- Doing something unique;

- Being involved over a long time in doing something well or successfully.

If any one of these four characteristics is present in your story, you get a point for *achievement imagery*; if more than one of these features is present, you still get only one point. If none of these features is in your story, *no further scoring for achievement need is possible* and the final score is zero. The full scoring of such a story is a more complex undertaking which leads to maximum scores of up to 11.

Now swap your story for that of a colleague and see if you can reach agreement on the achievement imagery content. The scoring process is subjective, and the instructions have been abbreviated for our purposes here. Spend some time discussing why you may have reached different conclusions in your assessments of each other's stories.

The procedure that you have now worked through is called a "thematic apperception test". It was invented by Henry Murray in 1938 and has been developed by David C. McClelland as a means of measuring the strength of individuals' need for achievement. The test can also be used to measure needs for power and affiliation, but we will focus here on achievement. In a full test, you would be asked to write stories about between 4 and 20 pictures. The minimum duration of the test is therefore 20 minutes.

Definition

The *need for achievement* is a general concern with meeting standards of excellence and a desire to be successful in competition.

What kind of a personality test is this ? You have been asked to write a short, creative, imaginative story in response to a picture and the story has been scored according to the presence or absence of achievement imagery and themes. What can this tell us about your distinctive and stable personality characteristics?

The thematic apperception test, also known as the TAT, is called a *projective test* because subjects are given the opportunity to "project" their personalities into the stories they write. The famous Rorschach inkblot test is another form of projective test in which subjects are asked to state what kinds of images they see in random inkblots. So any strong needs, preoccupations, interests, goals or motives should find expression in the stories that you write.

The pictures used in the test are chosen for their ambiguity. They do not suggest any one particular story or set of events. They therefore evoke a range of different types of story from different people. So the story that the individual creates draws on the channels of thought predominant in the individual's mind. McClelland argues that it is reasonable to assume that the person with a strong concern with achievement is likely to write imaginative stories with lots of achievement imagery and themes in them. This assumption seems to be supported by the research evidence.

Research also suggests that this test does measure a stable personality characteristic because people who sit a thematic apperception test a second time at a later date tend to get scores similar to those they got on the first attempt. Of course, nobody gets exactly the same scores. The association between test and retest scores is not strong. But any similarity between scores is striking when one considers the nature and length of the test.

The achievement need score that you now have for your story is based on five minutes' work. Can we regard this as "objective data" about your personality? You should have discovered that the scoring procedure involves a lot of subjective judgement. Judges who have been trained in the full test procedure and scoring manuals can however reach good agreement on their scoring of stories.

People with a high need for achievement tend to have the following characteristics:

- They prefer tasks in which they have to achieve a standard of excellence rather than simply carrying out routine activities;
- They prefer jobs in which they get frequent and clear feedback on how well they are doing to help them to perform better;
- They prefer activities that involve moderate risks of failure — high risk activities lead to failure, low risk activities do not give them a challenge or an opportunity to demonstrate skill and ability;
- They have a good memory for unfinished tasks and do not like to leave things incomplete;
- They can be unfriendly and unsociable when they do not want others to get in the way of their performance;
- They have a sense of urgency, appear to be in a hurry, to be working against time and have an inability to relax;
- They prefer sombre Scottish tartans with lots of blues and greens and dislike bright tartans with reds and yellows — the unobtrusive background allows them to stand out better.

People with low need for achievement are concerned more with security and status than with personal fulfilment, are preoccupied with their personal ideas and feelings, worry more about their self-presentation than their performance, and prefer bright Scottish tartans. (The Buchanan tartan is mainly bright red and yellow and the author does not wear it.)

We hope that some readers may recognize features of themselves in this analysis. This seems to be broadly consistent with our popular or intuitive understanding of what high achievement need actually is.

How do people acquire the achievement need? A study by Marian Winterbottom showed that this depends on the process of early socialization. She asked 29 American boys aged 8 to 9 years to tell her stories in response to spoken instructions (not pictures) and scored their answers for achievement imagery and themes. She then interviewed their mothers and asked them questions about how they raised their sons. She found that the mothers of the high scoring sons had treated them as children in the following ways:

- They had expected their sons to become independent and to do things on their own at an earlier age than the mothers of the low scoring boys;
- They rewarded independence with affectionate hugging and kissing;
- They imposed fewer restrictions on the behaviour of their children and relaxed any restrictions at an early age;
- Their total home atmosphere emphasized competitiveness, self-re-ance, independence, accomplishment and aspiration.

The mothers of the low scorers believed more in the value of restrictions on their children and kept restrictions in force for longer. Domineering and authoritarian parents thus tend not to have children with high needs for achievement.

Can the thematic apperception test be used to identify people whose early socialization has given them a high need for achievement and who may therefore be good at a particular job or occupation? Organizations typically want to employ people with drive, ambition, self-motivation and so on. The TAT looks like a promising organizational selection test.

It is probably not a very good test for this purpose. Once you know what the test is all about, it is fairly easy to fake a moderately good score. The general definition of achievement imagery is close to popular understanding of the term, although the detailed scoring may not be obvious to the untrained. If the test ever became widely used, the scoring procedure would become widely understood. So we are left with the same conclusion here as with Eysenck's personality test questionnaires. Personality measures are not good predictors of job performance.

McClelland has argued that individuals' achievement needs can be increased by teaching them the scoring system and helping them to write high scoring stories. This may increase the need for achievement by encouraging the individual to see and understand daily life more vividly in achievement terms. This retraining in mental habits may thus be translated more readily into action.

NOMOTHETIC VERSUS IDIOGRAPHIC?

In this chapter we have presented two approaches to the study of human personality. They are summarized and compared in this table:

The nomothetic approach:	The idiographic approach:
Has a positivist bias	*Has a phenomenological bias*

Is generalizing: it emphasizes the discovery of laws of human behaviour	Is individualizing: it emphasizes the richness and complexity of the unique individual
Is based on statistical study of groups	Is based on intensive study of individuals
Uses objective questionnaires	Uses projective tests and other written and spoken materials
Describes personality in terms of the individual's possession of traits	Describes personality in terms of the individual's own self understanding
Views personality as composed of discrete and identifiable elements	Believes that personality has to be understood and studied as a unified, indivisible, intelligible whole
Believes that personality is determined by heredity, biology, genetics	Believes that personality is determined by social and cultural processes
Believes that personality is given at birth and is unalterable	Believes that personality is adaptable, open to change through experience

How should we choose between these competing perspectives? We might resort to academic criteria and examine the logic of the arguments, consider how adequately the evidence relates to and supports the theory, and consider how comprehensive the explanations are. We might resort to practical considerations and consider the techniques used to treat personality disorders, and to analyse and predict behaviour.

But this misses the point that these two approaches are based on deeply contrasting and conflicting views of human nature. Here the evidence is such as to leave us debating for considerable time without satisfactory resolution. We may therefore have to resort to criteria that are in some respects unsatisfactory, such as:

- Which theory is more aesthetically pleasing?
- Which approach "feels" right?
- How does each approach fit in with other aspects of my world view?

Another way of resolving the competition, however, is to regard these approaches as *complementary*. They offer two broad research strategies each of which is capable of telling us about different aspects of human psychology. So perhaps we should use both approaches and not concentrate on one alone. This leaves one residual argument that we are not going to deal with here: should psychology be *predominantly* nomothetic or idiographic? Our preference here may not be your preference. But as we argued earlier, there is value in disagreement and debate.

SOURCES

Allport, G. W., 1937, *Personality*, Holt, New York.

Atkinson, J. W. (ed), 1958, *Motives in Fantasy, Action and Society: A Method of Assessment and Study*, D. Van Nostrand Inc., Princeton, New Jersey.

Berger, P. and Luckmann, T., 1966 *The Social Construction of Reality*, Penguin Books, Harmondsworth.

Eysenck, H. J. and Wilson, G., 1975, *Know Your Own Personality*, Penguin Books, Harmondsworth.

Kagan, J. and Havemann, E., 1976, *Psychology: An Introduction*, Harcourt Brace Jovanovich, New York, third edition.

McClelland, D. C., 1961, *The Achieving Society*, The Free Press, New York.

McClelland, D. C. and Steele, R. S., 1972, *Motivation Workshops: A Student Workbook for Experiential Learning in Human Motivation*, General Learning Press, New York.

Mead, G. H., 1934, *Mind, Self and Society*, University of Chicago Press, Chicago.

Rogers, C. R., 1947, "Some observations on the organization of personality", *American Psychologist*, vol. 2, pp. 358-68.

Winterbottom, M. R., 1958, "The relation of need for achievement to learning experiences in independence and mastery", in John W. Atkinson (ed.), *Motives in Fantasy, Action, and Society: A Method of Assessment and Study*, D. Van Nostrand Company Inc., Princeton, New Jersey, 1958, pp. 453-78.

PART 2:

GROUPS IN THE ORGANIZATION

DAVID SMITH

George Elton Mayo (1880-1949)

Times Higher Education Supplement 26 December 1980

Overview

Social psychology is the study of how human behaviour is influenced by the presence, behaviour and products of other human beings, individually and collectively, past and present. Miller and Rice (1967, p. 17) have written that,

"An individual has ... no meaning except in relation to others with whom he interacts. He uses them, and they him, to express views, take action, and play roles. The individual is a creature of the group, the group of the individual."

In the first section of this book, the emphasis was placed on how the internal aspects of people such as their motivation, perception and personality affected their behaviour in general, and their behaviour within organizations in particular. The impression may have thus been created that a knowledge of the individual alone was sufficient to understand his behaviour. While such differences are important, they are not the whole story. In this section of the book we shall move up one level of analysis from individual psychology to social psychology. Group structures and modes of functioning are part of a social process which modifies individual behaviour and therefore influences organizational behaviour.

At this level, the focus is on aspects of the interaction between people and the environment which they inhabit. It is now accepted that man is influenced partly by his biological evolution and partly by his social and cultural development. This has sometimes been referred to as the "Nature–Nurture Debate". The social psychologist is interested in the way in which the organizations, groups, institutions and individuals around a person affect the way in which he views the world and acts in it. The discipline is concerned with the relationship between group experience and the psychology of the individual, and the influence on interpersonal relationships of group membership. Those relationships are mediated through face-to-face interactions with others.

Henri Tajfel and others have argued that social psychology is concerned with the effects of the environment on the basic social psychological processes of the individual. But this is not simply a one way influence; individual and social factors interact and affect one another. Groups constitute only part of the individual's social environment. Social psychologists are therefore interested in gathering information about how the various social structures, social systems or groups affect an individual's ways of viewing the world in which he lives and of acting in it. The focus is upon the individual's motives, emotions, perceptions and interpretations. These will in turn affect his functioning in groups and relations between groups.

Chapter 7

The formation of groups

Key Concepts:

Once you have fully understood this chapter, you should be able to define the following concepts in your own words:

Psychological group   Interpersonal relations
Aggregate   Group relations
Formal group   Hidden agenda
Informal group

Objectives:

On completing this chapter you should be able:

1. To place current thinking and research about group behaviour in a historical context.
2. To identify some of the different purposes which groups serve.
3. To list the key characteristics of a psychological group.
4. To distinguish between a formal and an informal group.
5. To outline George Homans' theory of group formation
6. To enumerate Barry Tuckman's four stages of group development.

INTRODUCTION

An important aspect of work is that it is usually done in groups. It does not matter whether the work concerned is learning to read at school, checking insurance claims forms in an office or assembling a car in a factory. The lone artist in his garret or the single window cleaner tend to be the exception rather than the rule. Groups play an important and pervasive role in our lives. The average person belongs to five or six different groups. About 92 per cent of group members are in groups of five people or less. Such groups may include the lunch time card school, the quality control section, the college engineering course, the local women's group, the church group and the sports club. Our colleagues, friends, bosses and customers form the groups which are the fabric of our society. Whether at school, in the home or at work, we participate in and interact with members of groups. It has even been argued that one can view large organizations as a collection of small groups.

In this section of the book we shall emphasize the way in which individuals and groups are related in the context of the organization. Irrespective of their environmental context, groups are of interest because they represent mini-societies in which social interaction takes place and in which the behaviour of individuals can be studied. A distinction will be made between the interpersonal level and the group level of analysis. The interpersonal level is concerned with the ways in which one person interacts with another person. Often such interaction is ordered and becomes predictable. This predictability in turn leads to persons playing specific roles.

Definition

Interpersonal relations are the simplest social bonds which occur when two people stand in some relation to each other such as husband and wife, or leader and follower. The term means "between persons" and does not imply that the relationship must be a "personal" one. It can be an impersonal or an intimate one.

The group level is the next level. The interperson behaviour builds up into group behaviour which in turn sustains and structures future interpersonal relations. Groups develop particular characteristics, and relate to other groups in specific ways.

Definition

Group relations focus on the interaction within and between groups and the stable arrangements that result from such interactions.

HISTORICAL BACKGROUND TO
THE STUDY OF GROUPS IN ORGANIZATIONS

Industrial Fatigue Research Board Studies

The earliest British interest in group behaviour in organizations dates back to 1917 when the Department of Scientific and Industrial Research and the Medical Research Council were asked to appoint a board to investigate industrial conditions. The purpose of this board was to continue the work that the Health of Munitions Workers Committee had done during the First World War.

Two contrasting views of organization

In his chapter entitled "The principle of supportive relationships", Rensis Likert attempts to derive a theory of organizational design with the group as the basic building block. He argues that:

1. Work groups are important sources of individuals' need satis-
    faction;
2. Groups in organizations that fulfil this psychological function are
    also more productive;
3. Management's task is therefore to create effective work groups
    by developing "supportive relationships";
4. An effective organizational structure consists of democratic/
    participative work groups, each linked to the organization as a
    whole through overlapping memberships;
5. Co-ordination is achieved by individuals who carry out "linking
    functions".

From Rensis Likert. *New Patterns of Management,* McGraw-Hill, New York, 1961, Chapter 8, pp. 97-118.

In his book *The Organization Man,* William H, Whyte offers a radical alternative to the view put forward by Likert. Whyte describes the horrors of:

> ". . . an environment in which everyone is tightly knit into a
> belongingness with one another; one in which there is no
> restless wandering but rather the deep emotional security
> that comes from total integration with the group".

From William H. Whyte *The Organization Man,* Penguin Books, Harmondsworth, 1955.

Can you match Likert's argument with Whyte's views?

STOP!

A person may be a member of several groups at the same time. Can you give an example of such overlapping group membership from your own experience?

What problems does it cause for you?

The Industrial Fatigue Research Board as it was named, had as its terms of reference, "... to consider and investigate the relation of the hours of labour and other conditions of employment, including methods of work to the production of fatigue, having regard to both industrial efficiency and the preservation of health amongst workers." In 1929, the I.F.R.B. became affiliated solely to the Medical Research Council and widened its scope of enquiries to become the Industrial Health Research Board.

In 1924 the Board launched a series of studies into the problem of monotony and the work cycle. One of these studies was conducted by Wyatt, Fraser and Stock (1928) on women wrapping soap, folding handkerchiefs, making bicycle chains, weighing and wrapping tobacco, making cigarettes and assembling cartridges. It was published in 1928 as Report No. 52 of the Medical Research Council Industrial Fatigue Research Board. Among its findings was one which stated, ". . . the social conditions of work were found to have significant (but not emphasized) consequences, boredom being less likely to arise when operatives worked in groups rather than alone". While great emphasis is placed on the early work of the American industrial psychologists such as Elton Mayo, F. J. Roethlisberger and William J. Dickson, it is worth remembering that the research which was carried out at the Western Electric Company in Chicago from the late 1920s, by staff of the Harvard Business School led to the creation of,

". . . a school of management thought based on the rediscovery of two subsidiary findings of the earlier British industrial psychologists; that workers improve their performance when someone (a researcher or a supervisor) takes an interest in what they are doing (Vernon, Wyatt and Ogden, 1924, p. 15), and that the opportunity to interact freely with other workers boosts morale. The researchers emphasised the distinction between "formal" and "informal" worker groups and the relationships between informal organization and performance. The resultant "human relations" school of management stressed the importance of the work group. Taylor's workers required only money, the human relations school's worker required group membership. The immediate impact of the Hawthorne studies concerned the role of the supervisor in handing work groups, and this became a major area of research for American industrial psychologists, inspired also by the work of Kurt Lewin and his associates."

Buchanan (1979 p. 19.)

The Hawthorne factory of the Western Electric Company

Photograph of Relay Assembly Test Room

A section of the Bank Wiring department showing Banks at different stages of completion.

Bank Wirers at Work

The Hawthorne Studies

The studies carried out at the Hawthorne works of the Western Electric Company in Chicago between 1927 and 1932 were amongst the most extensive social science research ever conducted. Thousands of workers were observed and interviewed. This research is most often associated with an Australian academic, George Elton Mayo. Mayo was born in Australia in 1880 and died in a Guildford nursing home nearly sixty nine years later. Initially a philosopher with psychoanalytical training, Mayo came to the United States in 1922, and became a professor of industrial research at the Harvard Business School two years later.

The Hawthorne studies revolutionized social science thinking. They began in 1924 at the Chicago factory of the Western Electric Company. At the beginning they sought to examine the relationship between output and workplace illumination. The researchers could find no such relationship. The intended results of these experiments were to have been the kind which appear as profits in company accounts rather than as papers in academic journals. They were intended to have direct financial benefits for the company. These experiments were at first carried out by a research division within the Western Electric company. However, the Harvard Business School became involved in this research from 1927 onwards, and their experiments demonstrated the overriding influence of social factors on workplace behaviour.

The precise nature of this work and the results have generated a high degree of controversy. The work did stimulate a vast amount of research on groups and group behaviour. The results of research on small group behaviour indicate that:

- Groups serve the needs of both the organization and the individual;
- Most groups have both formal and informal functions;
- The importance of groups in the organizational context rests on the ability of their members to unite against management and frustrate their policies;
- The informal functions and norms (called the "internal system") may go counter to the formal functions and norms (called the "external system");
- The satisfaction that an individual gains from group membership may constitute a more potent reward than management can and does offer;
- Individuals may thus be subjected to conflicting motivational forces;
- Group unity and solidarity (through the informal group or union) is also a means to force management to improve a group's rewards.

The fact that a group (and not merely its leader, whether appointed, elected or emerged) has an effect on its members has led to a great deal of research on how group attitudes can be changed. Researchers have paid attention to those aspects of the work situation and management policies which could be thought to have an effect on the attitudes and behaviours of employees.

THE CONCEPT OF A GROUP

Given the emphasis on face-to-face interaction, social psychologists have studied the behaviour of groups. The idea of a group is well known to most people who work, live and play in groups. Very often we may refer to persons standing at a bus stop or in a queue, as a group. It is important to maintain a distinction between mere aggregates of individuals and what are called *psychological groups.* The latter are so called because they exist not only through the (often visible) interactions of members, but also in the (not observable) perceptions of their members. The term group is thus reserved for people who consider themselves to be part of an identifiable unit, who relate to each other in a meaningful fashion and who share dispositions through their shared sense of collective identity. In the above example, only the football team would fulfil our criteria for a group.

Definition

A *psychological group* is any number of people who (a) interact with each other, (b) are psychologically aware of each other, and (c) perceive themselves to be a group.

The use of this definition enables one to exclude *aggregates* of people who are simply individuals who happen to be collected together at any particular time. Like the bus travellers, theatre audience or rain shelterers, they do not relate to one another in any meaningful fashion, nor consider themselves a part of any identifiable unit despite their temporary physical proximity. By the same token, the definition allows one to exclude classes of people who may be defined by physical attributes, geographical location, economic status or age. Even though a trade union in an organization may like to believe it is a group, it will fail to meet our definition if all of its members do not interact with each other, and if they are not aware of each other. This need for *all* members to interact has led to the suggestion that in practice, a psychological group is unlikely to exceed twelve or so persons. Beyond that number, the opportunity for frequent interaction between members, and hence group awareness, is considerably reduced.

It is possible for small aggregates of people to be transformed into a psychological group through outside circumstances. In fact, a whole series of "disaster movies" in the cinema have been made in which people fight for their lives on board sinking ships, hijacked aeroplanes and burning skyscraper buildings. The story involves aggregates of people setting out at the start of the film. The danger causes them to interact with one another, and this increases their awareness of one another and leads them to see themselves as having common problems. By the end of the film, the survivors demonstrate all the characteristics of the psychological group as defined here. The disaster movie example helps us to understand some of the characteristics of a psychological group:

1. *A minimum membership of two people:* while it is clear that one cannot be a group on one's own, the more members a group has, the greater the number of possible relationships can exist between them, the greater the level of communication that is required, and the more complex the structure needed to operate the group.

2. *A shared communication network:* each member of a psychological group must be capable of communicating with every other member. In this communication process, the aims and purposes of the group are exchanged. The mere process of communication interaction satisfies some of our social needs, and it is used to set and enforce standards of group behaviour.

3. *A shared sense of collective identity:* each group member must identify with the other members of the group and not see himself as an individual acting independently. He must believe that he is both a member of, and a participant in the group which itself is distinctive from other groups.

4. *Shared goals:* the goal concerned is therefore shared and only achievable by the members working together and not as individuals. The goal may be the production of something (e.g. student group project, company marketing plan) or enjoying oneself (e.g. playing in a football team). While the individual may want to attain some particular objective, he must perceive that the other members of the group share this same disposition. He must feel obliged to contribute to the attainment of the shared goal.

5. *Group structure:* individuals in the group will have different roles e.g. initiator/ideas man, suggestion-provider, compromiser. There roles, which tend to become fixed, indicate what members expect of each other. Norms or rules exist which indicate which behaviours are acceptable in the group and which are not (e.g. smoking, swearing, latecoming).

One can summarize this section by emphasizing the need to distinguish between aggregates of people and a psychological group. Not all groups will possess all the features listed above. Groups will differ in the degree to which they possess such characteristics. To the extent that they do have them, it will make the group more easily recognizable by others as a group, and this will give it more power with which to influence its members, The topic of influence and control in groups is dealt with in a later chapter. What will be said in the remainder of this chapter and this part of the book will refer only to psychological groups. For this reason we shall use the shorthand label of *group* to refer to a psychological group.

PURPOSES OF GROUPS

Groups serve both organizational and individual purposes. The problem is that the task objective of a group, that is, the job it has to do such as speedily processing insurance claims forms, may conflict with its social objective, which may involve members deriving pleasure from interacting with other group members. Where there is such a conflict, either the organization or the individual group members will lose out. Another problem arises where different individual members seek to satisfy different needs through membership of the same group. One person may seek to fulfil his need for power and try to direct the behaviour of others in a group. These members may have a primary need for friendship.

Group membership gives the individual new experiences which in turn may induce new desires. Thus once a group has formed, it may develop "accessory goals" i.e. goals which were not there initially. If members are satisfied with their group, they are likely to find some aim to pursue in order to maintain the group's existence after its main objective has been achieved or become outdated. Thus the "Build a Zebra Crossing in Byres Road" pressure group may turn itself into a permanent residents' association once the crossing has been built. Our group membership also influences the the view we have of ourselves. This is what psychologists call our self-image. Ask a person at a party who he is, it is very likely that he will answer your question by telling you the groups to which he belongs. This has been encapulated in the phrase, "Who I am is who we are". Thus we use groups to define our social identity and this has an effect both on our own behaviour and that of the individuals with whom we come in contact.

STOP!

(a)   make a list of the main purposes of the groups of which you are a member.

(b)   against each, indicate whether that purpose is primarily work-related or social.

FORMAL AND INFORMAL GROUPS

In the chapter on motivation, we learned that people had a variety of different needs among which were included those for love and esteem. Love needs are concerned with belongingness and relationships, while esteem needs focus on recognition, attention and appreciation. It was mentioned that while these two sets of needs may not be as essential to human existence as others, if they are not satisfied, then we may not feel confident, capable, necessary or useful members of society. These needs concern our relationships with others, and while we may spend time outside of work with our wives, girlfriends, boyfriends, children or social club members, the time that we do spend at work remains considerable. In our relationships with work colleagues, we frequently seek to satisfy our love and esteem needs.

The difficulty is that the organizations in which we work are not primarily designed to allow individuals to meet such needs at work. The collective purpose of an organization may be to make washing machines, provide a repair service, or earn £200,000 profit a year or achieve a 5 per cent return on investment. To achieve such collective purposes, the organization is structured in such a way so as to use the limited resources it has at its disposal as efficiently and effectively as possible. It does this by creating what is called a *formal organization*. The overall collective purpose or aim is broken down into subgoals or subtasks. These are assigned to different subunits in the organization. The tasks may be grouped together and departments thus formed. Job requirements in terms of job descriptions may be written. The subdivision continues to take place until a small group of people are given one such subgoal and divide it between themselves. When this occurs, there exists the basis for forming the group along functional lines. This process of identifying the purpose, dividing up tasks and so on is referred to as the creation of the formal organization. The groups which are formed as a result of the process are therefore known as formal groups.

Definition

Formal groups are those groups in an organization which have been consciously created to accomplish the organization's collective purpose. These formal groups perform formal functions such as getting work done, generating ideas, liaising and so on. The formal group functions are the tasks which are assigned to it, and for which it is offically held responsible.

It is through the division of labour that formal groups are created. A motor car company divides itself into departments responsible for sales, production, quality control, finance, personnel, training and so on. Within each such department one finds further subgroupings of individuals. It is the organization itself which gives the impetus for the formation of various smaller functional task groups within itself. Managers make choices represented as decisions, as to how technology and organization will be combined to create task orientated (or formal) groups. The purpose of the subgroups in the production department may be to manufacture 100 cars a day, while that of the group in the design department may be to draw up a set of construction plans. Whatever type of formal group we are interested in, they all have certain common characteristics:

- They have a *formal structure*;
- They are *task-orientated*;
- They tend to be *permanent*;
- Their activities contribute *directly* to the organization's collective purpose; and
- They are *consciously* organized by somebody for a reason

Two different types of formal groups in organizations can be identified. They are distinguished on the duration of their existence. Examples of *permanent formal groups* would include a permanent committee (e.g. union-management consultative board), a management team or a staff group providing specialist services (e.g. computer unit, training section). There are also likely to be *temporary formal groups*. For example, a task group which is formally designed to work on a specific project where its interaction and structures are pre-specified to accomplish the task. Such a task force might be formed when, for an unknown reason, a major delay or serious defect occurs in some area of manufacture. The aim of the task force would be to identify the causes and suggest remedies. This group would be disbanded once this objective had been achieved. What makes a formal group permanent or temporary is not the actual time it exists, but how it is defined by the company. Some temporary groups may last for years. What is important is whether the group's members feel that they are part of the group which might be disbanded at any time.

Alongside the formal groups there will exist a number of *informal groups*. These emerge in an organization and are neither anticipated, nor intended, by those who create the formal organization. They emerge from the informal interaction of the members of the formal organization. These unplanned-for groups share many of the characteristics of the small social leisure groups. These can function alongside the formal groups. The informal structure of a group develops during the spontaneous interaction of persons in the group as they talk, joke and associate with one another.

Definition

An informal group is a collection of individuals who become a group when members develop interdependencies, influence one another's behaviour and contribute to mutual need satisfaction.

Why do informal groups exist and what purpose do they serve? It was noted earlier that a formal organization is designed on rational principles and is aimed at achieving the collective purpose of the organization. To do this, staff are hired to perform clearly specified tasks and play clearly defined roles. The company only requires the worker to perform a limited range of behaviours, irrespective of whether he wants or can do more. This limitation of behaviour is related to the organization's need to be able to control and predict the behaviour of its members.

Nevertheless, the worker comes to the job as a whole individual. While the organization may wish to "hire a pair of hands", it gets the rest of the body and the brain thrown in! The individual brings his hopes, needs, desires and personal goals to his job. While the company may not be interested in these, the employee will, nevertheless, attempt to achieve his personal ambitions while at work. Many of these needs are in the area of love and esteem. Organizations are rarely designed to be able to fulfil these, or even feel that they have any responsibility to do so. This being the case, the employee will set about the job himself by developing relationships with other workers which will allow such need satisfaction to occur.

What if organizations were designed to meet workers' love and esteem needs?

NOTICE TO ALL SHOP FLOOR STAFF

As a result of management policy to meet the love and esteem needs of company personnel, the following changes to work arrangements will be introduced as from the first of next month:

1. The three maintenance teams which are currently composed of workers with the required range of skills will be disbanded. New teams will be formed and chosen by maintenance staff themselves. Team composition will be based on the criteria of who likes whom the best.
2. Five minute "Talk breaks" will be scheduled alongside the usual tea-breaks. This will allow intensive social interaction to occur between staff currently spread along the assembly line.
3. Appreciation sessions: All supervisory staff have been instructed to show intermittent appreciation of individual workers. Shopfloor workers will be greeted with a "Hello, mate!", will be told "what a bloody good job they're doing" and that if it was not for them, "the company would be in a right mess!"

The individual employee will try to manipulate his surroundings or situation in such a way so as to allow him to meet his motivational needs. Most other staff will generally be seeking to do the same so it will not be difficult to set up series of satisfying relationships. These relationships in turn will lead to the formation of informal groups. Because of man's social nature, there is a strong tendency for him to form informal groups. The task-orientated, formal groups rarely consider the social needs of their members. Indeed these are frequently considered dispensible and counterproductive to the achievement of the collective purpose of the organization.

STOP!

Consider the ways in which the college/institution in which you are studying this course has consciously organized the meeting of your social needs.

Suggest any specific things it could do to meet these to a greater extent.

The formal and informal organization are not totally separate. The composition, structure and operation of the informal groups will be determined by the formal arrangements that exist in the company. These provide the context within which social relationships are established and within which social interaction can take place. Such formal constraints can include plant layout, work shifts, numbers of staff employed and the type of technology used. It is important to understand that informal groups arise out of a combination of formal factors and human needs. The nature of the formal organization is based on the choices made by senior company managers. Both the formal organization and the ensuring informal counterpart that it generates can be changed when different choices are made.

Organizations only meet a small range of the individual's needs. The informal organization emerges to fulfil those needs neglected or ignored by the formal system. It differs from the formal system by being more casual in terms of its member composition and nature of interaction. To locate different informal groups, one does not look at the work flow or the organization chart, but needs to note who interacts with whom, and what friendship relations exists between individuals. To summarize therefore, one can say that formal groups exist to meet organizational objectives and fulfil the individual worker's lower level needs as identified on Maslow's hierarchy. The informal group can meet his higher level needs.

Individual Needs		Provision
Need to know and understand		
Freedom of enquiry	*Informal*	*informal work group*
Self Actualization needs	*Provision*	
Esteem Needs		
Love needs		

Safety needs		*wages, recognition, redundancy agreements, pension*
	Formal Provision	
Physiological needs		*lunch breaks, tea and coffee facilities*

The Informal and Formal Organizations

	Informal Organization	*Formal Organization*
A. *Structure*		
(a) Origin	Spontaneous	Planned
(b) Rationale	Emotional	Rational
(c) Characteristics	Dynamic	Stable
B. *Position Terminology*	Role	Job
C. *Goals*	Member satisfaction	Profitability or Service to society
D. *Influence*		
(a) Base	Personality	Position
(b) Type	Power	Authority
(c) Flow	Bottom up	Top down
E. *Control Mechanism*	Physical or social sanction (norms)	Threat of firing or demotion
F. *Communication*		
(a) Channels	Grapevine	Formal channels
(b) Networks	Poorly defined, cut across regular channels	Well defined, follows formal lines
G. *Charting*	Sociogram	Organization chart
H. *Miscellaneous*		
(a) Individuals included	Only those "acceptable"	All individuals in work group
(b) Interpersonal relations	Arise spontaneously	Prescribed by job description
(c) Leadership role	Result of membership	Assigned by organization
(d) Basis for interaction	Personal characteristics, status	Functional duties or position
(e) Basis for attachment	Cohesiveness	Loyalty

From Jerry L. Gray and Frederick A. Starke, *Organizational Behaviour: Concepts and Applications*, third edition, Charles E. Merrill, Columbus, Ohio, 1984, p. 412.

GEORGE HOMANS' THEORY OF GROUP FORMATION

The research into the behaviour of groups in organizations has focused on three main questions: Why do groups form? What keeps a group together? What makes it effective? The second and third of these questions will be dealt with in the ensuing chapters under the labels of group cohesiveness and group effectiveness. The search for the answer to the first question has produced a great deal of research data but few accepted theories.

Of the theories that have been put forward to explain the formation of groups, perhaps the most often cited is that of the sociologist George Homans. Homans had been a member of Elton Mayo's Department of Industrial Research at the Harvard Business School, and during his time there had been influenced by Mayo's thinking about group behaviour. Homans presented his ideas in 1951 in his book, *The Human Group*. He argued that any social system, such as a group, exists within a three part environment. This includes a physical environment (terrain, climate, layout), a cultural environment (norms, values and goals) and a technological environment (state of knowledge). The environment imposes certain activities and interactions on the people involved in the system. These activities and interactions in turn arouse emotions and attitudes (sentiments) among the people towards each other and towards the environment. This combination of activities, interactions and sentiments is primarily determined by the environment, Homans calls this the "external system". It is so called because it is imposed on the persons concerned from outside and may not be of their own choosing. The activities, interactions and sentiments are mutually dependent on one another. For example, the more two people interact with each other, the more positive their sentiments towards each other are likely to be. The reverse is also true, that is, the more positive the sentiments, the higher the rate of interaction.

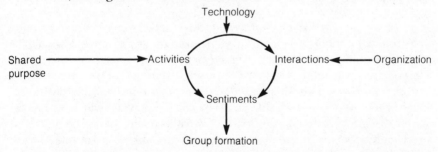

However, Homans noted that this external system did not exist alone. With increased interactions, people developed sentiments which were not specified by the external environment. That is, along with the new norms and shared frames of reference, new activities were generated which were not specified by the external environment. Workers were found to develop games, interaction patterns and sentiments not suggested and not sanctioned by the environment. Homans refers to this new pattern which arose from the external system as the *internal system.* This corresponds to what other theorists have called the informal organization.

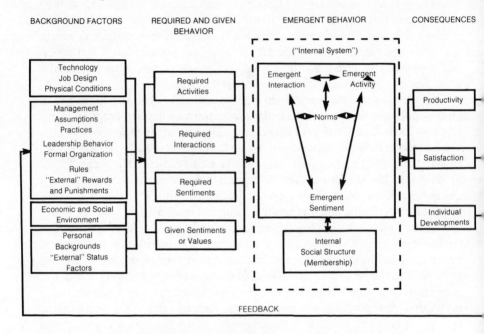

Figure 7.1   The Homans model of work group behaviour
From Arthur N. Turner, "A Conceptual Scheme for Describing Work Group Behaviour", in Paul R. Lawrence and John A. Seiler, et al., *Organizational Behavior and Administration; Cases Concepts and Research Findings.* Homewood, Ill.: Richard D. Irwin, Inc., 1965, p. 158. Copyright © 1961 by the President and Fellows of Harvard College. Reprinted by permission of the Harvard Business School.

Homans argued that the internal (informal) and external (formal) systems were interdependent. A change in work technology (external system) for example, would produce a change in interaction patterns which in turn would affect or disrupt the internal system. Conversely, if the internal system developed norms about how working life should be organized (as some of the Hawthorne Study groups did), this would often change the way in which work was performed, how much of it was done and what its quality would be.

Finally, Homans stressed that the two systems and the environment were interdependent. Changes in the environment would produce changes in the formal and informal work organization. The activities and the norms of the internal system would eventually alter the physical, cultural and technological environment. For example, the workers' informal method of solving problems might generate ideas for technological innovation, the redesign of work layout and the development of new norms about the nature of the relationship between workers and management. For example, new microcomputer developments in areas of production control mean that it is now possible for shopfloor level staff to monitor product output and quality themselves. This was a task previously carried out by first line management and would respresent a change in the relationships between the two groups. The most valuable aspect of Homans' conceptual scheme is its explicit recognition of the various dependencies.

In his theory, Homans distinguished between *required behaviour* and *emergent behaviour*. The concept is considered from the viewpoint of management. In designing a job, there are certain activities, interactions and sentiments which are required if the task is to be accomplished successfully. Other activities, interactions and sentiments emerge although they may not be required.

STOP!

Consider the person who is the checkout assistant at your local supermarket. What are the required activities, interactions and sentiments for her job?

As a regular customer at your local supermarket you will have been able to answer this question without difficulty. However, if you have stood in the queue on a Saturday morning you will have noticed some of the emergent behaviour. Checkout cashiers tend to have a friendly joke with the customers they know or with the other cashiers next to them. None of these interactions are specified by the required task system. Such behaviour may support the external system by making the work easier for the cashiers and makes the physical conditions more endurable. However, the emergent behaviour may function against the organization when the cashier fails to check out as many customers as quickly as she could. The point being made here is that there are, at the individual level, activities, interactions and sentiments which are required by management of the workers which further the collective purpose of the organization. However, such required behaviour forms the basis for the emergence of other activities which are not primarily geared towards this task attainment, but which contribute towards the satisfaction of individual employee needs.

STAGES OF GROUP DEVELOPMENT

Since we have been using the terms formal group and informal group, it is important to relate these to our organizational definition of the psychological group. While an informal group is always also a psychological group, a formal group may not necessarily be a psychological group. Consider for a moment the staff in a company finance office. As a task-oriented formal group they have a responsibility for the control of the company finances, costing and control. Of the twenty individuals who compose it, half may have been there for over twenty years, while others will have joined the company when it merged. Consider also the definition of the psychological group. There is no reason why these staff should all necessarily interact with each other or perceive themselves to be a single group. The finance department as a formally established group may consist of different informal groups. The question then arises as to how a collection of individuals becomes a psychological group.

Groups of whatever type do not come into existence fully formed. They grow and mature and it is possible to identify the stages of development through which a group goes before it becomes fully efficient and effective. Of course not all groups pass through all the stages and some get stuck in the middle and remain inefficient and ineffective. Progress through the stages may be slow, but appears to be necessary and inescapable. Barry Tuckman (1965) suggested that groups mature and develop, and have a fairly clearly defined four-stage cycle of growth which can be categorized as follows.

Forming
At this stage the set of individuals has not yet become a group. The persons are busy finding out who the other people are. They seek to know one another's attitudes and background. Members are also keen to establish their personal identities in the group and make a personal impression on the others.

Storming
This is a conflict stage in the group's life and can be an uncomfortable period. Members bargain with each other as they try to sort out what each of them individually, and as a group, want out of the group process. Individuals reveal their personal goals and it is likely that interpersonal hostility is generated when differences on these goals are revealed. The early relationships established in the forming stage may be disrupted.

Norming
The group develops a way of working to achieve its objectives. The questions of who will do what and how it will be done are addressed. Working rules are established in terms of norms of behaviour (do not smoke) and role allocation (Peter will be the spokesman). A framework is therefore created in which each group member can relate to the others.

Performing
This stage is concerned with actually getting on with the job in hand. The fully mature group has now been created which can get on with its work. Not all groups develop to this stage but may become bogged down in an earlier, and less productive, stage.

This four-stage model has been verified by research and can help us to explain some of the problems of group working. A group may be operating at half power because it may have failed to work through some of the issues at the earlier stages. For example, the efficiency of a project team may be impaired because it had not resolved the issue of leadership. Alternatively, people may be pulling in different directions because the purpose of the group has not been clarified, nor its objectives agreed. Members might be using the group to achieve their personal and unstated aims (so-called *hidden agendas*). For all these reasons, effective group functioning may be hindered.

CONCLUSION

A group can be considered as a society in miniature. A college department or company sales team will have a hierarchy with leaders and followers. It will have rules, norms and traditions as well as goals to strive for and values to uphold. It will change and develop, and will also adapt to and create changes in the environment and its members. Like a society it may experience a period of difficulty and decline. It is in such mini-societies as the family and the workgroup that an individual learns about, and is socialized into the wider society. It has been argued that small groups will reflect the social changes in the wider society, and it is likely that the individual will most directly experience these through the small group. For example, as there are changes about the value and organization of work, these may be reflected in changes in job design and workgroup organization.

Groups influence the behaviour, beliefs and attitudes of their members. While we may all like to believe that we are all free agents, and would resent being told that we are influenced by others or conform to others' views, research shows that this is in fact the case. In varying degrees and under certain circumstances, we are all influenced by others when we are in a group. If it is any consolation, we can remember that we in turn play an important role ourselves in influencing and controlling other group members. This is the topic of a later chapter in this part of the book.

SOURCES

de Board, R., 1978, *The Psychoanalysis of Organizations,* Tavistock, London.
Buchanan, D. A., 1979, *The Development of Job Design Theories and Techniques,* Saxon House: Farnborough.
Gray, J. L. and Starke, A., 1984, *Organizational Behaviour: Concepts and Applications,* third edition, Charles E. Merrill, Columbus, Ohio.
Homans, G. C., 1951, *The Human Group,* Routledge and Kegan Paul: London.
Likert, R., 1961, *New Patterns of Management,* McGraw Hill: New York.
McGrath, J. E., 1964, *Social Psychology,* Holt, Rinehart and Winston, New York.
Miller, E. J. and Rice, A. K., 1967, *Systems of Organization,* Tavistock, London.

Smith, J. H., 1980, "The Three Faces of Elton Mayo - a marginal man", *Times Higher Educational Supplement*, London, January 26.

Tajfel, H. and Fraser, C., 1978, *Introducing Social Psychology*, Penguin Books, Harmondsworth.

Tuckman, B., 1965, "Development Sequences in Small Groups", *Psychological Bulletin*, vol. 63, pp. 384-99.

Vernon, H. M. Wyatt, S. and Ogden, A. D., 1924, *On the Extent and Effects of Variety in Repetitive Work*, Medical Research Council Industrial Fatigue Research Board, Report no. 26, H.M.S.O., London.

Whitehead, T. N. 1938, *The Industrial Worker*, Harvard University Press, Cambridge.

Whyte, W.H., 1955, *The Organisation Man,* Penguin Books, Harmondsworth.

Wyatt, S., Fraser J. A. and Stocks, F. G. L., 1928, *The Comparative Effects of Variety and Uniformity in Work*, Medical Research Council Industrial Fatigue Research Board, Report no. 52, H.M.S.O., London.

Chapter 8

Group structure

Introduction
Why is there a group structure?
Status structure
Power structure
Liking structure
Role structure
Group structure and group processes
Leadership structure
Communication structure

Key Concepts:

Once you have fully understood this chapter, you should be able to define the following concepts in your own words:

Group structure   Social power
Group process   Social role
Group leadership   Communication structure
Position   Status incongruency
Social status   Sociometry

Objectives:

On completing this chapter, you should be able:

1. To understand the concept of group structure.
2. To understand group interaction represented symbolically.
3. To distinguish between two common uses of the concept of status.
4. To distinguish between group process and group structure and explain the relation between them.
5. To give examples of task roles and maintainance roles in a group.

INTRODUCTION

A central concept in helping us to examine the nature and functioning of groups is that of group structure. Structure refers to the way in which members of a group relate to one another. The formation of group structure is one of the basic aspects of group development. When people come together and interact, differences between individuals begin to appear. Some talk more while others listen. These differences between group members serve as the basis for the establishment of group structure. As differentiation occurs, relations are established between members. Group structure is the label given to this patterning of relationships.

Definition

Group structure is the relatively stable pattern of relationships among the differentiated elements in a group.

Group structure carries with it the connotation of something fixed and unchanging. Perhaps the picture of scaffolding is brought to mind. While there is an element of permanency in terms of the relationships between members, these do continue to change and modify. Group members continually interact with each other, and in consequence their relationships are tested and transformed. As we describe the structure of any group, it is perhaps useful to view it as a photograph, correct at the time the shutter was pressed but acknowledging that things were different the moment before and after the photo was taken. Differences between the members of a group begin to occur as soon as it is formed. This differentiation within a group occurs along not one, but several dimensions, the most important of which are:

Liking	Liking structure of a group
Status	Status structure of a group
Power	Power structure of a group
Role	Role structure of a group
Leadership	Leadership structure of a group

There are as many structures in a group as there are dimensions along which a group can be differentiated. Although in common usage we talk about *the* structure of a group, in reality, a group will differentiate simultaneously along a number of dimensions. Group members will be accorded different amounts of status and hence a group will have a status hierarchy. They will be able to exert differing amounts of power and thus a power structure will emerge. In examining group functioning, social scientists have found it useful to consider differences amongst group members in terms of liking for each other, status, power, role and leadership. While it is possible to examine each structural dimension of the group in turn, we need to remember that all are closely related and operate simultaneously in a group setting. Cartwright and Zander (1968) suggest that group structure is determined by:

1.   The requirements for efficient group performance;
2.   The abilities and motivations of group members;
3.   The psychological and social environments of the group.

The internal structure of the group

"Whyte's description makes it clear that the Nortons were a differentiated group in which individuals of different capacities and statuses were bound together in a common unity. Members formed a well understood and fairly stable hierarchy, from the peripheral members on the bottom to 'Doc' at the top. The activities in which the group engaged reflected this power structure: not only did the group usually do the things the leader suggested, but each member's behaviour tended to be a function of his position in the group. Whyte describes how the members' bowling scores reflected not only their innate skill but also their social standing. . . . When one skilled but low ranking member challenged a high ranking member to a bowling match, other members exerted enough group pressure (through razzing and other more subtle means) to make the challenger come out low scorer for the evening. More broadly, Whyte was interested in how the group arrived at its decisions, that is, in the patterns of influence which characterized the group. Beneath the casual and seemingly random surface activity, Whyte detected fairly consistent patterns of communication: remarks travelled 'up' the hierarchy during the planning of activities and, when a decision had been reached at the top, flowed 'down' to the lower ranks. It was not just a case of leaders telling followers what to do but of a far more complex give-and-take in which each 'rank' tended to interact with the rank adjacent to it. The result was a pattern which, though informal, resembled the chain-of-command communication flow in a bureaucracy."

From Michael S. Olmsted, The Small Group, Random House, New York, 1959, p. 35.

WHY IS THERE A GROUP STRUCTURE?

Why does a patterning of relationships between individuals in a group occur and what purpose does it serve? Robert Bales (1950, p. 15-16) argued that,

"The actions of other individuals . . . are always relevant to the problem of tension reduction of any given individual. . . . It is to the advantage of every individual in a group to stabilize the potential activity of other towards him, favourably if possible, but in any case in such a way that he can predict it. . . . All of them, even those who may wish to exploit the others, have interest in bringing about stability. The basic assumption here is that what we call the 'social structure' of groups can be understood primarily as a system of solutions to the fundamental problems of interaction which become institutionalized in order to reduce the tensions growing out of uncertainty and unpredictability in the actions of others.''

STOP!

Explain the following saying: "Better the devil you know than the devil you don't".

It is this basic need for predictability which causes structure to develop within a group. Members are differentiated several dimensions (e.g. status, role, power). One person will therefore simultaneously have high status and power since each person stands at the intersection of several dimensions. All the differentiated parts associated with an individual group member are referred to as his *position* in the group structure.

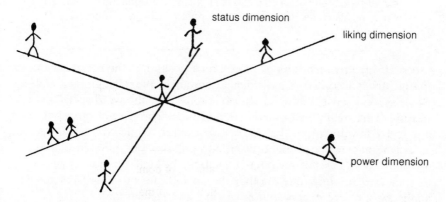

There is some confusion between the key concepts of *group structure* and of *position within the group*. Position is used refer to an individual's locus in a communication network. In order to characterize adequately any group member's relations to others in the group over a period of time and in different social settings, it is necessary to locate him along a number of dimensions, that is, in a number of different positions. Consider a typical group of work colleagues or fellow students. Usually, the number involved will not exceed seven. Each member of your group will occupy some position in it. It is the pattern of the relationships between the positions which constitutes the structure of the group. In the diagram overleaf, it is the lines which join the positions together.

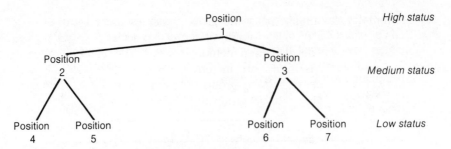

STATUS STRUCTURE

Each position in the group has a value placed upon it. Within the organization, a value is ascribed to a position by the formal organization e.g. Chief Controller, Vice-President, Supervisor and can be labelled formal status. Formal status is best thought of as being synonymous with rank as in the police or the armed forces and reflects a person's position on the organizational ladder.

Definition

Formal status refers to a collection of rights and obligations associated with a position, as distinct from the person who may occupy that position.

A second way in which value is placed on a position is the social honour or prestige that is accorded an individual in a group by the other group members. In this second sense, the word status is prefixed by the word social and is a measure of informally established value and its comparison with other positions as perceived by the informal group or organization. While one can view social status as a sort of badge of honour awarded for meritorious group conduct, it can also be viewed as a set of unwritten rules about the kind of conduct that people are expected to show one another. It can indicate the degree of respect, familiarity or reserve that is appropriate in a given situation.

Definition

Social status is the relative ranking that a person holds and the value of that person as measured by a group.

One of the powers possessed by an informal group is its ability to confer status on those of its members who meet the expectations of the group. These members are looked up to by their peers, not because of any formal position they may hold in the organization, but because of their position in the social group. Since many people actively seek status in order to fulfil their need for self-esteem, the granting of it by the group provides them with personal satisfaction. Similarly, the withholding of status can act as a group control mechanism to bring a deviant group member into line. The status given by the group to a member is immediate in terms of face-to-face feedback. The recognition and esteem given to group members goes to reinforce the individual's identification with the group and his dependence upon it.

Food preparers' social hierarchy

Whyte discovered the status rankings that were ascribed to food preparers in the restaurant industry. The usual hierarchy of status was:

1. Those who cook
2. Salad
3. Chicken preparation
   a. white
   b. dark meat
4. Meat
   a. beef
   b. pork
   c. roasts
   d. frying
5. Chicken cooking
6. Vegetables
   a. parsley
   b. chives
   c. celery
   d. beans — green
   e. spinach
   f. carrots
   g. potatoes
   h. onions
7. fish

From William Foote Whyte, *Human Relations in the Restaurant Industry*, McGraw Hill, New York, 1948, pp. 36-46.

An individual's formal status is based on hierarchical position and task ability. The organization is made up of a number of defined positions arranged in order of their increasing authority. The formal status hierarchy reflects the potential ability of the holder of the position to contribute to the overall goals of the organization. It differentiates the amount of respect deserved and it ranks individuals on a status scale. The outward symbols associated with formal status (e.g. size of office, quality of carpet) are there to inform other members in the organization of where exactly that person stands on the ladder. This topic leads ultimately to a consideration of organization structure, which is a topic of a later chapter.

Homans (1961) used the term *status congruency* to refer to a situation where the responsibility of a job that a person had was congruent with his superiority in other respects such as pay, perks and so on. By the same token, status incongruency may exist when, for example, an individual may be rich but uneducated, a successful businessman but a failed business student. Status incongruency can cause confusion in interpersonal relationships and social interaction. One does not know how to relate to that person, either individually or in a group. Rich people are usually ascribed high status while uneducated ones are ascribed a low one. Persons with high status are treated with deference and respect, while low status persons may be treated with impatience.

Status incongruency in group behaviour

How does status congruency affect group efficiency? Adams (1953) conducted a study of United States Army bomber crews and examined the variations in effectiveness. In the groups he studied, important status hierarchies were found. Those which were discovered as being of most significance were age, military rank, amount of flying time, education, reputed ability, popularity, length of service, combat time and position importance. Adams defined group congruence as existing when the individuals who composed the group stood in exactly the same rank in all the status hierarchies. Where a moderate degree of congruence existed, the groups performed better as measured by the number of targets hit during bombing practice.

Low status congruence was found to reduce the efficiency of the bomber crews. Adams suggested that this differing performance could be explained by the inconsistancy in the statuses leading to a reduced level of interperson communication. The minimum that was required to perform the technical task but no more. This led to a reduction in group cohesion and thereby to reduced performance. Adams also discovered that high status congruence was also associated with low performance. Perhaps it led to increased interaction between individuals on a social level thereby reducing the attention paid to the task in hand and shielding them from outside criticism through the security provided by the integrated group. Such a thesis is supported by the fact that high status congruence groups lead to the emergence of socially orientated leaders while low congruent groups lead to the emergence of task orientated ones. Since effective groups appear to require both types of leadership, it may be that it is provided by moderately status congruent groups.

From S. Adams, "Status congruency as a variable in small group performance", *Social Forces*, vol. 32, no. 1, 1953, p.p. 16-22.

Interaction with others perceived as lower in status can be threatening because of the potential identification of the person with the group or individual being associated with. Status is abstract and ascribed through the perceptions of others. One's status is therefore always tenuous. It may be withdrawn or downgraded at any time. The reference group with which one identifies and whose values and behaviour one adopts, plays an important part in establishing and maintaining one's status. To preserve one's status, one cannot leave the reference group for a lower status reference group.

POWER STRUCTURE

A second dimension on which differentiation occurs in a group is power — the control over persons. Individuals within the group are able to control the behaviour of others and may have to if the group is to achieve its goals. For this reason, it becomes necessary for the group to have established control relations between members. By having a power structure, the group avoids continued power struggles which can disrupt its functioning, and it can link goal achievement activities to a system of authority which is seen as legitimate.

Definition

Social power is the potential influence that one person exerts over another. Influence is defined as a change in the cognition, behaviour or emotion of that second person which can be attributed to the first.

John French and Bertram Raven defined power in terms of influence. They distinguished several different types of power base. A power base is the relationship between two people which is the source of that power. In a group the relationship between individuals will involve not one, but several power bases. For example:

Reward power: where one person perceives that another is able to offer him a reward, for example, mother and child.
Coercive power: when one person perceives that another can punish him, for example, traditional father and child concept.
Legitimate power: when one person perceives that another has a legitimate right to order him to do something, for example, person accepting a judge's ruling despite his own views.
Referent power: where one person identifies with the other, that is, he feels at one with him, or desires to identify with him, for example, a pop fan adopting the dress style of his idol.
Expert power: where one person perceives the second to have some expert knowledge, for example, certain types of teacher-pupil relationships.

French and Raven conclude that the broader the basis of power the individual has, the greater the power which he will exert. Referent power has the broadest range of coverage.

LIKING STRUCTURE

The liking (or affective) structure in the group refers to the way in which members differentiate themselves in terms of whom they like and do not like. To identify the affective structure of a group, one uses a technique called sociometry.

Definition

Sociometry is the name given to the technique of displaying patterns of human relationships that exist within groups. These relationships tend to depend upon personal choice (i.e. selection and rejection) and can be represented diagramatically using relatively few conventional symbols.

Sociometry was invented by Jacob Moreno (1934) who was responsible for the development of the technique. A sociometric test reveals the feelings which individuals have towards each other as members of a group. This feeling, the sociometric term for which is *tele*, may be one of attraction (positive tele), or repulsion (negative tele), alternatively there may merely be indifference. A written description of the affective structure of a group may be as follows:

Jim and Tim choose one another. Jim and Tim also choose Bob. Bob rejects Tim and is indifferent to Jim. Bob and Mandy choose each other. Mandy and Alice reject one another but Alice chooses Bob although this choice is not reciprocated in any way. Alan neither chooses nor is chosen. Louise chooses Bob but gets no response.

These liking relationships can be visually depicted in the sociogram below:

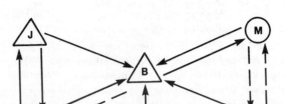

In a sociogram, the continuous line linking two individuals represents a positive choice (A———▶B), while a dotted line represents the negative aspect of choice — rejection (A— — — ▶B). Where no information is given about a relationship, and hence no lines can be drawn, the assumption is made of indifference between people. Choices are elicited by asking group members (in secret) to write down on paper, whom they would like to be with or work with and whom they would not like to be with or work with. The convention in sociometry is to represent a male with a $\triangle$ symbol, and a female with a $\bigcirc$ symbol.

Sociometric techniques are valuable in representing complex interpersonal feelings. If the question on which a sociogram is based is both meaningful and specific, it can provide information about possible group interaction.

Thus the question, "Who do you want to sit next to when the group discusses this topic?" is preferred to, "Who do you want to sit next to?"

STOP!

Select one of the questions below and ask members of some small group. Use the answers you obtain to draw a sociogram.

With whom do you want to do a joint class project? With whom do you want to spend your leisure time?

A sociogram represents a pattern of choice (selection, rejection, repulsion, indifference) at a given point in time and in relation to one aspect of the group's functioning (specified in the question asked). The pattern, and hence the liking structure of the group, will change over time. Thus several sociograms would therefore be needed to display changes over a period of time.

ROLE STRUCTURE

The occupant of every position in the group is expected to carry out certain functions when the members of the group interact with one another. The expected behaviours associated with a position within the group constitute the *social role* of the occupant of that position. This is the concept which relates the individual to the prescriptive dictates of the group. People's behaviour within the organization is structured and patterned in various ways, and an understanding of role help us to see and explain how this happens.

Definition

Social role is the set of behaviours that are expected of the occupant of a position by other members of the group.

Social scientists differ in the way in which they use the term role. The above definition emphasizes the expectations of other people. The term has also been used to refer to the behaviours which the occupant of the position himself believes are appropriate for him to enact (called *perceived role*) and also to the behaviours in which the person actually engages in (called *enacted role*). It is sufficient to note the existence of these different uses of the concept and remind readers that it will be examined in another context when organizational structure is discussed. For the present, it is sufficient that role be thought of rather like a script which actors have. The same actor changes his roles and can act out different parts in front of different audiences. Our concern here is with the different roles that exist within the group.

When we observe a group in action what we see are people behaving in certain ways or doing certain things. If we want to study how they behave in a group, it is necessary to have a precise and reliable way of describing what is happening within it. Social psychologists have developed precise techniques with which to describe and analyse the interactions of group members. Robert Bales (1958) was amongst the first to systematically observe the behaviour of people in groups and to develop a comprehensive and useable system of categorizing it, which he called Interaction Process Analysis (IPA). He specified twelve categories which he used to classify or "code" this behaviour. For example, "shows solidarity, raises other's status, gives help, reward" (category 1) and, "shows antagonism, deflates other's status, defends or asserts self" (category 12). Bales felt that with his twelve categories one could classify all the behaviours that were likely to occur in a group. He used his classification system to gather data with which to propose a theory of group functioning. In essence, he argued that group behaviour could be explained by showing how groups dealt with certain problems such as orientation, evaluation, control and so on.

Bales' scheme focuses on how people choose to express themselves in a problem solving situation. It neglects the content of what is said, its quality and any accompanying non-verbal communication. It also claims that every act plays some part in the problem solving process. While in reality a single comment can have several purposes, in IPA it is recorded in a single category and it assumes that the observer can accurately judge what the group member intended by it. These criticisms notwithstanding, Bales' observational technique is the most refined and exhaustive (empirically usable) method yet developed which can be used to study small group processes. It has been extensively tested, and an acceptably high agreement between observer–raters has been obtained. It has also provided the basis for other behaviour categorization schemes.

GROUP STRUCTURE AND GROUP PROCESS

When discussing groups, one often distinguishes group structure from group process. Process refers to the group activity which occurs over time. More specifically:

Definition

Group process is the sequence of interaction patterns between the members of the group.

Group process concerns itself with the verbal contributions of group members, how group problems are solved and how decisions are reached in the group. The observation of the process of a group gives us a clue to aspects of its structure. Group structure and group process are therefore clearly related. The structure of a group can affect its process and vice versa. The formal structure of a committee defines the persons appointed to sit on it, their roles and status within the group, their heterogeneity, etc. This determines in part the interaction that takes place. For example, high status members may be permitted to speak more and will exert more influence on group decisions than more junior staff. Equally, the processes that occur within an initially unstructured group can lead to the formation of a certain group structure. The individual who speaks most may be deferred to as the group leader. The valued contributions of some members may give them enhanced status in the eyes of others.

Group member roles

Within a group activity, such as a staff meeting or a tutorial discussion, some persons will show a consistant preference for certain behaviours and not for others. The particular behaviour, or set of behaviours a person demonstrates in a group can lead them to be seen to be playing a particular role within the group. Bales' work showed that people adopt specific roles.

STOP!

Overleaf is a list of seven behaviour categories with an explanation of each category alongside. Also provided is a chart for coding group member behaviours. Next time you are at a group discussion, listen to what is said and record the behaviours of each group member using the chart. Put the names of the group members along the top of the chart. Every time they speak decide what their behaviour is and place a tick or dot under their names, alongside the appropriate behaviour category. After you have watched and analysed the discussion, total up your ticks or dots horizontally and vertically. You may wish to share this information with the group members.

Category	Explanation
Proposing	Any behaviour which puts forward a new suggestion, idea or course of action.
Supporting	Any behaviour which declares agreement or support with any individual or his idea.
Building	Any behaviour which develops or extends an idea or suggestion made by someone else.
Disagreeing	Any behaviour which states a difference of opinion or a criticism of another person's statement.
Giving Information	Any behaviour which gives facts, ideas or opinions or clarifies these.
Seeking Information	Any behaviour which asks for facts, ideas or opinions from others.

Category	Names							Total
Proposing								
Supporting								
Building								
Disagreeing								
Giving Information								
Seeking Information								
Total								

After carrying out this exercise, did you have difficulty in knowing what the group was discussing, that is, the content of its conversation? What does this tell you about the difference between the *content* of a group's discussion and the *process* of its discussion?

Some roles are concerned with group maintenance issues, while others are more assertive and are concerned with getting on with the job.

Task roles	*Maintenance roles*
Initiator	Encourager
Information seeker	Compromiser
Diagnoser	Peacekeeper
Opinion seeker	Clarifier
Evaluator	Summariser
Decision manager	Standard setter

Charles Handy (1976) argued that when individuals decide about their behaviour in a group, they ask themselves three questions. These focus on issues of *identity* ("Who am I in this group? What is my occupational role? What are the role expectations of me?"), *power* (Who has the power? What kind of power is it? Do I want to change the influence pattern?) and *aims* (What are my needs and objectives? Are they in line with the group? What do I do about them if they are not?) The answers to these questions will influence which role(s) they will play in the group.

Roles in the gang

"Every member of a gang tends to have a definite status within the group. Common enterprises require a division of labour. Successful conflict (with other groups, the police or the community in general) necessitates a certain amount of leadership, unreflective though it may be, and a consequent subordination and discipline of members. As the gang develops complex activities, the positions of individuals within the group are defined and social roles become more sharply differentiated."

From Frederic Thrasher, *The Gang,* University of Chicago Press, Chicago, 1927, p.328.

LEADERSHIP STRUCTURE

As was pointed out earlier, there are many jobs to be done in a group if it is to be both productive and satisfying to its members. These functions can be either performed by the formal group leader or by the members. The leader and the members all play roles in the group. Through them a group atmosphere is created which enables communication, influence, decision making and similar processes to be performed. In much of the management literature, leadership is considered exclusively as a management prerogative. Authors write about "management style" rather than "leadership style". This material will be dealt with in a later chapter on leadership.

However, there is evidence to suggest that group performance and satisfaction is affected by the type of leadership exercised within a group. During the 1950s, Ralph White and Gordon Lippitt carried out research into leadership in a youth group under the direction of Kurt Lewin. They attempted to discover what effects different types of leadership style had on the behaviour of groups. One of their objectives was:

> To study the effects on group and individual behaviour of three experimental variations in adult leadership in four clubs of eleven-year-old children. These three styles may be roughly labelled as "democratic", "authoritarian" and "laissez-faire".

The research design involved creating a number of activity clubs, each of which consisted of five youngsters who were matched on characteristics such as age, leadership, IQ, popularity and physical energy. The children were given craft projects to undertake, and each group was under the direction of an adult leader who had been thoroughly briefed regarding the style of leadership he was to display. Each leader was to use a specific style, and each was rotated between the groups so that the effect of his personality on the group's behaviour was randomized. The characteristics of the three styles of leadership behaviour used were described by the researchers:

Autocratic style
All the policies of the group were determined solely by the leader. The leader told the children how the task was to be done in a step-by-step manner so that, at any one time, they were uncertain as to what the future steps were. The leader dictated what the work task was and with whom each member would work. He personally praised and criticized each member's work and remained aloof from the group except when demonstrating how the task was to be done.

Democratic style
Policies were determined by group discussion and decision. The leader encouraged and assisted the group in this process. The approach to the task emerged during group discussion. When technical advice was sought by members from the group leader he offered at least two alternatives from which the group could choose. The members chose their own work partners and the division of the task was left to them. The leader tried to be objective in his praise and criticism and sought to be a group member in spirit without doing the work for the group.

Laissez-faire style
There was a minimum of leader participation and members were left to make

their own individual or group decisions. The leader supplied materials for the group and indicated he would supply information if asked. He took no other part in the discussion of the techniques or activities to be carried out. He took no part in selection of work partners or in the division of the task. He made only infrequent and spontaneous comments on the activities, unless he was questioned. He did not attempt to either appraise or regulate what went on.

Careful observations were made by four researchers of the groups through spy-holes and the conversations and activities of the groups were recorded. A film was even made of what occurred. White and Lippitt discovered that each of the different leadership styles evoked different behaviour among group members as indicated in Table 8.1.

Table 8.1 Results of White and Lippitt's Research on Leadership Styles

	Leadership style		
	Authoritarian	Democratic	Laissez-faire
Percentage of the time spent by group members:			
Working	*74*	*50*	*33*
"Out and out loafing"	*0*	*1*	*5*
Playing	*2*	*13*	*33*
Working when adult present	*29*	*46*	*11*

What were the effects of the different leadership styles on the group members? Under *democratic leadership* there were personal and friendly relations among members. More individual differences were shown, but there was also a high degree of "group-mindedness". There was little scapegoating of individuals, a steadier work level when the leader left the room, and the group produced better results. When a *laissez-faire* leadership style was used with the same group, it was observed that the group lacked achievement, its members asked the leader more questions, it lacked a means with which either to make group decisions or to plan. The group spent a proportion of its time playing about. The leadership style was then changed again, and this time the same group experienced an *authoritarian style*. Two forms of group reaction were demonstrated, one was aggressive while the other was apathetic. Both reactions showed a high dependence on the leader by the group. The aggressive behaviour was rebellious and attention–demanding but showed mutual friendliness among members. Apathetic behaviour was characterized by outbursts of horseplay.

STOP!

What generalizations can you make about leadership from this study of adults and children in a summer camp?

What does it tell us about leadership style in organizations? Give the reasons for your views.

The concept of leadership suggests a process of goal attainment, follower satisfaction and group support. Actions and activities are performed for and by the leader. There has been an increasing interest in *group leadership* as opposed to the individual leadership research which in the past has sought to identify the characteristics of effective leaders. The group leadership approach aims to study the characteristics of small groups and tries to understand the social context in which they work. It seems therefore more useful to view leadership as an activity floating between members rather than a static status associated with an individual. Leadership is thus seen as a dynamic and innovative approach to problems commonly perceived by an individual or by a group of people. In helping to understand behaviour in organizations, it can be useful not to necessarily view the manager as the leader, although he could of course be. Not all formally designated supervisors or managers are leaders. By taking the group rather than the individual as the primary focus of study, an attempt is made to identify the way in which the group as a whole attempts to achieve its goals, and link it to the actions which may be required of the group members to achieve this end. From this standpoint, one discusses the roles that group members perform. It is now possible to offer a definition of leadership from a group, rather than from an individual perspective:

Definition:

Leadership is the performance of those acts which help the group achieve its preferred outcomes.

From D. Cartwright and A. Zander (Eds.) *Group Dynamics: Research and Theory*, Tavistock, London, 1968, third edition, p. 304.

The acts or "jobs-to-be-done" include defining group goals, promoting good relations between members of the group, and so on. Some acts are task focused, while others are maintainance focused. These leadership functions can be performed by different group members at different times. The group therefore will differentiate along the leader–follower continuum and will continue to redifferentiate as it progresses, with the leadership structure continually redefining itself.

The relationship between the leader-at-a-point-in-time and the followers may be thought of as one of social exchange. The leader provides rewards for the group by helping its members to achieve their own and the group's goals. They in turn reward the leader by giving him heightened status and increased influence. However, members can rescind that influence at any time if they feel that the leader is no longer worthy of their respect. Viewed as a social exchange process, the leader has power in terms of his ability to influence the behaviour of group members. But it is the group members who give him the power to influence them.

Collective leadership in groups

Thrasher studied boys gangs in the Chicago slums during the 1920s. He reported that while there was a natural leader in the group,

"In some cases leadership is actually diffused among a number of strong 'personalities' in the group who share the honours and responsibilities. The gang leader had a number of strong lieutenants which led to the central command being diffused. Another way of viewing it was that supplementary strengths of members were integrated. In addition to this collective leadership, a rotation of leadership relative to the aims or tasks of the group took place."

From Frederic Thrasher, *The Gang*, Chicago University Press, Chicago, 1927, pp. 345-52.

It is therefore useful to distinguish between a *leader* and *acts of leadership*. If we accept Cattell's (1951) view that the leader is any group member who is capable of modifying the properties of the group by his presence, then we can acknowledge that any member of the group can, in theory, perform acts of leadership, and not merely the individual occupying some formal position. Robert Bales found that a separation (or differentiation) in task roles and social roles occurred in a group. Many studies have since confirmed this finding and suggest that group frequently have both a social leader and a task leader. Bales himself does not view leadership as a single role, but as applying to several roles within the group. In a well organized group, in which leadership functions are being satisfactorily performed, the task-specialist and group maintainance specialist are found.

COMMUNICATION STRUCTURE

Group structure was defined as the relationships between different positions in the group. An important relationship between positions is in terms of the nature and frequency of interaction. A consideration of the communication structure of a group represents the final dimension to be considered, and the way in which it has been researched offers a link to a consideration of some of the research methods used in the study of small group behaviour.

The members of a group depend on information provided by others. Solving a problem, making a decision or reaching agreement all require information exchange between members. Usually, that information comes down a chain of people. A tells B, B tells C and so on. William Foote Whyte (1948) describes how a cook in a restaurant may receive an order from a customer via a runner, pantry worker and waitress. Such a communication link can produce a distortion in the message. When information arrives in this form, the cook is unable to check it, has no opportunity to negotiate with the message sender and cannot discuss any problems.

To discover which communication structure is most effective, Alex Bavelas (1953) conducted a laboratory experiment to test if certain communication patterns in a group had structural characteristics which limited the performance of the group in its task. While all the communication patterns studied were, in theory, adequate for the group to do the task, he wanted to know if any of them were significantly better. Were certain communication patterns superior in standing up to group disruption? Did some effect the emergence of leadership? Zelditch and Hopkins (1961) described the design of Bevalas' experiments and the equipment used.

Bavelas chose simple patterns of communication to study:

| Circle | Chain | Wheel | "Y" |

Patterns of communication

"Subjects in these studies sit in cubicles fashioned by partitioning a circular table. Each partition has a slot at the base through which messages may be passed. Communication is by written message only. The experimenter may form any pattern of communication he wishes by opening or closing the slots in the partitions. One may create, for example, a condition in which one subject is central and all the others peripheral by closing off all channels except those between the central subject and each of the others ... Typically subjects are given various problem solving tasks in the form of puzzles: they may, for instance, be given five cards, one per subject, among which six symbols are so distributed that only one symbol is common to all five cards, and the subject's task is to identify which is the common symbol. The experimenter measures such effects as the creation of social hierarchies, the speed and accuracy of the solution, and the morale of the subjects."

From Morris Zelditch Jnr. and Terence K. Hopkins, "Laboratory experiments with organizations", in Amitai Etzioni (ed.) *Complex Organizations: A Sociological Reader*, Holt, Rinehart and Winston, New York, 1961, p. 476.

Communication between individuals was permitted only along the channels prescribed by the pattern and subjects were insulated from any "cross talk". It was found that:

- The centrality of position in sending and receiving group messages produces group leaders.
- For organizing efficiency, the wheel is the fastest, followed by the "Y", the chain and the circle. Thus efficiency reduces with less centrality.
- For simple problems which required little interaction, the wheel was the fastest. Difficult problems which required interaction, the circle was the fastest.
- Satisfaction was highest in the circle network where everyone was involved in the decision making process.

SOURCES

Adams, S., 1953, "Status congruency as a variable in small group performance", *Social Forces*, vol. 32, no. 1, pp. 16-22.

Bales, R. F., 1950, *Interaction Process Analysis*, Addison-Wesley. Reading, Mass.

Bavelas, A., 1967, "Communication patterns in task-orientated groups" in D. Cartwright and A. Zander (eds) *Group Dynamics: Research and Theory*, Tavistock, London, 3rd edition.

Benne, K. and Sheats, P., 1948, "Functional roles of group members", *Journal of Social Issues*, vol. 4, pp. 41-9.

Cattell, R., 1951, "New concepts for measuring leadership in terms of group syntality", *Human Relations*, vol. 4, pp. 161-8.

Cartwright, D. and Zander, A. (eds), 1968, *Group Dynamics: Research and Theory*, Tavistock, London, 3rd edition.

French, J. R. P. and Raven, B. H., 1959, "The bases of social power" in D. Cartwright (ed.) *Studies in Social Power*, University of Michigan Press, Ann Arbor, Michigan.

Handy, C., 1976, *Understanding Organizations*, Penguin Books, Harmondsworth.

Homans, G. C., 1961, *Social Behaviour: Its Elementary Forms*, Harcourt Brace, New York.

Miller, D. C. and Form, W. H., 1969, *Industrial Sociology*, Harper: New York, 3rd edition.

Olmstead, M. 1959, *The Small Group*, Random House. New York.

Thrasher, F., 1927, *The Gang*, University of Chicago Press, Chicago.

White, R. and Lippitt, R., 1960, *Autocracy and Democracy*, Harper and Row, New York.

Whyte, W. F., 1943, *Street Corner Society*, University of Chicago Press, Chicago.

Whyte, W. F., 1948, *Human Relations in the Restaurant Industry*, McGraw Hill, New York.

Zelditch, M. and Hopkins, T. K., "Laboratory experiments with organizations" in A. Etzioni (ed.) *Complex Organizations: A Sociological Reader*, Holt, Rinehart and Winston, New York.

Chapter 9

Social control through groups

Key concepts:

Once you have fully understood this chapter, you should be able to define the following concepts in your own words:

Social influence   Shared frame of reference
Social facilitation   Sanctions
Social norm   Social organization
Conformity

Objectives:

On completing this chapter the reader will be able to:

1. Understand why groups are capable of exerting an influence on the behaviour and attitudes of individuals.
2. Know how such influence and control is exercised in the group situation.
3. Relate aspects of group control to the groups of which they are members.
4. Appreciate the organizational consequences of group influence and control.

INTRODUCTION

In the overview to this section it was pointed out that we were moving up one level of analysis from the individual to the group. A problem of choice faces us when we seek to study conformity and control in groups. From what we know already about the nature of psychological groups, it is clear that our interactions with other people can be studied from several different perspectives. Our behaviour is shaped by numerous factors. Amongst which one could list the following:

Intra-individual factors
Those considered in the first section of the book. Our personality, perceptual set, frame of reference, learning style and motivation. The strength of our attitudes and values and how they fit in with those of other people in the group and our need to feel accepted by other group members all play a part in how we behave in groups.

Group characteristics
Here the focus is not on the individual but on the structure of the group itself. We examine the hierarchy which exists, the roles people play and whether the group is a formal or an informal one.

Interaction process
From this perspective we consider the way in which the process of interaction itself between group members affects them in terms of their attitudes and behaviour.

　　　This chapter considers how the attitude and behaviour of an individual is changed or modified when that person joins and becomes member of a group.

- Why and how are individuals influenced by others in the group?
- Why do we as individuals conform to the dictates of society in general, and to that of our own group in particular?
- How do groups develop "rules of behaviour" to regulate the conduct of their members, and
- How are such rules enforced by the group?

SOCIAL INFLUENCES ON MOTIVATION

For the individual, group membership has benefits in the form of satisfaction of some psychological needs. But there are "costs" in the form of modifications to behaviour that the individual invariably must make in order to retain membership. The attraction that group members have for one another, that is, *group cohesiveness,* is influenced by various factors such as the homogeneity of members, amount of communication, isolation from distraction, group size, outside pressure or threat, group status and degree of past success. William F. Whyte (1955, p. 331) wrote that,

> "The group is a jealous master. It encourages participation, indeed it demands it, but it demands one kind of participation — its own kind —and the better integrated with it a member becomes the less free he is to express himself in other ways".

Cohesiveness affects the degree of dedication to group activities. Groups invariably establish rules of conduct in order to maintain consistency of behaviour among group members. These rules are generally referred to as norms and groups develop means by which they enforce such norms. Punishments such as practical jokes, social ostracism or even violence may be used against deviants. There is now impressive researach evidence which demonstrates the power of groups to exert profound social influence on individual behaviour. The mere presence of other people can affect what we do. The concept of social influence refers to this phenomenon. It has been found that a person's behaviour is affected by merely knowing that other people are present, or that they soon will be present to observe what they do.

STOP!

Think of *five* things that you do alone that you would not do if someone else was with you.

Why would you not do these things in the presence of others? What would be the consequences in each case if you did?

Definition

Social influence refers to the phenomenon that the mere presence of other people affects, and thereby alters, the behaviour of an individual from what it would otherwise have been.

The process of social influence can either facilitate or inhibit behaviour. The term social facilitation was coined by the psychologist Floyd Allport.

Definition

Social facilitation refers to the observation that whatever the person is doing alone, when he is joined by others, he frequently does it better, faster or more frequently.

At other times the effect is inhibitive, with performance reducing in the presence of others or else certain behaviours being totally eliminated. We all know how sportsmen can achieve an improved performance when they compete at a major international meeting attended by many spectators. Sports commentators frequently refer to the benefit a football team can derive by playing at home in front of its own crowd. In contrast, the presence of others can inhibit or eliminate certain behaviours. We may stop picking our nose in the company of others or a group of men may stop using swear words when they are joined by a female. Frequently it may be a mixture of both. When I join my daughter at the table for a meal, she stops wriggling around in her seat, uses her knife and fork more carefully, and stops hitting her brother.

Why do such changes in performance occur? It was believed at one time that the cause was diffuse excitability and hyperactivity. The presence of others was stimulating and led to an increased speed or quality of performance (higher output) or to a greater number of errors (lower quality). Research does show that the presence of others does sometimes have an encouraging effect, and at other times an inhibiting effect. It depends on the task being performed and on how the individual sees the group. If we accept that the individual's perception of his social environment (including other people) influences his behaviour, then this moves the explanation beyond the "general excitability" thesis, and accepts that different overt behaviour can result from the same internal stimulation. The presence of others (especially the opposite sex) can arouse us, but the way we behave as a result of that arousal is not direct. Each individual has acquired during his life, many ways of interpreting and reacting (his personality) and individuals differ too much to allow any simple laws to be stated.

Man has found in the struggle for survival that a strategy of co-operation is frequently useful but that the advantage of group membership which that co-operation entails, brings with it obligations. The need to be able to relate to and identify with a group is deep-seated within us. Many different psychologists have identified social or affiliation needs. Moreover, many of the tasks in which we engage cannot be completed alone but require the assistance of others. Thus for social and practical reasons, we work in and through groups. By virtue of that need and desire for membership of a group, we open ourselves up to the influences that the group can exert on our individual perceptions, values and behaviours. Thus from the viewpoint of individual freedom, group membership carries with it both costs and benefits.

Some agreement on perception and meaning is essential among the members of a group in order for them to interact, communicate, agree on goals and generally to allow members to act in concert on a common task. Such a shared framework is essential for the group if it is to continue and develop. Moreover, as we work in groups we find that our frame of reference becomes similar to that of the group.

Definition

Shared frame of reference is the assumption that we make about the kind of situation we are confronting. It is the context within which we view it. A frame of reference which is shared by the members of a group means that through their interaction and mutual education, the members of this group will tend to perceive a large range of phenomena in broadly the same way.

Why is a frame of reference important? Mainly because it determines the *meaning* which we attach to events and other people's behaviour. In the annual pay negotiations, for example, the frames of reference of the management representative and the union negotiator about the kind of situation they see themselves as being involved in will probably be radically different. The manager may see himself as concerned with resisting the excessive demands for increased wages by the workers and thereby defending the future of the company and the interests of the shareholders. The union man may see himself as representing the just demands of the workforce in a period of inflation. Both no doubt feel that the situation could be settled if the other person chose to act reasonably, but that reasonable behaviour involves the other side accepting completely the other's position. During any major strike, the radio and television interviews between the union and management representatives illustrate this point. They highlight the differences in values and meanings accorded to key concepts such a "a fair offer" and "co-operation".

How the negotiators see it

"A negotiating situation is therefore not merely one where two or more people discuss an issue. The people involved belong to groups (unions or management . . .) and a conflict between individuals is always in addition a conflict between groups. Mr A does not just perceive himself as Mr A and perceive Mr B as Mr B, he perceives himself also as a union member and Mr B as a member of management — these groups as well as the individuals are in conflict. The ethos or culture of a management group is in many ways opposed to that of a shop-floor group. Management norms emphasize efficiency, rational efforts to increase productivity and profitability, the orderly conduct of affairs, and a general stress on individual self-advancement through promotion, social progress and approval from others. As people adopt the management reference group and spend their lives with other managers, they come to take this so much for granted that they often hardly notice the existence of the norms and the accompanying social pressures.

Similarly the manual worker may be unlikely to recognize how far his actions and feelings are socially determined and he will probably have only a limited conception of norms different from his own. The typical shopfloor culture is one which is also based upon approval from others (for we have seen that self-esteem through group membership is a basic ingredient of mental health), but here the approval goes to other kinds of behaviour than efficiency and striving for promotion. Efficiency can of course be valued as an individual sign of skill, and promotion can be desired, but prospects are in many cases severely limited. The norms of the manual worker's group are often likely to emphasize an interest in horse-racing or football, an ability to mend cars or television sets, skill at extracting loose piecework rates from management, being one of the lads who sticks up for his mates, and (in some areas) a concern for improving the lot of the working class. The worker like the manager aims for group respect or status, but his status is an informal one in the group whereas the manager's is more a formal placement in a hierarchy of positions. In both cases their status comes largely from conformity, but the norms to which they may conform are different ones."

From Peter Warr, *Psychology and Collective Bargaining*, Hutchinson, London, 1973, pp. 15-16.

GROUP EFFECTS ON INDIVIDUAL PERCEPTIONS

Muzafer Sherif (1936), in a study which has now become a classic in experimental social psychology, showed how group norms emerged. He demonstrated that the way in which perceived motion can be affected by what others present at the time claim to see. Few of the subjects who took part in Sherif's experiments felt conscious that their judgements had been influenced by others. This reinforces the point that the process of social influence is covert and that its effects last a long time. Sherif's work showed that in a situation where doubt and uncertainty exist and where first hand information is lacking, a person's viewpoint will shift to come into line with those of other group members. In essence this situation leads to the creation of a group norm. This occurs quickly amongst group members who have had little previous experience of the group's work, but it also occurs amongst those who have had experience, although somewhat more slowly.

Sherif's work suggested that in order to organize and manage itself, every group developed a system of norms. What are norms and what is their purpose? Norms are behavioural expectations and they serve to define the nature of the group. They express the values of the members of the group and provide guidelines to help the group achieve its goals.

Definition

Norms are the "expected modes of behaviour and beliefs that are established either formally or informally by the group. . . . Norms guide behaviour and facilitate interaction by specifying the kinds of reactions expected or acceptable in a particular situation."

From E. E. Jones and H. B. Gerrard, *Foundations of Social Psychology*, John Wiley, New York, 1967.

STOP!

We would like you to do some social psychology research by studying your fellow students. You belong to a group of students following a broadly similar course of study, and you probably belong to a close subgroup within this larger class.

What modes of behaviour are expected of you within that subgroup? What beliefs do you share? How do these norms facilitate your interaction?

Norms develop in a group around those subjects and topics in the life of the group which are important to its functioning as defined by the group members themselves. Norms may apply to all group members or only to specific individuals. Norms may also vary in the degree to which they are accepted by the group, and can vary in the range of permissible deviation. In a workgroup, norms might exist regarding what is a fair days work, how to interact with the foreman and so on. Topics which are not central to a group's functioning will not have norms associated with them. There may thus be no norms about how one should dress or what is the appropriate length of time for a tea break. It is certain that a number of norms will develop in any group. However, around which topics these norms emerge, and what behaviour or attitude they specify, will vary from group to group. Similarly, a norm within a single group can change over time.

STOP!

Think of a group of which you have been a member for some time. Can you think of a group norm which has changed over time?

Sherif's study of the emergence of group norms

If you place yourself in a room which is completely dark and look fixedly at a small point of light, the light will appear to move in different directions. You can test this out yourself if you have a completely dark room and one small pinpoint of light. It is not that anything is actually moving, but the effect of fixing one's eyes on such a small point of light in the darkness makes the light seem to move. The apparent movement is an optical illusion known as the "autokinetic effect".

Sherif placed a group of subjects in such a darkened room and presented such a small spot of light. He then asked them to track the apparant movement of the spot. He also asked them to say, aloud, each in turn, the direction in which they thought the light was moving. Initially each group member differed. There were quite wide individual differences in the response to this situation. Some subjects saw little movement while others saw a lot.

However, Sherif discovered that they started to agree quite quickly. Having exchanged information on judgements, their behaviour changed. They began seeing the light moving in the same direction as those who had spoken earlier. Gradually all the members began seeing the light moving in the same direction at the same time. There was of course no "real" movement of the light. Each individual began to see the light in the same way as the group saw it. The results Sherif obtained with two-person and three person groups are shown below:

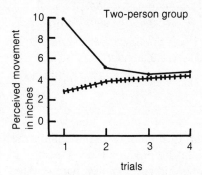 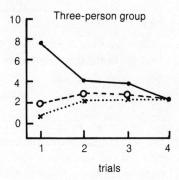

Each line of the graph represents the responses of one person

When a group norm emerged it was found that it became the basis for subsequent judgement when subjects were retested independently. The group norm therefore became a relatively permanent frame of reference for behaviour.

From Muzafer Sherif, *The Social Psychology of Group Norms*, Harper, New York, 1936.

Discovering the norm

Donald Roy, a researcher who acted as a participant observer in a factory, described the pressures that were placed on an individual to adhere to the group norm. Roy's earnings, and those of others, were based on a piece rate system. The more he produced the more he earned.

"From my first to my last day at the plant I was subject to warnings and predictions concerning price cuts. Pressure was the heaviest from Joe Mucha, . . . who shared my job repertoire and kept a close eye on my production. On November 14, the day after my first attained quota, Joe

Mucha advised: Don't let it go over $1.25 an hour, or the time-study man will be right down here! And they don't waste time, either! They watch the records like a hawk! I got ahead, so I took it easy for a couple of hours. Joe told me that I had made $10.01 yesterday and warned me not to go over $1.25 an hour . . . Jack Starkey spoke to me after Joe left. "What's the matter? Are you trying to upset the applecart?" Jack explained in a friendly manner that $10.50 was too much to turn in, even on an old job. "The turret-lathe men can turn in $1.35", said Jack, "but their rate is 90 cents and ours is 85 cents." Jack warned me that the Methods Department could lower their prices on any job, old or new, by changing the fixture slightly or changing the size of the drill. According to Jack, a couple of operators . . . got to competing with each other to see how much they could turn in. They got up to $1.65 an hour, and the price was cut in half. And from then on they had to run that job themselves, as none of the other operators would accept that job. According to Jack, it would be all right for us to turn in $1.28 or $1.29 an hour, when it figured out that way, but it was not all right to turn in $1.30 an hour.

Well now I know where the maximum is — $1.29 an hour."

From Donald Roy, "Banana time: job satisfaction and informal interaction", *Human Organization,* vol. 18, 1960, pp. 156-68.

The continued violation of norms by a group member therefore puts at risk the cohesion of the group. When there is disagreement on a matter of importance to the group, the preservation of group effectiveness, harmony and intactness requires a resolution of the conflict. Hence pressure is exerted on the deviating individual through persuasive communication to conform. While such pressure towards group cohesion ("going along with the other members of the group") may be beneficial in many respects for the group, it also carries costs. If conformity is allowed to dominate with individuals having little opportunity to present alternative and different views, this can lead to errors of judgement and the taking of unwise actions. The next chapter will consider the phenomenon of *groupthink.* Such pressure to conform on the individual is applied through the use of sanctions imposed by the group.

Definition

Group sanction refers to both punishments and rewards given by group members to others in the process of enforcing group norms. Reward is positive sanction and punishment is negative sanction.

The earliest examples of sanctions exercised in groups came from the Hawthorne studies. The researchers observed that persons producing either over or under the group norm were *binged.* This involved a group member flicking the ear of the norm transgressor or tapping him on the upper part of the arm. Both actions were intended to indicate physically that his behaviour was unacceptable. Other sanctions were also used by the group.

Controlling the deviants

"The mechanisms by which internal control was exercised varied. Perhaps the most important were sarcasm, "binging" and ridicule. Through such devices pressure was brought to bear upon those individuals who deviated too much from the group's norm of acceptable conduct. From this point of view, it will be seen that the great variety of activities normally labelled "restriction of output" represent attempts at social control and discipline and as such are important integrating processes. In addition to overt methods, clique membership itself may be looked upon as an instrument of control. Those persons whose behaviour was most reprehensible to clique A were excluded from it. They were in a sense, socially ostracized. This is one of the universal social processes by means of which a group chastizes and brings pressure to bear upon those who transgress its codes ... It can be seen, therefore, that nearly all the activities of this group may be looked upon as methods of controlling the behaviour of its members. The men had elaborated, spontaneously and quite unconsciously, an intricate social organization around their collective beliefs and sentiments."

From Fritz J. Roethlisberger and William J. Dickson, *Management and the Worker*, John Wiley and Sons, New York, 1964, pp. 523-4.

Group norms and sanction are not limited to the industrial context. They occur in all psychological groups, the family and the college class group.

Norms and sanctions on a Master of Business Administration programme

The part time Masters degree programme in Business Administration lasts three years. Each participant is therefore a member of one of the three large Year Groups, but additionally is a member of a smaller Syndicate Group. The latter operate as task-orientated, face-to-face primary groups. In these small groups, group norms are formed and established. These norms then control the behaviour of members. Deviant members are brought into line by the application of punishment mechanisms. Norms operating within the small Syndicate Group include the following:

- Keep up with the reading;
- Contribute positively to the discussions;
- Don't go isolate i.e. participate, don't "shut-off";
- Obtain or arrange copies of any handouts for absent members;
- Support each group member.

Syndicate members who did not contribute were at first gently repri-
manded, for example, by being accused of having a hectic social life or
by having criticism levelled at them ("nice of you to turn up").
Embarrassment was used as a major sanction. Continued failure by the
student to behave in accordance with group norms led to them initially
being temporarily, but deliberately, excluded from discussions and
conversations. The group would go to a different pub at lunch without
telling the "deviant". Further failure to conform would lead to exclusion
from the group. This was done by the sanctions on the member
becoming so regular, and being imposed with increasing magnitude,
that the attachment of the individual to the group would be reduced to
the extent that it would be negative. At this point he would resign from the
group. Embarrassment, reprimand and exclusion were the main sanctions available to members of the Syndicate groups.

The large Year Group which consisted of some fifty students and
met regularly in a lecture hall also had its own norms:

- Listen quiety and attentively — let the lecturer "bang on" about his
  particular subject;
- Behave courteously — don't shout the lecturer down or walk out
  even if you feel he is talking rubbish;
- Relatively static seating pattern;
- Ask brief questions, don't give mini-lectures, make relevant contri-
  butions;
- If you're late apologize to the lecturer, if you have to leave early get
  his permission;
- However old and mature you may be as a manager, in the classroom
  the lecturer (however young he may be) is superior to you;
- No smoking in the large group.

The sanctions available to members of the large Year Group to enforce
these norms were not as strong as those available within the smaller
Syndicate groups. Expulsion from the Year group was not open to
students since only the Department could exclude the student if he had
failed the exams or else not paid his fees. The group did show
disapproval of the behaviour of its members at times by visual and
verbal displays of apathy, boredom or restlessness. Shuffling, sighing,
groaning and students talking to each other while the deviant delivered
a mini-lecture were frequent. If these sanctions failed, students would
have an open discussion about the behaviour of the offender, within his
earshot, in the coffee queue during the intermission. It was agreed that
these sanctions were not however particularly effective.

A group member deviating from an important group norm has several
options. He can try to persuade others to join his position and thus alter the
group norm. Or he may be persuaded to conform to the original norm. The
higher his status (and thus power) in the group, the more likely he is to change
the attitudes of others and the less likely he is to change his own. If neither of
these alternatives take place then something else will happen. If he is free to

leave the group, and the group is of little importance to him, he may withdraw from it. Conversly, if he is of little importance to the group, he may be faced with the choice of conforming or else being rejected by the group. He may even be rejected by the act of deviance whether or not he is willing to recant. However, if he is of great importance to the group, that is, if he is a high status member in terms of power, popularity or special skills, the group may tolerate the deviation in order to avoid the greater threat of a loss of a valued member. The power which a group has to influence its members towards conformity to shared beliefs and actions depends on three main factors:

- The positive and negative sanctions (rewards and punishments) the group has at its disposal;
- The degree to which individual members value their membership of the group and its accompanying rewards (e.g. recognition, status, prestige, financial inducements);
- The member's desire to avoid negative sanctions such as social and physical punishments or expulsion from the group.

These were demonstrated by the differences between the Syndicate group and the Year group in terms of the power they had to exert of their members in order that they conformed.

GROUP EFFECTS ON INDIVIDUAL ATTITUDES AND BEHAVIOUR

Why is it that members do actually conform to group pressure? Part of the answer can be found in what has just been said. However, there is a little more to it. At the level of society level, there is a tacit agreement between people that for life to go on without producing continual problems, some general principles and rules need to be observed by members. For example, we drive on the left hand side of the road, we wear clothes and so on. Observation of such rules is of such individual benefit, that he or she is prepared to suppress any personal desires and is thus prepared to limit their freedom and abide by the rules. Moreover, the benefits which accrue, and the fear of the loss of these, encourage people to act in order to punish those who violate the rules. Thus we may report a car driver to the police who crosses a traffic light when it was at red, accusing him of dangerous driving. The more important of these norms have, over time, become backed by the rule of law.

A second reason why we conform to norms is that, at an individual level, we each have a desire for order and meaning in our lives. Numerous psychologists have demonstrated how people attempt to "make sense" of seemingly unconnected facts or events. For the individual, uncertainty is disturbing and is reduced to the absolute minimum. We like to know "what's going on" and we like to be in command of the situations in which we find ourselves. Norms, and the adherance to norms, provides the sense and predictabilty which most human beings desire. Finally, norm conformity can be explained at the intersubjective level. Evidence suggests that a person learns to adopt the attitudes and behaviour current in his society, either because he has an innate need for a response from others or because he acquires such a need very early in life through his interaction with his mother. Both explanations assume that one receives a satisfying response from others if they see you like themselves and if one behaves in accordence with their expectations. It seems that we need meaningful interaction and meaningful status from those we are with or with whom we compare ourselves.

STOP!

Suggest why the same people might behave differently in different situations or with different sets of people.

Eating offal

During World War II, the price of quality meat in the United States rose dramatically and the government wanted the population to eat the less popular cuts of meat such as offal which was both cheap and nutritious. However, kidneys and brains were not popular with family members. They were felt to be somewhat unattractive in appearance and more bothersome to prepare than, for example, steak meat.

A project was conducted in 1943 by Kurt Lewin to discover how best the public could be persuaded to change their eating habits towards offal. He did not think that a media campaign would work, since he considered eating behaviour to be a group norm. In his view, in order to change behaviour, one needed to change the norm. The key person in the family to do with eating was the housewife. Therefore, Lewin began using groups of housewives to investigate how best that behaviour could be changed.

Lewin's experiment consisted of six groups composed of housewife members of the Red Cross. Each group varied in size from between 13 and 17 people. Two approaches at influencing were attempted. In the first, lectures were given which linked the question of nutrition to the war effort, the health of the family, and the economic benefits. Different ways of preparing meat were discussed and recipes distributed to those attending. The lecturer attempted to arouse the interest of the listeners by explaining how she cooked herself and how successful it had been with her own family members. In the second approach, group discussion was the main vehicle in which a group leader raised the topic of diet and the war effort and this was followed by a discussion about what contribution the housewives could make to this. This discussion covered topics relating to the reasons which underlay the reluctance to change. Recipes were handed out again, and a vote was taken as to who would try out an offal meal the following week.

After a week all the housewives participating were interviewed at home. While only 3 per cent of the group who had attended the lecture had tried an offal recipe, 32 per cent of those participating in the discussion had. Lewin attributed this higher rate in the latter case to the establishment of a new group norm regarding offal eating which had emerged through the process of discussion.

From Kurt Lewin, "Group decision and social change" in Maccoby, E. E., Newcomb, T. and Hartley, E. L. (eds.) *Readings in Social Psychology*, Holt, Rinehart and Winston, New York, 1958, third edition.

A great variety of circumstances influence conformity to norms. The personality characteristics of individuals play a part in predisposing them to conform to group norms. The kind of stimuli eliciting conformity behaviour is also important. That people conform to norms when they are uncertain about a situation was demonstrated by the Sherif experiments. The amount of conformity to a group standard corresponds strongly to the degree of ambiguity of the stimulus being responded to. Situational factors are also involved. The size of the group, the unanimity of the majority, and its structure all have an effect. It has been found that conformity increases as the group size increases. It is also affected by a person's position in the communication structure of a group, conformity being greater in a decentralized network than a centralized one. Finally, there are the intra-group relationships referred to earlier. The kind of pressure exerted, the composition of the group, how successful it has been in the past, and the degree to which he identifies with the group, are all examples of this.

Conformity to group norms

Solomon Asch studied conformity (the tendency of an individual to "give in" to a group) in the laboratory setting. He demonstrated how difficult it was to resist other people's opinions. A group of six apparent subjects was shown a line of certain length and asked to say which of three other lines matched it (see figure below). This group in fact consisted only of one true volunteer. The other members were confederates of the experimenter. Subjects responded in a fixed order with the real subject always next to last. The "stooges" had been told secretly beforehand to select one of the "wrong" lines on each trial or in a certain percentage of trials. When for example the group was presented with the display, all the stooges said that line A was the same height as line X.

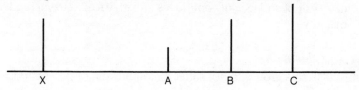

The naïve subjects were placed within earshot of the others so that they heard the answers of most of the group before they had to announce their own decisions. When the turn of the real volunteer subjects came to match line X with one of the others, would they resist the pressure to conform? Asch discovered that time and again the volunteers went along with the false statement of the stooges that line A was the same length as line X. Asch's measure of conformity was the number of times the real subject gave the wrong answer when the confederates did.

It is interesting to consider the pressure that a group can exert on an individual if it can influence something as unambiguous and familiar as judging the length of lines. How much more powerful the influence if individuals have to make subjective and unfamiliar judgements. The subjects in the experiments, both volunteers and stooges, were students who had only met during the experiment itself. They dispersed after it had been concluded. The degree of conformity tends to be increased when the group members have a higher status than the "deviant" individual and when the group must continue to work in the future. The research indicates how difficult it can be for individuals to express their opinions when these are not in line with those of other team members. In eighteen trials of the experiment, 25 per cent of his subjects never crumbled under group pressure, some 30 per cent went with the majority and against the clear evidence of their senses for half of the trials, while the other 55 per cent fell somewhere in between.

From Solomon E. Asch, "Effects of group pressure upon the modification and distortion of judgements", in Guetzkow, H. (ed.) *Groups, Leadership and Men,* Carnegie Press, New York, 1951, pp. 177-90.

Asch found that those who did yield, did so for different reasons. He distinguished three types of yielding:

Distortion of perception
In this category belong a very few subjects who yield completely under the stress of group pressure, but are aware that their estimates have been displaced or distorted by the majority. These subjects report that they came to perceive the majority estimates as correct.

Distortion of judgement
Most submitting subjects belong to this category. The factor of greatest importance in this group is a decision the subjects reach that their perceptions are inaccurate and that those of the majority are correct. These subjects suffer from primary doubt and lack of confidence and they feel a strong tendency to join the majority.

Distortion of action
The subjects in this group do not suffer a modification of perception, nor do

they conclude that they are wrong. They yield because of an overwhelming need not to appear different from or inferior to other. They are unable to tolerate the appearance of defectiveness in the eyes of the group. These subjects suppress their observations and voice the majority position with awareness of what they are doing.

CONFORMITY TO AUTHORITY

The Asch experiments demonstrated how group pressure affected individual internal standards by enforcing conformity within the group. Other research, by Stanley Milgram (1974), showed that a group can aid the individual to defy authority. When we conform, we are responding to pressures which are implicit. We consider our behaviour to be voluntary. If questioned about our actions we may have difficulty explaining why we went along with the group view. The subjects in Asch's experiments had this trouble and in fact many denied that this is what they did. They preferred to think they were acting independently. Even when their errors were pointed out, they preferred to attribute these to their personal error of judgement. The Milgram experiment presented a situation of conflict in which a group supported an individual member who rebelled against the authority of a superior.

Milgram's "electric shock" experiments

Would you torture another person simply because you were told to do so by someone in authority? Of course not, you would probably reply with little hesitation. In a series of now famous and highly controversial experiments, Stanley Milgram examined people's level of obedience to authority. The research involved ordinary people of different ages, sexes, races and occupations. A group of psychiatrists, post-graduate students and social science lecturers were asked by Milgram to predict how many of the research subjects would actually obey the experimenter's order. There was a high agreement that virtually all subjects would refuse to obey. Only one in a hundred would do it, said the psychiatrists, and that person would be a psychopath.

Milgram's experiment involved volunteers participating in a learning experiment They were to act as teachers of people who were trying to learn a series of simple word pairs. As teachers they were told to punish the student when he failed to learn by giving him an electric shock. At the start the shocks were small in intensity but every time the learner made a mistake, the teacher was told to increase the size of the shock. In carrying out the experiments Milgram found that *two out of every three* subjects tested administered the electric shocks up to a level which was clearly marked "fatal" simply because an authority figure told them to do so. In fact, no electric shocks were actually given although the volunteer teachers believed that the learners were really receiving the shocks they administered.

Our primarily interest in this chapter is in group influences. In his experiments, Milgram manipulated certain variables to see whether they had any effect on the behaviour of the subjects. One such variation involved placing two of the experimenter's confederates alongside the volunteer teacher so that the testing of the subject would be done by a group and not by the single volunteer. There is a similarity here with Asch's experimental situation. The trial began with one of the stooges administering the shocks. He then refused to continue, argued with the experimenter and withdrew sitting in the corner of the room. The second stooge took over, continued for a bit, and then refused as the previous one had done. The real volunteer now remained to administer the shocks himself. This procedure was repeated forty times. It was found that thirty of the subjects, once they had seen their group colleagues defy the experimenter, also defied him. When group pressure (or support) for such defiance was lacking, only fourteen subjects defied the authority figure. Milgram concluded that peer rebellion is a very powerful force in undercutting the experimenter's authority.

Milgram suggested seven reasons why the group was effective in helping the individual to do this. The reasons are the same as those which explain the power the group has over the individual:

"1.   Peers instil in the subject the idea of defying the experimenter.
2.   The lone subject has no way of knowing if defiance is a bizarre or common occurrence. Two examples confirm that it is a natural reaction.
3.   The act of defiance by the confederate defines the act of shocking as improper. It provides social confirmation for the subject's suspicion that it is wrong to punish a subject against his will, even in a psychological experiment.
4.   By remaining in the room, the confederates' presence carries with it a measure of social disapproval from the two confederates.
5.   As long as the confederates participated in the experiment, there was dispersion of responsibility among group members for the shocking. As they withdrew, the responsibility focused on the subject.
6.   The naïve subject witnessed two instances of disobedience and observed that the consequences of defying the experimenter are minimal.
7.   The experimenter's power is diminished by failing to keep the confederates in line."

From Stanley Milgram, *Obedience and Authority*, Tavistock, London.

The Milgram experiments have provoked a great deal of controvery and discussion on subjects such as the ethics of research, problems of experimental design and application of findings. They have be used to explain the behaviour of Nazi SS guards in the concentration camps during the Second World War.

When a person joins an existing group, he has an existing predisposition to accept the norms of the group. The group "educates" him into its frame of reference and he is often keen to learn. The new member's view on key matters are "corrected" by the group members when these differ from those of the group.

The power of the group

Lewis Yablonsky made a study of violent groups in New York City. Part of his study related to the structure of gangs. The following quotation from this study comes from a member of a group involved in the murder of Michael Farmer in 1959. Farmer was a partially crippled polio victim and, whilst walking home one evening through a park in central Manhatten, New York, he was set on by a gang of youths. They claimed membership of a gang called the Egyptian Kings. Some members felt that allegiance to the gang was such an overwhelming force that it superseded other, more normal values. From the transcript of the interview with these boys, the following extract is taken:

"I was watchin' him. I didn't wanna hit him at first. Then I kicked him twice. He was layin' on the ground lookin' up at us. I kicked him in the stomach. That was the least I could do, was kick 'im."

Another gang member questioned said he attacked the victim because he was afraid that the other members would "get him later" if he did not swing out.

From Lewis Yablonsky, "The violent gang as near-group" in *The Violent Gang*, Macmillan, New York, 1962, p. 37.

CONCLUSION

It has been argued that the studies which have been carried out on the effects of the group on the individual have dealt inadequately with both the internal group organization and have focused on the traits of individuals rather than their personalities. Studying the effects that a group has on an individual is relatively straightforward. One places the person in a group and sees what happens. Does he behave differently than when he is alone? However, such research activity needs to be distinguished from that which considers the effect of group life on the individual's personality.

Personality is a dynamic entity with an internal structure. Only psycho-therapy has really addressed this problem. To do this, we would have to make an analysis of all influences on the individual which can result in him reacting in a vast number of different ways. Moreover, since personality is deemed to be a system, what happens in one part of it has consequences for other parts. Thus this is more complex than a mere stimulus–response sequence. When we seek to understand the interrelatedness of group and personality, we take on a much bigger job than merely noting the reactions of individuals. This perspective requires us to have a theory of personality on which to base our investigations.

SOURCES

Asch, S. E., 1951, "Effects of group pressure upon the modification and distortion of judgements" in H. Guetzkow, (ed.) *Groups, Leadership and Men*, pp 177-90, Carnegie Press, New York.

Asch, S.E., 1952, *Social Psychology*, Prentice-Hall, New Jersey.

Broom, L. and Selznick, P., 1965, *Sociology*, Harper and Row, New York.

Jones, E. E. and Gerrard, H. B., 1967, *Foundations of Social Psychology*, John Wiley, New York.

Lewin, K., 1958, "Group decision and social change" in E. E. Maccoby, T. Newcomb and E. L. Hartley (eds.) *Readings in Social Psychology*, Holt, Rinehart and Winston, New York, 3rd edition.

Milgram, S., 1974, *Obedience and Authority*, Tavistock, London.

Roethlisberger, F. J. and Dickson, W. J., 1964, *Management and the Worker*, John Wiley, New York.

Roy, D. 1952, "Quota restriction and goldbricking in a machine ship", *American Journal of Sociology*, vol. 57, no. 5, March, pp. 427-42.

Roy, D., 1960, "Banana time: job satisfaction and informal interaction" in *Human Organization*, vol. 18, pp. 156-68.

Sherif, M., 1936, *The Psychology of Group Norms*, Harper and Row, New York.

Warr, P., 1973, *Psychology and Collective Bargaining*, Hutchinson, London.

Yablonsky, L., 1962, "The violent gang as a near-group" in *The Violent Gang*, Macmillan, New York.

Whyte, W.H., 1955, *The Organization Man*, Penguin Books, Harmondsworth.

Chapter 10

Group effectiveness

Introduction
Effectiveness, productivity and satisfaction
Factors affecting group behaviour
Making groups perform
Risk taking in groups
Group cohesion

Key concepts:

Once you have fully understood this chapter, you should be able to define the following concepts in your own words:

Group effectiveness   Risky-shift phenomenon
Member satisfaction   Group cohesion
Group productivity   Intermediate variable
Brainstorming   Groupthink
Synergy

Objectives:

On completing this chapter you should be able,

1. To distinguish between the concept of group productivity and group satisfaction and relate them to group effectiveness.
2. To describe the elements of the Kretch, Crutchfield and Ballachey model of group functioning.
3. To evaluate critically the research literature on the relative superiority of group performance over individual performance.

INTRODUCTION

Earlier, organizations were defined as, "social arrangements for the controlled performance of collective goals". Organizations were seen as being concerned with performance in the pursuit of their goals and that individuals and groups were tied to standards which were used to judge what was considered good, satisfactory or adequate. If we think of an organization as being a group of small groups, then organizational performance is the combination of the diverse group performances. For this reason, a great deal of attention has been paid in the research to increasing group effectiveness. Indeed, the earliest British and American studies on group behaviour which begun in the 1920s, addressed this very problem. The issue of group effectiveness centres around two fundamental questions. Firstly, are groups more effective than individuals, and secondly, in what ways can groups be helped to be made more effective? The individual-versus-the-group issue does not appear to have a single, universal answer. The research indicates that to obtain an answer one needs to specify the task to be performed and the circumstances involved.

Suitable situations for group working

"From the evidence that is available on the effectiveness and benefits of group working, it is possible to list some of the main features which would be indicative of a suitable situation for group working. These are:

1. When co-operative working is likely to produce a better end result (either in terms of speed, efficiency or quality according to which is most important) than working separately.
2. When the amalgamation of work into joint task or area of responsibility would appear meaningful to those involved.
3. Where the joint task requires a mixture of different skills or specialisms.
4. Where the system requires fairly frequent adjustments in activities and in the co-ordination of activities.
5. Where competition between individuals leads to less effectiveness rather than more.
6. Where stress levels on individuals are too high for effective activity".

From Angela Bowey and Ray Connelly, *Application of the Concept of Group Working*, University of Strathclyde Business School Paper, 1975, mimeo, p. 7.

EFFECTIVENESS, PRODUCTIVITY
AND SATISFACTION

The concept of group effectiveness within the context of the organization presents a number of problems which need to be addressed at the outset of this discussion.

STOP!

Consider the following situation:

"Two groups of workmen set out to build two comparable office blocks. One group takes two years to complete their block, but do so relatively uneventfully and then move on, as an experienced and cohesive workforce to tackle more demanding projects. The second group complete their block in only fifteen months, but have to work under such pressure, that two are killed in accidents, five more are seriously injured, and the remainder are so exhausted and disgusted that to a man they subsequently take up market gardening."

Which of the two groups described is the more effective?

From Henri Tajfel and Colin Fraser. *Introduction to Social Psychology*, Penguin Books, Harmonsworth, pp. 218-19.

You may have decided that, "it all depends". Clearly, one group was more productive and if you take a short term perspective, then as far as their employer was concerned, they were the more effective. However, if you look at the situation from the workers' point of view and take a longer term perspective the answer is different. Considering it with the values of the workers themselves, and judging by the continuity of the group, the former group now appears to be the more effective. What this analysis shows is that when we talk about the effectiveness of the group, we need to always consider both *group productivity* which refers to the external task achievement (e.g. building a house, solving a problem, making a decision) and *group satisfaction* which refers to the internal aspects of the groups. The criteria against which productivity and group satisfaction will be measured will be different in each case.

Productivity criteria	*Satisfaction criteria*
Quantity	Satisfaction with group
Quality	Satisfaction with group members
Economy	Pleasure in being in the group
Speed	Willingness to remain in group

The individual will judge the performance of the group in terms of fulfilling his needs for friendship, developing or confirming his sense of identity, establishing and testing reality and increasing his security and sense of purpose. These are the goals that groups and individuals have. We can use the label *member satisfaction* to refer to the extent to which such internal group goals are achieved.

One can ask if group productivity and group satisfaction are correlated with each other. Is not a happy group also a productive one? This was certainly one of the conclusions drawn from the studies at the Hawthorne plant. Observation of the women workers in the Relay Assembly Test Room led to the conclusion that the factor contributing most to the increases in output was not the change in the physical conditions at work, but the continually increasing cohesiveness and esprit de corps of the women workers. Mayo wrote that the satisfaction of social needs in face-to-face co-operative relationships with fellow workers should become a prime goal of enlightened management. Not only was it good for the soul in his view, but it was also good business since the policy was both humane and likely to increase productivity.

The Hawthorne studies signalled the birth of the Human Relations school of management. In the eyes of some managers, this in essence involved, "being nice to workers", and supervisors were sent on training courses which taught them leadership styles which would encourage this. It was not until some time had passed that people started to question this relationship between productivity and satisfaction. Perhaps it had been a fortuitous coincidence rather than some iron law? Sociologists who reviewed the findings and compared them with other data swung to the former explanation.

Whose output goals?

The women accepted management's goals regarding output and permitted their interpersonal satisfaction to contribute to increased productivity. Widespread unemployment, lack of alternative jobs may have influenced their performance. Had the group developed cohesiveness and esprit de corps as a result of deliberately defying management policy on some issue, then high satisfaction would have gone hand in hand with low productivity. A simple link between productivity and job satisfaction is not inevitable.

From Leonard Broom and Philip Selznick, *Sociology*, Harper, New York, 1965.

Competition and morale

A group of salesmen were studied in the clothing department of a department store. The morale of the salesmen was higher when they worked together in a co-operative system than when they competed with each other for customers and sales. However, when they competed they sold more units.

Nicholas Babchuk and William J. Goode, "Work incentives in a self-determined group", *American Sociological Review*, vol. 16, 1951, pp. 679-87.

STOP!

Can you describe a situation where *increased* group member satisfaction was accompanied by *decreased* group productivity?

A great deal of research has been conducted into the working arrangements and conditions of employees, their attitudes to work, individual and group member satisfaction and productivity. One way of looking at this work is to view it as an attempt to discover how one might seek to establish and maintain both high member satisfaction *and* group productivity. Research of this type has been done into work arrangements for the manufacture of Volvo cars, the composition and organization of coal mining teams and the introduction of new technology. It is no longer seen as simply a question of providing adequate financial incentives and specifying working methods (as Frederick Taylor would have argued) or of supervisors using a particular leadership style (as Elton Mayo would have seen it). Increasingly, economic, technological, social, psychological and organizational issues are being considered in parallel.

FACTORS AFFECTING GROUP BEHAVIOUR

A useful way of thinking about the influences on group productivity and satisfaction is provided by Kretch, Crutchfield and Ballachey (1962) and is set out in Figure 10.1. These authors distinguish between three sets of variables which they label independent, intermediate and dependent. Some writers have also given them the title of givens, emergent processes and outcomes respectively. Whatever the label, the idea in each case is the same.

Science attempts to discover relationships between such things as smoking and cancer. Social science has tried to do the same by investigating the relationships between, for example, job satisfaction and productivity. The term used to describe job satisfaction and productivity in this context is *variable*. When a social scientist studies productivity, job satisfaction, group size, physical setting or the nature of the task to be performed by the group, he is studying variables. Such a study involves manipulating one variable to see what effect it has on other variables. For example, the researchers conducting the Relay Assembly Test Room experiments manipulated the strength of the illumination in the room to see what effect it had on the productivity of the women. In this example, they were studying the relationship between two variables: illumination and productivity. Because it was the illumination level which was changed or manipulated, illumination was the *independent variable* in the experiment. Since interest was focused upon what effects this had on productivity, this became the *dependent variable*.

It is possible for there to be a direct causal relationship between an independent variable, such as group size, and a dependent variable, such as member satisfaction. For example, it may be found that as group size increases, the members' satisfaction decreases. However, it is equally possible for an independent variable to cause a change in the dependent variable through an *intermediate variable* such as leadership style. Thus member satisfaction may be found to decrease (dependent variable) when group size increases (independent variable) and the leadership style of the appointed leader is autocratic (intermediate variable). Such intermediate variables are also called "emergent processes". Let us now examine the Kretch, Crutchfield and Ballachey model. The given features of a group situation interact and lead to variations in emergent processes which in turn result in differences in outcomes. How might this work in practice? Take the example of a company which decides to establish a formal hierarchy in a plant with job titles which have a specific status position. Such a definition is intended to create a particular leadership style for those who occupy the positions. However, once people

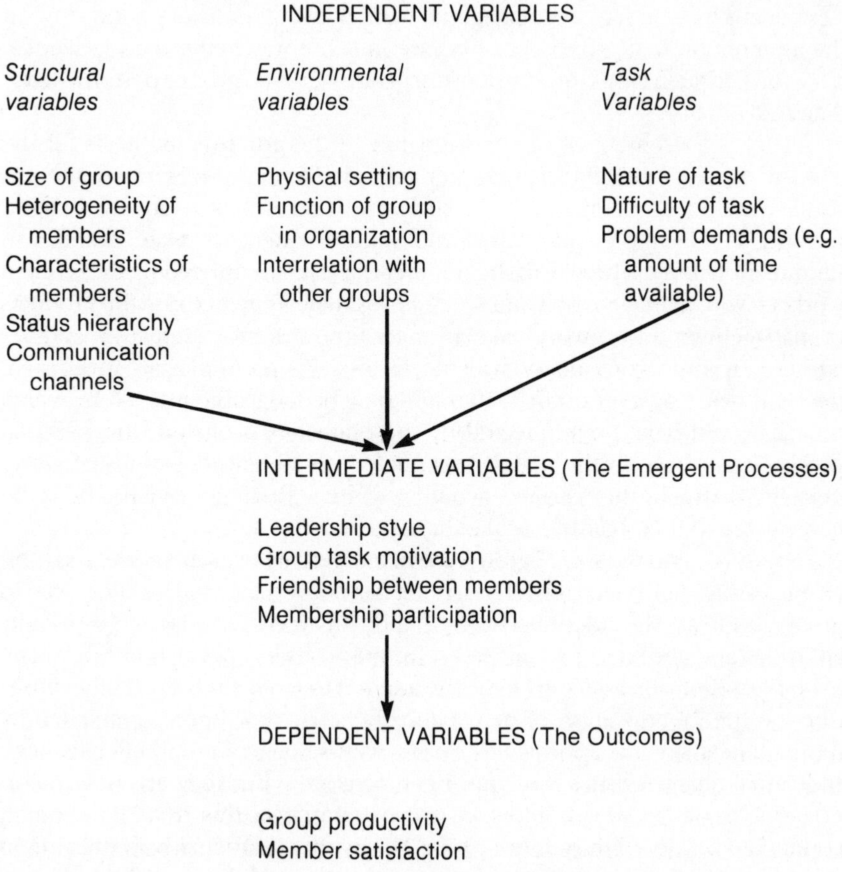

INDEPENDENT VARIABLES

Structural variables	*Environmental variables*	*Task Variables*
Size of group	Physical setting	Nature of task
Heterogeneity of members	Function of group in organization	Difficulty of task
Characteristics of members	Interrelation with other groups	Problem demands (e.g. amount of time available)
Status hierarchy		
Communication channels		

INTERMEDIATE VARIABLES (The Emergent Processes)

Leadership style
Group task motivation
Friendship between members
Membership participation

DEPENDENT VARIABLES (The Outcomes)

Group productivity
Member satisfaction

Figure 10.1: Kretch, Cruchfield and Ballachey Model of Group Functioning

begin to interact, differentiation will occur along the influence and leadership dimensions, irrespective of the formal pattern of communication prescribed by management. In reality, workers will organize their own communication pattern which is likely to be different from the formal one. The emergent processes will involve variations in group norms, task motivation and cohesiveness. All of these act to produce differences in the outcomes.

MAKING GROUPS PERFORM

Frequently in organizations there is no choice as to whether an individual or a group will perform a task. Legal, political, social and economic factors may dictate that a committee, a task force or some other group will carry out certain activities. The decisions and plans which guide large organizations are made by committees and groups. Organizations implicitly believe that the group is the best means by which to get managerial work done. Millions of pounds rest on the assumption that group decisions are in some way better than individual decisions. In such cases the key question to answer is do groups perform better than individuals?

The measurement of the performance of the group is the basis for the assessment of how well the group performs. In circumstances where there is some physical or countable task, such measurement is relatively straightforward. For example, the Hawthorne Studies sought to relate changes in illumination and tea breaks to the number of relays completed by the women workers. With management teams such assessment is rare because the products of management group work have a longer time scale for evaluation and are affected by numerous uncontrollable factors. For example, an investment decision made by a group in 1970 might only be judgeable in 1976 by which time it would have been affected by the dramatic rise in oil prices. Social psychologists have in the main concentrated on laboratory studies of group behaviour which they hoped would produce findings which could be generalized to the organizational context.

Research into the size of group, the heterogeneity of its members and their characteristics has been carried out, but it has not represented a major force in group studies. The identification of individual characteristics (especially aptitudes and abilities) for staff selection purposes has been more prevalent. Even in studies of leadership style, the attempt to focus on individual features through the identification of personality traits has now been superseded by more context specific approaches. So too with studies of group effectiveness. Individual characteristics have not been forgotten, but they are now incorporated into a broader context. A good example of this trend is research conducted by Meredith Belbin (1981). This work is particularly interesting in that it attempts to link individual variances (obtained through psychometric tests) with group role behaviour and relate both to output performance. The theories evolved are then tested in an organizational context. Belbin's work is rooted in the studies of Robert Bales who attempted to distinguish group member behaviours and to group these into separate and distinguishable group roles.

Various approaches and techniques have been developed to enable groups to be more effective. Research has also identified the pitfalls into which a group can fall and which reduces their performance. We shall now examine both of these.

Brainstorming

The ways in which groups operate to solve organizational problems have been investigated and constitute an alternative perspective from which to approach the question of group effectiveness. Brainstorming in particular is a technique which has received a great deal of attention. Intuitively one might expect that a group of people working together would solve their problems more creatively than if the same people worked as individuals alone. The group allows members to "bounce ideas off each other" or gives individuals the chance to throw out half-baked ideas which other group members might turn into more practical suggestions. The "brainstorming" technique was intended to stimulate such creative thinking and was invented in 1939 by the head of an American advertising agency.

Brainstorming stresses the superiority of the group approach over the individual method and contains four rules of procedure. First, individual ideas must not be criticized. Second, no suggested ideas are to be rejected, irrespective of how fanciful or bizarre they may be. Third, the group seeks to produce as many ideas as possible. The stress is placed on the quantity of suggestions and not on their quality. The discussion of the ideas takes place at a later stage and thus the more ideas there are, the greater is the chance of finding a winner. Finally, participants are encouraged to "hitch-hike", that is, to combine the ideas of others with their own to develop new ideas. It is argued that the flow of ideas in a group will trigger off further ideas whereas the usual evaluative framework will tend to stifle the imagination.

Designing a Management Team

Belbin (1981) and his colleagues conducted a study of different management teams in action. These included specially designed groups of participants playing a business game at a British management college as well as a collection of managers in industry who met frequently to achieve certain agreed objectives. The research showed that,

(a)   It was possible to identify and distinguish eight distinct management styles which the researchers labelled "team roles".

(b)   The managers studied tended to adopt one or two of these team roles fairly consistently.

(c)   Which role they became associated with was capable of prediction through the use of psychometric tests.

(d)   When team roles were combined in certain ways, they helped to produce more effective teams.

(e)   Such team roles were not necessarily associated with a person's functional role (e.g. accountant, production), but the way in which they were combined seemed to affect job success.

(f)   Factors which seemed to contribute to effective management by individuals included correct recognition of own best role; self-awareness of the best contribution they could make to their team or situation and their ability and preparedness to work out their strengths rather than permitting weaknesses to interfere with their performance.

The eight major roles Belbin identified were Chairman (co-ordinating styles); Team Leader (directive style - The Shaper); Innovator (creative thinking in the team); Monitor-Evaluator (critical thinking in the team); Company Worker (getting the work done); Team Worker (personal relationships in the team); Completer (keeping the team on its toes) and Resource Investigator (keeping in touch with other teams).

These roles are related to the personality and mental ability of individuals and reflect managerial behaviour in connection with the aims and demands of the manager's job. Since each role contributes to team success, a successful, balanced team will contain all roles. A team for example, needs a Chairman, Innovator, Monitor or Evaluator, one or more Company Workers, Team Workers, Resource Investigators or Completers and Specialists.

From R. Meredith Belbin, *Management Teams: Why They Succeed or Fail*, Heinemann, London, 1981.

A brainstorming group may often perform better than an individual who applies these rules to his own thought processes. However, if one has four individuals working alone, they can generally greatly outperform a group of four in terms of the number of ideas generated. Research has consistently shown that group brainstorming inhibits creative thinking. Taylor, Berry and Block (1958) carried out such a study and compared the performance of brainstorming groups with "pseudo-groups" (constructed by the experimenter from individual scores). The authors found that the brainstorming groups produced more ideas than individuals, that they produced more unique ideas, and that the ideas were of better quality as judged by various criteria. However, when the brainstorming groups' performance was compared with that of the pseudo-groups, the pattern was reversed. The pseudo-groups were superior to the brainstorming groups on all criteria. The research demonstrated that the superiority of groups over individuals is simply the product of the greater number of man hours they take up. Even under brainstorming instructions, the presence of others seems to inhibit rather than enhance the creativity of these *ad hoc* groups. It may be that brainstorming is effective with established or specially trained groups.

Brainstorming is based on two assumptions which can be questioned. First, it assumes that people think most creatively when there are no obstacles to the stream of consciousness and that among this torrent of ideas (actually associations), there are bound to be some good ideas. Brainstorming presumes that solving problems is a matter of letting one's natural inclinations run free. Second, it associates the quantity of ideas with the quality of ideas.

How effective are brainstorming groups?

The inferiority of group brainstorming over individual thinking may be the result of group members being shy about offering unconventional ideas in the belief that, despite the rules, they will be evaluated anyway. Maginn and Harris conducted an experiment in which they studied 152 psychology students who were split into groups of four and were asked to brainstorm answers to two problems. The first problem concerned, "the benefits and difficulties that would arise if people had found that they had suddenly grown extra thumbs". The second asked for, "ideas that if put into practice would reduce people's consumption of gasoline".

Some groups were told that their ideas would be assessed for quality and originality by the judges either observing from behind a one way mirror, or listening to a tape recording. The other group were told that, although fellow students would be listening, their ideas would not be evaluated. The authors predicted that the groups facing evaluation would produce fewer ideas.

But the findings showed that the output of both sets of groups was similar. If groups brainstorm badly, therefore, it is not due to diffidence. Maginn and Harris conclude with the suggestion that individuals put less effort into a task when they share responsibility for the outcome with others. Unless this diminished responsibility effect can be overcome, individual brainstorming is best, if lonelier.

From Barbara K. Maginn and Richard J. Harris, "Effects of anticipated evaluation on individual brainstorming performance", *Journal of Applied Psychology*, vol. 65, no. 2, 1980, pp. 219-25.

Synergy

The superiority of individual performance over group brainstorming is an example of how a taken-for-granted assumption can be disproved by social science research. Other studies have revealed that while groups are usually able to solve problems more effectively than individuals, they rarely do as well as their best member could do alone. This failure to achieve what has been called synergy has led to the devotion of much effort, especially in the area of applied social science.

Definition

Synergy is the ability of the group to outperform even its best individual member. It is akin to getting the whole to be greater then the sum of its parts.

Jay Hall (1971) conducted a number of laboratory-based group ranking and prediction tasks to which there existed correct answers. The tasks included predicting the behaviour of actors in the film called the "12 Angry Men" and achieving a correct answer to a task called, "Lost on the Moon" where participants had to pretend they were stranded on the moon and had to choose from a set of supplies in order to survive. He studied the typical behaviours of the effective groups and the strategies of the groups which did poorly. The answers he found and the conclusions he came to related to the processes apparent in the group. He found that the effective groups actively looked for the points on which they disagreed, and in consequence encouraged conflicts among participants in the early stages of the discussion. In contrast the ineffective groups felt a need to establish a common view quickly, used simple decision making methods such as averaging, and focused on completing the task rather than on finding a solution they could agree on.

Hall's Group Decision Instructions

On the basis of his studies, Hall (1971) identified the behaviours which characterized the effective teams which he studied. He presented these in the form of decision rules as follows:

Group-decision instructions

"Consensus is a decision process for making full use of available resources and for resolving conflicts creatively. . . . Here are some guidelines to use in achieving consensus:

1. Avoid arguing for your own rankings. Present your position as lucidly and logically as possible, but listen to other members' reactions and consider them carefully before you press your point.
2. Do not assume that someone must win and someone must lose when discussion reaches a stalemate. Instead, look for the next most-acceptable alternative for all parties.
3. Do not change your mind simply to avoid conflict and to reach agreement and harmony. When agreement comes too quickly and easily, be suspicious. Explore the reasons and be sure

everyone accepts the solution for basically similar or complementary reasons. Yield only to positions that have objective and
logically sound foundations.
4.   Avoid conflict reducing techniques such as majority voting,
averages, coin-flips and bargaining. When a dissenting member
finally agrees, don't feel that he must be rewarded by having his
own way on some later point.
5.   Differences of opinion are natural and expected. Seek them out
and try to involve everyone in the decision process. Disagree-
ments can help the group's decision because with a wide range of
information and opinions, there is a greater chance that the group
will hit upon more adequate solutions."

From Jay Hall, "Decisions, decisions, decisions", *Psychology Today*,
November, 1971.

Let us now turn to some problems of group functioning which researchers have
studied.

RISK TAKING IN GROUPS

The research has demonstrated the processes of social control in groups and
suggests that a group encourages compromise between individual views.
Group influences moderate extreme views and the group moves towards a
risk-avoiding compromise. Observers of groups at work have often commented
on their conservatism and lack of creativity. This element of compromise has led
to criticism of "management-by-committee". Research evidence quoted about
brainstorming also indicates that members self-censor their contributions so as
not to appear foolish.

Irving Janis studied a number of "disasters" in American foreign policy
including the Bay of Pigs, Korea and Vietnam. He attributed the reasons for these
failures to a phenomenon which he labelled "groupthink".

Definition

Groupthink is "the psychological drive for consensus at any cost that
suppresses dissent and appraisal of alternatives in cohesive decision-
making groups".

From I. L. Janis; *Victims of Group Think: A Psychological Study of
Foreign Policy Decisions and Fiascos,* Mifflin Houghton, Boston Mass,
1968, p. 8.

Studying these events, Janis argues that it was the cohesive nature of these
important committees which made these decisions, and which prevented
contradictory views being expressed. Thus, while group cohesion can make a

positive contribution to group productivity and satisfaction, it may also have negative consequences. The group loyalty instilled through cohesion can act to stifle the raising and questioning of controversial issues and thus lead to the making of bad decisions.

A number of symptoms of groupthink were identified. Amongst these were the illusion of invulnerability, there was excessive optimism and risk taking. Rationalizations by the members of the group were used to discount warnings. Those who opposed the group were stereotyped as evil, weak or stupid. Janis found self-censorship by members of any deviation from the apparent group consensus. Finally there was an illusion of unanimity in the group with silence being interpreted as consent.

Groupthink led to a failure by the group to solve its problems effectively. The group discussed a minimum number of alternatives; the courses of action favoured by the majority of the group were not re-examined from the view of hidden risks and other alternatives, nor were original, unsatisfactory courses. The group failed to use the expert opinion that it had, and when expert opinion was evaluated, it was done with a selective bias which ignored the facts and opinions which did not support the group view.

While individual doubt may have been suppressed and the illusion of group unanimity and cohesiveness maintained, the group paid a high price in terms of its effectiveness. As an antidote to the tendency towards groupthink, Janis suggested that the group should:

- Appoint one person in the group to critically evaluate the contributions of the other members;
- Make the discussion of doubts or uncertainties an important aspect of the group's work;
- Ensure the group leader is capable of taking criticism of his judgements from others.

Stoner (1961) carried out experiments that showed that groups of management students were willing to make decisions involving *greater* risks than their individual preferences. This counter-intuitive finding was supported by researchers using populations other than management students. This tendency for individuals in groups to take greater risks than the average of the prediscussion decisions became known as the *risky-shift phenomenon*. The research questionnaire which Stoner used was devised by Kogan and Wallace and described twelve hypothetical risk situations. Amongst these were the following:

A man with a severe heart ailment must seriously curtail his customary way of life if he does not wish to undergo a delicate medical operation which might cure him completely or might prove fatal.

An engaged couple must decide, in the face of recent arguments suggesting some sharp differences of opinions, whether or not to get married. Discussions with a marriage counsellor, indicate that a happy marriage, while possible, would not be assured.

From M. A. Wallach, N. Kogan and D. J. Bem (1962), "Group influence on individual risk taking", *Journal of Abnormal and Social Psychology*, vol. 65, pp. 75-86.

A number of explanations have been suggested for this shift towards risk. These include the following:

Diffusion of responsibility hypothesis
When a person makes a decision in a group situation, the responsibility for any failure which might result is assumed to be shared amongst the group members. Since each individual feels less of a personal responsibility for failure, the group consensus moves towards greater risk taking.

Cultural value hypothesis
In some cultures risk is valued and thus people in those cultures may hold boldness, courage and daring as things to be striven for. During a discussion in a risk-valuing culture, more arguments for risk taking are likely to be produced.

Social comparison hypothesis
The questionnaire used is ambiguous and while a respondent may consider himself too cautious in some situations he is not used to thinking in terms of numerical probabilities (3 in 10). Being uncertain of the choice he makes individually he is pleased to have the chance to compare it with others. Seeing himself as average, he compares his score with another group member whom he also considers to be average. But the group contains scores all along the range. On some items he argues for risk, on others for caution. The high risk takers and the low risk takers will also seek out suitable comparisons.

STOP!

The risky-shift phenomenon: evaluating the evidence.

Below is an item from the Choice Dilemma Questionnaire. Tick your own response, and then discuss it with three or four of the students around you and agree a single group choice.

Mr E is president of a light metals corporation in the United States. The corporation is quite prosperous, and has strongly considered possibilities of business expansion by building an additional plant in a new location. The choice is between building a new plant in the United States where there would be a moderate return on the initial investment, or building a plant in a foreign country. Lower labour costs and easy access to raw materials in that country mean a much higher return on initial investment. On the other hand there is a history of political instability and revolution in the foreign country under consideration. In fact, the leader of a small minority party is committed to nationalization, that is, taking over all foreign investments.

Imagine you are advising Mr E. Listed below are several probabilities or odds of continued political stability in the foreign country under consideration. Please tick the *lowest* probability that you would consider acceptable for Mr E's corporation to build in that country.

The chances that the foreign country will remain politically stable are:

1 in 10	☐
3 in 10	☐
5 in 10	☐
7 in 10	☐
9 in 10	☐

Please tick here if you think Mr E's corporation should not build a plant in the foreign country, no matter what the probabilities.   ☐

From N. Kogan and M. A. Wallach, "Risk taking as a function of the situation, person and the group" in *New Directions in Psychology: Volume III*, Holt, Rinehart and Winston, New York, 1967, pp. 111-278.

STOP!

Up until now we have discussed the existence of the risky-shift phenomenon as if we had accepted it unequivocally, and only needed to understand its causes and effects. In fact serious doubt has been cast on the findings. Consider the following objections:

- Risky shift experiments are conducted on artificial leaderless groups, the members of which have never met before;
- These artificial groups consist usually of five people and are asked to decide on entirely hypothetical risk situations;
- Real organizational committees are longer lasting, have an established leadership structure and deal with real decisions which have real consequences for their members;
- In the risky shift experiments, the magnitude of the shift to risk is small and by no means shown by all subjects;
- Researchers who have studied individual and group risk taking, and who have used different research methods, have obtained less consistent findings;
- Studies which use Stoner's questionnaire reveal that on the same question there is sometimes a shift to risk and at other times a shift to caution;
- On two of the twelve risk situations presented, participants in groups regularly demonstrate a shift to caution. The overall risky-shift effect rests on the shifts shown on the other ten items.

Read each of the above objections and decide whether it threatens the *internal* or the *external* validity of these research findings?

GROUP COHESION

Group cohesion is an important factor in keeping a group together and thus merits study when one considers group performance and member satisfaction. However, overall, does cohesion help or hinder group effectiveness?

Definition

"*Group cohesion* is that property which is inferred from the number and strength of mutual positive attitudes among members of the group".

From A.J. Lott and B.E. Lott, "Group effectiveness as interpersonal attraction", *Psychological Bulletin,* 1965, vol. 64, p. 259.

Group cohesion is sometimes loosely defined as the sum of all the factors influencing members to stay in the group. It is the result of the positive forces of attraction towards the group outweighing the negative forces of repulsion away from the group. How cohesive a group is can be judged by indicators such as whether members arrive on time, the degree of trust and support between them and the amount of satisfaction they gain from their group membership. Various theories of group behaviour emphasize the social exchange idea whereby individuals make a judgement about what they contribute to the group from what they receive back from it in terms of personal needs. Cartwright (1968) offered a scheme for analysing group cohesiveness when reflecting on empirical research studies:

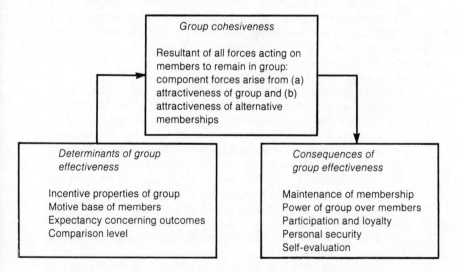

Figure 10.2: A scheme for analysing group effectiveness
Cartwright, 1968, p. 92.

Research studies which have investigated the consequences of high group cohesiveness on group productivity and member satisfaction show that there is a definite, and usually positive relationship. Members of cohesive groups appear to experience fewer work related anxieties than those in non-cohesive work groups and are better "adjusted" in the organization. They have higher rates of job satisfaction, lower rates of tension, absenteeism and labour turnover. This better adjustment comes partly from the psychological support provided by the group. The evidence favouring group cohesion is so great that both at shopfloor and management levels, attempts continue to be made to design strong teams. At the worker level this may take the form of work redesign which produces new forms of work organization, while at senior levels the trend is manifested by the use of multi-function project teams and team development approaches.

The redesign of work to increase group cohesion and thereby to reduce labour turnover can be the result of failure to achieve company goals in terms of cost reduction or profitability. At other times, the introduction of new technology can result in the unanticipated destruction of existing cohesive groups.

Coal mining groups

The introduction of the conveyor belt increased the length of coal face that could be worked. The longwall in the Durham pit became 100 yards long. To use this new technology, the organization of work had to be changed to deal with working on this longer coal face. . . . Initially all that happened was that Preparation and Getting were done together for the first two shifts and Advancing was done on the third (this method of working was called ("hewing longwalls"). When the electric coal cutter was introduced, the separation was completed with Preparation, Getting and Advancing being performed by a separate task group, each working a separate shift (this working method was called "cutting longwall"). Each shift had to finish its work before the next could begin.

The effect of this change was to abolish the composite autonomous workman. The job was broken down and task specialization introduced. Workers were allocated one task to do on one shift with no opportunity for rotation and thus no opportunity to extend their range of work skills. The group now only covered one stage of the cycle instead of all three. Given the work situation, this new form of work organization was inappropriate for underground working. The miner had to simultaneously complete physically demanding work and endure the psychological stresses which the location and nature of the work imposed on him.

The consequence of the reorganization was to destroy the cohesive groups which provided the individual miner with the psychological support he needed. Status differences immediately developed with the "cuttermen" who operated the new and powerful machinery becoming the "face aristocracy" while the "fillers" who shovelled coal, being accorded the lowest status. The unity of the traditional group became strained. Instead of the single group "paynote", each task group negotiated its pay separately since the basis for calculation for each was different. Intergroup competition to achieve a financial advantage replaced the task of performing the work cycle well. Negotiations of wages rates also meant that each shift group had a vested interest in the previous shift failing to complete its tasks.

In the coal mines example, the cohesive group did produce more. However, there is no general rule about this. Seashore (1954) argued that workers in cohesive groups were neither more nor less productive on average than workers in non-cohesive groups, but that cohesive workers were more uniform in their productivity. They all generally produced the same level of output. Such uniformity can be accounted for by group pressures against deviancy from group norms. However, high group cohesion under certain circumstances, while it may be functional to the group members themselves, may turn out to be dysfunctional to other groups in the organization and to the organization as a whole.

From David A. Buchanan, *The Development of Job Design Theories and Techniques*, Saxon House, Farnborough, Hants, 1979, pp. 99-102.

SOURCES

Babchuk, N. and Goode, W. F., 1951, "Work incentives in a self-determined group", *American Sociological Review*, vol. 16, pp. 679-89.

Belbin, R. M., 1981, *Management Teams: Why They Succeed or Fail*, Heinemann, London.

Bowey, A. M. and Connelly, R., 1975, *Application of the Concept of Group Working*, University of Strathclyde Business School, Glasgow, mimeo.

Broom, L. and Selznick, P., 1965, *Sociology*, Harper, New York.

Buchanan, D. A., 1979, *The Development of Job Design Theories and Techniques*, Saxon House, Farnborough, Hants.

Buchanan, D. A. and Boddy, D., 1983, *Organizations in the Computer Age*, Gower Publishing Company, Aldershot, Hants.

Cartwright, D., 1968, "The nature of group cohesiveness", in D. Cartwright and D. A. Zander (Eds), *Group Dynamics: Research and Theory*, Harper and Row, New York, pp. 91-109.

Hall, J., 1971, "Decisions, decisions, decisions", *Psychology Today*, November.

Janis, I. L., 1968, *Victims of Group Think: a psychological study of foreign policy decisions and fiascos*, Mifflin Houghton, Boston, Mass.

Kogan, N. and Wallach, M. A., 1967, "Risk taking as a function of the situation, person and group" in *New Directions in Psychology: Volume III*, Holt, Rinehart and Winston, New York, pp. 111-278.

Kretch, D. Crutchfield. R.S. and Ballachey, E.L. 1962, *The Individual in Society*, McGraw Hill, New York.

Lott, A. J. and Lott, B. E., 1965, "Group cohesiveness as interpersonal attraction: a review of relationships with antecedent and consequent variables", *Psychological Bulletin*, vol. 64, pp. 259-309.

Maginn, B. K. and Harris, R. J., 1980, "Effects of anticipated evaluation on individual brainstorming performance", *Journal of Applied Psychology*, vol. 65, no. 2, pp. 219-225.

Seashore, S. E., 1954, *Group Cohesiveness in the Industrial Work Group*, Survey Research Center, University of Michigan, Ann Arbor, Michigan.

Stoner, J. A. F., 1961, "A comparison of group and individual decisions involving risk", quoted in R. Brown (1965) *Social Psychology*, Free Press, New York.

Tajfel, H. and Fraser, C., 1978, *Introducing Social Psychology*, Penguin Books, Harmondsworth.

Taylor, D., Berry, P. C. and Bloch, C. H., 1958, "Does group participation when using brainstorming techniques facilitate or inhibit creative thinking", *Administrative Science Quarterly*, vol 3, pp. 23-47.

Wallach, M. A., Kogan, N. and Bem, D. J., 1962, "Group influences on individual risk taking", *Journal of Abnormal and Social Psychology*, vol. 65, pp. 75-86.

PART 3

TECHNOLOGY IN THE ORGANIZATION

Overview

> "We shall sing of the great crowds in the excitement of labour, pleasure or rebellion; of the multicoloured and polyphonic surf of revolutions in modern capital cities; of the nocturnal vibrations of arsenals and workshops beneath their violent electric moons; of the greedy stations swallowing smoking snakes; of factories suspended from the clouds by their strings of smoke; of bridges leaping like gymnasts over the diabolical cutlery of sunbathed rivers; of adventurous liners scenting the horizon; of broadchested locomotives prancing on the rails, like huge steel horses bridled with long tubes; and of the gliding flight of aeroplanes, the sound of whose propeller is like the flapping of flags and the applause of an enthusiastic crowd . . ."
>
> From the *Initial Manifesto of Futurism*, by F. T. Marinetti, 1909.

Technology presents two faces to modern society. It represents progress, change, affluence, leisure and mobility which most of us welcome. But it also represents unemployment, the dehumanization of work, pollution, the depletion of natural resources and the potential hazards of nuclear energy. It seems that we may not have the benefits unless we are willing to accept the disadvantages. Futurism was an artistic movement which developed in Italy early this century. Its members regarded the machine as a symbol of the new century, as a sign of the liberating potential of human creativity. It is rare to find technology written about in that style today.

Technical developments influence the ways in which we live and die, the relationships that we are able to form and maintain, our health and even the ways in which we think of ourselves. It is difficult to escape from motor cars and telephones, from televisions and tower blocks. It seems obvious to claim therefore that technology has a profound influence on the nature and functioning of organizations and on the experience of work.

Marinetti's metaphors imply that technology has a life of its own. Many scientific and philosophic commentators have argued that technical developments are driven by some kind of internal logic that puts technology beyond human control. Technology is therefore often regarded as a factor that determines key facets of organizations. The main theme of Part 3 is an exploration of this controversial question of "technological determinism".

Chapter 11

What is technology?

The problem of definition
Levels of mechanization
Determinism versus choice

Key concepts:

Once you have fully understood this chapter, you should be able to define
the following concepts in your own words:

Technology   Social technology
Apparatus   Levels of mechanization
Technique   Technological determinism
Material technology   Strategic choice

Objectives:

On completing this chapter, you should be able:

1. To recognize the problems of defining the term "technology".
2. To analyse and compare different definitions of the concept of
    technology.
3. To recognize different levels of mechanization.
4. To recognize "determinist" arguments about technology.

THE PROBLEM OF DEFINITION

As this book is being written, in 1983 and 1984, the popular press and television tell us that we are in the middle of an industrial revolution based on developments in computing and information technologies. The microchip, we are told, will invade all aspects of our working and private lives. The impact of these technical developments on organizations will be examined in detail in Chapter 14. But it is important to realize here that technology has to be studied as something that *changes*. It is not static. It is also useful to remember that technology is *pervasive*. Those aspects of our surroundings that are most familiar to us are often the most difficult to consider objectively.

If we are to examine the effect that technology has on anything at all, then we must be clear what we mean by the term. We have met this problem of definition before, for example in analysing how the word "personality" is used. The term "technology" is now used with such a wide variety of meanings that it has become ambiguous. We must therefore begin by exploring that variety and ambiguity.

Sociologists, and others, have "discovered" that technological developments are major sources of social, economic, and political change, for both good and evil. Alvin Toffler for example refers to ". . . that great, growling engine of change — technology". It has become fashionable to study and to make pronouncements on "technological implications". This concern began to replace the human relations school in the study of organizational behaviour in the 1950s. The promises, and threats, of the microprocessor revolution have revived this concern in the 1980s.

Langdon Winner, an American commentator on modern technology, has pointed out that the term has widened in meaning as concern for technological implications has grown. It has been transformed from a precise, limited and rather unimportant term and become a vague, expansive and highly significant one.

In the past:

> " . . . the term had a very specific, limited, and unproblematic meaning. Persons who employed the term spoke of "a practical art", "the study of the practical arts", or "the practical arts collectively". In the literature of the eighteenth and nineteenth centuries, such meanings were clear and were not the occasion for deliberation or analysis. *Technology*, in fact, was not an important term in descriptions of that part of the world we would now call technological. Most people spoke directly of machines, tools, factories, industry, crafts, and engineering and did not worry about "technology" as a distinctive phenomenon."

But today:

> "It is now widely used in ordinary and academic speech to talk about an unbelievably diverse collection of phenomena — tools, instruments, machines, organizations, methods, techniques, systems, and the totality

of all these and similar things in our experience."
(Winner, 1974, p.8)

How has this confusion arisen? Rapid technical developments leave the language behind. The word technology is a convenient blanket label that enables those of us with a poor technical understanding to talk about such important phenomena. So this ambiguity in the use of the term paradoxically reflects its pervasive and profound influence on modern society and our realization that we need to discuss and understand it. Winner also argues that this convenient way of using the language leads us to oversimplify and polarize technological issues. It is either a good thing or it is bad; you are either for it or against it.

We need a more precise definition in order to study technology and its implications from a social scientific point of view. Group psychotherapy, pocket calculators and space shuttles do not appear to have much in common. But they have all been described as "technology" at some time. The word that, " . . . has come to mean everything and anything . . . threatens to mean nothing" (Winner, 1974, p.10).

Winner identifies three broad but distinct uses of the term technology:

Apparatus
This simply means physical, technical devices such as tools, instruments, machines, appliances, gadgets and weapons that are used to accomplish a variety of tasks. This is probably the most common conception of technology.

Technique
This refers to technical activities such as skills, methods, procedures or routines which people perform to achieve particular purposes. The Greek work *techne* means art, craft or skill. Apparatus is not purposive. Techniques are related to specific human goals.

Organization
Winner uses this term for social arrangements such as factories, bureaucracies, armies, research and development teams and so on, that are created to achieve technical, rational productive ends.

So when someone uses the term technology, they could be speaking either about a physical device, a human skill, a social arrangement, or some combination, or all of these. This confusion can be seen in the work of those who have studied the implications of technology for organizational behaviour.

We are concerned here with technology applied to production and administrative *processes*. This is different from the application of technology in new *products*. Many researchers in the field of technical change use this distinction between process and product innovation. Here we are concerned with the former.

STOP!

Here are four definitions of technology that have been used by well known and influential organizational behaviour researchers.

Consider each definition and identify what, if anything, is being confused using Winner's distinctions as a guide.

Definitions of "technology" in organizational research

Charles Perrow

Technology is: "...the actions that an individual performs on an object, with or without the assistance of mechanical devices, in order to make some change in that object." (Perrow, 1967, p.194)

Joan Woodward

"The specific technology of the organization is, then, the collection of plant, machines, tools and recipes available at a given time for the execution of the production task and the rationale underlying their utilization." (Reeves, Turner and Woodward, 1970, p.4)

Louis E. Davis

Technology is: "...the application of science to invent technique and its supportive artifacts (machines) to accomplish transformations of objects (materials, information, people) in support of specific objectives." (Davis and Taylor, 1976, p.380)

Derek Pugh

Technology is: "...the sequence of physical techniques used upon the workflow of the organization .. the concept covers both the pattern of operations and the equipment used." (Pugh and Hickson, 1976, p.93)

Woodward uses the term "recipes";

Pugh speaks of "the pattern of operations".

What do you think these terms mean?

There seems to be confusion between apparatus and technique. In organizations, apparatus is the equipment, machinery and tools used in productive and administrative processes. Technique is the way in which work with the physical equipment of production is performed by employees.

A lot of research effort has been directed at the effects of "technology" on human work skills and experience. Skills and the experience of work can be regarded as being dependent on technology. In this research they are called "dependent variables". Technology is thus called an "independent variable". However, it is odd to approach this problem with a concept of the independent variable that overlaps with notions of the dependent variables. This confusion of apparatus with technique makes it difficult to interpret and compare research findings in this area.

The British industrial sociologist Alan Fox has suggested another way of looking at this issue. He makes a distinction between:

Material technology
". . . the technology that can be seen, touched and heard . . ."; and

Social technology
". . . which seeks to order the behaviour and relationships . . . of people in systematic, purposive ways through an elaborate structure of coordination, control, motivation and reward systems."

Material technology is what Winner calls apparatus. Social technology is Winner's "organization" and includes job definitions, payment systems, authority relationships, communications channels, control systems, disciplinary codes, " . . . all the many other rules and decision-making procedures which seek to govern what work is done, how it is done, and the relationships that prevail between those doing it". (Fox, 1974, p. 1.)

In these terms, many studies of technological implications in organizational behaviour can be seen as attempts to plot the impact of specific material technologies on various aspects of social technology. Again, there are clearly problems if the definition of technology straddles these two distinct dimensions.

The term technology can no longer be taken for granted in organizational behaviour. It is important to look carefully at the meaning which different commentators and researchers attach to it in order to understand and to compare their arguments.

LEVELS OF MECHANIZATION

There are many different approaches to the definition of technology. There are, however, no right or wrong definitions, only definitions that are more or less useful. The approach that one adopts to defining anything depends on why one is studying it in the first place. Engineers are not concerned with social relationships on the shop floor when they are designing new production machinery. Social scientists are not concerned with the intricacies of engineering design when they study group interaction in the factory. We have to decide which approach to technology will be the most useful in helping us to understand human behaviour in organizations.

The American Marxist sociologist Harry Braverman distinguishes two broad "modes of thinking" about technology:

The *engineering approach* "views technology primarily in its internal connections and tends to define the machine in relation to itself, as a technical fact."

The *social approach* "views technology in its connections with humanity and defines the machine in relation to human labour, and as a social artifact" (Braverman, 1974, p. 184).

Braverman argues that the engineering approach obscures the *relationship* between the machine and the user. The social approach to technology that takes into account the nature of this relationship thus promises to be a more useful one for our purposes. One obvious feature of the way in which this relationship has developed is that machines have progressively replaced human effort and skills, in the search for more speed, precision, standardization and efficiency. One researcher who tried to chart the development of this relationship was the American James R. Bright.

Bright devised a simple, but powerful, scheme to measure mechanical development in terms of the relationship between the capabilities of apparatus and the demands made on human muscles, mental processes, judgement and control over work operations. Bright identified seventeen levels of mechanization which are illustrated in Figure 11.1.

STOP!

Here is a short, non-technical, description of the functions and development of machine tools.

Trace the development of these machines, explained on page 217, through Bright's levels of mechanization.

Compare your analysis with that of colleagues. Your analyses should be similar, but may not correspond precisely.

A short history of the capabilities of machine tools

Machine tools are devices for cutting, bending and shaping pieces of cast or forged metal. The part that does the work of the machine is called the "tool", and the part being worked on is called the "workpiece". The kinds of operations that machine tools perform include:

Turning	Producing a circular surface
Drilling	Boring holes
Boring	Enlarging the diameter or "bore" of drilled holes
Tapping	Cutting screw threads inside holes
Milling	Shaving material off flat surfaces
Grinding	To produce a finer finish than milling
Shaping	Scraping the surface off metal plate
Shearing	Cutting metal plate into lengths
Profiling	Shaping the workpiece by cutting the profile into the tool, or moving the tool irregularly with a cam

Initiating Control Source	Type of Machine Response		Power Source	Level Number	LEVEL OF MECHANIZATION
From a variable in the environment	Responds with action	Modifies own action over a wide range of variation	Mechanical (Nonmanual)	17	Anticipates action required and adjusts to provide it.
				16	Corrects performance while operating.
				15	Corrects performance after operating.
		Selects from a limited range of possible pre-fixed actions		14	Identifies and selects appropriate set of actions.
				13	Segregates or rejects according to measurement.
				12	Changes speed, position, direction according to measurement signal.
	Responds with signal			11	Records performance.
				10	Signals preselected values of measurement. (Includes error detection)
				9	Measures characteristic of work.
From a control mechanism that directs a predetermined pattern of action	Fixed within the machine			8	Actuated by introduction of work piece or material.
				7	Power Tool System, Remote Controlled
				6	Power Tool, Program Control (sequence of fixed functions).
				5	Power Tool, Fixed Cycle (single function).
From man	Variable			4	Power Tool, Hand Control.
				3	Powered Hand Tool.
			Manual	2	Hand Tool.
				1	Hand.

Figure 11.1: Levels of mechanization and their relationship to power and control sources

From James R. Bright, Automation and Management, *Division of Research, Harvard Business School, Boston, 1958, p. 45. Reprinted by permission.*

Operating a conventional machine tool is a highly skilled task. The operator positions the workpiece, selects the appropriate tools in their correct sequence for each job, and manually operates the handles and levers that control the relative positions and speeds of the tool and workpiece to produce parts with the required dimensions and features. Machine tools have passed through the following broad phases of development.

1. Machine tools are often used to produce large numbers of identical components. Towards the end of the nineteenth century, it became possible, using a complex arrangement of cams and ratchets, to make machine tools carry out a sequence of operations automatically. It was therefore no longer necessary to have one operator at each machine. The operator's job was reduced to loading the workpiece, switching on the machine, removing the finished part, and replacing dull tools. Stripping and resetting the machine to carry out different sequences of operations was a skilled and time consuming job. These machines could be altered to carry out a wide range of different functions, but the long set up times and high costs of new hardware programmes meant that they were only effective with comparatively long production runs.

2. The computerization of machine tools began in the 1950s. To make the task of setting and resetting the machine tool easier and quicker, the automatic mechanical controls were replaced with "hard wired" electronic logic circuits. Beside the machine tool stood a plug board (like a telephonist's switchboard) on which the operator plugged in the sequence of operations required. This was the first version of what is now called numerical control (labelled NC).

3. In the early 1960s, machine tools were joined to small computers. The sequence of instructions or program that the machine followed was stored on paper tape. To change the sequence of operations, the operator had to change the tape which was prepared by a programmer.

4. The next step, during the 1970s, was to give the machine tool a built in programmable computer with a "conversational" video display unit and keyboard. This removed the need for paper tape. The availability of small, cheap, reliable computer components in the form of microprocessors has hastened the development of what is now called computer numerical control (CNC). These machines are also capable of "adaptive control"; they can adjust their speed and other operating characteristics to take account of adverse working conditions as they arise, such as tool wear, heat and deflection torque. Human intervention is at this stage reduced to loading and removing workpieces, and replacing dulled tools.

5. If each machine tool can be operated and controlled by its own computer, it is possible to schedule and control the work of several machines from one central computer. This will develop further in the 1980s, and is termed direct numerical control (DNC). The central computer tells the operator, through a video screen, which workpieces to fit on which machines.

Machine tools are the foundation of all sectors of the engineering industry. Automated machine tools are thus one of the basic components of the hypothetical "unmanned factory".

Bright's scheme emphasizes *the way in which the operations of the machinery are controlled*. This scheme does not measure technical development in terms of speed, complexity or size — which may be important to the engineer. Apparatus in levels 1 to 4 in Bright's scheme are human operated and controlled. From levels 5 to 8, the machine movements follow a fixed pattern. In levels 9 to 17, the machine is controlled by information coming from outside the apparatus. The key element is therefore the way in which the relationship between the machine and the user changes. This relationship depends on developments in the machine's capability to determine and control its own cycle of operations.

The systematic reduction of human intervention and control in work has advantages in making work less tiring and more safe. It also enables the managers of organizations to overcome the problems that arise through human idleness, dishonesty and carelessness. But it brings some disadvantages also. Braverman argues that technical change has dehumanized work:

> "... the remarkable development of machinery becomes, for most of the working population, the source not of freedom but of enslavement, not of mastery but of helplessness, and not of the broadening of the horizon of labour but of the confinement of the worker within a blind round of servile duties in which the machine appears as the embodiment of science and the worker as little or nothing." (Braverman, 1974, p. 195)

These comments give the impression that, as machines do more, people do less. That impression is however an oversimplification and it is not supported by the evidence. Braverman certainly never intended to give such an impression and does so here only because of the selection from his work that has been used so far. The demands that are made on the members of an organization may depend in part on the material technology that they use, but also depend on the social technology of the organization. In the following section, we will consider more closely the general proposition that technology determines skills and other facets of organizational life.

DETERMINISM VERSUS CHOICE

Different technologies make different demands on those who work with them. It is clear that the technology of an organization determines, at least to some extent, the nature of work in that organization. If we compare a hospital with a biscuit making factory, a consultancy firm with a coal mine, it seems reasonable to argue that the technology of these organizations determines:

- The kinds of tasks that have to be done;
- Job design, or the the horizontal division of labour;
- The organization of work or the grouping of jobs;

- The hierarchy through which work is planned and coordinated, or the vertical division of labour, or organization structure;
- The knowledge and skills required to carry out the work;
- The values and attitudes and behaviour of workers.

The argument that technology can be used to explain the nature of jobs, work groupings, hierarchy, skills, values and attitudes in organizations is called *technological determinism.* The determinist assumption that work has to be organized to meet the requirements of the machinery is widespread.

Technology can be used to explain organizational behaviour . . .

". . . this research started with the concept that every industrial job contained certain technologically determined task attributes which would influence the workers' response. By 'task attributes' we meant such characteristics of the job as the amount of variety, autonomy, responsibility, and interaction with others built into the design."

From A. N. Turner and P. R. Lawrence, *Industrial Jobs and the Worker: An Investigation of Response to Task Attributes,* Harvard University Division of Research, Graduate School of Business Administration, 1965.

Another facet of the determinist argument is the notion, mentioned earlier, that technology is somehow beyond human control and is not influenced by social or cultural factors. Alvin Toffler, for example, argues that technological innovation can be analysed in three main phases. The first phase is invention; someone has a creative new idea. The second phase is exploitation; practical applications of the new idea are developed. The third phase is diffusion; more and more people see the advantages of the new idea and apply it. But this third phase in turn triggers off more creative new ideas:

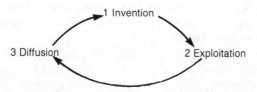

Technical change thus seems to encourage more technical change. The process is intrinsically self-stimulating and self-perpetuating. From this perspective, technology does appear to be out of our control and organization structures appear to be locked in to its demands. The logic of technical development appears to block any choices as to the direction of those developments and their application. Organizations may simply be forced to use new technologies as a result of competitive pressures.

Continuous innovation is also a way of life in the capitalist industrialized world, both in the development of new products and services and in new production processes. Technical innovation is central to maintaining "competitive advantage" in international trade. There is therefore an economic determinism behind technical innovation. Companies that do not introduce the improved technologies that their competitors use must inevitably fail when their customers desert them.

Technical change is simply the result of competitive pressure . . .

"It is widely assumed that we must employ new information and computing technologies to remain competitive in world markets. It is also generally accepted that, because microprocessor technologies are widely applicable, faster, smaller, cheaper and more reliable, their application will be inevitable, rapid and beneficial. A report by the British Advisory Council for Applied Research and Development concluded in 1979 that, 'The rate of technological innovation in United Kingdom industry will need to increase if its products and manufacturing processes are to match those of our major competitors. This is a necessary condition of our future survival as a trading nation.'"

From David A. Buchanan, 'Using the new technology: management objectives and organizational choices', *European Management Journal*, 1982, vol. 1. no. 2, pp. 70-9.

But Toffler also argues that:

"Important new machines do more than suggest or compel changes in other machines — they suggest novel solutions to social, philosophical, even personal problems. They alter man's total intellectual environment — the way he thinks and looks at the world." (Toffler, 1970, p.36)

There is now evidence to show that the technological determinist argument is oversimplified. In Toffler's view, technology *suggests* ways in which it may be used. That is different from the claim that it *determines* what happens. There are three broad areas of *choice* in the process of technical change which weaken the technological determinism argument.

First, there are choices in the design of equipment, tools and machines — apparatus. The main choice appears to be the extent to which the control of operations is built into the machine or left to human intervention and discretion. There are cases of automated controls being taken out of aircraft cockpits, ships' bridges and railway engine cabs when it was discovered that pilots and drivers lost touch with the reality of their task, surrounded by sophisticated automatic controls which functioned without their help. The task in each case had been automated to the extent that when human intervention really was required, mistakes were made.

Second, there are choices in the goals that technologies are used to achieve. Competitive pressure is just one reason for using a particular technology. Organizations also innovate to reduce costs and solve production bottlenecks and other problems. These reasons may reflect the demands of internal accounting procedures as well the desire to improve price and delivery for the customer. Managers also promote technical innovation for personal and political reasons, to give them more power over resources and influence over decisions, more status and prestige in the competition for promotion, and tighter control over their subordinates.

Third, there are choices in the way in which work is organized around technology. The applications of job enrichment presented in Chapter 3 illustrate that the demands made on human skill and knowledge depend partly on the technology and partly on the design of jobs. Job design depends on management decisions as well as on the type of machinery in use. The redesign of car assembly work by the Swedish company Volvo described in Chapter 10 shows how even this type of work is not dictated by the machinery of production. There are thus choices about the ways in which given technologies can be used by an organization.

These are called *strategic choices* because they depend on management decisions about the strategy behind the development and application of specific pieces of apparatus. Managers have discretion about the design of technology and about the organization of jobs around technology. The use of that discretion depends more on the assumptions that managers make about human capabilities and constraints than on the technical capabilities of specific pieces of apparatus. These are called "psycho-social assumptions" because they concern managers' beliefs about the behaviour of individuals and groups of people at work.

To consider the impact of a particular technology is to consider the wrong question, or at best to consider only a part of the issue. Both technology and its effects are the result of a series of management decisions about the purpose of the organization and the way in which people should be organized to fulfil that purpose. This implies that we should not be studying technology at all, but that we should instead be analysing managers' beliefs, assumptions and decison making processes.

The strategic choice alternative to technological determinism has been developed by sociologists adopting an *action perspective*. "Action" is the term given to purposive, meaningful behaviour, and action theorists have argued that links between technology and organization reflect choices based on management perceptions. There is no inescapable technological or bureaucratic logic. Applications and the implications of technology and technical change are firmly within our control. One of the strongest and most influential statements of this argument has been set out by John Child for whom strategic choice is, "an essentially political process in which constraints and opportunities are functions of the power exercised by decision makers in the light of ideological values" (Child, 1972, p. 2).

This argument regards technical change as a decision making process with five related components:

1. *What:*   The characteristics of the technology

2. *Why:*   The goals pursued by management

3. *How:*   The organization of work around the technology

4. *Consequences:*   Human, organizational, financial

5. *Feedback:*   The effects of past changes on future decisions

In this perspective, technical change acts as a *trigger* to processes of management decision making. The choices that form in those processes, concerning why and how the technology is to be used, determine the outcomes of technical change. Technology thus has no impact on people or performance in an organization independent of the purposes of those who would use it and the responses of those who have to work with it. The technological determinism case is therefore weak; the strategic choices are crucial. We will be able to say more about the what, why and how of technical change in Chapter 14 where this argument will be re-examined in more detail in relation to contemporary technological developments.

The management approach to these questions throughout this century has been influenced by a school of thought known as *scientific management.* That school has systematically presented a set of guidelines to management decisions about the use of technology and the organization of work. The influence of scientific management pervades management thinking and organization functioning in all industrialized countries in the world today and it is therefore necessary to examine its content and implications in more detail.

SOURCES

Braverman, H., 1974, *Labour and Monopoly Capital: The Degradation of Work in the Twentieth Century,* Monthly Review Press, New York.

Bright, J., 1958, *Automation and Management,* Harvard Business School, Boston.

Buchanan, D. A., 1982, "Using the new technology: management objectives and organizational choices", *European Management Journal,* vol. 1, no. 2, pp. 70-9.

Buchanan, D. A., 1983, "Technological imperatives and strategic choice", in G. Winch (ed.), *Information Technology in Manufacturing Processes: Case Studies in Technical Change,* Rossendale, London, pp. 72-80.

Buchanan, D. A. and Boddy, D., 1983, *Organizations in the Computer Age: Technological Imperatives and Strategic Choice,* Gower Publishing Company, Aldershot.

Child, J., 1972, "Organization structure, environment and performance: the role of strategic choice", *Sociology,* vol. 6, no. 1, pp. 1-22.

Davis, L. E. and Taylor, J. C., 1976, "Technology, organization and job structure", in R.

Dubin (ed), *Handbook of Work, Organization and Society*, Rand McNally, Chicago, pp. 379-419.

Fox, A., 1974, *Man Mismanagement*, Hutchinson, London.

Perrow, C., 1967, "A framework for the comparative analysis of organizations", *American Sociological Review*, vol. 32, no. 2, pp. 194-208.

Pugh, D. S. and Hickson, D. J., 1976, *Organization Structure in its Context: The Aston Programme 1*, Saxon House, Aldershot.

Reeves, T. K., Turner, B. A. and Woodward, J., 1970, "Technology and organizational behaviour", in Joan Woodward (ed.), *Industrial Organization: Behaviour and Control*, Oxford University Press, London, pp. 3-18.

Toffler, A., 1970, *Future Shock*, Pan Books, London.

Turner, A. N. and Lawrence, P. R., 1965, *Industrial Jobs and the Worker: An Investigation of Response to Task Attributes*, Harvard University Division of Research, Boston.

Winner, L., 1977, *Autonomous Technology: Technics-Out-of-Control as a Theme in Political Thought*, The MIT Press, Cambridge, Massachusetts.

Chapter 12

Scientific management

Frederick Winslow Taylor (1856-1915)

Henry Lawrence Gantt (1861-1919)

Frank Bunker Gilbreth (1868-1924)

Key concepts:

Once you have fully understood this chapter you should be able to define the
following concepts in your own words:

Scientific management·   Work rationalization
Efficiency   Systematic soldiering
The one best way   Functional foremanship

Objectives:

On completing this chapter you should be able:

1. To describe the main characteristics of the "scientific approach to
    management" as expounded by Taylor, Gilbreth and Gantt.
2. To distinguish their approach from that of other writers who make up
    the classical school of management.
3. To identify the model of man that underpins the "scientific" approach
    to management.
4. To evaluate the strengths and weaknesses of the "scientific"
    approach to management.

INTRODUCTION

The scientific management movement which arose during the first two decades of the 20th century has had a tremendous and lasting impact on organizational practice. Its chief exponent was an American, Frederick Winslow Taylor, whose ideas were developed by Frank Bunker Gilbreth and Henry Gantt. The concern of these writers was with the workers who performed routine manual tasks which meant an emphasis on shopfloor organization and management. The movement paid great attention to the organization member, to the details of his work behaviour and to his job motivation. All three writers were in broad agreement that the physical movements involved in shovelling earth or laying bricks could be regarded as those of a machine. For this reason, the label "modern machine theory" is sometimes given to this school of thought.

The scientific management objective was to plan workers' movements in the most efficient and least tiring ways. Taylor's ideas and those of his followers led to time and motion experts with their stop watches and clipboards observing workers and seeking to discover the 'one best way' in which every job could be performed.

Taylor's writings in particular still have enormous influence on management practice. In many organizations today, work is organized in the ways that Taylor suggested. But modern academic writers tend to be critical of Taylor and his "scientific" approach to management. They accuse him of being naïve, of contradicting himself, and of calling his personal ideas "principles". He claimed that these principles could be applied to any organization, but they have been found to have fairly limited application.

While it is easy to criticize Taylor's work today, we must take account of the conditions at the time that he was writing. The book *Principles of Scientific Management* was published in 1911. The United States was undergoing a major industrial reorganization. Complex forms of organization were emerging, with new technologies of production and large workforces. Many of the large industrial organizations, such as General Motors and Ford, with which we are now familiar, were created around the turn of the century. These organizations were broken down into plants and subunits. The workers employed in them came often from agricultural regions or were immigrants from Europe, seeking security and wealth in the new world. Directing the effort of workers with little knowledge of the English language, and no experience of the disciplined work of a factory, was a key organizational problem.

Scientific management was thus a reasonable approach to managing the technical, economic and social problems of America around the turn of the century. One question that we have to ask, therefore, is why his ideas are so influential today.

The first solutions to America's production problems came from practical men like Taylor who recorded their experiences and their successes, not from university professors or researchers. Taylor's writings are among the first systematic efforts to analyse and institute management practices that could be applied to organizations in general. The fact that Taylor tended to treat workers as machines was partly the result of his own training and experience in engineering.

FREDERICK WINSLOW TAYLOR

Taylor was born in Philadephia in 1856 and became an apprentice machinist in a firm of engineers before joining the Midvale Steel Company in 1878. The ideas which were to form the basis of his "scientific approach to management" were developed in this company in which he rose to the position of shop superintendent. His main concern here was with the individual worker and his job. He managed to increase production by reducing the variety of methods that were used by different workers. Taylor was appalled by what he regarded as the inefficiency of industrial practice and set out to show how management and workforce could mutually benefit by adopting his approach. His objectives were to achieve:

1. Efficiency, by increasing the output per worker and reducing deliberate "underworking" by employees;
2. Standardization of job performance, by dividing tasks up into small and closely specified subtasks;
3. Discipline, by establishing hierarchical authority and introducing a system whereby all management's policy decisions could be implemented.

As a supervisor, Taylor observed that few machinists ever worked at the speed of which they were capable. He gave the label *systematic soldiering* to refer to this conscious and deliberate restriction of output by operators. He attributed their behaviour to a number of factors:

1. The view among workmen that a material increase in the output of each man in the trade would have the end result of throwing a large number of men out of work;
2. Poor management controls which made it easy for each workman to work slowly, in order to protect his own best interests;
3. The choice of methods of work was left entirely to the discretion of the workmen who wasted a large part of their efforts using inefficient and untested rules of thumb.

To overcome these problems, Taylor sought to develop a true "science of work". He advocated the scientific selection, education and development of workers. Taylor was not clear in his use of the term "scientific", but he seems to have meant "detailed and careful" analysis of tasks and functions. He hoped that his approach would engender intimate, friendly and co-operative relationships between management and workers.

Taylor aimed to standardize and simplify the job so that, where possible, a job was broken down into its elements which were then distributed between several workers, each of whom performed one set of actions.

Taylor's approach first involved a detailed analysis of each work task. He chose routine, repetitive tasks performed by numerous operatives where study could save time and increase production. A wide range of variables was measured, such as size of tools, height of workers, and type of material worked. Through his studies he tried to answer the question, "How long should it take to do any particular job in the machine shop?" He wanted to replace rules of thumb with scientifically designed methods. Taylor experimented with different combinations of movement and method to reveal *the one best way* of performing each task.

A second aspect of the approach was the scientific selection of the person to perform each task. This meant the selection of workers on the basis of fitness for the job rather than on the basis of friendship or personal influence. We would nowadays take Taylor's suggestions on employee selection for granted, but they were considered new and even revolutionary at that time.

A third aspect of the approach was to encourage the selected worker to use the quickest and most effective "one best way". Taylor's motivational device was the piecework incentive system of pay. The more pieces the worker produced the higher the pay. Management had to decide the extra pay that was needed to encourage the worker to produce the effort required.

Scientific approach to shovelling . . .

I. Select suitable job for study which has sufficient variety without being complex, which employs enough men to be worthwhile and would provide an object lesson to all when installed.

2. Select two good steady workers.

3. Time their actions.

4. Get them to use large shovels on heavy material. Total amount within a set time period is weighed and recorded.

5. Shovel size reduced so that weight of shovel-load is decreased, but total amount shovelled per day rises.

6. Determine best weight per shovel-load. Identify correct size of shovel for all other materials handled.

7. Study actual movements of arms and legs.

8. Produce "science of shovelling" which shows correct method for each material and amount which should be shovelled per day by a first class man.

In 1898 Taylor was hired by the Bethlehem Iron Company (which later became part of the Bethlehem Steel Corporation) to introduce more efficient work methods. One of his tasks was to improve the work of pig iron handlers, gangs of men who loaded 92-pound pigs on to railroad cars. Taylor was warned

Taylorism is alive today . . .

Why the minutes matter to Joe Hughes

In the minute or so it takes you to read this, Joe Hughes will have done his bit on a new Maestro, moving down track 3 in Cowley's assembly plant at the rate of 34 an hour. On each one, he has just 100 seconds to screw two rubber buffers to the edge of the raised tail-gate with a power tool and then fix three earths to metal plates next to the wheel arches in the rear of the car, two on the left, one on the right. Hughes has been on the Maestro track for just three weeks, having been moved from the Rover Ambassador line where he fixed back arm rests and interior plastic trim on the columns between the windscreen and front windows. "I had only one night's training to do this job", he said. "The job is simple but keeping up isn't."

On the day shift, Hughes begins work at 7.15 a.m. The line in the assembly plant will keep going relentlessly until, 153 cars later, everything stops for lunch. It restarts an hour later until the shift ends at 4.15. If Hughes wants to go to the lavatory or have a smoke when the line is moving, he must ask the foreman to assign someone to cover him and wait until his relief arrives. He is allowed a total of 46 minutes off in each shift – known as his "relaxation allowance". At the end of his eight hour day and supposing that the line has not slowed or stopped for any reason, Hughes will have put in 1,792 screws and fixed 492 buffers and 938 earths in 246 cars.

From D. Macintyre, *"Death wish or desperation"*, Sunday Times, 3 April 1983, p. 51.

that these men who handled about twelve and a half tons of iron a day, "were steady workers, but slow and phlegmatic, and that nothing would induce them to work fast" (Taylor, 1911, p. 48). Undaunted, Taylor studied their work and concluded that with proper, less tiring methods, first class workers could handle 47 or 48 tons a day, or about four times the average. To introduce his method, Taylor selected a "little Pennsylvania Dutchman", called Schmidt, who he felt would be receptive to his approach. Taylor explained the method to Schmidt in the following terms:

"The task before us, then, narrowed itself down to getting Schmidt to handle 47 tons of pig iron per day and making him glad to do it. This was done as follows. Schmidt was called out from among the gang of pig-iron handlers and talked to somewhat in this way:

'Schmidt, are you a high-priced man?'

'Vell, I don't know vat you mean.'

'Oh come now, you answer my question. What I want to find out is whether you are a high priced man or one of these cheap fellows here. What I want to find out is whether you want to earn $1.85 a day or whether you are satisfied with $1.15, just the same as all those cheap fellows are getting.'

'Did I vant $1.85 a day? Vas dot a high-priced man? Vell yes, I vas a high priced man.'

'...Now come over here. You see that pile of pig iron?

'Yes.'

'You see that car?'

'Yes'

'Well, if you are a high priced man, you will load that pig iron on that car tomorrow for $1.85. Now do wake up and answer my question. Tell me whether you are a high-priced man or not.'

'Vell — did I got $1.85 for loading dot pig iron on dot car tomorrow?...'

'Certainly you do — certainly you do.'

'Vell den, I vas a high priced man.'

'Now hold on, hold on. You know just as well as I do that a high priced man has to do exactly as he's told from morning till night. You have seen this man here before, haven't you.'

'No I never saw him.'

'Well, if you are a high priced man you will do exactly as this man tells you tomorrow, from morning till night. When he tells you to pick up a pig and walk, you pick it up and you walk, and when he tells you to sit down and rest, you sit down. You do that right straight through the day. And what's more, no back talk. Do you understand that? When this man tells you to walk, you walk, and when he tells you to sit down, you sit down, and you don't talk back at him. Now you come on to work here tomorrow and I'll know before night whether you are really a high-priced man or not.'" (Taylor, 1911, pp. 45-6)

Schmidt loaded the car as instructed, and earned his $1.85 a day. As Taylor did not have access to the modern technology of tape recording, we may assume that he invented that conversation with Schmidt. This probably tells us more about Taylor than about Schmidt.

It was not only workers who had their jobs fragmented. Taylor felt that every worker in an organization should be confined to a single function. He proposed a system of *functional foremanship* (which never became popular). The job of the general foreman was to be divided and distributed among eight separate individuals. Each of these would oversee a separate function of the work, and would be called:

1. Inspector
2. Order of work and route clerk
3. Time and cost clerk
4. Shop disciplinarian
5. Gang boss
6. Speed boss
7. Repair boss
8. Instruction card clerk

Taylor's scientific management was a powerful attempt to institutionalize a system of organizational control and to change the role of management. Before Taylor, an initiative and incentive system had operated in the Bethlehem Steel Company, where management specified production requirements and provided an incentive in the form of a piece rate bonus. But the workers decided how targets should be achieved. Taylor could not accept the wasted effort this produced. He argued that responsibility for planning, co-ordinating and controlling work should be exercised by management. The worker had to concentrate on the task. Management concentrated on planning, organizing and controlling workers efficiently.

TAYLOR'S VIEW OF WORKERS AND MANAGERS

Taylor's approach and methods were embedded in an ideological position which is often forgotten. The methods and techniques for which he is famous were a means to improve the efficiency and social harmony of industrial life, which required a "mental revolution" on the part of both managers and workers. The elements of this revolution were:

- A clear division between manual and mental work;
- Acceptance of new responsibilities by both management and workers;
- The replacement of management's arbitrary power over workers by scientifically determined practices and procedures;
- The acceptance of these views and their strict implementation.

He believed that scientifically established work techniques could change the relationship between management and workers. By their mutual submission to the scientific method, workers would be rewarded by large increases in pay and managers would get higher productivity and profits.

Taylor also said:

> "Now one of the very first requirements for a man who is fit to handle pig iron as a regular occupation is that he shall be so stupid and phlegmatic that he more nearly resembles in his mental makeup the ox than any other type. The man who is mentally alert and intelligent is for this very reason entirely unsuited to what would, for him, be the grinding monotony of work of this character." (Taylor, 1947, pp. 53-60)

To Taylor, the human being was an economic animal who responded directly to financial incentives. Taylor regarded the worker as a machine fuelled only by money; shovel in more money and, given the right methods and working environment, the machine goes faster. The worker was guided in his actions by a pleasure-pain calculation that would lead him to exert effort in proportion to the rewards offered and the sanctions applied.

Taylor's unit of analysis was the individual. He considered the worker in isolation, unaffected by, for example, the structure and culture of the work group, management policies and procedures, or even the individual's own feelings, attitudes and goals. From this narrow focus, he emphasized the detailed study of the physical operations relevant to the performance of each task. All theories of organization are based on an implicit or explicit model of human behaviour — on a conception of how people behave in organizations. The Taylor model is a machine model.

In analysing the individual at work and by building up a standard set of procedures, Taylor concentrated on the instrumental aspects of human behaviour. He saw workers as units of production. Provided one knew the laws of scientific management, they could be handled as easily as other tools. He thus neglected the psychological and social variables which affect organizational behaviour. Taylor was aware that workers had feelings and that they associated with others in the factory. He assumed that these aspects were irrelevant to the problems of productivity.

TAYLORISM IN ACTION

Exceptional results were achieved by some of Taylor's followers. They redesigned individual tasks and the relationships between production tasks. Materials were systematically scheduled and routed through a plant. Inspection took place between operations. Standardization and simplification of methods and equipment and more systematic ways of distributing tools and materials became commonplace. By the third year of working under his plan, the following results had been obtained at Bethlehem Steel (Taylor, 1911, p. 71):

	Old plan	New Plan
Yard labourers	500	140
Tons per man per day (average)	16	59
Earnings per man per day (average)	$1.15	$1.88
Cost of handling a ton (average)	$0.072	$0.033

Symphonic engineering . . .

'Here is the way in which a literal minded industrial engineer reported on a symphony concert.

'For considerable periods the four oboe players had nothing to do. The number should be reduced and the work spread more evenly over the whole concert, thus eliminating peaks and valleys of activity.

'All the twelve violins were playing identical notes, this seems unnecessary duplication. The staff of this section should be drastically cut. If a larger volume of sound is required, it could be obtained by means of electronic apparatus.

'Much effort was absorbed in the playing of demi-semi-quavers; this seems to be an unnecessary refinement. It is recommended that all notes be rounded up to the nearest semi-quaver. If this were done, it would be possible to use trainees and lower grade operatives more extensively.

'There seems to be too much repetition of some musical passages.

Scores should be drastically pruned. No useful purpose is served by repeating on the horns something which has already been handled by the strings. It is estimated that if all redundant passages were eliminated the whole concert time of 2 hours could be reduced to 20 minutes and there would be no need for an intermission.

'In many cases the operators were using one hand for holding the instrument, whereas the introduction of a fixture would have tendered the idle hand available for other work. Also, it was noted that excessive effort was being used occasionally by the players of wind instruments, whereas one compressor could supply adequate air for all instruments under more accurately controlled conditions.

'Finally, obsolescence of equipment is another matter into which it is suggested further investigation could be made, as it was reported in the program that the leading violinist's instrument was already several hundred years old. If normal depreciation schedules had been applied, the value of this instrument would have been reduced to zero and purchase of more modern equipment could then have been considered."

From R. M. Fulmer and T. T. Herbert, *Exploring the New Management*, Macmillan, New York, 1974, p. 27.

The savings achieved with Taylor's new plan were between $75,000 and $80,000 (per annum at 1911 prices). However, the dramatic improvements in productivity were matched by the negative and often violent reactions to Taylor's techniques among workers, technicians, managers and government. The fragmented tasks designed by Taylor were boring, the worker required a much lower level of skill, which meant that management could offer lower wages, and the psychological needs and feelings of the worker were ignored. Taylor's methods were disliked by those who had to work under them.

Scientific management was used in other countries. In Britain, it was first applied in the J. Hopkinson works at Huddersfield in 1905. The Iron and Steel Institute evaluated the techniques and criticized them. In Germany, the Director of the Borsig Works noted the hostility of his workmen to the methods. In 1912, Renault introduced scientific management principles at Billancourt which resulted in violent conflict and strikes. The zealous application of time study in Renault had the following result: "The workman . . . had to adapt his human machine to the rate of the mechanical one; and workmen incapable of making all the necessary movements with their hands within the measured time aided themselves by using their heads as a third arm" (Friedmann, 1955, p. 42). Lenin encouraged the application of scientific management to transform Russian industry after the 1917 communist revolution (Wren, 1980).

Taylor's work in America was equally controversial. In 1898, he was appointed management consultant at Bethlehem Steel and tried to implement all aspects of his approach. Michael Rose (1975) noted that following Taylor's success with Schmidt, local newspapers calculated that his methods would lead to mass redundancies. Since this did not improve the company's industrial relations, and as the company benefited from the houses and shops that it owned near the works, management asked Taylor to moderate his efforts. Taylor could not tolerate such interference. Eventually he got a one line letter which said, "I beg to advise you that your services will not be required by this company after 1st May 1901".

The application of scientific management methods at the American Watertown Arsenal was a turning point for Taylor. General Crozier, Controller of Ordnance at the Arsenal, was interested in scientific management methods, but was hesitant to implement them. He was not convinced that bonuses should be paid for methods which reduced job times, and he thought that time studies themselves might to lead to a strike. When the approach was adopted, it led almost immediately to a strike among moulding workers.

The Watertown Arsenal strike led to a House of Representatives Committee to investigate Taylor's methods. He presented his case before the Committee in person, arguing that his methods could increase industrial efficiency and harmony. The Committee reported in 1912, and concluded that scientific management did provide useful techniques. However, in 1914, an attitude survey of Arsenal workers was conducted, revealing the hostility and resentment of the workers to the system. Concerned about industrial unrest in government arms factories in wartime, the American Congress banned Taylor's time study methods in its defence industry.

FRANK BUNKER GILBRETH — THE DEVELOPMENT OF TAYLORISM

In the work of those who followed Taylor we see a refinement and development of the measuring techniques applied to the study of work and an increased acknowledgement of the need to apply scientific thinking to solve the problems of work performance. Gilbreth's background resembled Taylor's but his work experience was in bricklaying and construction. His wife Lilian was a trained psychologist and her influence can also be seen in her husband's work.

Gilbreth is best remembered for the development of motion study. He wanted to refine and document Taylor's work more precisely. Gilbreth was the first to advocate the universal application of time and motion study.

He gave detailed instructions on how to find out the best way of doing any job. The nature of the building industry meant that there was a need to develop a way of controlling work carried out at a distance from head office. He set down for his workers, supervisors and managers what he called his "Field System". This was a set of written rules and procedures which were designed to establish uniform practice on all work sites. Apart from the Field System, there were the "Concrete and Bricklaying Systems" which detailed such matters as mixing concrete, transportation, training of apprentices, methods of scaffolding, and so on.

Gilbreth's approach clearly resembled that of Taylor. The work to be studied was carefully selected and the factors influencing performance (worker, surroundings, tools) were noted. The job was recorded by observation, the result analysed, unnecessary motions were deleted and the new method was installed. Gilbreth improved observational techniques by using photography and developed a more comprehensive system of noting actions based on eighteen elements called "therbligs" (a variation of his name spelt backwards). He developed a standard time for each job element, combining time study with motion study. This was used as a basis for designing wage payment systems.

While Gilbreth developed Taylor's ideas and produced a system of time and motion study, the major advances from the social science perspective came from his association with his wife Lilian. The study of motions, and the elimination of unnecessary motions and wasteful actions, was intended to reduce the level of fatigue experienced by workers. Since all work produced fatigue for which the remedy was rest, the aim was to find the best mix of work and rest to maximize productivity.

The Gilbreths addressed the problem of fatigue reduction in several ways. One approach was to shorten the working day and introduce rest periods and chairs. Another was the scientific study of jobs to eliminate the fatigue producing elements. Changes were also made to heating, lighting, and ventilation. The final ingredient was termed the "betterment of work". It included introducing rest rooms, canteens, entertainment and music into the factory. In the work of the Gilbreths we see the first realization that workers may have a variety of different needs. The Gilbreths thought that individual work performance depended on attitudes, needs and the physical environment as well as correct work methods and suitable equipment.

HENRY LAURENCE GANTT —
THE HUMANIZATION OF TAYLORISM

Henry Gantt worked for Taylor at the Bethlehem Steel Works. He supported Taylor's approach, but he did much to humanize scientific management to make it more acceptable. He believed in consideration for and fair dealings with workers. He felt that scientific management was being used as an oppressive instrument by the unscrupulous. His system was based on detailed instruction cards in the best scientific management tradition. These showed the time allowed for a job, the operations to be carried out, and the methods to be used. However, he replaced the "one best way" of Taylor with his own "best known way at present". This involved a much less detailed analysis of jobs than Taylor suggested.

Gantt also substantially modified the pay system which had caused such bad feelings between management and workers in the past. The piece rate system was replaced by a set day rate plus a 20–50 per cent bonus. The time for the job was set by Gantt, and if it was met, the worker would get the day rate plus the bonus. There existed detailed times for each part of the job, and if the worker could not meet these, the foreman had to demonstrate that it could be done. At the same time the initiative and responsibility was given to the supervisor to

ensure that his men performed satisfactorily. There was no functional foremanship here. The supervisor received a bonus for every man who achieved his
target and a further payment if all his team achieved it.

Gilbreth in action . . .

"All Gilbreth's work had one objective — to discover the best method of
doing a job. Once at an exhibition in London he gave a devastating
display of his ability to do this. This example was quoted by Henry L.
Gantt in his introduction to Gilbreth's book on Motion Study:
    'While in London with the American Society of Mechanical Engi-
neers, Mr. Gilbreth cornered an old friend of his and explained to him the
wonderful results that could be accompanied by motion study. He
declared that he did not care what the work was, he would be able to
shorten the time usually required, provided that nobody had previously
applied the principles of motion study to the work.
    'A few days before, his friend had been at the Japanese–British
Exposition and had seen there a girl putting papers on boxes of shoe
polish at a wonderful speed. Without saying what he had in mind, Mr.
Gilbreth's friend invited him to visit the Exposition, and in a most casual
way led him to the stand where the girl was doing this remarkable work,
with the feeling that here at least was an operation which could not be
improved upon.
    'No sooner had Mr. Gilbreth spied this phenomenal work than out
came his stop watch and he times accurately how long it took the girl to
do twenty four boxes. The time was forty seconds. When he had
obtained this information he told the girl that she was not working right.
She, of course, was greatly incensed that a man from the audience
should presume to criticize what she was doing, when she was
acknowledged to be the most skilled girl that had ever done that work.
    'He had observed that while all her motions were made with great
rapidity about half of them would be unnecessary if she arranged her
work a little differently. He had a very persuasive way, and although the
girl was quite irritated by his remark, she consented to listen to his
suggestion that he could show her how to do the work more rapidly.
Inasmuch as she was on piece work the prospect of larger earnings
induced her to try his suggestion. The first time she tried to do as he
directed she did twenty-four boxes in twenty-six seconds; the second
time she tried she did it in twenty seconds. She was not working any
harder, only making fewer motions.
    'This account the writer heard in Manchester, England from the
man himself who had put up the job on Mr. Gilbreth, and it is safe to say
that this man is now about as firm a believer in motion study as Mr.
Gilbreth.'"

From A. Tillett, T. Kempner and G. Wills (eds), *Management Thinkers*,
Penguin Books, Harmondsworth, 1970, pp. 102-3.

Gantt's view of the worker was different in some ways from that of Taylor and Gilbreth. He wrote, "The general policy of the past has been to drive. The era of force must give way to that of knowledge; the policy of the future will be to teach and to lead", and, "Time is needed to overcome prejudice and change habits. This is a psychological law. Its violation produces failure just as surely as the violation of the laws of physics or chemistry" (Rathe, 1961, p.9). More than the other two scientific management writers, he realized that the worker was a human being with needs and dignity that deserved consideration by management.

Nevertheless, he believed that the opportunity to earn money was all the motivation the workers needed to accept the improved methods. Management's job was to create the conditions in which this could happen.

CONCLUSIONS AND ASSESSMENT

In spirit, scientific management resembles in its cold rationality the classic bureaucratic and administrative theories of organization. The conception of the human being is that of an automaton whose performance can be improved by the application of logical engineering principles and simple economic incentives. Taylor developed what appeared to be an unbeatable combination — efficient motions, efficient tools, optimum working arrangements and good financial incentives.

Scientific management did not always work effectively. The problem was people. Such approaches either ignore human needs and behaviour or treat them in a naïve and simplistic way. Scientific management in particular:

1. Assumed that the motivation of the employee was to secure the maximum earnings for the effort expended. It neglected the importance of other rewards from work (achievement, job satisfaction, recognition) which subsequent research has found to be important.
2. Neglected the subjective side of work — the personal and interactional aspects of performance, the meanings that employees give to work and the significance to them of their social relationships at work.
3. Failed to appreciate the meanings that workers would put on new procedures and their reactions to being timed and closely supervised.
4. Had an inadequate understanding of the relation of the individual incentive to interaction with, and dependence on, the immediate work group. Taylor did attribute "underworking" to group pressures but misunderstood the way in which these worked. He failed to see that these might just as easily keep production and morale up.
5. Ignored the psychological needs and capabilities of workers. The one best way of doing a job was chosen with the mechanistic criteria of speed and output. The imposition of a uniform manner of work can both destroy individuality and cause other psychological disturbances.

6.   Had too simple an approach to the question of productivity and morale. It sought to keep both of these up exclusively by economic rewards and punishments. However, the fatigue studies of the Gilbreth during the 1920s did signal the beginnings of a wider appreciation of the relevant factors than had initially been recognised by Taylor. Incentive – productivity approaches under the scientific approach tended to focus on the worker as an individual and ignored his social context.

Despite the criticisms, the technical achievements of Taylor and his followers have stood the test of time with remarkably little modification. Despite its weaknesses, scientific management has had a tremendous impact on factory and office management practice and on the organization of production workers.

Taylor's concept of measurement has contributed to the study of "ergonomics", concerned with the measurement of human movements, machinery, and the physical work environment. An example of this can be seen in old people's homes and hospitals where the siting of electrical points and switches is based on measurements of chair height and arm reach.

Taylor has often been described as a "man of his times", whose ideas and techniques were born in and applicable to the period in history in which he lived and worked. But as we have illustrated, Taylor's work received a lot of opposition from the workers to whom it was originally applied. It is perhaps more readily applied and accepted today. It is commonplace in factories and offices today to see people with clipboards and stop watches timing the motions of workers, and "work study" and "organization and methods" specialists are still in demand, as a glance through newspaper job advertisement columns will show.

STOP!

If Taylor's approach is so outdated and inhuman, why do you think it is still commonly used by modern management?

SOURCES

Friedmann, G., 1955, *Industrial Society: The Emergence of the Human Problems of Automation*, Free Press, Glencoe, Illinois.

Fulmer, R. M. and Herbert, T. T., 1974, *Exploring the New Management*, Macmillan, New York.

Gantt, H., 1919, *Organizing for Work*, Harcourt, Brace and Hove, New York.

Gilbreth, F. B., 1908, *Field System*, The Myron C. Clark Publishing Company, New York and Chicago.

Gilbreth, F. B. and Gilbreth, L., 1916, *Fatigue Study*, Sturgis and Walton, New York.

Leavitt, H. J., Dill, W. R. and Eyring, H. B., 1973, *The Organizational World*, Harcourt, Brace, Jovanovitch, New York.

Rathe, A. W. (ed.), 1961, *Gantt on Management*, American Management Association, New York.

Rose, M., 1975, *Industrial Behaviour: Theoretical Development Since Taylor*, Penguin Books, Harmondsworth.

Tannenbaum, A. S., 1966, *Social Psychology of the Work Organization*, Tavistock Publications, London.

Taylor, F. W., 1911, *Principles of Scientific Management*, Harper, New York.

Tillet, A., Kempner, T. and Wills, G. (eds), 1970, *Management Thinkers*, Penguin Books, Harmondsworth.

Wren, D. A., 1980, "Scientific management in the USSR, with particular reference to the contribution of Walter N. Polakov", *The Academy of Management Review*, vol. 5, no. 1, pp. 1-11.

Chapter 13

Technology and work organization

The politics of technology
Characteristics of mass production
Organizations as systems
Socio-technical system analysis and design
Assessment

"We begin to find today the symptoms of a new type of industrial illness. We invent machines to eliminate some of the physical stress of work, and then find psychological stress causing even more health and behaviour problems. People don't want to be subservient to machines and systems. They react to inhuman working conditions in very human ways: by job-hopping, absenteeism, apathetic attitudes, antagonism, and even malicious mischief. From the worker's point of view, this is perfectly reasonable.

"People entering the workforce today have received more education than ever before in history. We have educated them to regard themselves as mature adults, capable of making their own choices. Then we offer them virtually no choice in our overorganized industrial units. For eight hours a day they are regarded as children, ciphers, or potential problems and managed or controlled accordingly."

From Pehr Gyllenhammar, *People at Work,* Addison Wesley Publishing Company, 1977, p. 4. Pehr Gyllenhammar is President of the Swedish company Volvo.

Key concepts:

Once you have fully understood this chapter, you should be able to define the following concepts in your own words:

Technology as a political tool   Composite autonomous work group
Job rotation   Closed system
Job enlargement   Open system
Mass production characteristics   Socio-technical system

Objectives:

On completing this chapter you should be able:

1. To identify the ways in which technology can be used to manipulate control over decisions in organizations.
2. To identify the advantages and limitations of job rotation, job enlargement and autonomous group working.
3. To understand and apply the view of organizations as socio-technical systems.
4. To recognize the limitations of the socio-technical system perspective.

THE POLITICS OF TECHNOLOGY

The production demands of the Second World War made managers and academics more aware of the effects of job design and work organization on employee morale and productivity. The notion that good human relations meant happy and productive workers began to lose its appeal. The significance of technology for worker attitudes and behaviour was recognized.

One critic of the human relations approach, the American sociologist Robert Merton, argued in 1947 that technology had several social implications. He claimed that technological change increased task specialization, took skill and identity from work, and increased discipline in the workplace.

This argument identifies *technology as a political tool* — as something that managers use to manipulate workers and conditions of work. This is an important argument because the apparatus of production is commonly regarded as politically "neutral". But if management can increase task specialization and reduce the level of skill required in a job, they can offer lower wages. If management can increase the discipline in work, they gain tighter control over the activities of workers. Reduced skill and tighter control mean less discretion for the worker over work methods.

The organization of work around a given technology can be used to control labour costs, to control decision making, to control the relative status of different groups in an organization and to control promotion and career prospects. Managers may be able to manipulate employees in these ways by appealing to the technological determinist argument: "We have to do this because the technology demands it." Technological determinism may thus be used to justify unpopular management decisions.

Managers get two main advantages from improved control. First, it can lead to lower costs and higher profits. Second, it maintains the role and status of managers as a controlling group. "Technological implications" can thus be regarded as the result of managers' attempts to improve their control by the way in which work is organized around the technology. The consequences of technical change are not simply the inescapable results of the demands of the machinery. These implications are not just the results of applications of the "efficient" techniques of scientific management.

At the end of the previous chapter, we asked you to consider why scientific management techniques are still used although the evidence suggests that they are inhuman and inefficient. Merton's argument about the political use of technology provides a partial answer to that question. Another possible answer is that scientific management is self-perpetuating, in the manner illustrated in Figure 13.1 (based on Clegg and Dunkerley, 1980).

The adverse human reaction to specialized, repetitive work may simply confirm management's feeling that tight control over work and workers is necessary to produce goods and services efficiently. In this way, scientific management becomes a self-justifying technique. The circle can only be broken by a change in managers' perceptions.

In the 1950s, some managers did begin to see that scientific management took task specialization too far. Morris Viteles, for example, argued in 1950 that the combination of increasing mechanization and scientific management techniques created routine, repetitive tasks which most people found boring and monotonous. The experience of boredom can have an adverse effect on the rate of work and on output, reduces employee morale and leads to higher levels of absenteeism and complaints.

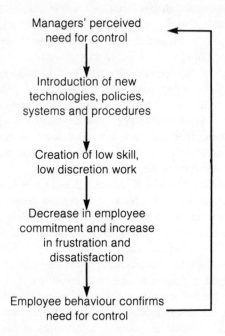

Figure 13.1: The vicious circle of control

The popular solutions to boredom in the 1950s were:

Job rotation   operators were switched from task to task at regular intervals

Job enlargment   tasks were recombined to widen the scope of individual jobs

The problem and its solution were simple:

The problem:

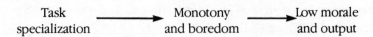

The solution:

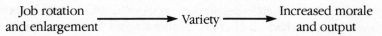

| Job rotation and enlargement | → Variety → | Increased morale and output |

This definition of the problem ignores the political role of technology in work. The main difficulty was seen as restoring the *variety* in work that scientific management had eliminated. Job rotation and enlargement techniques are still used today, although they have been superseded by more sophisticated job enrichment techniques. They do certainly reduce some of the monotony in work and increase variety. But they do this in a superficial way, and they do not touch the root of the problem which seems to lie with management control.

Job design techniques can be regarded as ways of improving employee motivation and performance while leaving organizational structures and the role of management intact. Job enrichment may affect the work of first line supervisors but rarely affects higher levels of the management hierarchy. These techniques do not, therefore, affect the overall balance of power, influence and control in organizations.

We have argued here that:

- Technology is a political tool;
- Which managers use to justify decisions about work organization;
- To achieve both financial and personal objectives.

This argument is not popular with managers. The counter-argument is that the organization of work depends on the technology, not on managerial political manoeuvres and decisons. Now let us look at the evidence.

CHARACTERISTICS OF MASS PRODUCTION

One major and influential investigation of the relationships between technology and the experience of work was carried out by Charles Walker and Robert Guest and published in 1952 in a book called *The Man on the Assembly Line*. Under the influence of the human relations school, they argued that some technologies prevent the formation of work groups and frustrate the social needs of workers. They conducted an attitude survey of 180 American automobile assembly workers. From their results, they identified six key characteristics of mass production work:

Mechanical pacing of work
Repetitiveness
Minimum skill requirement
No choice of tools or methods
Minute subdivision of product
Surface mental attention

The jobs of the car workers were scored on each of these characteristics. The workers said that they were happy with their pay and working conditions. But those in jobs with a high "mass production score" disliked those characteristics of their work and had a higher rate of absenteeism than those in low scoring jobs.

STOP!

Which of those six mass production characteristics are inescapable consequences of the motor car assembly line production?

Which of those characteristics are the result of reversible management decisions about the organization of assembly work?

Other studies in the 1950s produced similar results, and similar recommendations for alleviating the problem with job rotation and enlargement. Walker and Guest and other researchers at the time believed that machinery — the physical apparatus of production — was a key determinant of human behaviour in organizations and that very little could be done to overcome the problems that it created.

The first reported account of job enlargement was from Charles Walker in 1950. The project was carried out in the Endicott plant of the American company IBM on the initiative of the Chairman of the Board (not an academic). In 1944, the jobs of the machine operators were enlarged to include machine set-up and inspection of finished products. These two jobs were previously done by two other groups of workers.

There was nothing in the technology of machining that meant that machine operators could not have these extra tasks and responsibilities. These task allocations were determined by management. The benefits of job enlargement at Endicott included improved product quality and a reduction in losses from scrap, less idle time for men and machines, and a 95 per cent reduction in set-up and inspection costs. This simple technique thus had far reaching consequences.

Work that has mass production characteristics can cause stress and illness as well as boredom and dissatisfaction. Arthur Kornhauser's study of car assembly workers in Detroit was published in 1965. From the results, he argued that low grade factory work led to job dissatisfaction and poor mental health. The workers that he studied had a long list of complaints, including:

Low pay	Simplicity of job operations
Job insecurity	Repetitiveness and boredom
Poor working conditions	Lack of control over the work
Low status	Non use of abilities
Restricted promotion opportunities	Feelings of futility
The style of the supervisors	

Workers in jobs with these characteristics had lower mental health, which meant that they:

Were anxious and tense
Had negative self concepts
Were hostile to others
Were socially withdrawn
Were less satisfied with life in general
Suffered from isolation and despair

Each of these characteristics taken alone does not imply very much as most people have such feelings at some times in their lives regardless of the work they do. But Kornhauser argued that work with mass production characteristics tends to produce this *pattern* of psychological reactions.

Swedish car manufacturers were among the first to show that mass production characteristics can be avoided with novel approaches to work organization. The Swedish Employers' Confederation, the Swedish Central Association of Salaried Employees and the Confederation of Manual Workers' Unions established a Union Management Development Council for Collaborative Questions in 1966. The Council's objective was to carry out experiments of various kinds aimed at improving both job satisfaction and productivity.

By 1974, it was estimated that over 1,000 such experiments had been started, although many had failed and some were used mainly for publicity purposes (Valery, 1974). The work organization movement in Sweden appears to have rested on the projects of three companies: Volvo, Saab-Scania, and Atlas Copco. The work organization experiments of those companies became major management tourist attractions and Volvo received the most publicity.

Mass production characteristics cause stress . . .

Work that is fast, repetitive and strenuous usually creates stress. Stress can affect anyone, but most of the research has however concentrated on shop floor workers. The relationships between job characteristics and stress are therefore not well understood.

Robert Karasek attempted to clarify these relationships in an analysis of the results of two surveys of employee attitudes carried out by the University of Michigan and the Swedish Institute for Social Research. These surveys used random samples of the American and Swedish working populations and asked similar questions about the experience of work.

Karasek argued that stress was related to two main job characteristics:

• Workload;
• Discretion in how to do the work.

Jobs in which workload and discretion are low require little mental or physical activity.

Jobs with high workload and discretion are challenging and provide opportunities to develop competence.

Jobs with high discretion and low workload may be frustrating and create some stress.

Karasek argued that the most stressful jobs were those that combined high workload and low discretion.

This argument was confirmed by both the American and the Swedish data. Examples of high stress jobs in America included assembly workers, garment stitchers, goods and materials handlers, nurses' aids and orderlies and telephone operators.

The two main symptoms of stress were:

- Exhaustion, including problems waking up in the morning and extreme fatigue in the evening;
- Depression, including nervousness, anxiety and sleeping difficulties.

The Swedish data also showed a strong link between high stress work and the consumption of tranquilizers and sleeping pills.

Karasek argues that it is not usually stressful to use one's mental abilities, exercise judgement and make decisions. He argues therefore that stress can be reduced if workers are given more discretion in how work is performed. Discretion can be altered without changing workload, so mental health can be improved without affecting productivity.

From Robert A. Karasek, "Job demands, job decision latitude, and mental strain: implications for job redesign", *Administrative Science Quarterly*, 1979, vol. 24, no. 2, pp. 285-308.

The Saab-Scania Group's experiments in work organization began in 1970. Forty production workers in the chassis shop of a new truck factory were divided into small production groups (Norstedt and Aguren, 1973). Group members were responsible for deciding on their own rotation between the different tasks, and also carried out maintenance and quality control functions. The company also set up "development groups" which included a supervisor, a work study specialist and a number of operators. These groups met monthly and issued a report on their decisions stating who was to be responsible for any actions they recommended. These arrangements were designed to reduce labour turnover and absenteeism. The project had the following results:

- The new work methods spread to the rest of the chassis works, affecting about 600 manual workers;
- Productivity increased;
- Unplanned stoppages of production were significantly reduced;
- Costs were reduced to 5 per cent below budget;
- Product quality improved;
- Labour turnover was cut over 4 years from 70 to 20 per cent;

- Absenteeism was not affected;
- Co-operation between management and workers improved.

The Group's best known experiment was in their engine factory at Sodertalje which began production in 1972. From the results of their earlier experience, the company decided to design the factory layout and the work organization of the new factory from scratch. The layout consisted of an oblong conveyor loop which moved the engine blocks to seven assembly groups each with three members. An island of potted plants enclosing a café with a telephone was placed alongside the assembly line. Visitors noted the quiet, clean, relaxed and unhurried atmosphere of the plant (Thomas, 1974).

Each production group had its own U-shaped guide track in the floor to the side of the main conveyor loop. Engine blocks were taken from the main track, were completely assembled by the group, and were then returned to the main track. The engine blocks arrived with their cylinder heads already fitted and the groups dealt with the final fitting of carburettors, distributors, spark plugs, camshafts and other components.

Each group assembled a complete engine and decided themselves how their work was allocated. The guide track of each group was not mechanically driven. The group was simply given thirty minutes to complete each engine and they decided how that time would be spent. Individual jobs on the conventional assembly line had a cycle time of less than two minutes.

This form of work organization is known as the *autonomous work group* and was also used by the other Swedish car manufacturer Volvo.

It was estimated in 1974 that Saab-Scania were saving around 65,000 Swedish kroner on recruitment and training costs and that reductions in absenteeism were saving another 5,000 kroner a year.

Volvo also used the autonomous work group . . .

"We decided. . . to bring people together by replacing the mechanical line with the human work group. In this pattern, employees can act in cooperation, discussing more, deciding among themselves how to organize the work — and, as a result, doing much more. In essence, our approach is based on stimulation rather than restriction. If you view the employees as adults, then you must assume that they will respond to stimulation; if you view them as children, then the assumption is that they need restriction. The intense emphasis on measurement and control in most factories seems to be a manifestation of the latter viewpoint."

From Pehr Gyllenhammar, *People at Work*, Addison-Wesley Publishing Company, Reading, Massachusetts, 1977, p. 15.

Autonomous work groups have become a technique, with job enrichment, in the toolkit of the quality of working life movement. There are three different ways in which we can regard these experiments today:

1. Were these attempts by humanistic managers to alleviate the frustrations of conventional assembly line work?
2. Were these attempts by politically conscious managers to return discretion and control over working methods to employees?
3. Were these attempts by managers concerned with performance and control to find techniques that were more effective than scientific management?

STOP!

Which of these three views would you expect managers to support?

What evidence would you use to support your conclusion?

There are different ways in which we can regard these experiments...

"The problem as it presents itself to those managing industry, trade, and finance is very different from the problem as it appears in the academic or journalistic worlds. Management is habituated to carrying on labour processes in a setting of social antagonism and, in fact, has never known it to be otherwise. Corporate managers have neither the hope nor the expectation of altering this situation by a single stroke; rather, they are concerned to ameliorate it only when it interferes with the orderly functioning of their plants, offices, warehouses, and stores.

"For corporate management this is a problem in costs and controls, not in the 'humanization of work'. It compels their attention because it manifests itself in absentee, turnover, and productivity levels that do not conform to their calculations and expectations. The solutions they will accept are only those which provide improvements in their labour costs and in their competitive positions domestically and in the world market."

From Harry Braverman, *Labour and Monopoly Capital: The Degradation of Work in the Twentieth Century*, Monthly Review Press, New York, 1974, p. 36.

ORGANIZATIONS AS SYSTEMS

The concept of autonomous group work is one aspect of a wider perspective on the way in which organizations function — *the systems approach.* Swedish managers did not invent the idea of autonomous group working. The systems approach was developed by British researchers and consultants in the Tavistock Institute of Human Relations in London. It was their influence on Norwegian industry in the 1970s that prompted Swedish managers to copy their example, with more public success.

The word "system" is in common everyday use in the English language. We talk about the solar system, traffic management systems, telecommunications and computer systems, waste disposal systems and so on. The word is not difficult to understand, but it is difficult to define without ambiguity.

A system may be defined as something that functions by virtue of the interdependence of its component parts. But that is a superficial definition and it has limited value. It could apply (like the term technology) to almost anything. We could describe both a can opener and the human body as systems. The human body is clearly a system that works as an interdependent whole. Human perception, however, can also be analysed as a system in its own right. The same applies to the digestive system, the nervous system, and to any other subsystem of the body as a whole. What one defines as a system, therefore, or where one defines the system boundaries, depends on what one wants to study and why.

Can openers and human bodies have obvious and fundamental differences. The most important difference, from the systems perspective, is that the human body interacts purposively with its environment. The can opener does not. The human body takes into itself (imports) air, food, drink and a variety of perceptual information. The body transforms (converts) these imports into energy. The body disposes of (exports) waste products and uses up energy in selected behaviours.

The can opener is a *closed system*. Its existence does not depend on transactions with its environment. The human body, on the other hand, in common with all living things is an *open system* because it has to trade with its environment in order to survive:

Open system processes:

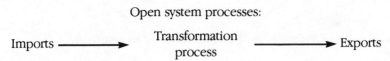

Imports ⟶ Transformation process ⟶ Exports

Living systems are also able to maintain their internal states after disturbances. The human body for example has built-in mechanisms that maintain the body's core temperature within certain extremes of ambient temperature. This self-regulating ability is called "homeostasis".

Open systems are also capable of achieving a particular end result from a variety of starting places. Some garden weeds continue to flourish after the gardener's attempts to chop their roots with the spade. The autonomous work groups at Volvo and Saab-Scania can assemble an engine in many different ways. A chemical reaction on the other hand is a closed system in which the final result depends on the concentrations and quantities of the chemicals used to begin with.

Open systems thus have the following properties:

- They depend on exchanges with the environment to survive;
- They are self-regulating;
- They are flexible and adaptable.

The systems approach is based on the assumption that work organizations can be treated as open systems. Consider how an organization survives. It has to import capital, materials, equipment, labour and information. It has to transform these somehow into goods and services. It then exports waste materials, finished products or satisfied customers to get money to begin the cycle again. An organization's activities can therefore be described in terms of its import, transformation and export processes.

This view of organization is also called the "organic analogy" because it implies that organizations have properties in common with living organisms (Rice, 1963; Miller and Rice, 1967). So we should expect to find that organizations are self-regulating, flexible and adaptable. Unlike closed systems which maintain or move towards states of homogeneity, organizations as open systems become more elaborate and diverse in structure in their attempts to cope with their environments (Emery and Trist, 1960).

Eric Trist, one of the Tavistock researchers, was responsible for the idea that an enterprise can be considered not just as an open system but as an *open socio-technical system* (Trist and Bamforth, 1951). The socio-technical system idea is summarized in Figure 13.2.

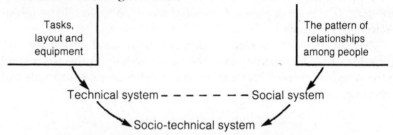

Figure 13.2: The socio-technical system idea

The concept of an open socio-technical system arises from the fact that any production system requires both a material technology and a social organization of the people who operate the apparatus. Trist argued that the social organization had social and psychological properties that were not dependent on the demands of the technology. In other terms, the socio-technical systems approach is not a technological determinist approach.

The socio-technical system design problem is to find the "best fit" between the social and technical components — which are not completely independent. They must be designed in such a way that the needs of each aspect are met to some extent. If the technical system is designed without taking into account the needs of the social system, then the system as a whole will not operate effectively. Conversely, the social system design must be consistent with the demands of the technical system.

Trist and his colleagues argued that an effective socio-technical system design could not completely satisfy the needs of either the social or the technical subsystem. This "sub-optimization" is a necessary feature of good socio-technical system design. The point, however, is that the design of each system is not dependent on the design of the other. The final design depends on human choices, not on technological imperatives.

The socio-technical systems approach is a useful way of looking at organizations. Organizations are of course not independent living systems. But the approach highlights important aspects of the way in which organizations function. The organic analogy prompts interesting questions about what one might expect to find in an organization. The approach provides a framework of related ideas that can be used to order the mass of information that can be collected about an organization.

The approach is sometimes called "socio-technical system theory". Like all analogies, the organic concept of organization can be taken too far. The approach is not a theory. It is simply a stimulating way of looking at organizational phenomena.

SOCIO-TECHNICAL SYSTEM ANALYSIS AND DESIGN

The socio-technical system approach was developed through two major studies carried out by Tavistock researchers. The first of these studies took place in the coal mines around Durham in Britain. The second was in a textile mill at Ahmedabad in north-west India. Here we will look at the Durham study in some detail. The concepts of the systems approach can be unfamiliar and awkward at first. It is therefore useful to discover their origins and to see how they were first applied.

The north-west Durham coal mines

Eric Trist and his colleagues appear to have had problems in deciding on the title of the book in which this research was published. The full title is, *Organizational Choice: Capabilities of Groups at the Coal Face Under Changing Technologies; The Loss, Rediscovery and Transformation of a Work Tradition* (Trist, Higgin, Murray and Pollock, 1963). The book deals with several related issues and a brief summary can give little indication of the wealth of detail to be found in the original.

The main argument of that research was that the form of work organization introduced when mechanical coal getting methods replaced traditional techniques was not determined by the new technology. In other words, they argued, technical change is consistent with "organizational choice". This is the strategic choice that we introduced in the previous chapter.

Britain's coal mining industry was nationalized by a Labour government in 1946. The predicted improvements in productivity and industrial relations did not occur. Labour turnover and the incidence of stress illnesses among coal face workers stayed high. Trist felt that these problems arose from the organization of work associated with mechanized mining methods. So an alternative form of work organization, which had developed in some pits, was studied to see if it made any difference. The research thus compared two different kinds of work organization in coal mines that were comparable in other ways — such as underground conditions and equipment.

The first report of the study, published in 1951 described the social and psychological disadvantages of the "conventional longwall" method of getting (that is obtaining) coal. This method had gradually replaced conventional "hand got" methods since the turn of the century. Trist's colleague K. W. Bamforth had been a miner himself for 18 years.

The coal getting cycle in the 1950s had three stages:

Preparation	The coal was either cut by hand — previously with a hand pick and now with a pneumatic pick — or it was undercut and blown down into the cleared space.
Getting	The coal was loaded onto tubs or a conveyor for removal to the surface.
Advancing	The roof supports, gateway haulage roads and conveyor equipment were moved forward.

Mechanization had replaced "single place" working where one or two miners worked with picks at faces (or places) up to eleven yards long. These men worked in self-selecting groups, shared a common paynote, and worked the same place on the same or different shifts. Each miner performed a *composite work role*, carrying out all the necessary face tasks:

"He is a 'complete miner' — the collier — who supervises himself and is the person directly responsible for production." (Trist et al., 1963, p. 33).

The traditional system organized around the composite autonomous miner had several advantages. The production tempo was slow but was maintained across and throughout shifts. This avoided periodic overloading of the winding gear and ensured the constant use of services such as haulage and the flow of supplies. Very little management organization was needed to keep production up because work on the coal seam as a whole was virtually self-regulating. The pit deputy's main responsibilities concerned safety regulations, keeping the miners supplied, and shotfiring when necessary.

The length of coal face that could be worked at any one time was greatly increased by the use of belt conveyors. In the Durham pits, straight longwall faces were generally 80 to 100 metres long — which explains the term "longwall". The advantage of the face conveyor was that the amount of stonework involved in advancing the gateways, in relation to the area of coal extracted, was significantly reduced. The coal-to-stone ratio becomes more important to the economics of a pit with thinner seams.

The extension in the length of the coal face led to a novel organization of work at the face. The first longwalls were simply extensions of single place working. Preparation and getting were carried out together for the first two shifts and advancing was done in the third. These were called "hewing longwalls". But the cycle was separated into its three discrete stages with the introduction of the electrical coal cutter. The "cutting longwall" was the most widespread longwall technology in Britain at the time of the Tavistock study.

The three stages, preparation, getting and advancing, were each performed by separate task groups working on separate shifts. This meant that coal was removed on only one of the three shifts. The task group on each shift had to finish its stage of the work before the next shift could begin. Balancing the work of the three shifts thus became a serious problem.

The most significant change to the organization of facework that the longwall method introduced was the abolition of the composite autonomous workman. Trist compared the conventional longwall technique with the mass production characteristics of manufacturing industry. The new mining technique also involved maximum job specialization. Workers were allocated to one task on one shift only. They thus had no opportunities for job rotation and no means of developing their skills. The close relationships between miners was retained to some extent in the new single task groups which covered one stage of the mining cycle. But on the whole, the new work organization was not appropriate to work underground.

The miner has to deal with two types of task at the same time — the work of the production cycle, and the background task of coping with the difficulties that arise from underground working conditions and dangers. The production skills were physically demanding, but were not complex and could all be learned by one person fairly quickly. But skill in dealing with the underground dangers was of a much higher order and was only developed through experience over several years. The organization of work underground should ideally ensure that this experience can be gained. Trist's team argued that the conventional longwall method prevented the underground worker from developing these skills.

The nature of the task breakdown and the resulting payment system in the conventional longwall pits created new status differences between miners. The Cuttermen who worked the entire length of a face with a large and powerful piece of machinery formed a "face aristocracy". The fillers on the other hand worked on their own shovelling coal in confined spaces and had comparatively low status. The pay of each task group was calculated on a different basis and each group conducted separate negotiations with management. The primary concern of each task group was to improve its relative financial position, not to win coal.

The conventional longwall method was not self-regulating. Management became responsible for co-ordinating the production cycle. Because self-regulation was impossible, management had to rely on wage negotiations to control the work of the three shifts. This became a key feature of the conventional longwall pits and "management through the wage system" developed into a highly complex bargaining process. Subtasks and ancillary activities, as well as the main production work, were the subject of separate agreements. No common factor could be used to establish rates of pay for the different task groups. Several different criteria were used, such as tonnage, yardage, cubic measure or number of operations completed. Each task group would typically ask for special payment for work not carried out by the shift that preceded them. Each shift thus had a vested interest in the previous shift failing to complete its stage in the production process. The negotiating procedures consumed vast amounts of the time and energy of workers and management.

But some pits had developed a form of "shortwall" work organization with characteristics similar to those of single place working. These "composite shortwalls" were worked by multi-skilled groups responsible for the whole coal getting cycle on any one shift, and paid on a common paynote.

In one of the Durham pits, roof conditions had meant a return to shortwalls as long faces had become impossible to support. Increasing costs however forced the management to consider a return to longwall working. The miners resisted this because they did not want to give up the "composite" form of work organization to return to a system which tied them to specific tasks and shifts. Instead, an agreement was negotiated which tried to preserve the social and psychological advantages of composite groups but still exploit the economic advantages of longwall mining. The result was the creation of self selected groups of forty-one men who allocated themselves to tasks and to shifts and who again received pay on a common note. This became known as the "composite longwall" system.

The composite longwall method had four main characteristics. First, the continuity of production was restored. Each shift took up the cycle at the point at which the preceding shift stopped. When the main task of a shift was complete, they automatically went on the the next stage of the cycle.

Second, the method required multi-skilled miners. Each man did not have to possess all the necessary skills as long as the group as a whole contained the skills required on each shift. The groups were therefore *composite* in terms of the range of skills contained in the group as a whole. They were also *autonomous* as they operated their own shift and job rotations.

Third, the work groups were self selected.

Fourth, each group was paid on a common paynote as all the members were regarded as making equivalent contributions to the work.

These composite autonomous groups were leaderless. Their "team captains" acted as representatives, not as managers. The workers themselves arranged all their shift and task rotation. This allowed them to retain their skills and gave them constant reminder of the conditions under which the other shifts had to work. The whole atmosphere of life and work in the mine was completely different under the composite longwall method.

The whole atmosphere of composite longwall working was different . . .

"The astonishing change in the physical appearance of the workplace, which would be the first thing to impress itself on a visitor, has come to be recognized as almost a hallmark of a composite group . . . Although the men were not responsible for equipment in the gates, they would use their lunch break to check and, if necessary, do repairs to the mothergate belt which leads to the face, anticipating and preventing possible disturbance of their work. No man was ever out of a job. If he finished hewing or pulling before others he would join and help them, or go on to some other job which was to follow. If work was stopped owing to breakdowns in the transport system on which the group was dependent for its supply of tubs, the men would go on to do maintenance work."

From P. G. Herbst, *Autonomous Group Functioning*, Tavistock Publications, London, 1962, p. 6.

The task and shift rotation arrangements developed away from the terms of the original union — management agreement. But the management never considered it necessary to investigate these changes or to prevent them. The arrangements operated to the mutual satisfaction of both parties. The composite longwalls were more productive, miners preferred them and absenteeism was much lower than on coventional longwalls.

The composite longwall method also affected the work of management. The composite organization, like traditional single place working, was self-regulating. The pit deputies were freed from their responsibility of "propping up" the conventional longwall cycle that was always collapsing on itself. Management and workers in the composite method were not involved in the endless wage rate negotiations of the conventional technique.

This study, and other similar Tavistock researches, led socio-technical systems thinkers to the following main conclusions:

- Work in groups is more likely to provide meaningful work, develop responsibility and satisfy human needs than work that is allocated to separately supervised individuals.
- Work can be organized in this way regardless of the technology.

Composite autonomous group working can thus be regarded as another kind of job enrichment technique. But job enrichment is usually applied to individuals. Autonomous group working is applied to groups of people whose work is related or interdependent. Job enrichment and autonomous group working thus adopt different levels of job analysis and design. The approach of the socio-technical system school is summarized in Figure 13.3.

STOP!

Figure 13.3 sets out the approach to the organization of work that the socio-technical system school advocates.

Compare this with the expectancy theory approach to the design of jobs in Figure 4.2 in Chapter 4.

We have mentioned one main difference between these approaches —the level of analysis. What other differences can you identify?

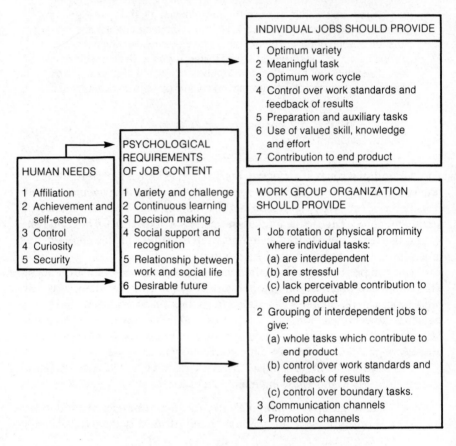

HUMAN NEEDS

1 Affiliation
2 Achievement and self-esteem
3 Control
4 Curiosity
5 Security

PSYCHOLOGICAL REQUIREMENTS OF JOB CONTENT

1 Variety and challenge
2 Continuous learning
3 Decision making
4 Social support and recognition
5 Relationship between work and social life
6 Desirable future

INDIVIDUAL JOBS SHOULD PROVIDE

1 Optimum variety
2 Meaningful task
3 Optimum work cycle
4 Control over work standards and feedback of results
5 Preparation and auxiliary tasks
6 Use of valued skill, knowledge and effort
7 Contribution to end product

WORK GROUP ORGANIZATION SHOULD PROVIDE

1 Job rotation or physical promimity where individual tasks:
 (a) are interdependent
 (b) are stressful
 (c) lack perceivable contribution to end product
2 Grouping of interdependent jobs to give:
 (a) whole tasks which contribute to end product
 (b) control over work standards and feedback of results
 (c) control over boundary tasks.
3 Communication channels
4 Promotion channels

Figure 13.3: The work organization approach to job design

From David A. Buchanan, *The Development of Job Design Theories and Techniques,* Saxon House, Farnborough, 1979, p. 112.

ASSESSMENT

The main thesis of the Durham study was that the work organization associated with conventional longwall technology was not wholly determined by that technology. Organizational choice exists because the social system has properties and flexibilities that are independent of the technical system. The social system can be designed in a way that meets technical demands as well as the needs of the human beings involved.

Let us attempt to summarize here the arguments of this chapter as they are in danger of being lost in the details of car assembly and mining:

1. The organization of work around a given technology for a given task depends on management decisions about job allocations, the formation of work groups, and the amount of discretion allowed to workers.

2. Technology can be used to justify changes to the organization of work in ways that give managers more control and reduce worker discretion.

3. Scientific management is self justifying because it has consequences that suggest further more rigorous application of its techniques.

4. The "mass production characteristics" of car assembly or mining can be avoided in ways that may improve worker performance.

5. A given technical sytem can be operated by different social systems. The problem is to find the best "fit" to meet both their demands.

6. Composite autonomous group working is advocated by socio-technical system thinkers as the best work organization solution to meet both technical demands and human needs. Give a multi-skilled group of workers a meaningful stage in a production process, and the time, materials and equipment to carry it out, and the responsibility for planning and controlling their own work activities.

We have throughout this chapter argued that organizations face a choice in designing work around technology. Have the socio-technical systems approach and the Durham study really demonstrated that this is the case? One commentator (Michael Rose, 1975) has argued that it does not.

STOP!

The "choice" seems to be between an effective and an ineffective form of work organization. What kind of choice is that?

SOURCES

Braverman, H., 1974, *Labour and Monopoly Capital: The Degradation of Work in the Twentieth Century*, Monthly Review Press, New York, 1974.

Buchanan, D. A., 1979, *The Development of Job Design Theories and Techniques*, Saxon House, Farnborough.

Clegg, S. and Dunkerley, D., 1980, *Organization, Class and Control*, Routledge and Kegan Paul, London.

Emery, F. E. and Trist, E. L, 1960, "Socio-technical systems", C. W. Churchman and M. Verhulst (eds), *Management Science, Models and Techniques*, vol. 2, Pergamon Press, London, pp. 83-97; reprinted in F. E. Emery (ed), *Systems Thinking*, Penguin Books, Harmondsworth, 1969, pp. 281-96.

Gyllenhammar, P. G., 1977, *People at Work*, Addison-Wesley Publishing Company, Reading, Massachusetts.

Herbst, P. G., 1962, *Autonomous Group Functioning*, Tavistock Publications, London.

Karasek, R. A., 1979, "Job demands, job decision latitude, and mental strain; implications for job redesign", *Administrative Science Quarterly*, vol. 24, no. 2, pp. 285- 308

Kornhauser, A., 1965, *Mental Health of the Industrial Worker: A Detroit Study*, John Wiley, New York.

Lindestad, H. and Norstedt, J. P., 1973, *Autonomous Groups and Payment by Results*, Swedish Employers' Confederation, Stockholm.

Merton, R. K., 1947, "The machine, the worker and the engineer", *Science*, vol. 105, pp. 79-84.

Miller, E. J., 1975, "Socio-technical systems in weaving, 1953-1970: a follow-up study", *Human Relations*, vol. 28, no. 4, pp. 349-86.

Miller, E. J. and Rice, A. K., 1967, *Systems of Organization: The Control of Task and Sentient Boundaries*, Tavistock Publications, London.

Norstedt, J. P. and Aguren, S., 1973, *Saab-Scania Report*, Swedish Employers' Confederation, Stockholm.

Rice, A. K., 1958, *Productivity and Social Organization*, Tavistock Publications, London.

Rice, A. K., 1963, *The Enterprise and its Environment*, Tavistock Publications, London.

Rose, M., 1975, *Industrial Behaviour: Theoretical Behaviour Since Taylor*, Allen Lane, London.

Thomas, H., 1974, "Finding a better way", *Guardian*, January 17.

Trist, E. L. and Bamforth, K. W., 1951, "Some social and psychological consequences of the longwall method of coal-getting", *Human Relations*, vol. 4, no. 1, pp. 3-38.

Trist, E. L., Higgin, G. W., Murray, H. and Pollock, A. B., 1963, *Organizational Choice*, Tavistock Publications, London.

Valery, N., 1974, "Importing the lessons of Swedish workers", *New Scientist*, vol. 62, no. 892, pp. 27-8.

Viteles, M. S., 1950, "Man and machine relationship, the problem of boredom", in R. B. Ross (ed), *Proceedings of the Annual Fall Conference of the Society for Advancement of Management*, New York, pp. 129-38.

Walker, C. R., 1950, "The problem of the repetitive job", *Harvard Business Review*, vol. 28, no. 3, pp. 54-8.

Walker, C. R. and Guest, R. H., 1952, *The Man on the Assembly Line*, Harvard University Press.

Chapter 14

Advanced technology and work organization

What is advanced technology?
Will computers take over?
Computers in manufacturing
Computers in the office
Assessment

"During a normal lifetime, most people don't have the chance to watch a revolution. For us, though, it's different. Not only can we watch a revolution, we're all actively taking part in it.

"The revolution we're talking about is that of Information Technology — two words that until recently were unknown to all but a small number of people. But they are two words with an impact so widespread that none of us can avoid being affected by them. Nor would we want to.

"Turn on a television, go to the bank, visit a supermarket, attend school, work in a factory or office, drive a car, or do the countless other things involved in daily living, and you'll find Information Technology is increasingly obvious and is making possible totally new services.

"It is no exaggeration to say that the impact of Information Technology, or IT, will be greater than that of any other technological developments that have come before — the invention of steam power, the telephone or electricity all included."

From Kenneth Barnes, Director, Information Technology Year, in *There's no Future Without IT,* Information Technology Year, 1982, London.

Key concepts:

Once you have fully understood this chapter, you should be able
to define the following concepts in your own words:

Microprocessor   Computer aided equipment control
Information technology   Word processing
Replacement effects   Complementarity
Compensatory mechanisms   Distancing
Computer aided process control

Objectives:

On completing this chapter you should be able:

1. To appreciate the diversity of modern technological advance based
    on computing power.
2. To understand the effects of technical change on employment.
3. To appreciate the barriers to radical organizational change as a result
    of technical developments.
4. To appreciate the role of managerial choice in influencing the
    consequences of applications of advanced technology

WHAT IS ADVANCED TECHNOLOGY?

To most people, advanced technology today means a combination of computers, robots, information technology and silicon chips. It has become difficult to escape from newspaper and television reports of the ways in which microprocesssors — the main components of modern computer systems — will affect all our lives rapidly and radically.

Definitions

A *microprocessor* is a miniature integrated electrical circuit based on a sliver of semiconducting silicon which is designed to perform the functions of the central processing unit of a computer.

Information technology is the term now used for all types of computer hardware (machines) and software (programs that tell computers what to do), telecommunications and office equipment. Some definitions are wider and include other applications of computers and electronic controls in manufacturing equipment and processes. We will use the wide definition here.

It is the aim of this chapter to develop *concepts* and a *framework* for examining the nature and consequences of technical change. Information technology promises to be a rich field of study, but consequently a very wide one. It is not possible here to cover the whole field and we have to be selective in the choice of applications to examine.

The press and television in Britain "discovered" the microprocessor or silicon chip in 1978, although it had been available since 1971. The prospect of a new industrial revolution has been popular ever since. Most media accounts of the "microprocessor revolution" adopt a technological determinist tone. It is however difficult to make realistic general statements about the impact of information technologies for two reasons:

- Microprocessors are simply building bricks, components of a wide range of different types of devices from computer aided design systems to children's games;
- The consequences of technical change depend on factors other than the capabilities and features of the apparatus.

Contemporary advanced technologies fall into two broad categories — computer aided manufacturing and computer aided administration. These are listed in Figure 14.1. You may be familiar with some of the names, but many of these may be strange. Do not worry about the unfamiliar terms in that list because they are not essential to understanding this chapter.

In 1978, the number of people who could say that they had experience of working with computers was very limited. Now almost everyone has used a computer in some respect. Digital watches, games like "space invaders", automatic bank terminals and some toys all have computer power. Computer components are now small, reliable, use little energy, and are comparatively cheap. The prediction of a wide-ranging revolution based on electronics developments is thus based on the wide range of potential applications for such devices.

Computer aided manufacturing	Computer aided administration
Computer aided design	Word processing
Numerical control	Electronic mail
Computer numerical control	Electronic filing
Direct numerical control	Computer aided order processing
Automated storage	Data base management
Robots	Standard payroll and accounting
Flexible manufacturing systems	Distributed processing
Computer aided stock and production control systems	Management forecasting, modelling, and decision making aids
Computerized instrument and equipment monitors and controls	Local area networks
Computer aided measurement and testing	Viewdata or teletext systems
Automatic vehicle guidance	Expert or intelligent knowledge based systems
Programmable conveyors	Electronic funds transfer (banking)
Computer integrated manufacture	Electronic point of sale (retailing)

You can add to this figure as the technology develops into new areas and as your awareness of the topic increases.

Figure 14.1 The new computing and information technologies

Computers have thus moved from "background" accounting and administrative activities in organizations into "foreground" tasks in product and process design, order processing, typing, and the control of domestic as well as manufacturing equipment. Conventional computers were too large and too expensive for most of these visible foreground activities.

Computing devices have four information handling capabilities which make them different from "old" mechanical and electromechanical technology.

Information capture

They gather, collect, monitor, detect and measure. The term capture implies an active process. Some devices gather information through sensors without human intervention. Computerized equipment monitors and controls are examples of active information capture. Word processing, where a typist has to put information into the machine through a keyboard, is an example of passive information capture.

STOP!

Modern computing and information technology is varied in its nature and capabilities and we cannot expect to cover all of them in one chapter. We are not going to offer any definition of "advanced technology" beyond the brief statements about microprocessors and information technology at the start of the chapter. In any case, technical advances put a chapter like this quickly out of date.

So we are going to ask you to do one major exercise in conjunction with your work for this chapter — to add to the content of the chapter for yourself.

Start a collection of newspaper and magazine articles dealing with the technologies that are listed in Figure 14.1 and any other computing and information technologies that you learn about.

For each article, first answer the following questions:

1.   What issue or issues made the technology interesting to the reporter?
2.   What evidence is there in the article of a "technological determinist" perspective on technical change?

There is a "popular image" of advanced technology which has the following components:

1.   Computers replace people in manufacturing;
2.   Office automation does away with clerical and administrative work;
3.   Robots will soon be able to make everything for us;
4.   Work where people are still necessary will be simple, routine and "dehumanized";
5.   The days of craft skill and worker autonomy are gone;
6.   There is a natural fear of and resistance to technical change.

To what extent do your newspaper and magazine articles support this popular image?

Compare your findings with those of your class colleagues.

This will keep your understanding of the technology up to date and give you an insight into how technological change is presented in the media.

You should also compare your findings with the material of this chapter to evaluate the validity of the popular image.

Information storage

They convert numerical and textual information into binary, digital form and retain it in some form of permanent computer memory from which the information can be retrieved when required. Machine tools and typewriters cannot store information. Numerically controlled machine tools and word processors can do this. Computers also store their own operating instructions, called programs or "software".

Information manipulation

They can rearrange and perform calculations on stored information. Manipulation means organizing and analysing, tasks for which computers are particularly appropriate, especially where repetitive calculations are necessary, such as working out the monthly payroll and generating standard accounting figures for an organization. As the size and cost of storage media has fallen, it has become possible to develop fast and flexible ways of manipulating text and graphical information.

Information distribution

They can transmit and display information electronically, on video screens and on paper. Word processors can exchange information, typewriters cannot. A numerically controlled machine tool can tell a central computer that it has finished a particular task. Sensors can be used to give operators displays of production progress information.

Technical change is currently a British national media obsession. We tend however to forget two things:

- Technical change is not new. It is a feature of human history.
- Technical development is not confined to computing and electronics.

In this chapter we will concentrate on contemporary developments in computing and information technology. This provides an interesting study in its own right and will be an important organizational issue for the next decade and beyond. We also want to develop the arguments presented in Chapter 11. It would help you to refer back to remind yourself of the argument about technical change as a management decision making process.

Research in this area has adopted three broad but distinct research traditions, each with a different unit and focus of analysis.

Ergonomists have analysed the relationship between the operator and the computer controls. These studies have portrayed the process operators as skilled and knowledgeable decision makers with responsibility, discretion and good working conditions (Singleton, 1974, 1979; Vine and Price, 1977; Bainbridge, 1978; Paternotte, 1978; Landeweerd, 1979; Umbers, 1979).

Psychologists concerned with employee attitudes and the quality of working life have argued that process automation eliminates dirt and danger, and can create a motivating work environment in which the operator has autonomy, task variety, meaning and opportunities for learning (Herbst, 1974; Davis, 1976, 1977; Davis and Taylor, 1975, 1976).

Sociologists have been concerned with the effects of technology on social structure, conflict and the relationship between operators and managers. These studies depict the process operator as a victim of managers' use of technology to create work that is unskilled, boring, lonely, repetitive, paced, controlled, and lacking in meaning (Braverman, 1974; Dickson, 1974; Nichols and Beynon, 1977; Gallie, 1978).

We are thus faced with conflicting reports on the impact of advanced technology. Ergonomists ignore the motivational and political implications of technical change. Sociologists and work psychologists overlook the physical nature and capabilities of computing technology and the skills required to operate it effectively.

The extension of automation with microelectronics may alter the skill demands made on operators and the quality of working life. Maddock (1978) argues that microelectronics will replace mechanical and electromechanical devices and displace human reasoning. But Barron and Curnow (1979) argue that electronic controls lack human adaptability and could create systems which enhance job skills and interest. We will look at British research which has tried to establish which of these views is correct.

But we will look first at an issue that threatens to make this whole question a purely academic one: will computers take over completely?

WILL COMPUTERS TAKE OVER?

Frightening headlines from 1978 . . .

The job killers of Germany	*New Scientist*
Society with chips and without jobs	*New Society*
New technology hits tyre plant	*Financial Times*
New technology could put 5 million out of work	*The Guardian*
4 million jobs threatened by electronics	*The Guardian*
Electronic revolution "may lead to the dole"	*The Times*
Computers will lift jobless total to 2.5 million	*Financial Times*

Those headlines represent part of the popular image of the impact of technical change in Britain and Europe in the 1980s. If they are correct, then the problems of technology and work organization may soon cease to be of any practical interest. If few people have work at all, then it may not be worthwhile to devote effort to studying the effects of technology on people at work. So we must clear up this matter before we proceed.

The headlines however are certainly wrong, and are probably very wrong. You may have already detected a hint of technological determinism in them. That is where their underlying assumptions begin to break down. We shall therefore first explore why they present an inaccurate picture of contemporary technical change.

Technical change may have two effects on an individual organization. First, the skill and knowledge requirements of employees may change as new devices are introduced. Second, to the extent that information technologies replace people (a general assumption that we will challenge later) then some people will lose their jobs. The difficulty is that the impact at the level of the organization may not reflect the overall, or "aggregate" impact of technical change in the economy as a whole.

The popular image, reinforced by the claims of information technology salesmen, claims that these new devices will increase productivity through *replacement* effects. These claims are based on the assumption that as machines do more and more, people will be required to do less and less. This kind of productivity increase will therefore reduce job opportunities and create unemployment.

Definition

Replacement means substituting intelligent, or at least clever, machines for people at work, in manufacturing and in offices.

But rapid technical change since 1945 has been consistent with increasing employment. Why should this not continue? A recent British report on the employment effects of microelectronics concluded that, " ... the evidence from the economic history of the entire industrial age is that technological change has been beneficial to aggregate employment" (Sleigh *et al.*, p. 9). The unemployment experienced by western industrial countries since the late 1970s was not "technological unemployment" but was caused by a deterioration in world trade. That report also argued that " ... it cannot be stressed too strongly that the overall impact on jobs will depend crucially on an unforeseeable economic climate" (Sleigh *et al.*, 1979, p. 1).

It is however possible that electronics will be so pervasive, so radically productive, and so rapidly introduced that previous relationships between technology and employment will no longer prevail. These technologies may be so new and so different that they may create an entirely new pattern of production of goods and services, and a new pattern of employment.

The overall effect of these technical developments may thus depend on the operation of a number of *compensatory mechanisms.*

Definition

Compensatory mechanisms are processes that overcome the replacement effects of technical change.

There are six main compensatory mechanisms at work:

1. *New products and services*
   Technical innovation generates new products and services, like electronic calculators, video cassette recorders, personal computers, and commercial data bases. These innovations change the pattern of consumer demand for goods and services. This leads organizations to invest in factories and offices to make the new products and provide the new services, which in turn leads to new employment opportunities.

2. *Lower costs increase demand*
   Higher productivity means producing the same output with fewer resources, or more output with the same or fewer resources. So lower costs can be passed on to the consumer in reduced or stable prices. This in turn means that consumers will have more money to spend which may increase demand for other goods and services in the economy. It is not realistic to assume that consumer tastes and demands are static and unchanging, although it may be hard to guess how they will change.

3. *Time lags*
   It takes time to incorporate new devices into existing systems. There are technical problems to overcome in linking electronic devices to mechanical and electromechanical machines. These are not insurmountable problems, but they do take time to resolve. Organizations do not adopt innovations as soon as they become available. It is expensive to replace existing facilities completely. Most organizations have investments in factories, machinery and offices that they simply cannot afford to write off overnight.

4. *Risks*
   Most organizations adopt new, experimental and untried technologies slowly at first. The risks are thus avoided or reduced by introducing technical change piecemeal and cautiously.

5. *Expectations of demand*
   Expensive investment in new technology (and information technologies

are still very expensive) is not likely unless an organization expects the market for its goods and services to expand. In that case, an organization may need to employ more people to handle the increase in business, not fewer. If on the other hand an organization expects that the demand for its output is stagnant or declining, then it is not likely to introduce any new technology or to do so very slowly.

6.   *Technical limitations*
New technologies do not always live up to the claims of the salesman. They may in fact not be able to do everything that the "old" technology was capable of doing. So existing jobs, skills and machinery may be required to work alongside the new devices for some time.

The way in which these compensatory mechanisms may work must be considered in the context of world demand for goods and services. A lot of the pressure to adopt new technology arises from competition from other countries whose organizations may innovate faster or more effectively than we do. They can then sell better products more cheaply than we can, our organizations lose sales, and eventually people lose their jobs. Technical change can thus be seen as a way of preserving jobs.

It is therefore not realistic to assume that new technology and increases in productivity will increase unemployment. It is equally plausible to argue that new technology could create as many jobs as it eliminates, and could create more. How this will work in practice is impossible to predict. It will depend on the complex inter-relationships between the replacement and compensatory mechanisms over time.

There are some remaining problems. The compensatory mechanisms may work slower than the replacement effects. And there will be skill and job losses in individual companies.

Replacement means substituting intelligent machines for people . . .

Will computers ever replace doctors? Would you trust a machine to treat your ailments? Research on the use of computer systems by doctors in Sheffield has shown that patients' health may be at risk.

The research was carried out at a hospital out-patient clinic which specialized in stomach disorders. Three doctors each had a computer terminal, with a video screen and a keyboard, in their consulting rooms. As their patients described their problems, the doctors keyed their symptoms into the computer which then worked out which diseases the patient could have.

The research first covered seventy-eight patients who were treated without the help of the computer. They filled in a questionnaire twice, before and after their consultation, to assess the stress they suffered when dealing with the doctor. The same procedure was then applied to sixty-seven patients whose diagnosis was computerized.

As might have been expected, all the patients were nervous before they saw a doctor and most of them were relaxed afterwards. But 22 per cent of the computerized consultations had *increased* the patient's stress. Only 9 per cent of the conventional consultations had this effect.

Another questionnaire was then given to 233 patients, including those in the first part of the study, to assess their attitudes to computers in medicine. The patients were asked to rate their agreement with statements like, "computers could save money for the health service", "with a computer around, you'll lose the personal touch of the doctor", and "a computer could be a useful check against mistakes".

The older and female patients were less enthusiastic about computerized consulting than younger and male patients. Those who had experienced a computerized diagnosis without any increase in stress supported the system. But those whose stress had risen in the presence of the computer disliked it.

If doctors can reach accurate diagnoses faster with the aid of a computer, does it matter if some patients suffer more stress? It does matter, because other research has shown that patients under stress are more likely to forget their doctor's instructions, and are less likely to follow the advice they do remember.

From P. J. Cruikshank, "Patient stress and the computer in the consulting room", *Social Science and Medicine*, 1982, vol. 16, no. 14, pp. 1371-6.

COMPUTERS IN MANUFACTURING

This section examines a study by David Buchanan and David Boddy (1983) which analysed how new computing technologies had affected work in a factory making biscuits in Glasgow. Each biscuit making line in the factory was staffed by a control room operator, a "doughman", a machineman, an ovensman and a packing team. Computer controls had affected several jobs, but here we concentrate on the doughman and the ovensman who were affected in significant and contrasting ways.

Biscuits were made in three stages; mixing, baking, and wrapping.

The recipe for each product was stored on punched paper tape which was fed into a computer by the control room operators. Computer controls fed the flour, water and sugar to the mixing machines. The control room operators had a wall display called a "mimic board", which showed the state of the process for each line. This was being replaced with a "recipe desk" device which allowed adjustments to be made to the recipes for individual mixes much faster, using small thumb-wheels on the desk panel.

The doughman first checked that the control room operators had loaded the correct recipe tape and made sure that enough "sundries" (ingredients added in small quantities) were available. The doughman then pressed a "call button" to start the mixing cycle. When the main ingredients had been delivered to the mixing machine, a light told the doughman to start the mixer. The sundries were added manually during the process.

The computer controlled the mix recipe, time, speed, temperature, and timing of interruptions. Mixing normally involved three stages; dissolving (the sugar), creaming (mixing in the fat) and doughing (mixing everything). Each mix took about 20 minutes with up to three interruptions for the sundries to be added. While a mix was taking place, the hoppers above the mixer were refilled and the cycle was ready to begin again.

A sample of dough from each finished mix was passed through an "oven test". If the doughman decided that the mix was all right, it was emptied into a dough hopper and fed to the cutting machine. The dough was then rolled to the right thickness by passing it through gauge rollers adjusted and monitored by the machine operator. The flat dough sheet then passed through a cutter which stamped out biscuits of the appropriate shape.

From the cutting machine to the packing benches, the process was conveyor run and continuous. The biscuits were baked as they travelled, in about 4 minutes, through the 90 metres long oven. The ovensman checked the thickness, or "bulk", of each batch of biscuits by measuring the length of a set number of biscuits in a graduated tray or gauge. If the bulk was wrong, the ovensman could change the temperatures in the zones of the oven to correct it. The colour and moisture content of the biscuits could also be adjusted in this way.

When they were cool, the biscuits were wrapped in an automatic wrapping machine. Each packet then passed over a "checkweigher" and was rejected if it was underweight. The wrapping machine operator got a digital readout from the checkweigher of the actual weight of each packet. If the weight was wrong, she could adjust the number of biscuits that the machine put into into each packet. This information, in summary form, also appeared on a video display screen in the ovensman's work area. Accepted packs were then boxed and palletized, ready for despatch.

One well known study of the impact of technological advance is that by the American Robert Blauner who analysed working conditions in:

- Printing, dominated by craft work;
- Cotton spinning, dominated by machine minding;
- Car manufacture, dominated by mass production;
- Chemicals manufacture, dominated by process production.

Blauner identified four components of *alienation*, concerning the individual worker's feelings of:

1. *Powerlessness* loss of control over conditions of work, work processes, pace and methods

2. *Meaninglessness*   loss of significance of work activities
3. *Isolation*   loss of sense of community membership
4. *Self estrangement*   loss of personal identity, of sense of work as a central life interest

Printing workers set their own pace, are free from management pressure, choose their own techniques and methods, have powerful unions, practise a complex skill, have good social contacts at work, have high status, identify closely with their work, and are not alienated.

Textile workers perform simple, rapid and repetitive operations over which they have little control, work under strict supervision and have little social contact through their work. Alienation among textile workers, however, was low. Blauner argues that this is because they lived in close rural communities whose values and way of life overcame feelings of alienation which arose in work. (It is interesting to note here the break in the technological determinist argument.)

Car assembly workers have little control over their work methods, see little meaning in the limited tasks they perform, are socially isolated and have no opportunities to develop meaningful skills.

Chemical process workers operate prosperous, technically advanced plants where manual work has been automated. They control their work pace, have freedom of movement, social contact and team work. They develop an understanding of the chemical reactions which they monitor and also develop a sense of belonging, achievement and responsibility. In addition they have close contact with educated, modern management.

Blauner's conclusion, therefore, was that advanced technology, like chemicals processing, would eliminate alienation.

From Robert Blauner, Alienation and Freedom: *The Factory Worker and His Job*, The University of Chicago Press, Chicago, 1964.

The doughman's story

The company's first production computer was installed in 1971 to control the mixing process. To change a recipe it was necessary to prepare a new paper tape which usually took about half an hour and required basic computer programming skills. The new recipe desk system carried out much the same functions, but ingredient quantities could be changed quickly by adjusting the small thumb-wheels. This required no special skills.

The doughman's job was repetitive, with a cycle of around 20 minutes, and was classed as semi-skilled. The job used to be done by time served master bakers, but the computer now controlled the mixing process, doing 60 mixes every 24 hours. Bored doughmen sometimes forgot to add sundries, such as salt. This was only discovered at the end of the mix or at the oven test.

The skilled and varied craft of the doughman had been replaced by the computer controls, and management preferred to call the job that of a "mixer operator". The doughman was previously responsible for getting the flour, with the help of other manual workers. The mixing was done in "spindle mixers", which were open vats like large domestic food mixers. When they could see and hear it, the doughmen could tell by the feel of the dough, and by the sound that it made during mixing, if it was too dry or too wet and add small amounts of required ingredients to compensate.

Factory managers commented:

> "There was more variation in the things he did. Now they seem to lose all interest. There are three or four operators who've been here longer than the computer, and I can see they've really switched off. I've seen it happen to new people coming in as well. It destroys the human contact."

> "One problem with the whole mixer set up seems to be that the new generation of operators don't appreciate as fully as before the consequences of what they do. It's all so automatic they have difficulty visualizing the effects of, say, half a minute extra mixing time on later stages in production."

The mixing vessel was enclosed and the operator could not see or hear the mix, and rarely had to leave it. When the equipment failed, skilled electronic technicians were required to track down the cause and repair it.

The doughmen commented:

> "We used to have much more humour. You had your own group of manual workers working with you doing the manhandling and this gave a lot more fun. It's much more routine now."

> "It's much less interesting, more routine, very little scope for human error now. Initially, it's more skilled, till you get to know the set up, then there's a fair amount of boredom. Except when something goes wrong."

Buchanan and Boddy argue that the introduction of computerized mixing had adversely affected the job of the doughman. It replaced his craft skills, but did not overcome the need for human intervention at that stage of the process. It created what they describe as a *distanced* role with the following features:

1.   Operators had little understanding of the process and equipment;
2.   Operators could not visualize the consequences of their actions;
3.   Operators could not identify the causes of equipment faults;
4.   There was no backup system for them to operate;
5.   Specialist maintenance staff were needed;
6.   Operators became bored, apathetic and careless;
7.   Operators rejected responsibility for breakdowns;
8.   Operators developed no skills to make them eligible for promotion.

Buchanan and Boddy conclude that these *distancing* features may be typical of jobs in "nearly automated" systems, where traditional skills are replaced, but where the work experience equips the operator with neither the capabilities nor the motivation to carry out residual but key functions effectively.

The Ovensman's Story

The ovensman was responsible for baking biscuits that had the correct bulk, weight, moisture content, colour, shape and taste. This was complex because action to correct a deviation on one of these biscuit features could affect the others. The training time was twelve to sixteen weeks.

Two of the most important features were biscuit bulk and weight. The ovensman checked these manually at least once during the baking of every mix. This allowed him to adjust the baking process to ensure consistency, and tell the wrapping machine operators of any potential difficulties. Every mix could have different properties. Some flours absorbed more moisture than others; some doughs were soft and others were tough.

At the end of every baking line, after the biscuits had been wrapped, there used to be a "checkweighing" device. The biscuit packets travelled on a conveyor over this machine which contained a weigh cell that weighed each individual packet and compared this weight with a (manually) preset standard weight. Light packs were pushed off the conveyor, opened later, and good biscuits were fed back into the line. This machine captured no information on packet weights and a manual check was made every half hour.

A microprocessor controlled checkweigher was installed in 1979 to replace the old electromechanical system. As each packet passed over the weigh cell, its weight was recorded by the computer and was displayed on a panel near the wrapping machine. The computer also gave summary information on packet weights to the ovensman through a video display unit. This display was updated every two minutes and was presented in graph and digital form. The computer also printed production analyses for management.

The new system gave the ovensman information on the performance of the line that enabled him to make rapid adjustments to the oven controls and to reduce turn of scale by producing more accurate packet weights. If the packet weights were too high, and the wrapping machine could not compensate, the ovensman could tell the machine operator to adjust the weight of the dough blanks, or he could increase the oven temperature to increase the bulk and reduce the number of biscuits per packet.

The information fed back from the new computer system showed that something was going wrong, but did not show what was causing the problem or what action to take to correct it. The ovensman and machine operator had to take into account the properties of the flour being used and the dough that it made. When the packet weights wandered, the ovensman and machine operator decided what to do to correct it. It was vital that they took this decision together, otherwise they may have overcompensated by taking independent action simultaneously to correct the same fault.

The ovensman felt that the new system had reduced the pressure on him; management kept out of the way when there were no problems. The system was used to settle disputes about the responsibility for errors. The ovensman also felt that the system had increased the interest and challenge in the job because it gave him a goal that he could influence, related to packet weights, and the number of packets of biscuits that left the factory. This was reflected in the bonus payment, and he felt that he now had the satisfaction of knowing that he was cutting waste and costs.

One supervisor commented:

> "There is now no need for a constant physical check. The new system highlights problems making it easier to make corrections quicker. The operators are continually on top of the job, and the feedback from the package makes operators more aware of passing problems down the line. The system is an assistant, a second opinion. The new system gives more information faster, whereas before those 'unforgiving minutes' were lost."

The ovensman had become a "process supervisor". He commented, "That's what our job is all about, really. The equipment does all the work and our job is essentially to make sure that it is doing everything correctly." But he also commented:

> "When everything is computer controlled, and the computer breaks down, the manual skills will still be needed, but there will be nobody around who has them."

Buchanan and Boddy argue that the introduction of computerized packet weighing affected the job of the ovensman beneficially. The new technology *complemented* his skill and knowledge and created a role in which he:

1. Retained discretion to monitor and control the process;
2. Got rapid feedback on performance;
3. Had good understanding of the relationships between process stages;
4. Was able to control the process more effectively;
5. Had a visible goal that could be influenced;
6. Felt that the job had more interest and challenge.

As machines do more, people do not necessarily do less. Computer technology may be tools that complement human skills and create more interesting and meaningful work. But the example of the doughman illustrates that the outcome depends to a large extent on management decisions on how to organize the work around the new devices.

Management here could have designed the equipment to let doughmen see and hear the mixing process, or give the doughman the recipe desk to adjust ingredient quantities himself, or establish autonomous work groups each responsible for one production line. These choices were closed mainly by management's preoccupation with production information and control.

COMPUTERS IN THE OFFICE

This section looks at the findings of a another study in Scotland by David

Buchanan and David Boddy which analysed the effects of word processing in one of the largest marine engineering consultancy firms in Europe.

Word processors have three components: a video display screen and keyboard; a "central processing unit" with an electronic memory; and a printer. As the video typist hits the terminal keys, words appear on the screen and are sent by the central processor to the machine's memory. Stored text can be retrieved any number of times without retyping. Once the text is stored, it can be edited to remove mistakes before it is committed to paper. The typist can also correct mistakes as they appear on the screen.

The company's consultancy work was presented to clients in written technical reports which usually had several authors and went through several revisions. Before the introduction of word processing, each group of specialist consultants had a secretary and one or two copy typists. Reports were typed on conventional electric typewriters. Secretaries and copy typists worked close to each other and to the authors of the reports.

The company formed a "working party" in 1977 to examine how word processing could cut the costs of typing staff. The working party decided to establish two word processing "pools" or centres in which all the video typists would be grouped, with a supervisor in each centre. The centres were the responsibility of a technical services manager, whose line of authority extended down through a word processing section head, a typing services co-ordinator, and the two supervisors to the nine video typists.

This reorganization was determined by the perceived need to control more effectively the flow of work to and from the typists. The other advantages of the centres were easier training, flexible staffing, less cable and fewer printers. It was recognized that the typists would lose contact with authors who would not be able to follow the progress of their typing through the system. But it was felt that the advantages of improved control over the typing work would offset this. There was nothing in the technology of word processing that determined the pooling arrangement.

Copy typing and word processing staff, as a percentage of technical staff, fell from 8.3 to 4.5 per cent between December 1975 and June 1980. Before word processing, in 1975, twenty-eight typists worked for 338 authors. After word processing was introduced, in 1980, sixteen typists worked for 352 authors.

The output of the typists increased dramatically. Copy typists used to produce less than six pages a day on average. The video typists produced over forty pages a day. But despite these obvious improvements, the overall impact of the new technology on typing productivity was hard to assess. The dissatisfaction of the authors had risen with the typists' output rate. They saw no reduction in the amount of time that they spent waiting for drafts to be typed, and they also spent more time correcting drafts.

Buchanan and Boddy interviewed the two centre supervisors and nine video typists to find out how their jobs had changed with the introduction of word processing. The results of the interviews were analysed in terms of the "work organization" model presented in Chapter 13, Figure 13.3. It would help you to refer back to that briefly.

Task variety and work cycle

The copy typist worked for a group of authors who all did similar work. In the word processing centres, each video typist worked for several different groups, with different report styles and preferences. In this respect, the variety of their work had increased.

But the video typist spent almost all her time sitting in one location, entering and editing text. The frequent breaks in the work rhythm of the copy typist did not occur. Everything was done at the keyboard, and the typists found this mentally and physically more demanding. The video typists varied their work patterns by switching between input and editing tasks. Typing the input for a large report was considered particularly monotonous, and these jobs were often divided among several typists.

Meaningful task and contribution to end product

Some of the video typists preferred to work on major jobs rather than on short notes, letters and memos. After a long input typing and editing job, they felt it satisfying to watch the computer print out perfect copy. But the copy typist followed a complete job through for one author or for one group of authors. This rarely happened with video typing. Successive drafts were often done by different typists. Work was normally allocated by the supervisor to the first typist available who could handle the job, whether it was a first or later draft. This loss of identity with the whole job was reinforced when a large job was divided among several typists, when the typist did not know the author whose work was being typed, and when the typist did not know when she was typing the final copy.

Control over the work

The copy typists handled authors and their requests individually. To give a particular job priority was a matter for negotiation between the author, the group, and the copy typist. These negotiations had become a major part of the work of the centre Supervisors, the Typing Services Coordinator, and the Section Head. Although typists could share jobs in the system, control over work scheduling passed to management. The video typists felt, however, that they had more control over the quality and appearance of the end product through the word processing system. An item that was "retyped" carried its corrections without the introduction of new errors, as may be the case with the retype of a document by conventional means.

Feedback of results

The video typist could not see on the screen the precise format of the copy to be typed and had to judge the appearance of the printed text from the format codes attached to the input. There was no instant printout. The typist had to wait until the printer had finished its work before being certain that the text and format instructions had been entered correctly. As the printers were in a separate room, the typists did not normally see their work being printed out. The centre supervisors supervised the printers, separated each author's copy, and personally returned it. This lack of feedback on job performance was a serious hindrance to learning the system. Feedback from authors did not occur when editing was not given to the typist who did the input.

Preparation tasks

Most of the preparatory work was carried out either by the supervisor or the computer. The supervisor checked that the printers were set up and working properly, replaced when necessary the print heads and ribbons, loaded the printers with paper, removed the finished printout and collated jobs for authors. The supervisors received the work from the authors, discussed their needs with them, and often returned the printout to them. The computer performed many of the tasks of the conventional typist, such as arranging page layout and storing text.

Skill and knowledge

In some respects, the video typing job was less skilled than conventional typing. Little or no paper handling was required. The touch of the terminal keyboard was light and led to faster typing. Corrections were simple, and the fear of making a mistake at the bottom of a page (which sometimes slows down the conventional typist) did not arise. The video typist did not have to be concerned with the paper edges as the computer positioned the text on the paper. The keys on modern terminals are closer together and involve less finger stretching than typewriters. The keyboard is flatter and is more comfortable to operate. The terminals are quieter than typewriters and although the printers were noisy, they were kept in another room. Through experience with a group of authors, the copy typist built up a knowledge of their handwriting, technical terms, and report layout needs and preferences. The video typists in the word processing centres could neither acquire nor exploit this knowledge.

The job required more skill and knowledge than conventional typing in three respects. First, the video typist had to learn the codes for formatting and editing text and be able to assess the appearance of printed text by interpreting the format codes attached to input. As the system developed, the typist's knowledge of it had to be updated. Second, the job required more concentration and was physically more demanding than conventional typing for reasons discussed earlier. Third, the system editor on the computer could cause files to be lost and erase the work of others if not used carefully. Much of the training concerned computer file management.

The overall pattern of skill and knowledge required by the typist had therefore changed.

Rotation and proximity

The typists did not feel that their work was stressful. But their organization into typing centres did not reflect the interdependence between typist and author.

Grouping to provide meaning, control and feedback

It has been established already that the reorganization reduced the meaning, contribution and performance feedback of video typists, and gave them less control over work scheduling.

Communication channels

The formal company rules encouraged interaction between typists and authors, but the changes to the way in which the typists' work was organized and controlled, and the equipment itself, inhibited this.

Authors were instructed to hand work to the supervisor of the appropriate centre or the typing services co-ordinator, not direct to the typist. The supervisors handled problems and clashes of priority over typing. Authors did not know which typists were doing their work and the typist no longer controlled those aspects of the typing of interest to the author — the amount and timing of the work. The formal rules and the re-allocation of control led the authors to supervisors and higher levels of management.

Authors could see what the copy typist did with her machine and her time, but were uncertain about the nature of the job of the video typist. Their knowledge of the capabilities of the new technology was imperfect. As the equipment discouraged the typists from leaving their terminals, they tended not to check spelling and formatting requirements with authors but would "have a go" because corrections were simple.

The pooling of the typists established their separation from the authors of the documents that they typed. Authors were not likely to develop the personal, informal working relationships that they had with the copy typists. The typists and authors both regretted this loss of contact.

Promotion opportunities

Video typists were given a salary increase of one grade over copy typists, and had the opportunity of promotion to supervisor.

Conclusions

The job of the typists was affected in several ways by the introduction of word processing. Video typing reduced task variety, meaning and contribution to end product, control over work scheduling, feedback of results, involvement in preparation tasks, skill and knowledge requirements (in some respects), and contact with authors. The change had on the other hand increased control over typing quality, skill and knowledge requirements (in some respects) and pay and promotion prospects. The overall quality of the typing service was felt to have been reduced.

The technology of word processing has powerful information management capabilities, but the findings of this research suggest that the video typist can only fully exploit these capabilities in an appropriate form of work organization. The video typist can experiment with a range of different page layouts and print formats to produce better looking documents faster than with conventional typing. Word processing thus increases the skill requirements of the typing job where the typist has to visualize, create and amend the presentation of text to improve the quality of written communications. This skill, combined with the typist's knowledge of the needs and preferences of individual authors, can potentially create a highly effective typing service.

Management's belief in the need for control to achieve productivity seems to have displaced such considerations.

ASSESSMENT

The function of this section is to sum up the arguments of the chapter. We have dealt in detail with two technologies because many readers will have a limited understanding of computer capabilities and applications. But it is easy to lose sight of the main argument among the details.

The main conclusions of this chapter, and of Part 4 as a whole, are summed up in Figure 14.2 which sets out the argument that the consequences of technical change in an organization depend on the capabilities of the technology used, why it is used, and how work is organized around it.

The central issue is management *choice*, of:

- Technical design and layout;
- Objectives;
- Work organization.

We are not looking at "technological implications" as such. We are instead looking at the implications of managerial choices. Technical change simply acts as a *trigger* to processes of management decision making.

What?: the capabilities of computing technologies

New technologies have new capabilities that open up new areas of management choice, for products, processes and for organizational arrangements. The capabilities of a new technology are *enabling characteristics*. They do not on their own "determine" organization functions or structures. So computerized controls in biscuit making enable operators to control the process more effectively, and also enable management to distance operators from the process. Word processing facilitated the reorganization of typists into centres, but did not determine this arrangement. Technology has no impact on people or performance independent of the purposes of those who would use it and the responses of those who have to operate it. The technological imperatives are weak; the choices are vital.

New technologies open up new choices . . .

"An automatic system of machinery opens up the possibility of the true control over a highly productive factory by a relatively small corps of workers, providing these workers attain the level of mastery over the machinery offered by engineering knowledge, and providing they then share out among themselves the routines of the operation, from the technically advanced to the most routine."

From H. Braverman, *Labour and Monopoly Capital*, Monthly Review Press, New York, 1974, p. 230.

Why?: management objectives

We have had to challenge the assumption that new technologies are introduced only to combat the pressures of competition. Technical change is undertaken for a variety of motives which may reflect the career aspirations of individual managers as well as the overall goals of the organization. In the Scottish studies, managers spoke about three types of objectives behind the introduction of computing technologies:

Strategic objectives. These are external, economic, customer orientated objectives, such as the desires to increase capacity to meet increasing demand, give better delivery, be leaders in the use of new technology to attract customers, and improve quality and price to meet competition.

Operating objectives. These are internal, technical, performance orientated objectives, such as the desires to reduce production costs, replace obsolescent equipment, overcome bottlenecks in production, control energy use and cut other plant running costs, and reduce numbers and costs of support staffs. These operating objectives are clearly related to strategic objectives.

Control objectives. These objectives included the desires of managers to:

- Reduce human intervention;
- Replace people with machines;
- Reduce dependence on human control of equipment and processes;
- Reduce uncertainty, increase reliability, predictability, consistency and order in production operations;
- Increase the amount of performance information and the speed at which it is generated.

Control objectives concern reduction of human intervention . . .

" . . . the remarkable development of machinery becomes, for most of the working population, the source not of freedom but of enslavement, not of mastery but of helplessness, and not of the broadening of the horizon of labour but of the confinement of the worker within a blind round of servile duties in which the machine appears as the embodiment of science and the worker as little or nothing."

From H. Braverman, *Labour and Monopoly Capital*, Monthly Review Press, New York, 1974, p. 195.

How?: the organization of work

We have had to challenge the assumption that the logic of technology precludes organizational choice by determining the division and control of labour in an organization. The choice of forms of work organization that may accompany a given technology is wide.

Managers are preoccupied with control objectives . . .

" . . . engineers and managers share a design philosophy of producing machinery which eliminates as far as possible the 'human factor', in order to achieve the regularity and predictability that managers regard as necessary for profitable operation."

From S. Hill, *Competition and Control at Work*, 1981, Heinemann, p. 113.

The assumptions that managers seem to make about people and technology emphasize the need for more control by machine and less human intervention. This preoccupation may be because machines, even computers, are more easily understood than people. But even where human skills are made redundant, people are still required to carry out some tasks.

The problem is that discretion, skill and motivation go hand in hand. The pursuit of control objectives can lead to the design of forms of work

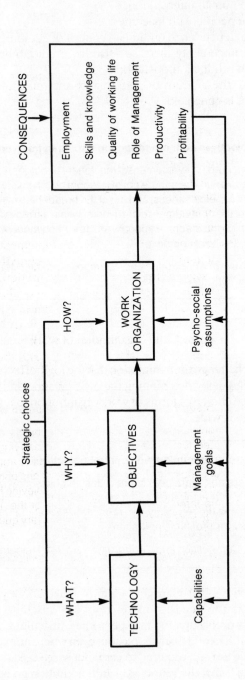

Figure 14.2: Technical change: the management decision making process

Based on David A. Buchanan, "Technological imperatives and strategic choice", in G. Winch (ed), *Information Technology in Manufacturing Processes: Case Studies in Technical Change*, Rossendale, London, 1983.

organization that eliminate discretion and thus give operators neither the skills nor the motivation to perform their functions effectively. Control objectives are therefore not necessarily consistent with strategic and operating objectives.

The theme of management control is dealt with separately and in more detail in Part 5.

The consequences — the future

It seems that the "popular image" of computers taking over the world of work is not an accurate one. There are several reasons why this is not likely to happen, and if it does, it is not going to happen very quickly. You should by this point know what those reasons are, and also be in a position to recognize and take issue with those who insist on arguing from a "technological determinist" perspective.

Computing technologies are however likely to shift the emphasis away from manual skills in work to information processing and problem solving skills. But this depends on recognition of the *complementarity* between the technology and the people who operate it. This complementarity thus needs to be taken into account in the organization of work around the technology.

But the research suggests that human and organizational implications are often disregarded or their importance underestimated, although they have a significant effect on the degree of success of technical change. The organizational choices that accompany applications of new technology are rarely recognized and evaluated. Physical layouts and organizational structures created by past decisions tend to be taken as given and the possibilities and opportunities of new arrangements are not explored.

Impact of technology ? It all depends on what you do with it . . .

"Technology is only a *means*, it is a piece of machinery or equipment with an associated technique which is used for carrying out certain tasks. Developments in technology may have massive implications for individuals and for society at large. Those implications only arise when people choose to adopt them and apply them to achieving human ends. Technology is no force in its own right. To talk of the 'iron hand of technology' . . . is to avoid the important and necessary question of who is applying technology and *to what ends*."

From T.J. Watson, *Sociology, Work and Industry*, Routledge and Kegan Paul, London, 1980, p. 77.

SOURCES

Bainbridge, L, 1978, "The process controller", in W. T. S. Singleton (ed), *The Study of Real Skills, Volume 1: The analysis of practical skills*, MTP Press, Lancaster, pp. 236-63.

Barron, I. and Curnow, R., 1979, *The Future With Microelectronics*, Frances Pinter, London.

Blauner, R., 1964, *Alienation and Freedom: The Factory Worker and his Industry*, The University of Chicago Press, Chicago.

Braverman, H., 1974, *Labour and Monopoly Capital: The Degradation of Work in the Twentieth Century*, Monthly Review Press, New York.

Buchanan, D. A., 1979, *The Development of Job Design Theories and Techniques*, Saxon House, Farnborough.

Buchanan, D. A., 1982, "Using the new technology: management objectives and organizational choices", *European Management Journal*, vol. 1, no. 2, 70-9.

Buchanan, D. A., 1983, "Technological imperatives and strategic choice", in G. Winch (ed), *Information Technology in Manufacturing Processes: Case Studies in Technical Change*, Rossendale, London.

Buchanan, D. A. and Boddy, D., 1982, "Advanced technology and the quality of working life: the effects of word processing on video typists", *Journal of Occupational Psychology*, vol. 55, no. 1, pp. 1-11.

Buchanan, D. A. and Boddy, D., 1983, "Advanced technology and the quality of working life: the effects of computerized controls on biscuit-making operators", *Journal of Occupational Psychology*, vol. 56, no. 2, pp. 109-19.

Buchanan, D. A. and Boddy, D., 1983, *Organizations in the Computer Age: Technological Imperatives and Strategic Choice*, Gower Publishing Company, Aldershot.

Cruikshank, P. J., 1982, "Patient stress and the computer in the consulting room", *Social Science and Medicine*, vol. 16, no. 14, pp. 1371-6.

Davis, L. E., 1976, "Developments in job design", in P. Warr (ed), *Personal Goals and Work Design*, John Wiley, New York, pp. 67-80.

Davis, L. E., 1977, "Evolving alternative organization designs: Their sociotechnical bases", *Human Relations*, vol. 30, no. 3, pp. 261-73.

Davis, L. E. and Taylor, J. C., 1975, "Technology effects on job, work, and organizational structure: a contingency view", in L. E. Davis and A. B. Cherns (eds), *The Quality of Working Life: Problems, Prospects and the State of the Art*, The Free Press, New York, pp. 220-41.

Davis, L. E. and Taylor, J. C., 1976, "Technology, organization and job structure", in R. Dubin (ed), *Handbook of Work, Organization and Society*, Rand McNally, Chicago, pp. 379-419.

Dickson, D., 1974, *Alternative Technology and the Politics of Technical Change*, Fontana/Collins, London.

Gallie, D., 1978, *In Search of the New Working Class: Automation and Social Integration Within the Capitalist Enterprise*, Cambridge University Press, Cambridge.

Herbst, P. G., 1974, *Socio-technical design: Strategies in Multi-disciplinary Research*, Tavistock Publications, London.

Landeweerd, J. A., 1979, "Internal representation of a process, fault diagnosis and fault correction", *Ergonomics*, vol. 22, no. 12, pp. 1343-51.

Maddock, I., 1978, 'Beyond the protestant ethic', *New Scientist*, vol. 80, no. 1130, pp. 592-5.

Nichols, T. and Beynon, H., 1977, *Living with Capitalism: Class Relations and the Modern Factory*, Routledge and Kegan Paul, London.

Paternotte, P. H., 1978, "The control performance of operators controlling a continuous distillation process", *Ergonomics*, vol. 21, no. 9, pp. 671-9.

Singleton, W.T., 1974, *Man – Machine Systems*, Penguin Books, Harmondsworth.

Singleton, W. T., 1979, *The Study of Real Skills, Volume 2: Compliance and Excellence*, MTP Press, Lancaster.

Sleigh, J., Boatwright, B., Irwin, P. and Stanyon, R., 1979, *The Manpower Implications of Micro-Electronic Technology*, Department of Employment, HMSO, London.

Umbers, I. G., 1979, "A study of the control skills of gas grid control engineers", *Ergonomics*, vol. 22, no. 5, pp. 557-71.

Vine, D. R. and Price, F. C., 1977, "Automated hot strip mill operation: a human factors study", *Iron and Steel International*, vol. 50, no. 2, pp. 95-101.

Teaching materials to support this chapter

"Fifty Years On" is a teaching package which illustrates the impact of mechanization, computerization and microprocessor technology on the production process and its operators. The programme is set in a biscuit making factory and examines the technical changes that have taken place over the last fifty years. The programme contains a video tape, case notes and supporting materials.

"Fifty Years On" is available from the Centre for Staff Development in Higher Education, 55 Gordon Square, London, WC1H 0NU (01-636 1500 ext 489).

PART 4

STRUCTURAL INFLUENCES ON BEHAVIOUR

Overview

A man enters a doctors surgery smoking. He reads the no smoking sign, and extinguishes his cigarette. A woman feels she has been underpaid, and fills in a DX 218 form and hands it in at the wages office in the factory. The "No Smoking" sign and the DX 281 form are both examples of aspects of an organization's structure. They are important because they direct the behaviour of people in certain directions and away from others. In the first case, the man adhered to the rule established by the doctor and changed his behaviour by ceasing to smoke. In the second example, the woman had a number of ways in which to voice her grievance but chose to follow the procedure established by mangement through which such issues were dealt. The use of rules and procedures acts to guide organizational members' behaviours in certain directions and thus helps to control it and make it predictable. Other structural devices do the same. For example, payment systems, physical objects, physical layout and technical systems. In the previous sections it was noted that people's behaviour in organizations can only partly be explained by their personal characteristics. The organizational situations in which they work also play a part. One can summarize this by saying;

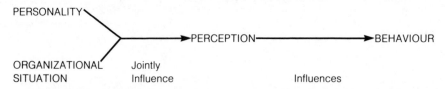

PERSONALITY

ORGANIZATIONAL SITUATION   Jointly Influence   PERCEPTION   Influences   BEHAVIOUR

Social scientists now generally agree that human behaviour is not solely, or even predominantly determined by psychological attributes such as personality, learning, motivation or perception. The organizational situation has to be taken into account. It is the way in which that situation is perceived, based on the person's personality, that leads to him acting in certain ways. In the previous section we examined one important aspect of the organizational situation, technology. In this section we shall turn our attention to another crucial one, the organizational structure. It will be seen that these are related.

Charles Perrow (1971, p. 176) has argued that it is possible for designers of organizations to consciously change the behaviour of people in an organization by changing its organizational structure:

> ". . . there is enormous potential in organizations for a direct attack on behaviour, without intermediate efforts to alter attitudes or personalities. It is possible to control reward structure (in particular the kind of behaviour that receives positive rewards)."

The way in which an organization is structured, that is, how its bits are assembled, does not affect what satisfactions members obtain from their jobs and what behaviours they exhibit. In the first chapter, the elements of structure will be outlined and defined, and the questions regarding organizational design considered. The three subsequent chapters describe and evaluate some of the answers proposed by different writers.

Chapter 15

Organization Structure

Defining organizational structure
Types of jobs
Types of structural relationships
Designing organizational structure
Operating mechanisms

Henri Fayol
(1841-1925)

Mary Parker Follett
(1865-1933)

Key concepts:

Once you have fully understood this chapter, you should be able to define the following concepts in your own words:

Organizational structure	Job specialization
Basic structure	Organization chart
Operating mechanisms	Line, staff and functional relationships
Job description	Authority
Hierarchy	Reward system
Span-of-control	Responsibility

Objectives:

On completing this chapter, you should be able to:

1. Explain the influence which organizational structure has on the behaviour of people in an organization.
2. List the main elements of organizational structure.
3. Distinguish between job specialization and job definition.
4. Relate the concept of span-of-control to the shape of the organizational hierarchy.
5. Identify line, staff and functional relationships on an organizational chart.
6. Describe five different criteria on which jobs might be grouped in an organization.

DEFINING ORGANIZATIONAL STRUCTURE

At the start of the book, organization was defined as a goal orientated system seeking effectiveness and efficiency. One aspect of this view is that those designing and managing organizations need to control the activities within them, including the behaviour of members. John Child (1984, p. 4) stressed this point:

> "The allocation of responsibilities, the grouping of functions, decision-making, co-ordination, control and reward — all these are fundamental requirements for the continued operation of an organization. The quality of an organization's structure will affect how well these requirements are met".

STOP!

The objective of organizational structure appears to differ depending on whether one is designing and managing it, or being managed within it. Compare Peter Drucker's definition with the one that follows it:

"Structure is a means for attaining the objectives and goals of an organization."

From Peter Drucker, "New templates for today's organizations", in *Harvard Business Review*, January-February, 1974, p. 52.

"... the extent to which and the ways in which organization members are constrained and controlled by the organization and the distribution of activities and responsibilities and the organizational procedures and regulations".

From DT 352, *People in Organizations: Course Book*, Open University Press, 1974, p.61.

These two statements refer to the perceived purpose of organizational structure. In what ways do they differ?

If one is seeking a definition of organizational structure, one can usefully go back to the work of Derek Pugh and David Hickson (1968, pp. 374-96) who, in addition to defining the term, also highlight the possibility of having different structural arrangements:

> "All organizations have to make provision for continuing activities directed towards the achievement of aims. Regularities in activities such as task allocation, supervision and co-ordination are developed. Such regularities constitute the organization's structure, and the fact that these activities can be arranged in various ways means that organizations can have differing structures."

Sociologists claim that people's attitudes are shaped as much by the organizations in which they work as by their pre-existing personality variables.

The constraints and demands of the job can dictate their behaviour. For this reason, it is impossible to explain the behaviour of people in organizations solely in terms of individual or group characteristics. Alan Fox (1966) has argued that, in seeking to make such explanations, "the structural determinants of behaviour be included".

It is not just a question of changing people's attitudes and behaviour by changing the structure of the organization in which they work. Transferring people from one part of the company or hospital to another involves moving them from one structural situation to another. Transferring a lecturer from the business studies department of a college to the management studies department, or a sales manager from headquarters to the regional office can change his behaviour. The changes may be more to do with the organizational setting in which he now operates, for example, the methods used, the type of communication system in operation, and the method of judging performance and so on, than any particular characteristic of the person himself.

Fox's description stresses an important element in the structural view of organizations. He argues that attention should be paid to the roles that people play, and not just to the personalities in these roles. The emphasis is on the structures in which the roles are played, and he criticizes analyses which do not take this dimension into account.

Structural determinants of behaviour at work

"... the failure lies in the popular tendency amongst managers and the general public to exaggerate the importance of personalities, personal relationships, and personal leadership as determinants of behaviour. This often results in the wrong kinds of questions being asked and the wrong kinds of remedies being proposed ... The so-called 'Human Relations' movement, in its more naïve and simplified forms, could be taken to imply that the 'social skills' — or lack of them — of managers and supervisors were the main determinants of how subordinates behaved at work. Such views were highly acceptable to 'common-sense', which is ever ready in this field to seek explanations in terms of personalities and personal relationships ... The presumption thus created is that in any situation of difficulty, the way out lies through those involved choosing or being compelled to 'change their attitudes', or making a resolve to ensure that the situation works better in future, or exercising more 'inspired leadership' of a personal kind ... the industrial behaviour of individuals and the relations between them are shaped not only by their being the sort of people they are, but also by the technology with which they work, the structure of authority, communication and status within which they are located, the system of punishments, rewards and other management controls to which they are subjected, and the various other aspects of 'the structure of the situation.'"

From Alan Fox, *Industrial Sociology and Industrial Relations*, Royal

Commission on Trade Unions and Employers Associations, Research Papers 3, London, H.M.S.O., 1966, p. 15.

There is a danger of taking the structural perspective to the extreme and ignoring the human element altogether. In this view, individuals are seen as playing only a minor role. Some authors, while acknowledging that it is people who do the work, consider them as incidental. They are a taken-for-granted element in the organization puzzle and are viewed as expendable, replaceable, interchangeable and generally capable of being fitted into the organizational scheme as required. Therefore, the structural view of organizations stresses the logical and rational elements, and de-emphasises people's preferences or feelings. If organizational efficiency and effectiveness are to be achieved, the structuralists argue, then people need to adopt organizational plans as their own, and adapt to them if necessary.

Some social scientists, particularly those who have become involved in management training and development, operate at the other end of the spectrum, and ignore the structural aspects of organizations preferring instead to focus on individual and group characteristics. Tom Lupton (1978, p. 129) has argued that what some social scientists and management writers were saying was that:

> "... with a few weak caveats, ... it is universally the case in organizations that improvements in productivity, economic performance and personal satisfaction with work arise from changes in the context of interpersonal relationships in which individuals work whatever the context of size, product or client environment, form of ownership, location, cultural or social setting, technology, etc. The degree of dogmatism with which this proposition is asserted varies from writer to writer, but one is justified in describing the position of all of them as psychological universalist."

STOP!

Consider the behaviour of your organizational behaviour lecturer.

Identify aspects of their behaviour which you like and do not like.

Decide if these positive and negative behaviours are influenced by that person's personality or the organizational structure in which they work?

Elements of organizational structure

Jay Lorsch (1970) and John Child (1984) make a useful distinction between two aspects of an organization's structure, its Basic Structure and its Operating Mechanisms. Each aspect contains its own group of elements.

Basic Structure (intended to signal the behaviour expected of organizational members)

Concerned with	Involves	Exemplified in
How the work of the organization is divided and assigned to individuals, groups, and departments	Allocating tasks and responsibilities to individuals (e.g. how much choice they have about how they work)	Organization chart Job descriptions Establishing boards committees and working parties
How the required co-ordination is achieved	Specifying and defining jobs Designing the formal reporting relationships Deciding on the number of levels in the hierarchy Deciding on the span-of-control of each supervisor and manager	

Operating Mechanisms (To indicate to individuals in greater detail what is expected of them, to motivate them).

Specifying expected behaviour in greater detail Motivating members	Delegating authority and monitoring its use Providing a control system for objective setting, monitoring and motivating	Control procedures (budgetary accounting financial systems) Information system Staff appraisal Training and development
Attempting to ensure they strive towards organizational goals		Rules and procedures Operating procedures Planning procedures Spatial arrangements in Office or factory

A useful framework suggests that organizations can be viewed as complex systems which consist of five mutually interacting independent classes of variables: organizational objective, technology, structure, people and environment.

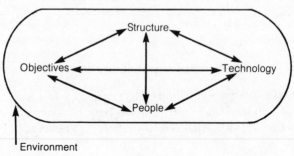

The variation in organizational structure can be accounted for by the interactions of these elements as will be shown later. Which features of the organizational structure are affected by these elements?

TYPES OF JOBS

Job specialization

An important series of decisions on organizational design relate to what types of jobs should be created. How narrow and specialized should these be? How should the work be divided and what should be the appropriate content of each person's job. The detailed answer will of course depend on the type of job considered. Is it the job of a nurse, engineer, car assembly worker, teacher or politician that is being designed? Certain general principles need to guide the design. Decisions here relate to the issue of *specialization* by which is meant the narrowing of the work to be done by the individual.

Specialization is a feature of both knowledge jobs and of manual or clerical jobs. After their general training doctors become paediatricians, while on the assembly line some workers fit car tyres while others fit on the doors. The choice concerning the extent and type of specialization depend on criteria used by the organizational designer. These in turn will be affected by his values, beliefs and preferences. It may be a case of trading off efficiency of production against job satisfaction. A value position might be to seek to maximize both elements.

Job definition

A second major question concerns how well-defined jobs ought to be? There is a school of thought which will be discussed in the next two chapters which argues that newly-appointed staff ought to know exactly what their duties are in detail. They suggest that this high degree of definition (or *specification*) helps to motivate employees by letting them know exactly what is expected of them. Such detail can also assist in the appraising of their past performance. Others believe that far from being motivating, a high level of job definition acts to control people's behaviour and sets minimum performance standards. What is needed instead, they say, is for the employee to create his own job. In practice, detailed job definition is applied to low level manual and clerical jobs while at more senior levels there is a greater degree of own job making. The physical manifestation of the choice about how much to define the job is the piece of paper on which is written the job description. Rosemary Stewart (1973) suggested that a job description will usually contain the following information:

- Job title and the department in which it is located;

- Job holder's position in the hierarchy;
- To whom the job holder is responsible;
- The objectives of the job;
- Duties required of the job holder (regular, periodical and optional);
- Responsibility — the number of persons supervised or the degree of judgement required for the process;
- Liaison with other workers, staff, supervisors, and managers.

The specialization of work activities and the consequent division of labour is a feature of all large complex organizations. Once tasks have been broken down (or "differentiated") into subtasks, these are allocated to individuals in the form of jobs. Persons carrying out the jobs occupy positions on the organization's hierarchy. Particular levels of responsibility and authority are allocated to these positions. The division of labour and the relationship of one position to another is reflected in the organizational chart which can act as a guide to explain how the work of different people in the organization is co-ordinated and integrated.

Part of a job description for a hospital catering manager

TITLE: Catering Manager

GRADE: 10

RESPONSIBLE TO: District Catering Manager

OBJECTIVES: To ensure the efficient management of all catering services for patients and staff at the hospital

DUTIES: Monitor and issue food to all departments

Organize and monitor kitchen work

Recruit and train catering staff

Menu planning within the framework of district policy

RESPONSIBILITIES: Responsible for the supervision of ten cooks

LIAISON WITH: Hospital administrator, Senior Nursing Officer and other Heads of Department on day-to-day matters

Environmental Health Officer to maintain a high standard of hygiene and to ensure standards in accordance with the Health and Safety at Work Act.

Once specified and defined, the jobs and the authority and responsibility relations between them are represented on an organizational chart such as the one shown below.

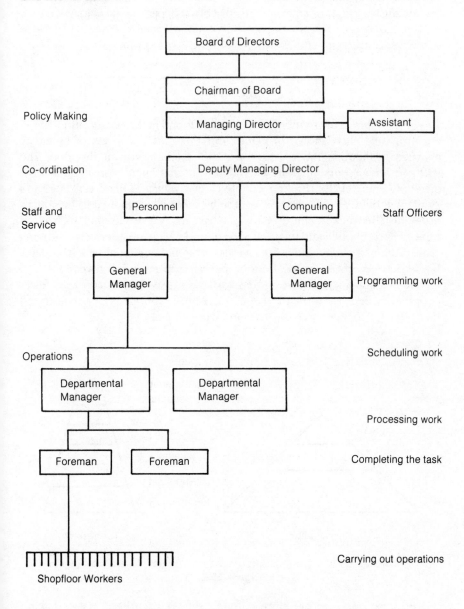

Figure 15.1 Organizational Chart

An examination of Figure 15.1 can help to explain and clarify some of the basic concepts associated with organizational structure.

Span of control

From the organizational chart, it can be seen that the foreman's span of control is twenty-one shopfloor operatives while that of the departmental manager is two.

Span of control refers to the number of subordinates who report to a single supervisor or manager and for whose work he is responsible.

Hierarchy

Hierarchy refers to the number of levels to be found in the organization. In the organizational chart shown in Figure 15.1 there are six levels of hierarchy between the Board members at the top and the operatives on the shopfloor. The staff and service personnel are excluded from this calculation because only direct or "line" relationships are counted. The distinction between "line" and "staff" will be dealt with shortly. For the moment it is sufficient to be able to distinguish between organizations which have many levels or tiers, such as the Armed Forces, police and the Civil Service, and which are referred to as being "tall" in their hierarchy, and organizations with a "flat" hierarchy which have few levels between those at the bottom and the top such as universities. Flat hierarchies are distinctive, not necessarily because they incorporate fewer people, but because the typical span of control is much wider than in tall hierarchies. The difference is shown in Figure 15.2.

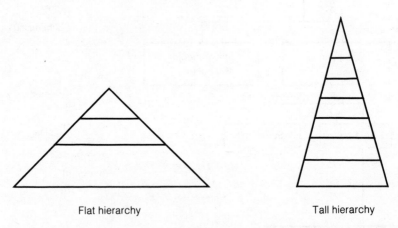

Flat hierarchy   Tall hierarchy

Figure 15.2

Because resources are always limited, they restrict the decision-making process. Because of this, some managers in an organization are given authority to control more resources than others. For this reason, the managers who occupy a position lower down the hierarchy are forced to integrate their actions with those above them by having to ask their bosses to approve some of their actions. In this way, managerial control is exercised from the top of the organizational hierarchy downwards.

The concepts of span of control and hierarchy are closely related. The greater the span of control, the poorer will be the contact between members between each of the levels. A foreman responsible for twenty-one workers will have less contact with each operative than if he was responsible for only ten. However, this broad span of control means that there will be fewer levels in the hierarchy and thus a flatter organizational structure. A narrow span of control, e.g. one foreman to ten workers, will tend to improve contact and communication between levels. Increasing the number of levels in the hierarchy (making the organization "taller") offers more rungs in the promotion ladder.

Although flat hierarchies imply a broader span of control and fewer promotion opportunities, they also force managers to delegate their work effectively if they are not to be faced with an intolerable workload. Evidence suggests that individuals with high self-actualization needs prefer flat hierarchies, while those who emphasize security tend to gravitate towards tall hierarchies. Hierarchy is a co-ordinating and integrating device intended to bring together the activities of individuals, groups and departments which were previously separated by the division of labour and function.

Organizational charts

"Now, obviously, to know who is to do what and to establish authority and responsibility within an institution are the basic first principles of a good administration, but this is a far cry from handing down immutable tablets of stone from the mountaintop. Not even the Ten Commandments undertook to do more than establish general guidelines of conduct. They contained no fine print and no explanatory notes. Even the Almighty expected us to use our own good judgement in carrying them out . . ."

From C. Randell, *The Folklore of Management*, Boston: Atlantic-Little, Brown, 1962, pp. 24-5.

TYPES OF STRUCTURAL RELATIONSHIPS

As organizations become larger and more complex, tasks such as recruiting staff, training them, keeping accounts and paying wages, providing technical assistance and so on cannot be performed by those who either manufacture the product or who offer the service. Special individuals may be engaged to provide such services or advice. These are referred to as *staff specialists* in an organization. Where a number of them are recruited, such as a number concerned with advising on industrial relations matters, these may be designated as a staff department. Because these people offer a service to those engaged in production, they are also referred to as *service departments*. It is this which leads to the distinction between line and staff relationships within an organization. Before elaborating on the differences between these types of relationships, it is important to define the concepts of *authority* and *responsibility* which have been introduced into this section and which will be further used here.

Definitions

"*Authority* is a form of power which orders the actions of others through commands which are effective because those who are commanded regard the commands as legitimate".

From G. Duncan Mitchell (ed), *A Dictionary of Sociology,* Routledge and Kegan Paul, London, 1968, p. 14.

Responsibility is an obligation placed on a person who occupies a certain position.

Line relationship

These are the relationships which exist between a senior and a subordinate. Between a person who has *authority* and anyone who has a *responsibility* directly to that person. A person at one point in the line has the authority to direct the activities of those in positions below it on the *same* line. Thus in the organizational chart shown in, Figure 15.1 the General Manager has the authority to direct the activities of the Departmental Managers below him on the same line. He in turn, can be directed by the Deputy Managing Director above him. All these people are in line relationships with each other.

Staff relationship

Individuals may offer specialist advice to others on certain technical matters. The person concerned may be an "assistant to" a manager appointed to assist with the workload of a superior. He has no authority of his own, but acts in the name of his superior and on his authority. Thus the Managing Director in the chart in Figure 15.1 has such an assistant. Alternatively, an individual may be appointed to offer specialist information on, computing or industrial relations, to managers in the line structure, but without the authority to insist that such advice is taken. Thus in the chart, financial staff may only be able to offer such advice. Because these staff are not in a line relationship, they do not constitute a level in the hierarchy.

Functional relationship

A third type of relationship exists when a specialist is designated to provide a service which the line manager is compelled to accept. The specialist's authority comes by delegation from a common superior. The General Manager in the chart may decide that rather than have each piece of advice from the financial staff cleared through him for onward transmission to his Departmental Managers, the finance person can issue an instruction directly to the Departmental Manager. The functional specialist concerned remains accountable to the boss in whose name he issues the instructions. If the manager requires *functional assistance* to be given to his subordinates in some area such as training, the manager concerned would have to delegate some of his own authority to the functional specialist concerned, and the organizational chart will look like this,

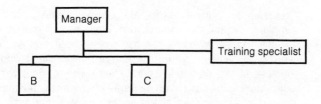

Departments such as technical, personnel and training in an organization tend to use this structure of functional authority.

STOP!

In Figure 1, does the assistant have the authority over and responsibility for the work of B and C? In Figure 2, is it the manager or the assistant who exercises authority over B and C?

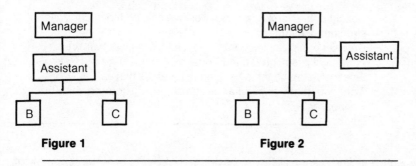

Figure 1   **Figure 2**

Authority relationship

The organizational chart shows the formal relationships which exist between

positions or offices in an organization. The chart there indicates *positional authority*, i.e. the authority to direct the activities of persons below in the line relationship based on the position which one occupies. Formal authority in an organization is assigned to positions and not people. The Private in the army salutes the office of the Lieutenant, not the man personally, since that man can change. Positional authority is distributed hierarchically in that persons occupying positions at upper levels in the organization have more power and exercise more control than those at successively lower levels. One of the functions of hierarchical authority is to provide predictability. Its exercise increases the probability of orderly, regular institutionalized behaviour.

The organization of a professional football team

Professional football teams are business enterprises that use a simplified organizational structure. While not all football teams follow exactly the same pattern, most professional teams are owned by wealthy individuals (some of whom are millionaires) who enjoy being involved in this particular sport. Their owner(s) usually makes major policy decisions, but a hired manager oversees the business side of the operation — such as ticket sales, travel, contracts for facilities, equipment, vendors and personnel matters. The manager usually has responsibility for player/personnel decisions — as in trades, drafts of new players, and assignment of personnel to minor leagues. The field manager or head coach is in charge of the team's actual performance. This person assists the manager in matters concerning players. In some cases the manager is also the field manager. Other personnel employed by professional teams include team physicians, scouts and ticket sales personnel.

Questions

1. Describe the strengths and weaknesses of the organization structure of a professional football team.
2. Draw an organizational chart for a professional football team.
3. What conflicts might an individual experience if he were simultaneously a manager, a field manager and a player.
4. Can you think of similar organization structures in other businesses?

Authority and responsibility were defined earlier in this chapter. Authority relationships can be traced on an organizational chart by following the lines of an organizational chart *downwards*. Responsibility relationships can be traced by following those same lines *upwards*. It is now appropriate to introduce a third related concept, that of *accountability*.

Accountability

Difficulties may arise when an individual has responsibility for some work but lacks the concomitant authority. For example, the foreman may be held responsible for the punctuality of his workers but is not given the authority to discipline them over latecoming. The converse of this situation may also cause difficulties when a person is empowered to take decisions but is not held responsible for what results, for example, recruitment decisions taken by personnel specialists in some companies.

Definition

Accountability is the subordinate's acceptance of a given task to perform because he or she is a member of the organization. It requires that person to report on his or her discharge of responsibilities.

STOP!

Explain the differences and relationships between the concepts of responsibility, authority and accountability.

There are other bases of authority, other than position. Charismatic authority, based on the personality characteristics and reputation of the individual, and sapiential authority, based on the wisdom and knowledge displayed by an individual. In contrast referent authority is that authority which is delegated by a superior to a junior.

Society without authority

A hierarchy of authority as a way of distributing power among people is not a universal human phenomenon. It was found that the Central Algonkin Indians of North America, neither had one nor appeared to have needed one. Miller reported two accounts of how authority was delegated amongst them. The first account comes from Nicholas Perrot, a French fur trader:

"Subordination is not a maxim among these savages; the savage does not know what it is to obey. . . . It is more necessary to entreat him than to command him. . . . The father does not venture to exercise authority over his son, nor does the chief dare give commands to his soldier . . . if anyone is stubborn in regard to some proposed movement, it is necessary to flatter him in order to dissuade him, otherwise he will go further in his opposition. . . ."

From W. B. Miller, "Two Concepts of Authority", *The American Anthropoligist*, vol. 57, April, 1955, p. 271.

STOP!

Start with your own position in the organization, institution or college. Indicate the different levels of authority above you and the levels below you for which you are responsible.

Add in any other relationships (staff or functional) which clarify your position.

DESIGNING ORGANIZATIONAL STRUCTURE

There are many different types of organizations. They include businesses, trade unions, hospitals, schools and local authorities. All of these have a purpose and hence a policy. Those who design them, or change their design, can be seen as attempting to translate that policy into practices, duties and functions which are allocated as specific tasks to individuals and groups. As Derek Pugh and David Hickson (1968) pointed out at the start of this chapter, different organizations will have different structures. These represent goals and policies. The structure that emerges results from the choices made about the division and grouping of tasks into functions, sections and divisions.

Grouping jobs

Having decided on the degree of job specialization and job definition, there is the need to group them into sections, place the sections into units, locate the units within departments and co-ordinate the departments. Thus job grouping or the "departmentalization of jobs" constitutes a second major area of organizational design. Jobs can be grouped on several criteria. For example, by:

Product or service (e.g. car, insurance)
Educational institutions are structured on the basis of the service. Thus all lecturers teaching management are located in the management department.

Functions (e.g. finance, production, sales)
Grouping of jobs based on the function which they perform. For example, the jobs in a manufacturing organization will be grouped according to production, marketing, sales, finance and so on. In a hospital grouping will be physiotherapy, nursing, medical physics.

Customers (e.g. retail, wholesale)
Separate groups organized for different types of customers. Sales departments that sell in different markets.

Place/Territory (e.g. Northern England, Scotland)
Geographical grouping may be used where the service is most economically provided by a limited distance.

Time (e.g. shift, non-shift)
Hospitals and factories offering a 24 hour service or producing round the clock will have different groups for different shifts.

Technology Used (e.g. small batch, mass production, process)
The type of technology employed can be a criterion especially when several different types are used in a single plant.

An organizational chart shows which type of grouping has been adopted. Usually an organization will use not one but a mixture of groupings.

Function-based organizational structure

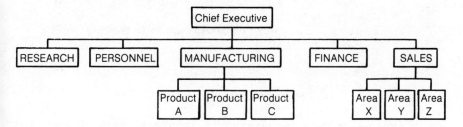

Product-based organizational structure

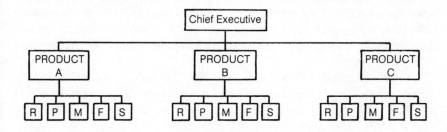

Geography-based organizational structure

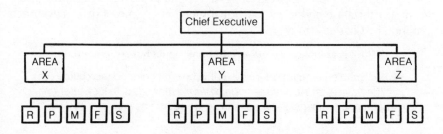

OPERATING MECHANISMS

Up to now the basic structure of an organization has been examined. Attention will now turn to the operating mechanisms which complement and reinforce that basic structure. These mechanisms seek to structure further the behaviour of individuals and motivate them towards the organizational goals. Two mechanisms will be examined briefly — staff appraisal and training. If this were a management textbook it would be unlikely that these topics would be considered under the heading of organizational structure.

STOP!

Read over the definitions of organizational structure presented at the start of this chapter.

(a)   Consider whether or not it is appropriate to consider staff appraisal and training under the heading of organizational structure. Give your reasons for your viewpoint.

(b)   Explain why management textbooks might avoid dealing with this topic under this heading.

Staff appraisal and training

A staff appraisal scheme is a procedure whereby every boss in an organization discusses the work of all his subordinates. He sees each person individually and considers the progress that they have been making in their job, their personal strengths and weaknesses, and whether they may need further training. Not all companies have such a formal system, although most of the larger employers have some version of it. Staff appraisal schemes differ between organizations in their detail although all contain the central idea of a meeting between a boss and his subordinates.

Graeme Salaman (1978) has argued that, "behind the claimed common-sense of modern appraisal schemes lurk a number of assumptions about organizational structure and functioning". His fundamental criticism is that both staff appraisal and management development schemes accept the organizational structure as fixed and unchangeable, and that an individual should change, or be made to change, in order to fit in with such a structure. In the management literature, the benefits of staff appraisal are held to accrue equally to the organization and to its individual members. Some of these have been outlined by Charles Handy (1975):

"The organization needs a data bank on its human resources.

- To enable some broad-scale manpower planning to take place (of the nature 'do we have enough potential managers to look after our proposed expansion? If not should we recruit now or later?').

- To provide an objective and comparative base for promotion and transfer decisions.
- To allow some systematic planning to be done to give potential senior managers the right sort of developmental experiences.

The individual on his part has some complementary needs

- He needs feedback on his work. Man like nature abhors a vacuum. The architect can look at his building, the actor hear his audience, the farmer see his crops, the tradesman his takings, the doctor his satisfied patients. Only the corporate manager lacks feedback fed to the senses. For him some artificial mechanism must be created.
- He needs to see his work in context, have some idea of what is expected of him, how he will be judged, and where his goals are in that job.
- He will from time to time appreciate friendly counselling, in difficulties, in career decisions, in planning his own development, in working to improve his talents and modify his shortcomings."

From Charles Handy, "Organizational Influences on Appraisal", *Industrial and Commercial Training*, vol. 7, no. 8, 1975, pp. 326-7.

STOP!

Do you argee with Handy's views, especially as they refer to the individual?

Would you welcome this type of feedback on performance? Under what circumstances would you find it useful or harmful?

Salaman went on to suggest that appraisal schemes appeared to regard most, if not all of the problems an organization (as well as the successes it achieved), as being entirely the result of the personal qualities of the people who composed them. The psychological characteristics of individuals, their intelligence, motivation, communication skills, loyalty and flexibility were all stressed in both appraisal documents and appraisal interviews. In the same way he felt, interdepartmental relationships tended to be explained in terms of the personalities involved.

This "psychologistic" approach, i.e. explaining all behaviour solely in terms of individual characteristics without reference to contextual factors, was what Alan Fox (1966) had complained of when he argued for a "situationally-determined" analysis of organizational behaviour. Appraisal schemes are one of the operating mechanisms of an organizational structure. It is because they focus on an individual's behaviour that they emphasise its significance.

STOP!

Consider the following comments. What evidence, from research or from your own experience, would you produce to challenge the three ideas or assumptions presented below.

In short it is possible to see modern appraisal schemes as assuming three interrelated ideas:

- "That organizations are goal-oriented phenomena, within which, short of something going wrong, members, levels and departments work together co-operatively in the realisation of their inherent mutuality, interdependence and harmony.
- That variations in levels of performance are due to personnel or communication problems — people being unable, or unwilling, to see the benefits of commitment and co-operation — or people being unable or unwilling to understand, or perform their job responsibilities.
- That the structure of organizations — the way in which work and control are divided and distributed and then re-integrated and orchestrated — is something given by the nature of the organization —its goal and technologies merely the context within which appraisal is performed beyond choice politics or change."

From Graeme Salaman, "Management development and organization theory", *Journal of European Industrial Training*, 1978, vol. 2, no. 7, p. 8

From the perspective of those within the organizational structure who design such schemes (the personnel staff), those who are required to operate them (line management personnel) as well as those who prepare managers for their use (training department), the organization structure is perceived as given, as something which cannot be changed. Indeed their job definition may require them to operate such schemes successfully. Any appraisal scheme can only be understood within the organizational structure of which it is a part.

How can such appraisal schemes contribute to increasing the predictability of the behaviours of people, and thus warrant being included within the definition of organizational structure which is presented here? The appraisal process has been extensively researched and documented. It involves a rational approach which is based on the formal basic structure of the organization. The process usually involves:

- Clarifying a person's job (considering his job specification);
- Assessing competence (how well is the person doing in the job);
- Interviewing the individual concerned;
- Identifying and agreeing future goals and targets;
- Agreeing action points, e.g. listing training needs, altering job responsibilities.

The aim is to achieve efficiency based on rationality. It is grounded in the belief that feedback on past performance influences future performance, and that the process of isolating and rewarding good performance is likely to repeat it. The efficiency sought comes from both organizational planning that the appraisal scheme facilitates, and also from the control of members which comes from them agreeing to strive for certain organizational goals, knowing that they will be rewarded for doing so.

Management training and development can both be considered as socializing agents, although they are rarely viewed this way either by managers themselves or in the management literature. Having surmounted the recruitment hurdle, new organizational members are initiated to organizational values and practices through the induction training programme. They subsequently receive further inputs of training and development which the organization can choose to define as either rewards or punishments. Salaman argues that both training and appraisal aim to control and make predictable the behaviour of people in organizations.

CONCLUSION

In this chapter we have defined some of the key concepts that are used in the discussion of organizational structure. Two points are worth stressing First the creation of organizational structures, that is, "designing organizations", is a complex task. Those managers who have had to do it sought ideas, principles, guidelines and theories to help them. The following chapters will go on to consider and evaluate these. Second, the type of organizational structure that will be designed will vary, and will do so along the dimensions that were described and defined in this chapter. Figure 15.3 summarizes the characteristics of two very different types of organizational design which are labelled *organic* and *mechanistic.*

STOP!

Compare the list of organic and mechanistic organizational structures. Decide which organizations that you know of predominantly have one type of structure or the other.

Type of organization structure

Organizational Characteristics Index	Organic	Mechanistic
Span of control	wide	narrow
Number of levels of authority	few	many
Ratio of administrative to production personnel	high	low
Range of time span over which an employee can commit resources	long	short
Degree of centralization in decision making	low	high
Proportion of persons in one unit having opportunities to interact with persons in other units	high	low
Quantity of formal rules	low	high
Specificity of job goals	low	high
Specificity of required activities	low	high
Content of communications	advice and information	instruction and decisions
Range of compensation	narrow	wide
Range of skill levels	narrow	wide
Knowledge-based authority	high	low
Position-based authority	low	high

From Ralph M. Hower and Jay W. Lorsch, "Organizational inputs" in John A. Seiler (ed.) *Systems Analysis in Organizational Behaviour*, Richard D. Irwin and Dorsey Press, Homewood, Ill., 1967, p. 168.

Figure 15.3 Organizational characteristics of organic and mechanistic organizational structures

SOURCES

Child, J., 1984, *Organization: A Guide to Problems and Practice*, Harper and Row, London, 2nd edition.

Drucker, P. F., 1974 "New templates for today's organizations", *Harvard Business Review*, January – February, pp. 45-65.

Fox, A., 1966, *Industrial Sociology and Industrial Relations*, Royal Commission on Trade Unions and Employers Associations, Research Papers 3, HMSO, London.

Handy, C., 1975, "Organizational influences on appraisal", *Industrial and Commercial Training*, vol. 7, no. 8, pp. 326-30.

Hower, R. M. and Lorsch, J. W., 1967, "Organizational inputs" in John A. Seiler (ed.) *Systems Analysis in Organizational Behaviour*, Richard D. Irwin and Dorsey Press, Homewood, Ill.

Lorsch, J. W., 1970, "Introduction to the structural design of organizations" in G.W. Dalton. P. R. Lawrence and J. W. Lorsch (eds), *Organizational Structure and Design*, Richard Irwin Inc., Homewood, Ill.

Lupton, T., 1971, *Management and the Social Sciences*, Penguin Books, Harmondsworth, Middlesex.

Miller, W. B., 1955, "Two concepts of authority", *The American Anthropologist*, vol. 57, April, pp. 271-89.

Mitchell, G. D. (ed), 1968, *A Dictionary of Sociology*, Routledge and Kegan Paul, London.

Open University, 1974, "Structure and system: basic concepts and theories" in DT 352, *People and Organizations*, course book.

Perrow, C., 1971, *Organizational Analysis: A Sociological View*, Tavistock, London.

Pugh, D. S. and Hickson, D. J., 1968, "The comparative study of organizations" in D. Pym (ed.) *Industrial Society*, Penguin Books, Harmondsworth, Middlesex.

Randall, C.,1962, *The Folklore of Management*, Atlantic-Little Brown, Boston.

Salaman, G., 1974, "The management development movement", *Industrial Training International*, vol. 9, no. 10, pp. 319-22.

Salaman, G., 1978, "Management development and organizational theory", *Journal of European Industrial Training*, vol. 2, no. 7, pp. 7-11.

Stewart, R., 1973, *The Reality of Management*, Pan Books, London, 5th edition.

Chapter 16

Bureaucracy and roles

Max Weber (1864-1920)
Reproduced by permission of Leif Geiges

Key concepts:

Once you have fully understood this chapter, you should be able to define the following concepts in your own words:

Bureaucracy	Role
Charismatic authority	Role set
Traditional authority	Role expectation
Rational legal authority	Role conflict
Socialization	Focal person

Objectives:

On completing this chapter, you should be able to:

1. List the main questions which those designing organizational structures need to answer.
2. Distinguish between charismatic, traditional and legal-rational forms of authority.
3. State the main characteristics of a bureaucratic organization as specified by Max Weber.
4. Construct your own role set depicting yourself as the focal person.
5. Explain the different ways in which the concept of role is presented in the social science literature.
6. Following Argyris, give an example, from your own experience, of the way in which organizational structures affect personality development.

INTRODUCTION

This chapter will examine the development and characteristics of a form of organizational design called *bureaucracy.* Although bureaucracy is not the only form of organizational structure that is possible, in large, modern organizations it has tended to dominate. Since bureaucracy stresses the definition of roles and their relationships between one another, this chapter will also consider the concept of role in organizations. It should be emphasized that at the present time, there is an increasing questioning about the appropriateness of bureaucratic forms of organization to the needs and objectives of companies and individuals. These concerns are not just academic discussions conducted in textbooks. We are seeing experiments in new forms of organizational designs taking place in Britain and elsewhere.

ORGANIZATIONAL STRUCTURING

Anyone seeking to design an organization needs to make certain decisions about how it should be structured. Child (1984) identified five main questions which a designer of an organization needs to ask:

"1. Should jobs be broken down into narrow areas of work and responsibility, so as to secure the benefits of specialization? Or should the degree of specialization be kept to a minimum in order to simplify communication, and to offer members of the organization greater scope and responsibility in their work? Another choice arising in the design of jobs concerns the extent to which the responsibilities and methods attaching to them should be precisely defined.

2. Should the overall structure of an organizational be "tall" rather than "flat" in terms of its levels of management and spans of control? What are the implications for communication, motivation and overhead costs of moving towards one of these alternatives rather than the other?

3. Should jobs and departments be grouped together in a "functional" way according to the specialist expertise and interests that they share? Or should they be grouped according to the different services and products which are being offered, or the different geographical areas being served, or according to yet another criterion?

4. Is it appropriate to aim for an intensive form of integration between the different segments of an organization or not? What kind of integrative mechanisms are there to choose from?

5. What approach should a management take towards maintaining adequate control over work done? Should it centralize or delegate decisions, and all or only some of the decisions? Should a policy

of extensive formalization be adopted in which standing orders and written records are used for control purposes? Should work be subject to close supervision?"

From John Child, *Organization: A Guide to Problems and Practice*, Harper and Row, London, 1984, p. 8, second edition.

STOP!

Select one of the five issues raised above. With one or two fellow students, think about an organization which you all have had experience of, and discuss your views with each other.

BUREAUCRACY

Amongst the first writers to offer answers to these questions was a German sociologist called Max Weber. Weber did not invent the term *bureaucracy*. That distinction is often credited to a Frenchman, de Gournay (1712-59), who wrote that, "We have an illness in France which bids fair to play havoc with us; this illness is called "bureaumania" (Albrow, 1970, p. 16). However, it is to Weber that one goes when considering modern developments of the concept. His work, which was carried out at the turn of the nineteenth century, stemmed from his study of power and authority. In his view:

power was the ability to get things done by threats of force or sanction,

while,

authority was managing to get things done because one's orders were seen by others as justified or legitimate.

Taking a historical perspective, Weber studied earlier societies and was able to identify three different types of authority:

Traditional authority based on the belief that the ruler had a natural right to rule. This right was either God-given or by descent. The authority enjoyed by kings would be of this type.

Charismatic authority based on the belief that the ruler had some special, unique virtue, either religious or heroic. Hitler and the prophets had this.

Legal-Rational authority based on formal written rules which had the force of law. The authority of present day prime ministers, and college principals is of this type.

Because of the process of rationalization in modern society, the authority which predominates is of the legal-rational type. We obey and do what managers and civil servants tell us not because we think they have a natural right to do so or possess any divine powers, but because we acknowledge that they have a legal right.

Definition

Bureaucracy is the typical apparatus corresponding to the legal type of domination. It is also characterized by this belief in rules and the legal order.

From Nicos Mouzelis, *Bureaucracy and Organization*, Routledge and Kegan Paul, 1969, p. 17.

Weber's "Ideal Type" Bureaucracy

According to the German sociologist, Max Weber (1864-1920) bureaucracy is the most efficient way of running large organizations. He wrote:

"The fully developed bureaucractic mechanism compares with other organizations exactly as does the machine with the non-mechanical modes of production."

The bureaucratic form of organization as Weber saw it has the following characteristics:

Specialization. "Each office has a clearly defined sphere of competence."

Hierarchy. "A firmly ordered system of super- and subordination in which there is a supervision of the lower offices by the higher one."

Rules. "The management of the office follows general rules, which are more or less stable, more or less exhaustive, which can be learned."

Impersonality. "*Sine et studio* without hatred or passion, and hence without affection or enthusiasm. Everyone is subject to formal equality of treatment. This is the spirit in which the ideal official conducts his business."

Appointed officials. "Candidates are selected on the basis of technical qualifications. They are *appointed*, not elected."

Full time officials. "The office is treated as the sole, or at least primary, occupation."

Career officials. "The job constitutes a career. There is a system of promotion according to seniority, or to achievement, or to both."

Private/public split. "Bureaucracy segregates official activity as something distinct from the sphere of private life. Public monies and equipment are divorced from the private property of the official."

Weber used the term bureaucracy to describe a type of formal organization which was both impersonal and rational. Whereas in the past, authority had been based on nepotism, whim or fancy, in bureaucratic organizations it was based on rational principles. For this reason, it offered the possibility of the most efficient service ever, in comparison with what had preceded it. Now the term bureaucracy tends to be used in a derogatory manner to refer to inefficiency, waste and "red tape". Weber's view was in direct opposition to this. For him it was the most efficient form of social organization precisely because it was coldly logical and did not allow personal relations and feelings to get in the way of achieving goals.

Weber was a sociologist, not a manager or management consultant. As such he did not advocate bureaucracy as the answer to the questions posed at the start of this chapter. He did believe that, historically, bureaucracy was the most efficient form of organization available. He feared that its success would produce a deadening effect on people. It was the unintended consequences of bureaucratic forms of organization that have now given the word such negative connotations which, as de Gournay's quotation suggests, was evident even in eighteenth century France. Nevertheless, Weber's outline of bureaucracy, of rationally ordered activity, based on a set pattern of behaviour and distribution of work, did offer guidelines for the design and structuring of organizations. Moreover, while his main focus was on organizations such as the army, government and the church, bureaucratic forms of organization have come to be adopted by many other organizations such as hospitals, schools and industrial and commercial companies.

RULES

Amongst the key features of a bureaucratic organization is the pattern of rules which it contains and which are intended to guide, and hence structure, the behaviour of members.

Definition

A rule is a procedure or obligation explicitly stated and written down in company manuals

---

Weber laid great stress on the organized patterning of relationships between people through the use of rules. He felt that rules, based on rational and logical needs, contributed significantly to the efficient operation of his bureaucratic form of organization. William Buckley (1968) found that in the organizations that he studied, the areas of human interaction which were covered by clearly defined rules were small. He noted the existence of certain house "ground rules", but beyond that there were continued negotiations with rules being argued, ignored, lowered or stretched as the situation appeared to require. The rules did not act as universal prescriptions which provided the neutral impersonal direction that Weber had imagined. Instead, human action and choice continued to be demanded in their application.

Research studies on rules suggest that the behaviour of people in organizations cannot be explained in terms of them conforming to rules. In many instances, it is only by ignoring company rules that work can get done. This is what makes "working-to-rule" such an effective union weapon during the time of an industrial dispute. Individuals all have their own personal view as to what constitutes right and proper behaviour. They often will not accept other people's views which may be represented in certain organizational rules and procedures.

BUCKINGHAM WORKS.
RULES AND REGULATIONS.
FINES.

	s.	d.
1. For smoking in the Works	1	0
2. For bringing in malt liquors or spirits during the working hours	1	0
3. For introducing a stranger into the Works without leave	2	6
4. Any workman taking chips, tools, or any other thing belonging to his employers, from the premises, otherwise than for the purpose of the business, will be regarded as guilty of felony.		
5. For taking another person's tools without his permission	0	6
6. For altering any model, pattern, standard tool or measure, without leave	2	6
7. For tearing or defacing drawings	1	0
8. For neglecting to return to their proper places within a quarter of an hour from the time of having used them, any taps, screw stocks, arbors, or other tools, considered as general tools	0	6
9. For injuring a machine or valuable tool, through wantonness or neglect, the cost of repairing it.		
10. For striking any person in the Works	2	6
11. For ordering any tool, smith's work, or castings, without being duly authorized	1	0
12. For reading a book or newspaper in the working hours, wasting time in unnecessary conversation or otherwise, or whistling	0	6
13. For washing, putting on his coat, or making any other preparation of a similar kind for leaving work before the appointed time	0	6
14. For neglecting after his day's work is done to note down correctly on his time slate the various jobs he may have been engaged upon during the day, with the time for each job	0	6

	s.	d.
15. For leaving work without having carefully extinguished his light	0	6
16. For using any stores, such as wood, iron, steel, oil, paint, tallow, candles, or waste improperly, or cutting and using large wood where small would do, or wasting brass turnings	1	0
17. For being in any other than his own workship without leave, or sufficient cause	1	0
18. For handling work not his own	0	6
19. For picking or breaking any drawer or box lock	2	6
20. For swearing or using indecent language	1	0
21. Any apprentice absenting himself without leave from Messrs. Cooke or the Clerk, be fined	1	6
22. For writing or sketching anything indecent upon, or defacing any part of the Works, or the Rules, Regulations, or Notices therein fixed up	2	6
23. For neglecting to hang up his cheque when leaving work, or for losing it	0	6
24. Windows broken will be charged to the parties working in the same room, unless the person who did the damage be ascertained.		
25. Boys' fines to be only one half, except the Rule which applies to the breaking of windows; in which case the full amount will be levied.		
26. That every man sweep and make tidy his bench or lathe every Saturday commencing not before ten minutes to One.		

☞ The above Fines and Regulations are intended solely for the purpose of maintaining better order in the Works, preventing wasteful and unnecessary expense, and for promoting the good conduct and respectability of the workmen.

August, 1865   T. COOKE & SONS.

From *Thomas Cooke* © Brendan Heane and David Johnson, 1975, p.3.

Alvin Gouldner investigated the application of rules in a plant owned by the General Gypsum Company in the United States. Weber had assumed that members of an organization would comply with and obey company rules. Gouldner, however, rejected Weber's view that rules created order and regularity. Instead he asked for whom do rules make things regular, and in terms of whose goals are the rules a rational device?. He identified three classes of rules.

"The 'No-Smoking' Rule: Mock Bureaucracy

Analysis of the plant rules can begin by turning to the 'no-smoking' regulations. As comments of people in the plant emphasised, one of the most distinctive things about this rule was that it was a 'dead letter'. Except under unusual circumstances, it was ignored by most personnel.

Thus while offering a cigarette to a worker, one of the interviewers asked: 'What about the "No Smoking" signs? They seem to be all over the place, yet everyone seems to smoke'.

(Laughing) 'Yes, these are *not really Company rules*. The fire insurance writers put them in. The office seems to think that smoking doesn't hurt anything, so they don't bother us about it. That is, of course, until the fire inspector (from the insurance company) comes around. Then as soon as he gets into the front office, they call down here and *the word is spread around for no smoking*.'

The workers particularly seemed to enjoy the warning sent by the front office, for they invariably repeated this part of the story. For example another worker remarked: 'We can smoke as much as we want. When the fire inspector comes around, *everybody is warned earlier* . . . The Company doesn't mind.'"

The Safety Rule: Representative Bureaucracy

"In the mill there were rules specifying the manner in which the large dehydrating vats were to be cleaned out. Still others rules, indicating proper procedure to be followed if a tool fell into the mixture, applied only to the board building.

Not only was the system of safety rules complex, but considerable stress was placed upon conformity to them. Unlike the no-smoking rules, the safety regulations were not a 'dead letter'. Specific agencies existed which strove energetically to bring about their observance. These agencies placed continual pressure upon both workers and management, and sought to orient the two groups to the safety rules during their daily activities. For example, the Company's main office officially defined accident and safety work as one of the regular responsibilities of foremen and supervisors."

The "Bidding System": Punishment Centred Bureaucracy

The 'bidding system' is an example of rules enforced by 'grievances'. Originally incorporated into the labour-management contract at the union's initiative, the bidding rules specified that:

'All job vacancies and new jobs shall be posted within five (5) days after such a job becomes available, for a period of five (5) days, in order to give all employees an opportunity to make application in writing for such jobs. Such application shall be considered in the order of seniority in the department, provided, however, that the ability of the applicant to fill the requirements of the job shall also be considered. If no one in the department bids for the job, bidding shall be opened to other employees.'

The workers were usually determined that the supervisors should conform to the 'bidding system'. Supervisors, however, responded to the bidding rules with considerable resistance, much of it covert. They would sometimes strive to evade these regulations by posting a job at a lower rate than it would have carried. This discouraged bids from all individuals except the worker whom the super wanted for the job. He would bid for the job on the super's private advice, get it, and shortly thereafter be upgraded.

The 'bidding system', in brief, involved a pattern from which local management withheld full support and which it sometimes deliberately evaded, but which was strongly supported by most workers."

From Alvin W. Gouldner, *Patterns of Industrial Bureaucracy,* Free Press, New York, 1954, pages 182-3, 188 and 208

STOP!

Think of an organization with which you are familiar, e.g. school, college, university or a company. Give one example of each of the three types of rules distinguished by Gouldner.

Peter Blau studied two American government agencies (a federal law enforcement agency and an employment office). His aim was to discover what consequences flowed from the introduction of bureaucratic procedures such as rules, job definitions and so on. Blau described how statistical performance records were used. He discovered that performance assessment not only acted as a control on the individuals concerned, but also encouraged them to substitute their work goals. That which was measured — the number of interviews conducted — became more important than the original aim which had been to ensure the number and quality of job placements for agency clients.

Statistical records: a mechanism of control

"Quantitative records were used widely in the employment agency. They provided accurate information of various phases of operations, such as the number of requests for workers received from different branches of the industry and the number of placements made. This information enabled higher officials to take the actions they considered necessary to improve operations. Statistical reports were intended to facilitate the exercise of administrative control. However, the collection of data for these reports had consequences that transformed them from an indirect means of controlling operations into a direct mechanism of control. . . .

The knowledge that his superior would learn how many clients he (the subordinate) had interviewed and would evaluate him accordingly induced him to work faster. Far from being a disadvantage, this direct effect constituted the major function of performance records for bureaucratic operations. The supervisor wanted to know the number of interviews completed by each subordinate only in order to take corrective action in case any of them worked too slowly. The fact that the very counting of interviews had induced them to work faster facilitated operations by making such corrective steps superfluous. The use of statistical records not only provided superiors with information that enabled them to rectify poor performance but also obviated the need for doing so.

Until the beginning of 1948 the number of interviews held per month was the only operation that was statistically counted for each interviewer in Department X. (Although detailed reports were kept in the agency, they were presented only for departments as a whole, not for individuals.) As long as jobs were plentiful during the war, this rudimentary record seemed to suffice. However, when jobs became more scarce after the war and time and effort were required to find one for a client, this count of interviews had a detrimental effect on operations. One interviewer, perhaps slightly exaggerating, described the behaviour of her colleagues at the time in the following terms, 'You know what happened then? They used to throw them (clients) out. The same interviewers who engage in all the bad practices now in order to make placements never made a referral then; maybe, when the superior was looking. Otherwise they tried to get rid of them as fast as possible.'

Except for the information obtained by direct observation, the number of interviews completed by a subordinate was the only evidence the superior had at that time for evaluating him. The interviewer's interest in a good rating demanded that he maximize the number of interviews and therefore prohibited spending much time on locating jobs for clients. This rudimentary statistical record interfered with the agency's objective of finding jobs for clients in a period of job scarcity. There existed an organizational need for a different evaluation system."

From Peter M. Blau, 1966, *The Dynamics of Bureaucracy*, University of Chicago Press, Chicago, second edition, pp. 37-8.

STOP!

Can you think of an example of any similar measuring device or rule which goes against organizational aims?

The formal rules and procedures of most organizations encourage co-ordination and conformity amongst employees. But well qualified professionals such as doctors, engineers, and college lecturers usually want to be free to do their own thing and to develop themselves and their personalities through work. A study of this contradiction was carried out by Dennis Organ and Charles Greene (1981) who tried to find out whether bureaucracy cramped the style of this category of company employee. Two hundred and forty researach scientists and engineers completed a questionnaire which aimed to measure six different aspects of the respondent's work experience. As expected, organizations with an engineering orientation were found to be more formalized than those engaged in basic research. Formalization, that is bureaucracy, was associated with role-conflict and self-estrangement, but it was also to linked low role ambiguity, high organizational identification, and low self-estrangement. The authors drew the conclusion that bureaucracy can be beneficial in managing professional employees. Formalization avoids the frustrations of uncertainty about job requirements, and gives the professional "a gestalt within which he can define the nature of his own contribution". To avoid the drawbacks, administrators have to make rules that are consistant with professional standards, and avoid rules that create job conflict.

ROLES

Organizational structuring also occurs through the specification of the roles members are expected to play.

Definition

Role is the pattern of behaviour expected by others from a person occupying a certain position in an organizational hierarchy.

It follows that if individuals at different points in the hierarchy have mutual and complementary expectations, then the patterning and predictability of their behaviour is increased. Following Weber, the formal positions (identified on an organizational chart) in a company can be considered as "offices". The behaviour expected of any person occupying an office then becomes his "role". Roles are thus associated with positions in the organization and are involved in interactions. A single office holder, such as a foreman, will have regular interactions with a limited number of other office holders such as workers, the department manager, trade union officials and so on.

Each individual in an organization therefore has his or her own particular role set. It is important not to confuse this concept with the notion of a single person playing a number of different roles in their life (e.g. mother, wife, counsellor).

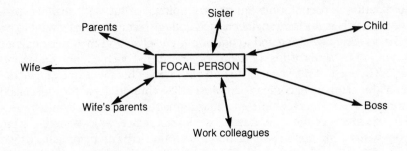

Definition

Role set refers to the set of roles with which a person interacts by virtue of occupying a particular position.

From David Katz and Robert L. Kahn *The Social Psychology of Organizations*, John Wiley, New York, 1966.

The concept of role is one which has been used extensively to understand the behaviour of people in organizations. A person may be observed in a single role e.g. nurse, engineer, trade union official, but he may play many different roles at the same time in his normal working life.

The priest's story

The officiating priest has two roles. He has the task of managing the act of worship, through instructions and more elaborate exhortations. He also has the traditional priestly role of representing the congregation to God and God to the congregation. On certain occasions he addresses God on behalf of the congregation. On others he speaks in the name of God and with his authority. On no occasion does he unequivocally take the part of God, although in the Holy Communion service he in effect takes the part of Christ at the Last Supper. His role is a subtle one, in that it constitutes both a series of acts by which God confronts, instructs, feeds, absolves and blesses the congregation, and also a screen between God and the congregation, in that God's initiatives are always mediated through the priest.

From Bruce Reed and Barry Palmer, "The local Church in its environment" in Miller, E. J. (ed.), *Task and Organization*, John Wiley, Chichester, 1978, p. 266.

Defining Roles

Roles may be viewed in different ways. There is disagreement on this issue amongst social scientists. Definitions of role depend on how they are to be used. We shall consider a prescriptive, evaluative, descriptive and action definition of the concept of role.

Prescription
Here the concern is with what the person should do when he plays a specific role.

STOP!

With the person next to you make a list of what the person studying this course should do,

or

Choose an occupation you know little about and quickly state what someone in that occupation should do.

Your replies to the first question are likely to be much more specific than those to the second. In that sense, your response to the former question resembles the prescriptive statements found in job descriptions. These are compiled by the organization and refer to what is expected of an individual in a certain position, e.g. ward sister in a hospital. Difficulties can arise when individuals disagree as to what the role holder ought to be doing.

Evaluation
In order to evaluate how well or badly a role is being performed, one needs to establish criteria or standards against which to make an assessment. A role prescription supplies such standards.

STOP!

With the person next to you list the behaviours of someone who occupies the role of a student. Then, individually, rank yourself and the other person on a 1-5 scale (1 = always does this, 5 = never does this). Now compare your rankings.

In organizations, staff appraisal schemes aim to set criteria in order to monitor and evaluate individual role performance. Earlier we saw how staff appraisals could be considered to be part of the procedure intended to pattern, and make predictable the behaviour of organization members.

Descriptive
This is based on the actual duties performed by the person being studied. Such a

descriptive role statement can be developed by observing and noting in minute detail what a person does. Such forms of analysis have been carried out by researchers who have studied how managers spend their time. These analyses contain the content of the work done alone as well as the nature of the interactions.

STOP!

List the main activities you have engaged in today in your role as a student. Rank them in order of importance.

Actions

A job description gives an account of the duties which should be undertaken by someone playing a specific role (e.g. a teacher should motivate students to learn). In pursuing these duties, many actions may be performed. Lecturers establish rapport, joke with students, ask them questions and so on. A role can therefore be specified in terms of actions involved in its performance.

STOP!

- What actions do you perform when meeting a stranger?
- Does your behaviour form a set pattern irrespective of who the stranger is?
- If not, how and why does your behaviour change in meeting different strangers in different circumstances?

Any role may thus be considered under the four aspects of prescription, evaluation, description and action. All four are interrelated and interdependent.

ROLE RELATIONSHIPS AND SOCIALIZATION

These are the relationships that one has with the individuals occupying other positions or "offices" in the organization by virtue of them being a member of your role set.

Definition

Role relationship is that intangible mixture of feelings and emotions which exist between two or more people.

Relationships can be considered as the way in which one uses oneself in a disciplined and responsible way when dealing with a group or individual. In achieving his goals and fulfilling his duties, the organization member can use his "good" relationships with colleagues, bosses, clients and customers to help him to achieve his aims at work, for example, getting support for some new plan of action. The individual needs however to be aware that the other people also have needs and feelings, and should show concern for these and be aware of others responses. Failure to do his can lead to a breakdown in relationships.

Individuals have role relationships with each other and organizations can be thought of as a set of overlapping and interlocking role sets. In the chapter on groups, the concept of norm was introduced and defined. Here, norms can be seen as the general expectations of how people ought to behave in a given organizational role. Roles are thus more restricted expectations about what behaviour is appropriate in which specific situations. A role influences the behaviour of an individual by setting limits within which he is expected to act.

Roles in organizations are learned through socialization,

Definition

Socialization is the process by which an organization seeks to make the individual more amenable to the prevalent mode of influence.

From Charles Handy, *Understanding Organizations*, Penguin Books, Harmondsworth, Middlesex, 1975, p. 134.

Many of the tasks involved in the job have been learned and assimilated so well that they become accepted as being part of the person. It raises the question of whether, in behaving in a certain way, we are ourselves or just conforming to what the organization (and society) expects of us. Role relationships therefore are the field within which behaviour occurs. People's behaviour at any given moment is the result of:

- Their personalities;
- Their perception and understanding of each other;
- Their attitudes to the behavioural constraints imposed by the role relationship;
- The degree of their socialization with respect to constraints;
- Their ability to inhibit and control their behaviours.

An important function of role relationships is to reduce the areas of possible uncertainty to manageable proportions. Michael Argyle (1964) has argued that occupants of similar positions, for example firemen, tend to behave in similar ways in certain situations and share various attitudes and beliefs. In many standardized situations, the behaviour which takes place can be accurately predicted from knowledge of the organization and its rules, while knowledge of the personality characteristics may be of little use. A person's behaviour is thus not necessarily the result of personality factors, but the consequence of the various influences which mould people to the standard role behaviour for that position.

Such sharing of behaviour, attitudes and personalities can come about in an organization through the staff selection process (self-selection and company selection), through training (role behaviour results from carefully created training courses and spontaneously created initiation ceremonies) and not least through the job itself (new organization members are exposed to job demands and are pressured to perform in certain ways). In practice, it is a mixture of all three. The way in which individuals behave and the attitudes which they develop are strongly influenced by the roles which are assigned to them in a set of structured relationships, e.g. tutor-student, boss-subordinate. The expectations of other people in related roles, and an individual's own beliefs learned through the process of socialization inside and outside of the organization, will effect their decisions as to what is and is not appropriate behaviour in a specified role.

Role Expectations

"Gouldner shows, in his analysis of the Gypsum factory, how useful the notion of *role expectations* can be, in explaining how human behaviour in organizations is influenced and controlled. Regularity and predictability in social relationships are highly valued in individuals. They expect that the persons they associate with, at work or in the family, will behave in predictable ways. If they do not, the individual feels tense and uncomfortable and wants to do something to make life more predictable. In all human groupings there are mechanisms for punishing people who do not behave in predictable ways and for rewarding those who do. Gradually the norms of behaviour which emerge from the desire for predictability become part of the individual's personal make up. He sometimes does not know how to explain why he behaves regularly in the way he does. It's just 'the way we do things here'. In short, people cast other people in roles which are defined by their own expectations. These may be highly formal, as legal prescriptions and bureaucratic rules are, or they may be informal or implicit, as in custom. Because of the urge to predictability, role expectations, whether formal or informal, tend towards stable equilibrium in social systems and there is a pressure for them to remain that way. This is one reason why imposed social change, say as a result of new technology, may be a difficult problem."

From Tom Lupton, *Management and the Social Sciences*, Penguin Books, Harmondsworth, Middlesex, 1971, second edition, pp. 50-1.

Role conflict

The woman who is both a manager and a mother may experience role conflict when the expectations in these two important roles pull her in opposite directions.

Definition

Role conflict, is the simultaneous existence of two sets of role expectations on a focal person in such a way that compliance with one makes it difficult to comply with the other.

Role conflict and the shop steward

"On the one hand he is expected to represent his members by standing firm against management and arguing inflexibly for his just demands. This is his role as representative of his members. But he is also in the role of negotiator, and it is apparent that a successful negotiator has to adopt compromise and concession techniques if agreement is to be reached.

The role of representative thus implies a we-win-and-you-lose perspective (so that image loss is of great concern) but the role of negotiator involves a joint problem-solving approach where both sides' aim is to reach agreement. On the one hand the shop steward has to defeat management but on the other hand both he and management have to win together (by achieving a settlement). There is no doubt that such a conflict of roles can present difficulties, especially for the inexperienced shop steward. (His more experienced colleague can be quite thick skinned about it all.) The situation is naturally one where a union negotiator can easily get out of step with his members who are less aware of the complexities of the issue and are liable to see any concession as a defeat. So the negotiating steward is the man in the middle who has to work to persuade his members as well as argue their case against management. As if that were not enough both of these roles are in effect part-time ones. For most of his time his role is also that of a worker who has his day-to-day job to carry on."

From Peter Warr, *Psychology and Collective Bargaining,* Hutchinson, London, 1973, p. 34-5.

PROBLEMS OF BUREAUCRACY

With the speed of environmental change increasing, Weber's views about the beneficial aspects of bureaucractic forms of organization have been challenged. Warren Bennis called bureaucracy, "a lifeless crutch that is no longer useful", while Michel Crozier referred to it as an organization that cannot learn from its errors. Chris Argyris (1957, 1973) offered a theory of personality development which argued that as an individuals' personality matured, the bureaucratic organization was an unsuitable place to work in. Argyris identified seven dimensions along which he claimed that the personality of an individual developed towards psychological maturity. These are as follows:

1.   An individual moves from a passive state as an infant to a state of increasing activity as an adult.
2.   An individual develops from a state of dependency on others as an infant to a state of relative independence as an adult.
3.   An individual behaves in only a few ways as an infant, but as an adult is capable of behaving in many ways.
4.   An individual has erratic, casual and shallow interests as an infant, but develops deeper and stronger interests as an adult.
5.   An infant's time perspective is very short, involving only the present, but with maturity this perspective widens into the past and future.
6.   An infant is subordinate to others, moving as an adult to equal or superior positions in relation to others.
7.   Infants lack self-awareness, adults are self-aware and capable of self-control.

Argyris argued that the healthy personality developed naturally along the continuum from immaturity to maturity. However, he also said that managerial practices within formal organizations can inhibit this natural maturation process. Lower level employees in particular are given minimal control over their work environment and are encouraged to be passive, dependent and subordinate. Widespread worker apathy and lack of effort are thus not the result of individual laziness. Employees behave immaturely, he believes, because they are expected to behave in this way. The design of formal organizations, or bureaucracies, frequently incorporates features such as:

- Task specification;
- Rigid chain of command;
- Principle of unity of direction;
- Limited span-of-control.

Power and authority lie with those at the top, those at the bottom are strictly controlled by the supervisors. Argyris thus points to a stark incongruity between the needs of the mature personality and formal organizations as they currently exist. In support of this argument he cites American cases — in a knitting mill and in a radio manufacturing plant — where mentally retarded people were successfully employed on unskilled jobs. Management found them exceptionally well-behaved, obedient, honest and trustworthy. Their attendence was good, and their behaviour was better than other employees of the same age.

The challenge for management, as he saw it, was to create work environments in which everyone has opportunity to grow and mature as individuals. This, in essence, meant moving away from bureaucratic organization and towards some other type of organizational design. But this is no longer a question of large companies "being nice to their workers". In the economic climate of the late twentieth century, organizations are finding that bureaucratic organization is expensive to maintain, incapable of responding sufficiently fast to change, and does not utilize the innovative resources of its members. Failure to achieve profit-targets resulted in the first instance in large scale redundancies of staff, including managers. Now that the slimming down has been completed, the new-look, leaner organizations are experimenting with radically different forms of structures. There have been *management-buy-outs* where the managers have bought a part of the company's operation and now run it as a separate small business supplying a service to the large organization (e.g. transport, printing). Individuals previously part of the company now supply a specialist service to it as individual subcontractors (e.g. computer software development, systems analysis). The label *networking* has been given to this . Finally, there are the *intrapreneurial groups* which are groups of employees within the organization who operate as group profit centres. These will be discussed in the next chapter. All these developments suggest that, in order to survive, organizations will be seeking to develop alternative organizational structures to the bureaucratic ones they currently operate.

SOURCES

Argyle, M., 1964, *Psychology and Social Problems*, Methuen, London

Argyris, C., 1957, *Personality and Organizations*, Harper and Row, London.

Argyris, C., 1973, "Personality and organization theory revisited", *Administrative Science Quarterly*, vol. 18, no. 2, pp. 141-167.

Blau, P. M., 1966, *The Dynamics of Bureaucracy*, University of Chicago Press, Chicago, 2nd edition.

Buckley, W., 1968, "Society as a complex adaptive system" in W. Buckley (ed.) *Modern Systems Research for the Behavioural Scientist*, Aldine Publishing Company, pp. 490-513.

Child, J., 1984, *Organization: A Guide to Problems and Practice*, Harper and Row, London, 2nd edition.

Gouldner, A. W., 1954, *Patterns of Industrial Bureaucracy*, Free Press, New York.

Handy, C. B., 1976, *Understanding Organizations*, Penguin Books, Harmondsworth.

Katz, D. and Kahn, R. L., 1966, *The Social Psychology of Organizations*, John Wiley, New York.

Lupton, T., 1971, *Management and the Social Sciences*, Penguin Books, Harmondsworth, 2nd edition.

Mouzelis, N. P., 1969, *Organization and Bureaucracy*, Routledge and Kegan Paul, London.

Organ, D. W. and Greene, C. N., 1981, "The effects of formalization on professional involvement: a compensatory approach", *Administrative Science Quarterly*, vol. 26, no. 2, pp. 237-52.

Reed, B. and Palmer, B., 1978, "The local church in its environment" in E. J. Miller (ed.) *Task and Organization*, John Wiley and Sons, Chichester.

Stewart, R., 1967, *Managers and Their Jobs*, Macmillan, London.

Warr, P., 1973, *Psychology and Collective Bargaining*, Hutchinson, London.

Weber, M., 1947, *The Theory of Social and Economic*, New York: Oxford University Press, translated by A. M. Henderson and T. Parsons (eds).

Chapter 17

Classical universal approach

Key concepts;

Once you have fully understood this chapter, you should be able to define the following concepts in your own words:

Scalar concept   Span-of-control
Principle of unity of command   Organizational specialization
Exception principle   Intrapreneurial group

Objectives:

On completing this chapter, you should be able to:

1.   Summarize the approach and main principles of the classical universal school of management.
2.   Identify the writers who comprise the school and state their main individual contributions.
3.   Discuss the strengths and weaknesses of the classical-universal approach to organizational structure and management practice.
4.   Identify the application of classical-universal principles in the design of contemporary organizations.
5.   Contrast classical-universal principles of organizational design with intrapreneurial forms.

CLASSICAL UNIVERSAL APPROACH TO ORGANIZATIONAL STRUCTURE

A second source of ideas about how to structure an organization came, and continues to come, from practising managers. In the early years of this century, various writers made suggestions about the principles which should guide how managers built up the formal structure of organizations and how they ought to administer it in a rational way. Their movement was labelled classical, according to Baker (1972), because it attempted to offer simple principles which claimed a general application. It was also classical in the sense that it followed architectural and literary styles which emphasized formality, symmetry and rigidity.

Classical theory was based primarily on the work experience and personal theories of certain key individuals rather than on empirical research. The publications of this so-called, classical–universal school of management, began in 1914 with the contribution of Henri Fayol, a French mining engineer. Fayol's work complemented and built upon many of the ideas of Frederick Winslow Taylor. However, he took a broader, organization-wide approach with James Mooney, Edward Tregaskiss Elbourne, Mary Parker Follett, Luther Gulick and E. F. L. Brech. These writers together constitute what is referred to as the classical–universal school of management. Their views have exerted a lasting impression right up to the present day. Despite the criticisms of their ideas, most major companies are organized in a way which incorporates at least some of their thinking.

The underlying philosophy of this school of thought was summarized by one of its main proponents:

> "It is the general thesis of this paper that there are principles which can be arrived at inductively from the study of human experience of organization, which should govern arrangements for human association of any kind. These principles can be studied as a technical question, irrespective of the purpose of the enterprise, the personnel composing it, or any constitutional, political or social theory underlying its creation. They are concerned with the method of subdividing and allocating to individuals all the various activities, duties and responsibilities essential to the purpose contemplated, and the correlation of these activities and the continuous control of the work of individuals so as to secure the most economical and most effective realization of the purpose".
>
> From L. Urwick "Organization as a Technical Problem", a paper of 1933 reprinted in L. Gulick and L. Urwick (eds) *Papers on the Science of Administration*, Columbia University Press, New York, 1937, p. 49.

This quotation puts in a nutshell the essential views of the classical school. In response to the questions "How does one structure an organization?", the writers in this school offered a remarkably similar set of principles and concepts to guide the organizational designer. They believed these were applicable to all organizations irrespective of their size, technology, environment or employees. For this reason, it is often written that these writers preached the doctrine of "structural universalism" as a way of achieving organizational efficiency. These principles concerned the issue of how to allocate tasks, control the work being done and motivate and reward those doing it. The answers which they offered were underlaid by the "logic of efficiency". This logic stressed:

- Bureaucratic forms of control;
- Narrow supervisory span;
- Closely prescribed roles;
- Clear and formal definition of procedures, areas of specialization and hierarchical relationships.

Moreover, the values which underpinned it, held that for a technically efficient organization, one needed to achieve a unity of effort and to do this meant limiting the freedom and discretion of organizational members. In this sense, the classical writers had a direct similarity with those in the scientific management school – Frederick Winslow Taylor, Frank Gilbreth and Henry Gantt. However, the latter focused on shopfloor arrangement while the former considered the company as a whole. The classical school was not a group of people who worked together. Rather it is the collective name for a number of individuals who came from different backgrounds, from different countries and who, over a period of some thirty years expounded a set of remarkably similar ideas in their writings and talks. Their experience of management was based on both commercial, industrial and governmental organizations. Some were managers, others were consultants. In their writings they sought to make sense of their experience, rationalize it, explain it and set it down as a set of principles which appeared to be consistent with their observed practice. They then went on to promote their ideas more widely.

CLASSICAL SCHOOL PRINCIPLES AND POSTULATES

The writers had both similar and differing views. Some emphasized certain points and not others. They did not have any single, common "manifesto". Nevertheless, Bruno Lussato (1972, p. 46) identified a group of concepts and principles which seemed to be common to the different classical school writers.

Scalar concept

This viewed an organization as a group of grades arranged in a sequence. Superior grades carried authority which could be delegated to the grade immediately below. The lower grades carried no authority. From this scalar concept stemmed the principle of hierarchy. It held that authority descended from the top to the bottom along a well defined scale of posts in a continuously clear line.

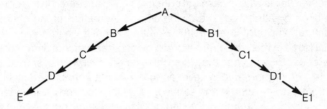

Principle of Unity of Command

This held that an individual must only receive orders from one hierarchical superior. A related principle, that of Unity of Direction, annunciated that there should be one head and one plan for a group of activities which contributed to the same objective.

Exception Principle

Delegation should be maximized with decisions being taken at the lowest level possible. The routine and ordinary (programmed) tasks should be performed by subordinates, while the exceptional tasks were to be entrusted to the hierarchical superior.

Span-of-control concept

The question of the optimal number of subordinates to be put under the authority of one hierarchical chief. General Sir Iain Hamilton once said that, "No one brain can effectively control more than six or seven other brains".

Principle of organizational specialization

Management activities should be differentiated according to their objectives, processes, clientéle, materials or geographical location.

Application of scientific method

Use of experimental methods in studying organizational and managerial practices were stressed. This involved observation, hypothesis formulation, experimentation, formulation of quantitative and universal laws and their checking and correcting.

Organizational structure as a function of divine intervention

"Another way in which classical principles have appeared in the church
has been by attributing to a divine source the nature of the church's
structure. The structure of the Roman Catholic church has been
understood in this way: there is the typical organizational pyramid with
the Pope at the apex and the hierarchies ranged below on ever widening
levels. The organization is believed to derive not from human initiative
but from a divine source and sanction. That is, a theological foundation
is provided for a church organized on classical lines; but the question
remains whether this foundation is adequate and whether the classical
model is appropriate — the extremes of ultramontanism, the mechanistic view of infallibility and the exercise of authority, the "pipe-line"
theory of apostolic succession are grounds for doubt. The new currents
of thought in the papacies of John XXIII and his successor in the second
Vatican Council may be evidence of the reshaping of the structure (and
perhaps also the doctrine) of the church on lines other than the classical
theory of organization."

From Peter F. Rudge, *Ministry and Management: The Study of
Ecclesiastical Management*, Tavistock, London, 1968, p. 40.

To these principles, Massie (1965) added a number of further postulates
which included the following:

- Efficiency can be measured in terms of productivity, irrespective of human factors.
- Men behave in a logical and reasonable manner.
- Men need to be supervised closely (because they cheat).
- Tasks must be strictly defined and must not overlap with each other.
- The worker seeks security and a clear definition of the limits of his work.
- The only exchanges between individuals which need to be considered are those that are official or formal, and which relate to be objectives of the firm.
- Activities must be defined in an objective and impersonal manner.
- The only motivation of the workers is their salary: the creation of a fair system of remuneration will be enough to obtain their co-operation.
- This calls for strict supervision. Such laziness decreases as one goes higher up the hierarchy.
- Co-ordination must be imposed and controlled from above, and dele-gation of authority is made from top to bottom.
- Simple tasks are easier to assimilate. To increase productivity therefore, as detailed a division of labour as possible should be carried out.
- It is possible to extract from experience, universal principles which are valid for any man or any situation.

STOP!

Consider the list of principles and postulates. Which are complementary and which are in conflict with one another?

CLASSICAL THEORY AND ITS ADVOCATES

When considering classical theories of organization it is important to locate them in their historical content. The managers of the period were dealing with larger, more complex organizations than had existed hitherto. At the beginning of the 20th century many new companies developed. They employed vast numbers of people, had numerous plants and employed new technologies. All of this needed co-ordinating. With no model or experience to fall back on, those who managed these organizations had no choice but to develop their own principles and theories as to what to do to run them well. Inevitably these principles were grounded in their day-to-day experience of managing.

Do not have an excessive span of control

"The principle is to have a chain of command, so that each man knows to whom he is responsible and there can be units of different managerial sizes for different purposes. For example, according to Xenophon counting on the fingers of two hands, the divisions of Cyrus's army were:

	Form	*Under*	
5 men	1 squad	corporal	5
2 squads	1 sergeant's squad	sergeant	10
5 sergeant's squads	1 platoon	lieutenant	50
2 platoons	1 company	captain	100
10 companies	1 regiment	colonel	1,000
10 regiments	1 brigade	general	10,000

With modifications in the numbers in different units, this is the principle on which armies have been organized. The general does not have to control 10,000 men directly, he controls the ten regimental colonels, and so on. In modern armies this would be considered an excessive span of control and two or three armies would form an army group, but the principle remains. Split the task up into manageable proportions and do not have an excessive span of control so that real control is lost."

From F. R. Jervis, *Bosses in British Business*, Routledge and Kegan Paul, London, 1974, p. 87.

Classical theory is generally held to have originated in France with the work of Henri Fayol. Fayol qualified as a mining engineer in 1860 after which he joined the Commentary-Fourchambault combine, a company in which he was to spend his entire working life. In 1866 he became manager of the Commentary colliers and in 1888, at the age of 47 he was appointed to the General Manager position at a time when the financial position of the company was critical. By the time he retired in 1918, he managed to establish financial stability in the organization.

It was in the year that Frederick Winslow Taylor died, that Fayol's *General and Industrial Administration* was published. Fayol had tried to put down, in as scientific form as possible, the experience he had gained while managing a

HENRI FAYOL'S ANALYSIS OF THE OPERATIONS WHICH OCCUR IN BUSINESS GOVERNMENT

("To govern an undertaking is to conduct it towards its objective by trying to make the best possible use of the resources at its disposal; it is in fact, to ensure the smooth working of the six essential functions.")

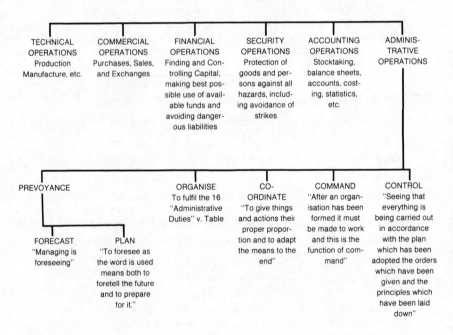

| TECHNICAL OPERATIONS Production Manufacture, etc. | COMMERCIAL OPERATIONS Purchases, Sales, and Exchanges | FINANCIAL OPERATIONS Finding and Controlling Capital, making best possible use of available funds and avoiding dangerous liabilities | SECURITY OPERATIONS Protection of goods and persons against all hazards, including avoidance of strikes | ACCOUNTING OPERATIONS Stocktaking, balance sheets, accounts, costing, statistics, etc. | ADMINIS-TRATIVE OPERATIONS |

| PREVOYANCE | | CO-ORDINATE "To give things and actions their proper proportion and to adapt the means to the end" | COMMAND "After an organisation has been formed it must be made to work and this is the function of command" | CONTROL "Seeing that everything is being carried out in accordance with the plan which has been adopted the orders which have been given and the principles which have been laid down" |

| FORECAST "Managing is foreseeing" | PLAN "To foresee as the word is used means both to foretell the future and to prepare for it." |

ORGANISE To fulfil the 16 "Administrative Duties" v. Table

From Henri Fayol, General and Industrial Management (1916), quoted in L. Urwick and E. F. L. Brech, *The Making of Scientific Management, Volume 1: Thirteen Pioneers*, Sir Isac Pitman, London, 1966, p. 47.

large scale company. In his writings, he stressed not personalities but methods. He tried to present the latter in a coherent and relevant scheme. This formed the basis of his *theory of organization*. While Taylor focused on the worker on the shopfloor — a bottom-up approach; Fayol began from the top of the hierarchy and moved downwards. However, like Taylor, he too believed that a manager's work could be reviewed objectively, analysed and treated as a technical process which was subject to certain definitive principles which could be taught. Fayol's book had two parts: (a) Theory of Administration; (b) Training for Administration.

In the first part he differentiated the main operations he found in a business — technical, commercial, financial, security, accounting and administration. The administrative function he further subdivided into organizing, co-ordinating, commanding, controlling and "prevoyance". This last label included the concepts of forecasting and planning.

It is said that Fayol's classification distinguished managing as a separate activity from the others for the first time. In a sense, therefore, Fayol "invented" management. Interestingly, the word "management" is not translatable into all languages, nor does the concept exist in all cultures. Managing of course occurs, but is not treated as anything special or separate. Fayol's second major contribution was to identify fourteen principles of administration. Elsewhere he also had sixteen administrative rules. He wrote that these were,

"some of the principles of management which I have had more frequently to apply".

He added that:

"it seems at the moment especially useful to endow management theory with a dozen or so well-established principles, on which it is appropriate to concentrate general discussion".

Classical theory is characterized by a plethora of rules, principles, hints, hunches and beliefs. This chapter contains numerous lists of dos and don'ts as suggested by classical theorists. Some of the principles are descriptive and prescriptive, while others are exhortative. Classical theory literature can be distinguished by the use of words such as must, ought, should and needs to. Some of Fayol's writings contain recommendations for managerial behaviour based on his personal opinion, while others are too abstract for application to practical situations. Following Fayol, many writers added to the list of principles which are now collectively referred to as the classical school of management.

STOP!

Review the list of principles and postulates. Distinguish between those which are descriptive, prescriptive and exhortative.

The main ideas of classical theory have already been mentioned. They do not represent a coherent body of thought since they were developed by a wide range of different managers and writers. This breadth can be shown by a brief description of their backgrounds. James Mooney and Alan Reiley had been senior managers in General Motors Company in the United States. Luther Gulick, born in 1892, had both practical public administration experience and was a director of the New York Institute for Public Administration. He was interested in how to bring together into a single area amounts of work to effect the best division of labour and specialization while at the same time maximizing machinery and mass production.

Oliver Sheldon worked under B. Seebohm Rowntree at the Cocoa Works in York in England during the 1920s. Lyndall Urwick was the main propagandist in Britain for classical management thought, Colonel Urwick's thoughts and writings had a heavily militaristic flavour. He had had many of his formative experiences in management in the British Army. In 1943, he published 29 principles of administration which reflect his belief that far from being contradictory and inappropriate, all management principles could be related to one another and had a universal application.

Mary Parker Follett is usually located among the classical theorists. However, Follett is at the junction between their thinking and that of the human relations school led by Elton Mayo. She is considered to be classical in the sense that she propounded certain principles. She offered a "law of the situation" which stressed the need for management to operate on the "logic of efficiency". However, at the same time she stressed democratic social relationships, and "creative collectiveness". She argued that as a "science of relationships", psychology could be developed and learned. It was her emphasis on group relationships and participative leadership in management which foreshadowed much of what was to emerge from the writings of Elton Mayo. For this reason she is seen as straggling the classical (universal) and human relations schools.

ASSESSMENT OF THE CLASSICAL SCHOOL

Writing critically about shortcomings of the classical - universal school, Herbert March and James Simon (1958) have pointed to,

1.   Its lack of concern with the interaction between people;
2.   Its underestimation of the effects of conflict;
3.   Its underestimation of the capacity of individual workers to process information;
4.   Its misunderstanding of how people think.

Other writers have criticized the classical-universal theorists for the naivity of their principles and the existence of contradictory and ambiguous propositions. Almost all the classical writers took for granted the right of managers to manage. That is, they accept unquestioningly the managerial prerogative but provided with few means of coping in situations where that "right" was challenged. Talk of managerial authority is hollow where such authority is not re-inforced by appropriate reserves of power.

STOP!

Individually make a list of the main strengths and weaknesses of the classical-universal approach from the point of view of someone designing or managing an organization.

CLASSICAL THEORY TODAY

It is fashionable, especially in academic circles, to relegate classical theory to a place in history. However, many of the principles are being applied today. Hunt (1979, p. 185) quotes a list of management principles produced in an American management magazine in the 1960s. While they are now referred to as "guidelines" and not principles, they are in all major respects the same:

> "There must be clear lines of authority running from the top to the bottom of the organization."

Clarity is achieved through delegation by steps or levels from the leader to the working level — from the highest executive to the employee who has least accountability to the organization. It should be possible to trace such a line from the chief executive to every employee. From military language, this vertical line is often referred to as "the chain of command" and the principle is often referred to as the "scalar" principle.

> "No one in the organization should report to more than *one* line supervisor. Everyone in the organization should know to whom he reports and who reports to him."

This is usefully referred to as the "unity of command" principle. Put bluntly, it means that everyone should have one boss.

> "The accountability and authority of each supervisor should be clearly defined, in *writing*."

Putting accountabilities in writing enables the supervisor to know both what is expected of him and the limits of his authority; it prevents overlapping of tasks and authorities.

Classical theories of organizations occupy an ambivalent position today. Ancient classical theory, as represented by Fayol, Sheldon, Sloan, Urwick and others has been found wanting. It may have worked when companies had a stable market, centralized decision-making, employees motivated by basic life needs, a long history of task orientated management and conservative and predictable governments. These circumstances have now changed. Nevertheless, those who manage organizations continue to seek advice on how best to do this. They seek clear, unambiguous, practical, simple to understand and apply rules, principles and recipes. Thus modern classical theory, as represented by those who contributed to Ray Wild's book (1983) attempt to offer a set of updated (but still universal) ideas.

To those who want to know how to manage

"This many be one of the most authoritative books on management ever published, since it has been written by 123 distinguished and experienced managers, from many types of organizations in several countries. Together, these contributors have over 3000 years of managerial experience to draw on. The objective of the book is to pass on some of this experience to those who want to know how to manage."

From Ray Wild (ed), *How to Manage*, Heinemann, London, 1983, p. 1.

Whether ancient or modern, these based-on-experience, this-is-how-I-did-it guidelines can only provide limited assistance to those running organizations. The particular circumstances of each organization make the "recipe-for-managing" uniquely relevant and not universally applicable. Moreover, even in a single organization, what worked yesterday may not work tomorrow because of technological, environmental or some other change.

STOP!

In the book, *How to Manage*, Tony Jacklin , the golfer, writes:

"The key to good management in my opinion is choosing the right people in the first place".

(a)   What does this statement mean?
(b)   To what extent is it universally applicable?
(c)   How would you choose, "the right people in the first place"?

For this reason, those concerned with structuring and designing organizations have had to look elsewhere. They have had to acknowledge the complexity of the task and reluctantly admit that they are no "laws" or "principles". Recipe knowledge is no longer adequate to meet the demands of organizational design and management. Instead the focus has shifted towards identifying and relating important variables. How does one combine organizational goals, human needs, technological opportunites and the need for some form of organizational control? These variables have been related to each other to produce a best fit for the circumstances of the particular organization at the time. New and innovative forms of organization are now emerging. The characteristics of these appear to be their temporary nature and the focus away from control by managers of workers and towards individual self-control and group-control. In this context, the issue of managerial prerogative to manage is once again raised.

Recipes for managing

"Since everyday life is dominated by pragmatic motive, recipe knowledge, that is, knowledge limited to pragmatic competence in routine performances, occupies a prominent place in the social stock of knowledge . . . I have recipe knowledge of the workings of human relationships. For example, I must know what I must do to apply for a passport. All I am interested in is getting the passport at the end of a certain waiting period. I do not care, and do not know, how my application is processed in government offices, by whom and after what steps approval is given, who puts which stamp in the document. I am not making a study of government bureaucracy — I just want to go on vacation abroad. My interest in the hidden workings of the passport getting procedure will be aroused only if I fail to get my passport in the end. At that point, very much as I call on a telephone repair expert after my telephone has broken down, I call on an expert in passport-getting – a lawyer, say, or my Congressman, or the American Civil Liberties Union. *Mutatis mutandis*, a large part of the social stock of knowledge consists of recipes for the mastery of routine problems. Typically, I have little interest in going beyond this pragmatically necessary knowledge as long as the problems can indeed be mastered thereby.

From Peter L. Berger and Thomas Luckmann, *The Social Construction of Reality*, Heinemann, London, 1972, pp. 56-7.

Small is beautiful (and fast!)

A study by Peters and Waterman looked at the management styles of sixty two American companies with outstandingly successful records in 1961-80 plus a sample of big companies which were going bust. They found that a failing big company will have a large matrix chart. One organizational chart they found set out 223 formal linkages between different people or divisions before a decision could be taken. Few decisions were ever taken. They were delayed by long feasibility studies which were carried out before any product was introduced. In contrast, a successful company would get a small team of ten or so people who would test market on a tiny sample and perhaps reject twenty-four of the twenty-five products thus allowing them to fail cheaply.

From Thomas J. Peters and Robert H. Waterman Jnr., *In Search of Excellence*, Harper and Row, New York, 1982.

THE INTRAPRENEURIAL GROUP

Norman Macrae (1982) predicted the decline of big business corporations. He felt that it was now inappropriate to have hierarchical managements sitting in offices deciding how "brainworkers", as he called them, could use their imaginations. One organizational trend which he identified was to have a company consider several different ways of doing the same thing. This involved creating a number of separate groups which would be in competition with each other. He labelled these confederations of workers *intrapreneurial groups*. An intrapreneurial group would consist of about twelve friends who worked together. Each day, they would seek the maximum productivity. How would this work in practice? It is well illustrated by Macrae's example of a typing pool.

	Role (Classic) organization	Intrapreneurial organization
Emphasis	*Bureaucracy*	*Enterprise*
Control	*Exercised by managers down*	*Internal within group by members*
Size orientation	*Single large unit*	*Many small units*
Inter-unit relation	*Co-ordination*	*Competition*
Relationship to centre	*Strictly controlled*	*Independent*
Work flexibility	*Low*	*High*
Sphere of operation	*Company*	*Company but can also take on outside work*
Leadership	*Appointed by management*	*Group's choice of leader accepted by management*
Work design	*Done by experts and managers*	*Done by group members themselves*

Each group of typists would be constituted as a sort of profit centre. The firm would not pay people for attendance at work, but for the output of work which they produced. Instead of having one large typing pool with perhaps thirty-six typists, there might be three groups of twelve. Each group would organize itself separately with management's help. Each would then be offered an index-linked contract for a set period such as six months. The services required by the company would be specified, such as audio typing, dictation, photocopying, filing and so on. In return they would receive a lump sum group monthly payment. The typists who constituted the group would apportion the work between them, devise their own flexible working hours, and choose how they wanted to do it. If one of them left or went part-time, the group would have the choice of either replacing the person or of accepting an increased workload, and dividing that person's salary between them. This group would also be allowed to tender for outside work in other departments in the organization. The three groups would compete with each other.

What makes intrapreneurialism diametrically opposed to classical universal theory? It is not the small number of people which tend to be involved. The optimum span-of-control discussed by some classical theorists is roughly equivalent to the intrapreneurial group. It is the other factors which are shown on the previous page.

Intrapreneurialism in Hungary

"Mr Timko has been the first at Kossuth to explore the government's newly launched scheme under which small groups of workers can "lease" equipment and supplies in their enterprises. His first move was to consult with a hand-picked number of colleagues in the composing room. Out of about 100 workers, 26 of the best skilled joined in a 'social agreement' among themselves; made a symbolic investment of 1,400 forints (about £25 each) and went on to negotiate a contract with the management. It was agreed that their earnings, as a group, would be distributed according to productivity, and not only according to the time spent on group work. Their contract also provides for agreed work tariffs, and gets away from the standard practice of hourly rates.

The group pays 10 per cent of its earnings for the lease of machinery and the supply of light, heating and materials. (In other enterprises where more energy and raw materials are used, the deductions are higher.) The group is not obliged to work exclusively for Kossuth, but can take up any outside work it drums up. During the eight months Mr Timko's group has operated, about 20 per cent of its activity has been devoted to outside orders. The scheme requires that the general manager of the enterprise must accept the group's choice for leader. Once formed the group also has to register itself with the authorities. Inevitably there have been growing pains when Mr Timko's group began to function. But now they are run in, working smoothly under an arrangement where each group member regularly tells Mr Timko how many extra hours he intends to work in the following week.

"Over exertion" by way of too much unsocial working time is discouraged. This means that, on average, the Timko group work an extra three to four hours a week, over the daily eight hour shift. They also work on "free Saturdays". Yet because of the money they charge for extra work, and the incentive to high productivity it provides, these extra hours have enabled the group's members to increase their earnings substantially.

Discussing these earnings, Mr Timko makes a point which is more familiar in Western countries than in the Communist bloc. He notes that

Hungary's progressive tax rates are such that it no longer pays to work after a certain point. A revision of the tax-system has just been promised."

From "Printer's group earns a bigger share of the pie", *The Guardian*, May 31, 1983.

CONCLUSION

This chapter has attempted to illustrate the considerable influence that the classical-universal school of management has had on the design of organizational structures during the last seventy years. It is certain that some organization of which you are a member — company, college, church — will be organized using classical principles. At the same time the serious weaknesses of the classical school have been pointed out. Environmental change in the economic and political spheres, together with a revolution in technology based on the microprocessor, have all forced large organizations to re-examine their structures with a view to adapting them so that they best fit the circumstances in which the organization now finds itself.

SOURCES

Baker, R. J. S., 1972, *Administrative Theory and Public Administration*, Hutchinson, London.

Berger, P. L. and Luckmann, T., 1971, *The Social Construction of Reality*, Penguin Books, Harmondsworth, Middlesex.

Child, J., 1969, *British Management Thought*, George Allen and Unwin, London.

Fayol, H., 1916, *General and Industrial Management* translated from the French by C. Storrs, 1949, Sir Issac Pitman and Sons, London, 1916.

"Five ways to go bust", *The Economist*, January 8, 1983.

Follett, M. P., 1926, Mary Parker Follett's papers given to the Bureau of Personnel Administration are reported in H. C. Metcalf and L. Urwick (eds.) *Dynamic Administration*, Sir Issac Pitman, London, 1926.

Hunt, J., 1979, *Managing People at Work*, Pan Books, London.

Jervis, F. R., 1974, *Bosses in British Business*, Routledge and Kegan Paul, London.

Lupton, T., 1978, "'Best fit' in the design of organizations" in E. J. Miller (ed.), *Task and Organization*, John Wiley and Sons, Chichester.

Lussato, B., 1972, *A Critical Introduction to Organizational Theory*, Macmillan, London.

Macrae, N., 1982, "Intrapreneurial now", *The Economist*, April 17.

Massie, J. L., 1966, "Management theory" in J. G. March (ed.), *Handbook of Organizations*, Rand McNally, Chicago.

March, J. G. and Simon, H. A., 1958, *Organizations*, John Wiley and Sons, New York.

Mooney, J. D. and Reily, A. C., 1931, *Onward Industry*, Harper, New York.

Peters, T. J. and Waterman Jnr., R. H., 1982, *In Search of Excellence*, Harper and Row, New York.

"Printer's group earns a bigger share of the pie", *The Guardian*, May 31, 1983.

Rudge, P. F., 1968, *Ministry and Management: The Study of Eccesiastical Management*, Tavistock, London.

Sheldon, O., 1965, *The Philosophy of Management*, Pitman, London, 1924, Reprinted with an introduction by A. W. Rathe

Urwick, L., 1933, "Organization as a technical problem" reprinted in L. Gulick and L. Urwick (eds.) *Papers on the Science of Administration*, Columbia University Press, New York, 1937.

Urwick, L., 1943, *The Functions of Administration*, Harper, New York.

Urwick, L., 1947, *The Elements of Administration*, Pitman, 2nd edition.

Urwick, L. and Brech, E. F. L., 1966, *The Making of Scientific Management: Volume 1: Thirteen Pioneers*, Sir Issac Pitman, London.

Wild, R. (ed.), 1983, *How To Manage*, Heinemann, London.

Chapter 18

Contingency approach

Key concepts:

Once you have fully understood this chapter, you should be able to define the following concepts in your own words:

Contingency approach   Strategic choice
Role culture   Technical complexity
Task culture   Environmental complexity
Power culture   Environment uncertainty
Person culture   Differentiation
Determinist perspective   Integration

Objectives:

On completing this chapter, you should be able to:

1. Explain in what sense the classical-universal school of management and the human relations approaches are both universal.
2. Give reasons for the shift away from the classical-universal approach towards the contingency approach.
3. Distinguish between different types of organizational activities and suggest the most appropriate structure for each.
4. Distinguish between the determinist and the strategic choice perspectives towards organizational design.
5. Understand and be able to contrast different types of determinist thinking as represented by the work of Woodward, Perrow and Lawrence and Lorsch.

DEVELOPMENT OF THE CONTINGENCY APPROACH

The antecedents of the contingency approach to the design of organizational structure have their roots in the search for the "one-best-way" of management. Both the classical theorists and those from the human relations school sought to offer panaceas, although of different varieties. Managers have received voluminous, although often conflicting, advice on topics such as how to plan plant layout, what reward system to introduce, how best to motivate staff and so on. Each suggestion claimed a universal application, and in so doing, paid little or no attention to the circumstances of the particular organization concerned — its objectives, environment, market or the kind of people it employed.

The 1960s represented a watershed in this kind of thinking. Such universal prescriptions began to be rejected as research findings became available which raised questions about the validity of the organizational principles preached by the classical theorists. Blain's (1964) research showed that there was no necessary correlation between organizational effectiveness and the industrial principles advanced by classical management theorists, for example, strictly limited span of control. Moreover, it was found that very different forms of organizational structure could be equally successful. This contradiction forced researchers to look more closely at organizational structure and management practice. Tom Burns and G. M. Stalker (1961) identified a number of crucial variables which needed to be considered when structuring an organization. Joan Woodward's (1965) major contribution was to increase our understanding of the influence of technology, a variable which was further studied by Charles Perrow (1967).

It was this work in the early part of the 1960s which established the basis for the *contingency approach*. Contributions came from many different researchers who studied diverse topics such as wage payment systems, leadership styles, organizational structures, environmental influences and job design. Despite their different interests and approaches, what these writers had in common, which distinguished them from previous organizational theorists, was their rejection of any "one-best-way". Instead, they studied the kinds of situations in which particular organizational arrangements and management practices appeared to be most appropriate. Having identified what they felt were the crucial factors for a company, e.g. its labour market, technology, product market, environment, they argued for an organizational design which "best fitted" the situation as it existed. With the coming of contingency theory, organizational design ceased to be "off-the-shelf", but became tailored to the particular and specific needs of an organization. In discussing organizational design, Tom Lupton (1971) identified three separate approaches to the study of organizational behaviour. Two of them have already been considered in this book. These were the human relations, classical and contingency approaches.

Human relations approach

The key to organizational design from this perspective was a clear understanding of the capacities and abilities of individuals. The approach drew on the work of Elton Mayo and the studies carried out at the Hawthorne plant of the Western Electric Company. It assumed that employees were both committed to company goals and that they worked towards them. The job of the organization designer was to identify and remove those aspects of organizational structure which acted to obstruct the commitment of the workforce. Such "obstructions" were held to exist in different organizations and thus a common design was recommended for all of them.

Classical approach

This viewpoint was initiated by Henri Fayol and developed further by Mooney, Reilly, Urwick, Brech and others. It focused on rules, roles and procedures. In stressing orderliness and predictability, it echoed the writings of Max Weber on bureaucracy. Amongst its guiding concepts were span-of-control, job descriptions, hierarchy, and the separation of line and staff. Its objective was the achievement of efficiency through rationality. Like the Human Relations approach, it considered that organizations had similar problems (although it disagreed with the Human Relations school as to what those problems were) and so offered a package of principles and checklists which could be applied to all organizations. Warren Bennis (1959), a famous American social scientist, coined an epigram which distinguished these two views. He felt that classical theory was about "organizations without people", while the human relations approach was about "people without organizations".

Contingency approach

Both the preceding perspectives to organizational design had their beginnings in the 1930s. The contingency approach, in contrast, is a product of more recent times. Underlying this perspective is the notion that organizations consist of tasks which have to be performed and people to perform them. Both exist in the same environment. The tasks need to be carried out while the people try to grow and develop in an environment which offers both opportunities and constraints. Those charged with the task of designing organizations, are seen, from this viewpoint, as trying to achieve some acceptable degree of "fit" between the tasks, people and the environment. This "fit" will depend on (will be *contingent* upon) the prevailing circumstances.

Universal prescriptions versus specific choices

"It is of great practical significance whether one kind of managerial 'style' or procedure for arriving at decisions, or one kind of organizational structure, is suitable for all organizations, or whether the managers in each organization have to find that expedient that will best meet the particular circumstances of size, technology, product, competitive situation and so on. In practice, managers do, indeed must, attempt to define the particular circumstances of the unit they manage, and to devise ways of dealing with these circumstances. I have often observed that their success in doing so is limited by their belief that there must be a universal prescription. This belief can obscure some of the alternatives that are open. To act in this way could also cause failure to develop criteria for choosing the alternative amongst those that are available and visible, which is best suited to the particular circumstances."

From Tom Lupton, *Management and the Social Sciences*, Penguin Books, Harmondsworth, Middlesex, 1971, second edition, p. 121.

The universal prescriptions of the human relations and the classical schools, and the "it-all-depends" approach of the contingency theorists, does capture the main distinction between the current views about organizational structuring. However, it is possible to see elements of one in the other. Ironically, Henri Fayol known as the father of classical management theory, may be credited with making perhaps the earliest contribution to the contingency approach. He wrote,

"If we could eliminate the human factor, it would be easy enough to build up an organization; anyone could do it if they had an idea of current practice and the necessary capital. But we cannot build up an effective organization simply by dividing men into groups and giving them functions; we must know how to adapt the organization to the requirements of the case, and how to find the necessary men and put each one in the place where he can be of most service; we need, in fact, many substantial qualities."

Thus Fayol demonstrated a greater degree of sensitivity and awareness of the complexity of organizational design than he is often credited with. In his book, *Administration Industrielle et General*, published originally in French in 1916, he made another statement which could be incorporated, unamended, into any book describing the contingency approach,

"For preference I shall adopt the term principles whilst dissociating it from any suggestion of rigidity, for there is nothing rigid and absolute in management affairs, it is all a question of proportion. Seldom do we have to apply the same principle twice in identical conditions; allowances must be made for different changing circumstances, for men just as different and changing and for many other variable elements".

From Henri Fayol, (1916) *General and Industrial Management,* Sir Isaac
Pitman, London, 1949, p. 19.

Following the elaboration of classical theory during the 1930s and 1940s,
concern began to be expressed about the univeral application of the principles
being expounded. Herbert Simon (1948, p. 240) commented on the, "... steady
shift of emphasis from 'principles of administration' themselves, to a study of the
conditions under which competing principles are respectively applicable". As
early as the 1950s, writers were considering alternative organizational forms.
William Foote Whyte (1959) used a scheme based on the work of George
Homans to depict the "it all depends" idea of structural design. He argued that
each interaction, activity and sentiment was part of the "environment of the
organization". By environment, Whyte meant the factory or company environment. It is as if he had drawn a circle or boundary around the company and
examined what happened to individuals and groups inside that circle. This
perspective is sometimes labelled "closed systems theory" because it does not
take into account factors outside of that boundary. Nevertheless, Whyte did
stress that the appropriate structure and management behaviour (i.e. the "good"
foreman) was context specific. For him it was technology, which he interpreted
as part of a company's environment, which was the crucial variable.

> "If we take seriously the statements presented here regarding the
> impact of the environment upon the social system, then we must
> recognise that there is no such thing as the good foreman and the good
> executive".
>
> From William Foote Whyte, " An interaction approach to the theory of
> organizations" in M. Haire (ed), *Modern Organization Theory,* John
> Wiley, New York, 1959, p. 181.

Modern thinking about different organizational structures can be related
back to the work of John Child (1972). Child argued that early contingency
theorists felt constrained in their organizational choices about the appropriate
structure by factors such as the size of the organization and its technology. In
fact, it was felt that there was limited choice possible because these variables
went a long way towards determining the structure of an organization. These
views were presented in the writings of people such as Joan Woodward, Charles
Perrow, Peter Blau, Tom Burns and G. M. Stalker as well as Jay Lorsch and Peter
Lawrence. Let us at this point define was is meant by contingency theory.

Contingency theory

"Contingency theory refers to attempts to understand the multivariate
relationships between components of organizations and to designing
structures piece-by-piece, as best fits the components. This approach
rejects earlier theories of universal models for designing formal
structures, and argues that each situation must be analysed separately.
Contingency means, 'it depends'. Moreover, choosing a design for the

whole is seen by contingency theorists to be restrictive: units of structure may be adopted from all along a design continuum, depending on the situation. Contingency implies that within the same organization there may be units of bureaucracy, units operating in a matrix structure, and units which are divisionalized. Single design types. neatness, symmetry and permanence are not indicative of 'good' design. The only criteria for good design are task performance and individual/group satisfaction."

From John Hunt, *Managing People at Work*, Penguin Books, Harmondsworth, Middlesex, 1979, p. 189.

It is worthwhile stressing that while writers talk about contingency *theory*, it is nothing of the sort. It is more correct to consider it as a way of thinking rather than as a set of interrelated causal elements which might be said to constitute a theory.

DIFFERENT FORMS OF ORGANIZATIONAL STRUCTURE

Derek Pugh, David Hickson and Diana Pheysey (1964) devised ways of measuring and "profiling" the many different structural characteristics to be found in organizations. They wanted to develop a "language" which could help to distinguish one organization from another with great precision. They considered activity, structural, contextual and performance variables. Each such variable was measured along a number of dimensions. An example of the structural variable and its dimensions are shown below:

Variable:

Structural

Dimensions measured:

Specialization: does the organization have a specialism dealing with specific functions, e.g. personnel?
Standardization: the extent to which jobs are codified and the range of variation that is tolerated within the rules defining the jobs.
Formalization: the extent to which rules, procedures, instructions and communications are written down.
Centralization: where is the locus of authority to make decisions?

The researchers sought to measure every organization they studied on the four variables among the different dimensions. In this way they sought to develop a profile of each organization in order to be able to compare them. They went on to define and measure the characteristics of the environment in which the organization existed in order to relate the two sets of information to see what organizational characteristics produced a high performance organization.

What structural forms are available to the person designing an organization? Four main different ones were originally identified by Roger Harrison (1972). His labels and descriptions offer a useful shorthand with which to discuss structural arrangements within organizations. This author distinguished four prevailing organizational ideologies or cultures, each of which gave rise to its own characteristic structural arrangements. Writing about these, Handy commented that:

> "In organizations there are deep set beliefs about the way work should be organized, the way authority should be exercised, people rewarded, people controlled. What are the degrees of formalization required? How much planning and how far ahead? What combination of obedience and initiative is looked for in subordinates? Do work hours matter, or dress, or personal eccentricities? What about expense accounts and secretaries, stock options and incentives? Do committees control or individuals? Are there rules and procedures or only results?"
>
> From Charles Handy, *Understanding Organizations*, Penguin Books, Harmondsworth, Middlesex, 1976, p. 177.

Handy's book describes Harrison's organizational cultures which are labelled Role, Task, Power and Person. Each has its own corresponding organizational structure.

Role culture
This reflects the structural/classical views of writers such as Weber and others. A bureaucratic form of organization is depicted by the shape opposite. The specialities or functions in an organization, e.g. production, marketing, finance, personnel constitute the pillars upon which the 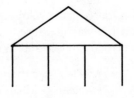 organization stands. It is viewed in terms of roles with procedures specifying each role (e.g. job descriptions), those specifying the nature of communication (e.g. number of copies required), and still other rules which specify how conflict is to be managed (e.g. who to appeal to). The different company functions (e.g. marketing, production, finance) are co-ordinated at the top by a group of senior managers. The organizations is seen as a collection of interlocking roles and role sets.

Anyone can fill the role if suitably selected and adequately trained. The showing of too much initiative can be disruptive. The power is exercised on the basis of position and rules and procedures are used to influence persons. Following Weber, efficiency is sought by rationally allocating work and responsibility. Role structures, such as the Civil Service, work well in stable environments but are slow to change.

Task culture

A task culture is job or project orientated and its structure reflects such a priority. Depicted as a net, the focus is on task to be done. The appropriate people are brought together in teams to achieve the task. The objectives of the group are more important than the differences in status between 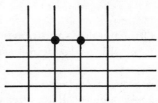 its members. The matrix structure is flexible, and individuals tend to exert a high degree of control over their work. The relationships between task group members are based on their contribution to goal achievement rather than status in some hierarchy. The control which is exercised tends to be loose and is achieved through the allocation of people and other resources to the projects.

Power culture

The focus here is on the power source which may be an individual or a small group. It is from this centre of power that influence and instructions generate out. Work is organized according to precedent, and staff anticipate the wishes of those in positions of power. There are few rules or  specified procedures, and control is exercised by appointing key individuals. The structure that is created is very dependent on the skill and presence of a few key individuals. Shopkeepers and small family firms frequently have this type of culture and associated structure.

Person culture

This organizational culture holds the view that the organization serves the needs of the individuals in it. It is created for them, rather than they being fitted into it. Individuals who share common aims and objectives may come together in order to pursue their individual aims collectively. This may 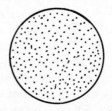 require the sharing of equipment and other facilities. Small consulting firms, social groups and architect partnerships represent examples of person cultures.

Four different types of organizational cultures and structures have been defined. It will be shown that contingency theory recommends matching an organizational structure to suit the prevailing situation and circumstances of companies. The approach does not exclude having a number of different organizational structures co-existing within the same organization. What circumstances and situations should be considered when designing a suitable structure? These include the activities which are performed within the organization, the technology used by the company and, not least, the environment in which it exists. Each of these will be examined in turn.

ACTIVITIES WITHIN THE ORGANIZATION

Of the hundreds and thousands of things that people do within organizations, it is possible to distinguish four main classes of activities.

Steady state activities
These include all activities which are routine and which are capable of being programmed. Every organization routinely keeps accounts, performs secretarial tasks, engages in sales activities, attends to the production of the output. Such programmed, routine activities may constitute up to 80 per cent of the tasks carried out by people.

Policy making activities
Here the activities concern identifying goals, setting standards, allocating scarce resources and getting people to do things.

Innovation activities
These are concerned with anything that changes in what the company does or how it does it. Research and development departments, organization and methods studies, developing new markets for old products are all examples of innovation activities.

Breakdown activities
Certain individuals, groups or departments in organizations deal with emergencies and crises. Parts of the personnel department during a period of an industrial dispute will be engaged in crisis activities.

STOP!

Think about your own work in an organization. Classify the activities in which you engage under these four headings.

The implication of this viewpoint is that within a single organization it is feasible to have a number of different structures existing in parallel. Moreover, within each type of structure there may be differences in:
- The types of people best suited to work in them;
- The appropriate means of motivating people;
- The style of management.

Different structures for different activities

"An example of this would be the 4077th MASH where to meet the demands of treating emergencies in battle they need to react quickly.

But to treat complex injuries with complex technology and maintain records etc. for the future treatment and other associated administration, a certain level of routine is necesary. Similarly when the unit is overloaded and necessary medical supplies are not available, considerable 'negotiation' and 'dealing' with other units etc. is undertaken. The organization that has evolved is a sort of Task Culture where everyone works as a team to process the work with easy working relationships etc. but it does have role elements in the efficiency with which paperwork is processed. It has power culture elements for Radar to negotiate and bargain with other units and the unit commander has to use personal intervention to keep the unit going and protect it from the rest of the organization in which it exists.

The problem of imposing an inappropriate organizational design exists in the shape of Major Burns, Hoolahan and the occasional CIA agent. These represent the dominant role organization in which the unit exists. Their attempts to impose military rules and procedures and impose the formal rank in the unit are seen as highly inappropriate, often farcical."

From John Parris, "Designing your organization", *Management Services*, October, 1979, p. 14.

DETERMINISM VERSUS STRATEGIC CHOICE

The debate concerning contingency focuses around the basic question of whether there is a single variable such as activity-to-be-performed, technology-used or environment-lived-in, which *determines* the structure of an organization. Or, whether organizational structure is always the outcome of a choice made by those in positions of power within organizations. These two schools of thought are labelled the *determinist school* and the *strategic choice school* respectively.

Definitions

Determinism is the belief that some variables such as technology or company size determine, that is, are the direct cause of, changes in other variables such as the degree of specialization, standardization, formalization and centralization that is to be found in an organization.

Strategic choice is the view that holds that organizational structure is wholly a company management decision. It is senior management which decides which technology to adopt, how it is introduced and used, what products are manufactured and in which markets they are sold. Thus decisions about the number of levels of hierarchy, the span-of-control and so on, are ultimately based on the personal values of those who make them.

Linked to these issues about the shape of the organization's structure, is the question of organizational performance and efficiency. Are particular structural arrangements more conducive to organizational success than others?

Technological determinism

The work of Joan Woodward and Charles Perrow is representative of the technological determinist school. Woodward (1965) investigated 100 firms in south east England which used different technologies. These companies were using unit and small batch production systems, large batch production, mass production and process production systems. She identified differences in the technical complexity of the process of production. By *technical complexity* she meant that as one moved from prototype production to small batch to mass production and then on to process production, there was a greater degree of control and predictability in the manufacturing system. She also examined the company's organizational structures. Following a statistical analysis, Woodward related the organization's technology to its structure. She argued that as the technology became more complex, so,

- The length of the chain of command increased;
- Chief executives' span-of-control increased;
- The proportion of indirect to direct labour increased;
- The proportion of managers to the total employed workforce increased.

She argued that a relationship existed between a company's economic performance (e.g. profitability) and its organizational structure. Having identified these statistical relationships, she went on to make observations about the effectiveness of performance of the companies. In her view, the companies which had a structure close to the norm for the category were more commercially successful than those whose structure deviated from the pattern. Her conclusion was that,

> "... there was a particular form of organization most appropriate to each technical situation." (Woodward, 1965, p. 72)

The reasoning underlying this conclusion is that the technology used to manufacture the product, or make available the service, places specific requirements on those who operate it. Such demands, for example, in the need for controlling work, or motivating staff, are likely to be reflected in the organization structure. The technology-structure link is complemented by the notion of effective performance which held that each type of production system called for its own characteristic organizational stucture. Within this technological determinist school one can also include the research of Charles Perrow. His work is based on two assumptions:

1.   Technology defined the character of the organization (Perrow, 1967, p.

194). The key point was whether the individual tasks to be performed were routine or non-routine. From this essential distinction flowed the methods of control and co-ordination, the degrees of individual discretion and power, and the type of social structure and motivation.

2.   Technology was an independent variable and "arrangements to get things done" (i.e. organizational structure) were considered to be a dependent variable.

Unlike Woodward who felt that it was the *complexity* of the technology that determined the appropriate organizational structure, Perrow argued that it was the *predictability* of the work task which determined the structure. He suggested that there was a continuum in technology from the routine to the non-routine. Organizations differed in their structures depending on the requirements of the *kind of search the technology required.* What Perrow meant by this was that the technology used affected the number of mini-crises or unpredictable cases which came up and which needed to be dealt with (e.g. machine breakdown). How these exceptional cases were dealt with (e.g. applying routine procedures, analysing them, and so on), determined the type of organizational structure which emerged. The greater the amount of predictability in the work, the more one could specify roles and reduce the discretionary elements to produce a role-type organizational structure. Perrow's argument can thus be summarized as follows:

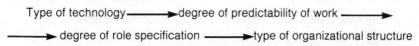

Type of technology ———▶ degree of predictability of work ———▶
———▶ degree of role specification ———▶ type of organizational structure

Perrow postulated a causal relationship between structure and technology arguing that certain aspects of job discretion, co-ordination and group interdependence were *caused* by the use of different technologies. In his view, the variable of technology was more important than others such as leadership style or the dynamics of small groups.

Environmental determinism

A second influential subschool within determinism considers that it is an organization's *environment* which determines its organizational structure.

Tell me what your environment is and I shall tell your what your organization ought to be.

Peter R. Lawrence quoted in Chris Argyris, *The Applicability of Organizational Sociology*, Cambridge University Press, Cambridge, 1972, p. 88.

The environmental determinists see the organization as being in constant interaction with the environment in which it exists. This would include the general economic situation, the market, the competitive scene and so on. They argue that because a company is dependent on its environment for sales, labour, raw materials, etc., this relationship constrains the kind of choices an organization can make about how it structures itself. As the environmental situation changes, so the organizational-environment relationship will change. To continue to perform effectively, the organization is seen to be forced to structure, and re-structure, in ways dictated by that environment. The environmental determinists use certain key concepts in their explanation.

Definitions

Environmental uncertainty is the degree to which the environments of the company change. It is measured by the speed of customer demands and responses.

Environmental complexity refers to the range of environmental activities which are relevant to what the organization does. For example, different customer groups, different supplier companies, central and local government, the labour market, other companies, its own competitors. The greater the number of these, the greater its environmental complexity.

Organizational environments and organizational structures

Tom Burns and G. M. Stalker studied the behaviour of people working in a rayon mill. They found that this contented, economically successful company, was run with a management style which, according to contemporary wisdom about "best" management practice, should have led to worker discontent and inefficiency. Some time later, the same authors studied an electronics company. Again it was highly successful, but used a management style completely different from that of the rayon mill studied earlier. This contradiction gave the authors the impetus to begin a large scale investigation to examine the relationship between the management systems and the organizational tasks. They were particularly interested in the way management systems changed in response to changes in the commercial and technical tasks of the firm.

The rayon mill had a highly stable, highly structured and bureaucratic character which would have fitted well into Weber's view of bureaucracy and would represent a role culture in Harrison's terminology. In contrast, the electronics firm violated many of the principles of classical management. It discouraged written communications, defined jobs as little as possible, interaction was on a face-to-face basis and staff even complained about this certainty. The authors gave the label "Mechanistic" to the first form of organization structure, and "Organismic" to the second. These represented ideal-types at opposite ends of a continuum.

They argued that neither form of organization was necessarily efficient or inefficient, but that rather it all depended on the nature of the environment in which a firm operated. The key variables in their view were the product market and the technology of the manufacturing process. These needed to be considered when the structure of a firm's management system was being designed. Thus, a mechanistic structure may be appropriate for an organization which uses an unchanging technology and operates in relatively stable markets. An organismic structure can be more suitable for a firm which has to cope with unpredictable new tasks.

From Tom Burns and G. M. Stalker, *The Management of Innovation*, Tavistock Publications, London, 1961.

Classifying environments

Fred Emery and E. L. Trist (1965) distinguished four types of environments in which organizations existed. These were the *placid-random* type which was stable and unchanging; the *placid-clustered* where organization had to develop a degree of internal specialization in its structure and adopt strategies to meet situations where parts of its environment were related to one another; the *disturbed-reactive* environment in which there were several organizations pursuing similar goals and each had to decide between co-optation, co-operation or competition with the others; and finally there was the *turbulent* environment which was volatile and ever changing. In this one, the organization needed to adopt a non-bureaucratic (task-type) organizational structure, in order to survive.

Peter Lawrence and Jay Lorsch also took an environmental determinist position. They argued that an organization exists within three main environments — market, research and development and technology. Each environment differs in terms of its rate of change and the time span of feedback, i.e. the time lapse between a decision/action taken inside of the organization and its consequences being known and evaluated. Since these are different for different environments and different organizations, argue Lawrence and Lorsch, companies had different needs for specialization which become reflected in their organizational structures.

Their research indicated that companies did not necessarily adopt the same organizational structures in the face of their environmental situations. Organizations which were similar in size and which had similar markets and technology, were found to have different structural arrangements. They do not adopt a single, common type of organizational structure. However, in terms of organizational performance and success, some structures appeared to be preferable to others. In considering this, Lawrence and Lorsch (1967) used two basic concepts — differentiation and integration.

Definitions

Differentiation was the degree to which the tasks and the work of individuals, groups and units should be divided.

Integration was the required level to which units should be linked together and their degree of independence. Integrative mechanisms include rules and procedures and direct managerial control.

Differentiation and integration were found to be inversly related in that highly differentiated units are difficult to integrate. The aim of Lawrence and Lorsch was to identify the characteristics which organizations needed to have in order to perform effectively under a particular set of environmental situations. A differentiated organization is one in which the tasks of policy, innovation, breakdown and steady-state are carried out by units with different structural forms operating within the *same* organization. A company's environments are likely to change at different speeds. Those parts of the company which face, and interact with that particular environment will be structured in a way which is most likely to be successful in dealing with that environment.

STOP!

Is your educational institution differentiated or integrated? What evidence do you base your answer on? What problems does such differentiation/integration give to you as a client, and to the staff?

University challenge

An example of a major environmental change from a "placid-random" to a "turbulent" environment is provided by the experience of British universities during the period 1968-83. (Gurth Higgin, 1983). The main contrasts are summarized in the table below:

1968◄───────────────────────────────────────►1980s

Placid environment certain-simple	Turbulent environment uncertain-complex
Numbers of undergraduates increasing	Student numbers falling
Ample supply of foreign students	Scramble among universities for falling number of overseas students
Five-year forward rolling grant system	Cuts in univeristy spending-annual allocation

Tenure for staff nearly automatic	Tenure under threat due to economic prssures
Acceptance by society of higher education for its own sake	Scholarship and knowledge values questioned. Pressure from vocational practicality.
Polytechnic institutions in public sector developing	Low-cost competition provided by public sector institutions
Full employment	Mass and structural unemployment
Settled view	Pressure for change in patterns of work, jobs and leisure
University lobby listened to and generally had demands met	Universities just another voice in the money queue

The universities experienced both a certain increase in environmental complexity, and a massive increase in environmental uncertainty. They no longer knew for certain what the pattern of relationships between themselves and other key institutions would be in the future.

STOP!

What are the implications of such environmental changes for the types of organizational structures that universities might now usefully adopt?

STRATEGIC CHOICE VIEW

The label that is given to the meaningful behaviour of individuals is "action". The action frame of reference pays particular attention to the purposeful behaviour of individuals. It seeks to understand their expectations, their beliefs about how their behaviour is constrained, and their choices of goals and the means to be used to achieve them. Those who adopt an action perspective therefore, argue that the relationship between an organization's structure and its technology is a reflection of a choice made by management based on its perception of the situation. These writers reject the arguments of Woodward and Perrow that organizational structure emerges out of some technological or bureaucratic demand. This opposing view, which is labelled the *strategic choice* perspective, has been summarized by John Child. This perspective sees the design of organizational structures as being:

> ". . . . an essentially political process in which constraints and opportunities are functions of the power exercised by decision makers in the light of ideological values." (Child, 1972, p.2)

Action theorists would argue that technology does not determine organizational structure, independently of the aims, beliefs and expectations of those who make the decision about how it is to be used. It is not the technology itself but rather how it is used, that is the crucial factor. To understand the impact of technology on organizational structure, one needs to study the nature of the managerial decision making process itself. After all, it is the managers who decide upon the design of an organization.

CONCLUSION

Amongst the strengths of the universal "panacea school" was the fact that it offered managers and others in organization a prescription for action. It told them what to do. In contrast, contingency approaches appear somewhat wishy-washy, and the notion of "it all depends" appears to suggest that this group of thinkers are not as informed. While contingency theorists do not offer ready made answers, they do have a set of questions and do provide a way of thinking which can help a manager analyse his organization in its environment in order to be able to make a more informed choice about the most appropriate organizational structure.

SOURCES

Argyris, C., 1972, *The Applicability of Organizational Sociology*, Cambridge University Press, Cambridge.

Bennis, W. G., 1959, "Leadership theory and administrative behaviour: the problem of authority", *Administrative Science Quarterly*, vol. 4, no. 3, December.

Blain, I., 1964, *Structure in Management*, National Institute for Industrial Psychology, London.

Burns, T. and Stalker, G. M., 1961, *The Management of Innovation*, Tavistock Publications, London.

Child, J. (1972) "Organizational structure, environment and Performance© the role of strategic choice", *Sociology*, vol. 6, pp. 1-22.

Emery, F. E. and Trist, E. L., 1965, "The causal texture of organizational environments", *Human Relations*, vol. 18, no. 1, pp. 21-31.

Fayol, H., 1916, *General and Industrial Management*, translated from the French by C. Storrs, Sir Issac Pitman and Sons, London, 1949.

Handy, C., 1979, *Gods of Management*, Pan Books, London.

Handy, C., 1976, *Understanding Organizations*, Penguin Books, Harmondsworth, Middlesex.

Harrison, R., 1972, "Understanding your organization's character", *Harvard Business Review*, May - June, pp. 119-28.

Hickson, D. J., Pugh, D. S. and Pheysey, D. C., 1969, "Operations technology and organizational structure: An empirical appraisal", *Administrative Science Quarterly*, vol. 14, no. 3, pp. 378-97.

Hunt, J., 1979, *Managing People*, Pan Books. London.

Higgin, G., 1983, "Unsteady state theory", *Times Higher Educational Supplement*, 19 August,.

Lawrence, P. R. and Lorsch, J. W., 1967, *Organization and Environment*, Division of Research, Harvard Business School, Boston.

Lupton, T., 1971, *Management and the Social Sciences*, Penguin Books. Harmondsworth, Middlesex.

Parris, J., 1979, "Designing your organization", *Management Services*, October, pp. 10-14.

Perrow, C., 1967, *Organizational Analysis: A Sociological View*, Tavistock, London.

Pugh, D. S., Hickson, D. J., Hinings, C. R. and Turner, C., 1964, "The context of Organizational structures", *Administrative Science Quarterly*, vol. 14, pp. 91-114.

Whyte, W. F., 1959, "An interaction approach to the theory of organizations" in M. Haire (ed.) *Modern Organization Theory*, John Wiley, New York, pp. 155-183.

Woodward, J., 1965, *Industrial Organization: Theory and Practice*, Oxford University Press, London.

PART 5:

MANAGEMENT IN THE
ORGANIZATION

Overview

"The manager is the dynamic, life-giving element in every business. Without his leadership 'the resources of production' remain resources and never become production. In a competitive economy, above all, the quality and performance of the managers determine the success of a business, indeed they determine its survival. For the quality and performance of its managers is the only effective advantage an enterprise in a competitive economy can have."

From Peter F. Drucker, *The Practice of Management*, Heinemann, London, 1955, p. 13.

Management can be viewed as a function, or as a set of functions, that must be carried out if an organization is to operate and survive. But *managers* can be viewed as a social group, as a profession, as an organizational elite. A good deal of confusion can arise from a failure to distinguish clearly between these two perspectives.

The management function is a set of indispensible activities. Regardless of the type or nature of an organization, there are a number of tasks that have to be carried out to ensure the organization's success. These functions were examined in Chapter 17. They are usually carried out by professional managers. But this is no more than a social arrangement. The management function or aspects of it could be carried out by people other than those who belong to the management profession.

We will explore some of the ways in which the simple equation of management with managers is inaccurate. We will also examine Peter Drucker's stereotype of the manager as an indispensible male leader.

The organizational dilemma introduced in Chapter 1 concerns the fact that the goals of the individual members of an organization are not necessarily consistent with those of the organization that employs them. People often prefer to question rather than follow orders, do not always accept change, and do not always agree with the goals and actions of others. Management therefore is not a set of routine administrative functions. The organizational dilemma creates a persistent problem for managers — how to manage unmanageable people.

The first three aspects of management that we examine here — leadership, and the management of change and conflict, are those which cause many managers and their employees serious problems. But it is possible also to argue that these are simply facets of a more fundamental problem. Karl Marx argued that conflict in capitalist organizations arises because the pattern of ownership and control establishes classes of owners and workers whose interests inevitably conflict. Owners and managers want bigger profits. Employees want bigger pay cheques. There is no way in which these fundamentally opposed interests can be reconciled within the capitalist system and Marx thought that the resulting conflict would eventually destroy capitalism. Problems of leadership, change and conflict are in this view all aspects of the central issue of management control in organizations.

Chapter 19

Leadership and management style

The functions of leaders and managers
Are leaders special people?
Leaders need followers
The importance of the context
Can leaders change their styles?

The roots of management . . .

manus agere	Latin	To work with the hand.
le manege	French	Horse training, horsemanship, a riding school.
maneggiare	Italian	To train and handle horses.
management	English	1 The action or manner of managing.
		2 The use of contrivance for effecting some purpose; often in bad sense, implying deceit or trickery.
manager	English	1 One who manages.
		2 One skilled in managing affairs, money, etc.
		3 One who manages a business, an institution, etc.

From *The Shorter Oxford English Dictionary*.

"The manager's job can, therefore, be broadly defined as 'deciding what should be done and then getting other people to do it'."

From Rosemary Stewart, *The Reality of Management*, Pan / Heinemann Books, London, 1963, p. 74.

---

y concepts:

Once you have fully understood this chapter, you should be able to define the following concepts in your own words:

Leadership

Consideration

Initiating structure

Great man theory

Reward power

Coercive power

Referent power

Legitimate power

Expert power

Contingency theory

Least preferred coworker score

Structured task

Unstructured task

Objectives:

On completing this chapter, you should be able:

1. To identify the main functions of leaders in organizations.
2. To understand why there is little relationship between personality traits and effective leadership.
3. To understand why there are few women managers.
4. To understand the bases of power in organizations.
5. To understand why effective managers typically adopt a democratic leadership style which takes into account the needs of subordinates as well as the task needs of the organization.
6. To identify the circumstances in which an autocratic leadership style can be effective.

THE FUNCTIONS OF LEADERS AND MANAGERS

"Leadership is the lifting of a man's vision to higher sights, the raising of a man's performance to a higher standard, the building of a man's personality beyond its normal limitations. Nothing better prepares the ground for such leadership than a spirit of management that confirms in the day-to-day practices of the organization strict principles of conduct and responsibility, high standards of performance, and respect for the individual and his work. For to leadership, too, the words of the savings bank advertisement apply: 'Wishing won't make it so; doing will'."

From Peter F. Drucker, *The Practice of Management*, Heinemann, London, 1955, p. 195.

Our interest in this section is with leadership in organizations, not with leadership in general. Most managers would probably claim to be able to exercise leadership in some form or another. A manager can be regarded as someone who by definition is assigned a position of leadership in an organization. It may therefore be reasonable to treat the terms leader and manager as meaning the same thing. But many people considered to be leaders are not actually managers. Many managers have duties and responsibilities that are not recognized as leadership. If we can first decide what leadership is, we can then ask which individuals possess or exercise it and which do not.

Interest in organizational leadership was stimulated by the human relations movement in industrial sociology after the Second World War. The Hawthorne studies demonstrated that if managers took an interest in their employees and involved them in decisions affecting their work they would work harder. Those studies thus claimed to have identified the style of supervision most likely to guarantee a happy, harmonious, motivated work force. Management style thus became a major interest and focus for research.

Many commentators have argued or assumed that the performance of an organization depends on the quality of leadership exercised by its managers. But in many organizations, tasks have been designed to be so routine, standardized and controlled that the dynamic, inspirational aspects of the leadership of other people may become redundant. These extreme views are probably incorrect and it is reasonable to claim that what managers do in their leadership capacity does affect organizational performance — along with many other factors.

The functions of management include:

1. Establishing the overall purpose or policy of the unit for which they are responsible;
2. Forecasting and planning for the future;
3. Organizing work, allocating duties and responsibilities;
4. Giving instructions or orders;

5.   Checking that performance is according to plan — control;
6.   Coordinating the work of others.

People prefer considerate leaders . . .

As psychiatrists are too expensive for most of us, managers at work end
up dealing with their employees' personal problems. Factory foremen
for example do not just give orders to subordinates to organize and
co-ordinate their work. They have to deal also with a range of employee
queries and difficulties. The *style* in which they carry out these extra
responsibilities may influence their effectiveness as foremen.

Elizabeth Kaplan and Emory Cowen studied how American factory
foremen felt about this counselling aspect of their work — which is
important as psychological well being and productivity can be related.

They asked ninety-seven foremen in twelve companies in New
York about the kinds of problems that their subordinates brought to
them, how much of their time this took up, how they went about solving
these problems, and how important they felt this part of their job was.

The average foreman spent 7 per cent of his working time — about
two-and-a-half hours a week — dealing with the personal problems of
subordinates. The most difficult problems for the foremen to solve were
those which concerned marriage, money, and other employees.

The foremen's most popular counselling technique was "the
sympathetic ear". They usually encouraged subordinates to work out
their own solutions and rarely suggested that they seek professional
help.

Most of the foremen were happy to have been approached for this
kind of help, felt that this was an important aspect of their work, and felt
satisfied when their advice had been successful.

The authors argue that this informal counselling service is important to subordinates and to productivity and that supervisors who
have to provide the service should be given formal training in listening
and advisory skills.

From Elizabeth M. Kaplan and Emory L. Cowen, 'Interpersonal helping
behaviour of industrial foremen', *Journal of Applied Psychology*, 1981,
vol. 66, no. 5, pp. 633-38.

But the exercise of these functions alone has little directly to do with lifting
vision, raising performance and building personality. Leadership it seems is
something more than the mere discharge of administrative functions. It is the
way in which these functions are discharged — in the *style* of the manager —that
the features of leadership are sought.

Some commentators have argued that communication and motivation are
two additional functions of management. But these are not administrative duties
such as planning and organizing. They are more concerned with how the
manager *influences* others to carry out the plan, to accept instructions. They are

again concerned with management style.

Definition

A leader is someone who exercises *influence* over other people.

This definition makes most managers leaders by virtue of their organizational role. But managers do not *automatically* become leaders. The ability to influence also needs the permission of those to be influenced. The functions of leaders in organizations may include:

Enabling people and groups to achieve their objectives;
Setting and communicating objectives;
Monitoring performance and giving feedback;
Establishing basic values;
Clarifying and solving problems for others;
Organizing resources;
Administering rewards and punishments;
Providing information, advice and expertise;
Providing social and emotional support;
Making decisions on behalf of others;
Representing the group to others;
Arbitrator in disputes;
Father figure;
Scapegoat.

This list could easily be extended. The point however is that you do not have to have the word "manager" in your job title to be able to carry out these functions. Almost anyone could perform most of these tasks, and it has been suggested that these functions are best distributed depending on who can do each most effectively. There is therefore no necessary connection between these functions and a formally appointed manager. Similarly, managers do not become leaders just because they have job titles such as "team leader" or "section leader". The notions of management and leadership thus overlap and there is no clear separation between them.

The studies of Edwin Fleishman and his colleagues at the Bureau of Business Research at Ohio State University in America in the late 1940s are a classic and influential attempt to make sense of the complexity and diversity of leadership behaviours. They first designed a Leadership Behaviour Description Questionnaire based on how people in leadership roles actually carried out their functions. Foremen in the International Harvester Company, and various employees in other organizations, then rated the frequency with which their own superiors behaved in the ways described in the questionnaire. Analysis of the questionnaire results revealed that the behaviour of leaders was described on two distinct categories:

democratic

Consideration

This type of leader behaviour is *needs and relationships orientated.*

> The leader is interested in and listens to subordinates, allows partici-
> pation in decision making, is friendly and approachable, helps sub-
> ordinates with personal problems and is prepared to support them if
> necessary. The leader's behaviour thus indicates genuine trust, respect,
> warmth, and rapport. This type of behaviour enhances subordinates'
> feelings of self-esteem as well as encouraging the development of
> close communications and relationships in a work group.

This is the kind of emphasis that the human relations management school
encouraged, except that some of its advocates tended to exaggerate the benefits
of superficial "first name calling" and the "pat on the back". The researchers first
called this leadership dimension *social sensitivity.*

In the Leadership Behaviour Description Questionnaire, subordinates
would rate their superiors as needs orientated if they agreed with the following
kinds of statement:

> He stresses the importance of high morale among those under him.
> He backs up his foremen in their actions.
> He does personal favours for the foremen under him.
> He expresses appreciation when one of us does a good job.
> He is easy to understand.
> He helps his foremen with their personal problems.
> He sees that a foreman is rewarded for a job well done.
> He treats all his foremen as his equal.
> He is willing to make changes.
> He makes those under him feel at ease when talking with him.
> He gets the approval of his foremen on important matters before going
> ahead.

Subordinates with inconsiderate superiors agreed with statements like:

> He refuses to give in when people disagree with him.
> He criticizes his foremen in front of others.
> He insists that everything be done his way.
> He rejects suggestions for change.
> He changes the duties of people under him without first talking it over
> with them.
> He refuses to explain his actions.

autocratic

Initiating structure

This type of leader behaviour is *task orientated.*

> The leader plans ahead, decides how things are going to get done,
> assigns tasks to subordinates, makes expectations clear, emphasizes

deadlines and the achievement of objectives, and expects subordinates to follow instructions closely. The leader's behaviour thus stresses production and the achievement of organizational goals as a main objective. This type of behaviour can stimulate enthusiasm to achieve objectives as well as encouraging and helping subordinates to get the work done.

This is the kind of emphasis that the scientific management school encouraged, except that here it is recognized that task orientation can have a positive motivating aspect. The researchers first called this leadership dimension *production emphasis.*

In the Leadership Behaviour Description Questionnaire, subordinates would rate their superiors as task orientated if they agreed with the following kinds of statement:

He rules with an iron hand.
He criticizes poor work.
He talks about how much should be done.
He assigns people under him to particular tasks.
He asks for sacrifices for the good of the entire department.
He insists that his foremen follow standard ways of doing things in every detail.
He sees to it that people under him are working up to their limits.
He stresses being ahead of competing work groups.
He "needles" foremen under him for greater effort.
He decides in detail what shall be done and how it shall be done.
He emphasizes the meeting of deadlines.
He emphasizes the quantity of work.

Subordinates whose superiors lacked task orientation agreed with statements like:

He lets others do the work the way they think best.
He waits for subordinates to suggest new ideas.

The Ohio State University study created a dichotomy that still survives in management and leadership thinking, between employee centred and job centred leadership. This is also often expressed as the distinction between *democratic* and *autocratic* leadership. These two dimensions have been found in numerous similar subsequent studies of the way in which leadership behaviour is perceived by others.

These dimensions do *not,* however, represent opposite poles of a continuum of leader behaviour. The Ohio studies consistently showed that the two types of behaviour are independent. A leader can emphasize either or both.

The Ohio State University studies and a lot of later research based on their findings show that the most effective supervisors are those who emphasize *both* consideration and structure. The leader thus has two main functions, to accomplish the task in hand and to maintain group relationships. Inconsiderate leaders who emphasize structure tend to have subordinates who complain a lot and leave the organization, and tend to have comparatively unproductive work groups. Most subordinates prefer considerate supervisors and dislike those who are task orientated.

Inconsiderate leaders are bad for your health . . .

Management style and employee burnout

Employees who have lost interest in their job, and who just go through the motions, always tired, having colds, flus and headaches, can be suffering from *burnout*. This phenomenon has been researched by Cary Cherniss who blames leadership style for the suffering of employees.

Cherniss argues that the condition begins with a mismatch between the demands of the job and the abilities of the individual. This mismatch causes stress. Stress in turn induces anxiety and exhaustion, which provoke either action to resolve the problem, or burnout which is a form of psychological escape from the problem. The burntout employee becomes cynical and works mechanically. This seems to be common in social work and education where the demands of the job are high, but where the effects of the individual's efforts are not always clear.

Cherniss analysed the experiences of two community mental health workers over nine months.

Karen worked with a large and geographically spread case load of mentally retarded patients who had little hope of rehabilitation. The goal was simply to meet their physical needs. Karen could not devote much time to individual cases and had little chance to use her skills. Her department was a medical one and did not appreciate the function of social workers. Staff meetings run by the director were formal and businesslike with no time for informal contact with colleagues to share experiences. The main concern of Karen's boss was that she did not "rock the boat" by breaking the rules. She got no emotional or technical support. Karen's attempts to overcome bureaucratic obstacles were not supported and she was labelled a troublemaker. After nine months she lost enthusiasm, and felt powerless and frustrated. She was even apathetic about looking for another job.

Diane worked with a small group of alcoholics. They initially resisted treatment, but were intelligent and responsive. Opportunities to work with families, employers and other agencies, and to mix individual and group therapies, gave her variety and a chance to use her abilities. The management trusted the staff and concentrated on support and development rather than on control. Diane became committed to her career in this field.

Cherniss argues that the outcomes in these cases were determined by the different styles of the managers. Cherniss suggests that to overcome Karen's problems:

- Staff have to be allowed to participate in management decisions.
- Managers have to understand the adverse effects on their subordinates of mistrust and lack of consideration.

From Cary Cherniss, *Staff Burnout*, Sage Studies in Community Mental Health, no. 2, 1980.

ARE LEADERS SPECIAL PEOPLE?

One of the quotations earlier in the chapter implied that leaders are men with special qualities. The early research into leadership thus concentrated on discovering what these special qualities might be. There is a widespread and persistent assumption that women are unsuited to positions in which management and leadership qualities are required. Women are thus poorly represented in the ranks of management and have been largely ignored, until recently, in leadership research.

The search for the qualities that made good leaders was influenced by the *great man theory* of history. Great man theory states that the fate of societies, and of organizations, is in the hands of key, powerful, idiosyncratic individuals who by the force of their personalities reach positions of influence from which they can direct and dominate the lives of others. Such men are simply born great and emerge to take power in any situation regardless of the social or historical context.

STOP!

List the five most powerful and influential figures that you know about, who are alive today, and who you would describe as leaders. They can be political or religious figures as well as organizational managers.

Now write down the special qualities which you believe each of these people has.

Compare your list of special qualities with that of your colleagues and see if you can agree on one general "master list" of the attributes of leaders.

You have now worked through one of the first stages of many typical research projects on leadership. It used to be thought that a good starting point would be to identify the *personality traits* that might make leaders effective. The next stage is to measure the extent to which good and bad leaders possess these personality traits. One would then hope to be in a position to be able to identify the traits which distinguish effective from ineffective leaders.

Rosemary Stewart cites an American study in which organization executives were asked to identify what they thought were the indispensable desirable qualities of top managers. They came up with the following fifteen attributes:

Judgement	Initiative
Integrity	Foresight
Energy	Drive
Human relations skill	Decisiveness
Dependability	Emotional stability
Fairness	Ambition
Dedication	Objectivity

Co-operation

How many of these attributes did you have in your own list of special leadership qualities?

Leaders of course may also have *undesirable* qualities and be stubborn, self-centred, vain and domineering.

Leaders are men with special qualities . . .

"Discussion of leadership is so often overloaded with vague but emotive ideas that one is hard put to it to nail the concept down. To cut through the panoply of such quasi-moral and unexceptionable associations as 'patriotism', 'play up and play the game', the 'never-asking-your-men-to-do-something-you-wouldn't-do-yourself' formula, 'not giving in (or up)', the 'square-jaw-frank-eyes-steadfast-gaze' formula, and the 'if . . you'll be a man' recipe, one comes to the simple truth that leadership is no more than exercising such an influence upon others that they tend to act in concert towards achieving a goal which they might not have achieved so readily had they been left to their own devices.

"The ingredients which bring about this agreeable state of affairs are many and varied. At the most superficial level they are believed to include such factors as voice, stature and appearance, an impression of omniscience, trustworthiness, sincerity and bravery. At a deeper and rather more important level, leadership depends upon a proper understanding of the needs and opinions of those one hopes to lead, and the context in which the leadership occurs. It also depends on good timing. Hitler, who was neither omniscient, trustworthy nor sincere, whose stature was unremarkable and whose appearance verged on the repellent, understood these rules and exploited them to full advantage. The same may be said of many good comedians."

From Norman F. Dixon, *On The Psychology of Military Incompetence,* Futura Publications, London, 1976, pp. 214-15.

Do women not have the right qualities . . .?

Top managerial jobs go to men who are rational, efficient, tough minded, and unemotional. Women have to fight the popular stereotype that says they are dependent, sociable, subjective and emotional — personality traits that disqualify them from positions of managerial responsibility. Research says these traditional stereotypes are wrong.

Rhona Steinberg and Stanley Shapiro used a series of questionnaires to test the personalities of twenty-nine female and forty-two male students on a university management course. The results showed that there were few personality differences between the sexes. All the students got high scores on the "managerial" characteristics like dominance, self-assurance, and the needs for responsibility and achievement.

The female students in fact had some strong "masculine" personality traits. They were more tough minded and suspicious of others than the men. The men were more tender minded, humble, trusting, imaginative and introspective — traditional "feminine" traits.

The researchers argue that women may exaggerate the masculine facets of their personalities to help them to compete more effectively for managerial jobs which they can perform just as well as men.

From Rhona Steinberg and Stanley Shapiro, "Sex differences in personality traits of female and male Masters of Business Administration students", *Journal of Applied Psychology*, 1982, vol. 67, no. 3, pp. 306-10.

STOP!

Remember what we said in Chapter 6 about the relationship between personality traits and job success?

On that evidence, what do you think has been the outcome of research that has tried to find the personality traits that are associated with effective leadership?

Does fear of success prevent women from becoming managers . . .?

In theory, women are afraid of success because they get anxious in situations where they are expected to behave in "masculine" ways. As one has to be aggressive and competitive to be a successful organizational leader, and as these traits are not usually considered "feminine", this theory might explain why there are so few female managers. Research suggests that this theory is wrong.

Gary Popp and William Muhs gave a questionnaire to 214 American civil servants who gave information about their sex, age, pay, background, work experience and attitudes to success.

The results showed that women were not more afraid of success than men. Fear of success was strongest among young employees in low pay grades.

The researchers argue that junior employees are more anxious because they face greater uncertainty over their careers than their older and more affluent and experienced superiors. They conclude that the stereotype of the female frightened by success is false.

From Gary E. Popp and William F. Muhs, "Fear of success and women employees", *Human Relations*, 1982, vol. 35, no. 7, pp. 511-19.

Discrimination prevents women becoming managers . . .

In Northern Ireland, about 40 per cent of the workforce are women but less than 5 per cent of them hold management jobs.

Stanley Cromie got ninety-nine female and seventy-nine male replies to a questionnaire which he posted to professional teachers, managers and secretaries in Belfast. The questions measured the importance of work to the individual, and attitudes to women as managers were assessed.

The results showed that women valued their jobs just as much as the men in the sample. Professional women in fact had higher degrees of commitment to their work than professional men, but the male and female managers had similar commitment scores.

The job involvement of the secretaries was low, but Cromie argues that this was due to the low status of their work, and not to their sex alone. The women all felt that women could happily handle management jobs, but the men felt that female managers were incompetent.

Cromie argues that management jobs are closed to women by male bias and discrimination, not because women lack ambition, capability or the "right" personality traits.

From Stanley Cromie, "Women as managers in Northern Ireland", *Journal of Occupational Psychology*, 1981, vol. 54, no. 2, pp. 87-91.

Attempts to identify the personality traits of effective leaders have failed for three main reasons:

1. It is very difficult to reach any agreement on how vague concepts such as "judgement" and "dedication" are to be defined and measured.
2. Personality traits and job success are not generally associated.
3. A leader in an organization is a person in a role. The characteristics of that role will influence the behaviour of a leader and the outcomes of that behaviour.

Effective leaders are not necessarily special people with special qualities. Women are not disqualified by personality from leadership positions. The qualities, characteristics and traits needed in a leader depend to a large extent on the demands of the situation in which he or she has to function. The two main aspects of the situation are the people being led — the "followers" — and the tasks that they have to perform.

LEADERS NEED FOLLOWERS

If leaders do not need special qualities, then we must turn to followers to find an explanation of leadership. The one essential attribute of followers is that they must be willing to comply with the instructions of their leader. If followers are for some reason unwilling to comply with the orders of their superior, then the leader can do nothing.

A leader can only be a leader if followers are willing to follow. The use of physical violence by thugs and bullies to get people to comply is not recognized as the exercise of "leadership". It is not just the individual's qualities that make someone a leader. The willingness of potential followers to comply with instructions is equally important.

Definition

Leadership is a *social process* in which one individual influences the behaviour of others without the use or threat of violence.

Leadership, in this definition, is a property of the *relationship* between leader and followers. It is not simply some property of the individual leader. This helps to explain why an examination of the properties of leaders alone has proved so fruitless. To understand leadership therefore we have to understand compliance. We need to know why people are willing to let themselves be influenced by some individuals and not by others.

The ability of an individual to function as a leader is thus in part dependent on the willingness of followers to be influenced. A problem with this view is that everyone exerts some influence on everyone else. Followers in many instances clearly influence their leaders. Those people who we call leaders however seem to be different in at least two respects. First, they have more influence than those around them. Second, they try to influence others to behave in ways that are beyond the mere compliance with the rules and routines of the organization.

Power is a useful concept with which to explain why different people exert different degrees of influence. As with leadership, power is a property of the relationship between the more and the less powerful. The exercise of power is thus a social process. Power is a critical dimension of leadership, and the two terms are often used with the same or similar meanings. Here we will define the use of power in the same way that we have defined leadership — as the ability of an individual to control or to influence others, to get someone else to do something. But we can distinguish between different types or *bases* of power.

John French and Bertram Raven in their classic study identified five main bases of power.

Reward power

A leader has reward power if followers believe that the leader is able to control rewards that they value, and that the leader will part with these rewards in return for compliance with instructions. In an organization these rewards may include pay, promotion, allocation to desirable work duties, responsibility, new equipment, and recognition for good performance.

If the leader controls rewards that followers do not value, then the leader has no reward power. If the leader has no control over valued rewards, but followers believe that such rewards will be forthcoming, then the leader has reward power.

Coercive power

A leader has coercive power if followers believe that the leader is able and willing to administer penalties that they dislike. The intensity of the penalties and the probability of them being applied are what really matter. In an organization, these penalties may include humiliation and other forms of oral abuse, withdrawal of friendship and emotional support, loss of favours and privileges such as allocation to desirable work, curtailment of promotion opportunities and delayed pay rises.

It is the subordinate's expectation of undesirable penalties which gives the leader coercive power. Employment legislation in Britain since the 1970s has given employees some protection against the coercive power of managers, particularly against the managerial practice of summary dismissal of disliked employees. But this power base is by no means redundant in contemporary organizations where other aspects are still used frequently.

Referent power

A leader has referent power if followers believe that the leader has character-istics that are desirable and that they should copy. Followers thus *identify* themselves with the leader, regardless of what he or she actually does. Referent power thus depends on the personality and attractiveness of the leader, as perceived by followers. Referent power has also been called *charisma*. Not many people have the charisma of, say, John F. Kennedy, but organization managers are sometimes able to command respect and admiration from their subordinates.

Legitimate power

A leader has legitimate power if followers believe that the leader has a right to give them orders which they in turn have an obligation to accept. Managers today rely on the widespread belief in the efficiency and legitimacy of managerial hierarchies, of the division between blue collar manual and white collar managing work.

This has also been called "position power" because it depends on the role of the leader in the organization. The leader's legitimacy may rely simply on a job title — professor, doctor, matron, director, captain, chairman and so on —which followers see as conferring on the leader the right to give orders.

Expert power

A leader has expert power if followers believe that the leader has superior knowledge and expertise which is relevant to the particular tasks or activities in hand. Expert power can thus confer leadership on anyone with the requisite knowledge and skills regardless of their job title or organizational position. The expert power of many organizational managers may be limited to narrow specialisms and functions.

The leader has to demonstrate relevant ability. The subordinates' perceptions of the leader's understanding, credibility, trustworthiness, honesty and access to information are fundamental to their perception of the leader as a person with expert power.

These five power bases have a number of important features.

First, they all depend on the beliefs of followers. These beliefs may be influenced by the abilities and behaviour of the leader but it is subordinates' beliefs that count. A leader may be able to control rewards and penalties, have superior knowledge and so on, but if subordinates do not believe that the leader has these attributes then they may not be willing to be easily led. Similarly, leaders may be able to manipulate subordinates into the belief that they possess power which they in fact do not have.

Second, these bases are interrelated and the use of one type of power may affect a leader's ability to use another. The leader who resorts to coercive power may for example lose referent power. The leader may be able to use legitimate power to enhance both referent and expert power. Leadership, power and influence are therefore not static.

Third, a leader can operate from multiple bases of power. The same person may be able to use different bases in different contexts and at different times. Few leaders may be able to resort to one power base alone.

STOP!

Which power base, or which combination of power bases would you expect to be most effective for an organization leader?

A prestigious job title may therefore give a manager in an organization a certain amount of legitimate power which he or she can then use to exert leadership over subordinates. The title creates a shared expectation that the manager gives the orders and the subordinates carry them out.

But legitimate power alone is not enough. Some subordinates may have sources of power of their own which they can use to subvert the leader's position. The "prerogatives" or "rights" of management in modern organizations are increasingly challenged and employment does not guarantee loyalty or commitment to the objectives of the organization. Many employees are suspicious of managers and their motives and react cautiously to what managers say and do. Fancy job titles no longer automatically confer legitimacy on the bosses' orders.

Leadership style has thus become a central problem for managers. How should leaders or managers handle their followers or subordinates? How can managers overcome suspicion and caution and ensure high work motivation and performance? What is the most effective management style? These questions have generated an enormous quantity of research and commentary. This is an issue in which there are no simple theories or solutions. But the evidence however all seems to point in the same direction.

Rules for leaders and followers . . .

". . . the job satisfaction and health of subordinates are better when supervisors establish a warm, friendly and supportive relation, and look after their welfare; and when supervisors consult them, allow them to take part in decisions, and explain and persuade rather than give orders. Our study showed the most important rules for supervisors to be:

- Plan and assign work efficiently;
- Keep subordinates informed about decisions affecting them;
- Respect the other's privacy;
- Keep confidences;
- Consult subordinates in matters that affect them;
- Advise and encourage subordinates;
- Fight for subordinates' interests;
- Be considerate about subordinates' personal problems.

There is no corresponding research on the skills of subordinates, and it is not clear what "success" consists of here. Research by colleagues and myself indicates these rules for subordinates:

- Don't hesitate to question when orders are unclear;
- Use initiative where possible;
- Put forward and defend own ideas;
- Complain first to superior before going to others;
- Respect other's privacy;
- Be willing and cheerful;
- Don't be too submissive;
- Be willing to accept criticism;
- Keep confidences;
- Be willing to take orders.

The rules we found for co-workers were:

- Accept one's fair share of the work load;
- Respect other's privacy;
- Be co-operative over shared physical working conditions (like light, noise);
- Be willing to help when requested;
- Keep confidences;
- Work co-operatively, despite feelings of dislike;
- Don't denigrate another employee to superiors.

If the rules are followed, it is probably easier to sustain these relationships without getting into further trouble. For example, saying nasty things about people very often gets back to them."

From Michael Argyle, *"Pleasures and pains of working together"*, New Society, 9 June 1983, pp. 382-3.

The most effective style of management seems to be one in which the manager shares power with subordinates. This style can increase both the satisfaction and effectiveness of those who are led. In other words the most effective managers are those who appear to relinquish power to their subordinates. Many managers however are not keen to share power, influence and decision making with people towards whom they feel superior. Many managers feel that they personally must lose the influence that they give to their subordinates. This is in fact not the case.

One influential study which demonstrated the effectiveness of this "power sharing" management style was that carried out by Rensis Likert at the University of Michigan Survey Research Center. Likert was concerned with the characteristics of effective supervisors. He interviewed twenty-four supervisors and 419 clerks in highly productive and less productive departments in an American insurance company.

One of Rensis Likert's less effective supervisors . . .

"This interest-in-people approach is all right, but it's a luxury. I've got to keep pressure on for production, and when I get production up, then I can afford to take time to show an interest in my employees and their problems."

One of Rensis Likert's more effective supervisors . . .

"One way in which we accomplish a high level of production is by letting people do the job the way they want to so long as they accomplish the objectives. I believe in letting them take time out from the monotony. Make them feel that they are something special, not just the run of the mill. As a matter of fact, I tell them if you feel that job is getting you down get away from it for a few minutes. . . . If you keep employees from feeling hounded, they are apt to put out the necessary effort to get the work done in the required time.

"I never make any decisions myself. Oh, I guess I've made about two since I've been here. If people know their jobs I believe in letting them make decisions. I believe in delegating decision-making. Of course, if there's anything that affects the whole division, then the two assistant managers, the three section heads and sometimes the assistant section heads come in here and we discuss it. I don't believe in saying that this is the way it's going to be. After all, once supervision and management are in agreement there won't be any trouble selling the staff the idea.

"My job is dealing with human beings rather than with the work. It doesn't matter if I have anything to do with the work or not. The chances are that people will do a better job if you are really taking an interest in them. Knowing the names is important and helps a lot, but it's not enough. You really have to know each individual well, know what his problems are. Most of the time I discuss matters with employees at their desks rather than in the office. Sometimes I sit on a waste paper basket or lean on the files. It's all very informal. People don't seem to like to come into the office to talk."

From Rensis Likert, *New Patterns of Management*, McGraw-Hill Book Company, New York, 1961, pp. 7-8.

He found that the supervisors in the highly productive sections were more likely to:

- Get general as opposed to close supervision from *their* superiors;
- Enjoy their job authority and responsibility;
- Spend more time on supervision;
- Give general as opposed to close supervision of their subordinates;
- Be employee rather than production oriented.

The supervisors in the sections where productivity was low had the opposite characteristics. They were close, production oriented supervisors who concentrated on keeping their subordinates busy with specified tasks and methods and achieving targets on time.

Likert's effective supervisors were not just concerned with the needs of their employees. They were seen by their subordinates as emphasizing high levels of performance and achievement and had a "contagious enthusiasm" for the importance of achieving these goals. This clearly supports Fleishman's argument that leaders need to stress both consideration and structure.

Likert and his research team at Michigan identified four main styles or *systems* of leadership in organizations, based on their research:

System 1: Exploitative autocratic, in which the leader

- has no confidence and trust in subordinates;
- imposes decisions on subordinates; never delegates;
- motivates by threat;
- has little communication and teamwork involving subordinates.

System 2: Benevolent authoritative, in which the leader

- has superficial, condescending confidence and trust in subordinates;
- imposes decisions on subordinates; never delegates;
- motivates by reward;

- sometimes involves subordinates in solving problems; paternalistic.

System 3: Participative, in which the leader

- has some incomplete confidence and trust in subordinates;
- listens to subordinates but controls decision making;
- motivates by reward and some involvement;
- uses ideas and opinions of subordinates constructively.

System 4: Democratic, in which the leader

- has complete confidence and trust in subordinates;
- subordinates allowed to make decisions for themselves;
- motivates by reward for achieving goals set by participation;
- substantial amount of sharing of ideas and opinions and cooperation.

Likert's research shows that effective managers are those who adopt either a System 3 or a System 4 leadership style which is based on trust and pays attention to the needs of the organization and the employees.

Many managers believe, like Likert's less effective supervisors, that a democratic leadership style is a luxury. It is too time consuming. Others believe that employee participation in management decisions can only lead to anarchy, disorder and inefficiency, and that democratic management is a contradiction of the rights, duties and prerogatives of management itself.

The research shows however that democratic management means involvement, mutual respect, openness, trust, motivation and commitment. It is an "alternative organizational life style" which has been found mainly in successful companies.

Democratic leadership seems to erode the influence of managers. Managers prefer formal, written rules and believe in the necessity of hierarchy to achieve order, discipline and control which they feel are essential to achieve high performance. But this view ignores the politics of organizational life in which people at all levels compete for power and influence – the ingredients of leadership.

Democratic leadership may *increase* a manager's ability to exert influence over subordinates. If a manager allows subordinates to take part in management decisions, the influence of that manager is not necessarily eroded. By demonstrating confidence and trust in subordinates, the manager's ability to exert further influence on them may be increased rather than diminished.

We have defined leadership as a property of the *relationship* between leaders and followers. This is not a simple relationship in which there is a straightforward division of labour with the leader carrying out all the functions and making all the decisions on the one hand, and the followers passively doing what they are told on the other. The functions of leaders are not the same as the functions of management. In some respects they are separate and in others they overlap.

Leadership functions are thus dispersed in an organization rather than being concentrated in the hands of formally appointed managers. Leadership functions, as we have identified them here, are best carried out by people who have the interest, knowledge, skills and motivation to perform them effectively. These people are not always formally appointed managers.

The leadership tasks of managers may therefore be:

1. To find ways of handling the inconsistency between organizational objectives and individual needs through a democratic leadership style that concentrates on both consideration and initiating structure.
2. To identify those individuals best able to carry out the various different aspects of the leadership function and to delegate accordingly.

THE IMPORTANCE OF THE CONTEXT

We have discussed in this chapter the nature of leaders and followers in organizations and how their characteristics may influence the effectiveness with which a leader operates. But there are other factors that can affect the behaviour and effectiveness of leaders — such as the nature of the task that is to be done and the organization in which it is set.

The nature of the organizational context in which the leader has to work complicates the management dilemma. Subordinates who are asked to dismantle a machine for repair will probably react differently from those who have to dismantle the machine because their department has been made redundant. People working constantly under severe time pressure, as in many restaurants and hospitals, behave differently from those whose daily routine is more relaxed. The organizational leader's behaviour may thus be affected by features of the task that has to be managed.

Leadership behaviour that is appropriate in one context may not be effective in another. People who are accustomed to harsh autocratic leadership may be suspicious of someone with a friendly, democratic, participative management style. People who are accustomed to participative management may on the other hand accept an autocratic style if they can see that pressure of work makes this necessary to achieve the work objectives.

This suggests that an organizational leader must be able to "diagnose" the human and organizational context in which he or she is working and be able to decide what behaviour will best "fit" the situation. As the best style to adopt is thus contingent on the situation, this approach is referred to as *contingency theory*.

The leadership research and contingency theory of Fred Fiedler provides a useful, systematic approach to diagnosing these contextual factors.

Fiedler worked with groups whose leaders were clearly identified and whose performance was easy to measure — such as basketball teams and bomber crews. Fiedler first developed a new measure of a leader's basic approach to managing people — the leader's *least preferred coworker* (LPC) score.

Leaders were asked to think of the person with whom they could work least well. They were then asked to rate that person on sixteen dimensions:

pleasant .... unpleasant	quarrelsome ... harmonious
gloomy .... cheerful	rejecting .... accepting
helpful .... frustrating	unenthusiastic ... enthusiastic
tense .... relaxed	distant .... close
self-assured .... hesitant	cold .... warm
friendly .... unfriendly	efficient .... inefficient
co-operative... unco-operative	open .... guarded
supportive .... hostile	boring .... interesting

The leaders who rate their least preferred coworkers negatively get low LPC scores and are task orientated: they regard anyone whose performance is poor in wholly negative terms. Leaders who rate their least preferred coworkers positively get high LPC scores and are relationships orientated: they tend to see positive values even in those they dislike.

The high and low LPC scores are similar to consideration and initiating structure — the Ohio study dimensions of leadership behaviour. Fiedler appears to have found with the LPC score another way of discovering an individual manager's orientations, biases, preferences and predispositions. It should not be surprising to find that Fiedler's attempts to correlate the LPC scores of leaders with the performance of their groups was not successful. This led Fiedler to the argument that the effectiveness of a leader is influenced by three main sets of factors:

1. The extent to which the task in hand is structured;
2. The leader's position power;
3. The nature of the relationships between the leader and followers.

A task is structured if it has clear goals, few correct or satisfactory solutions or outcomes, few ways of performing it, and clear criteria of success. A task is unstructured if it involves ambiguous goals, many correct solutions or satisfactory outcomes, many ways of achieving acceptable outcomes, and vague criteria of success.

STOP!

Would you describe the task of writing a term essay in organizational behaviour as structured or unstructured?

Fiedler identifies three typical or extreme sets of conditions under which a leader may have to work.

Condition 1.

- The task is highly structured.

- The leader's position power is high.
- Subordinates feel that their relationships with the boss are good.

Task orientated (low LPC score) leaders get good results in these favourable circumstances. The task orientated leader in this situation detects that events are potentially under his or her control, sets targets, monitors progress, and achieves good performance.

Relationships orientated (high LPC score) leaders get poor results in these circumstances. The relationships orientated leader tries to get the work done by building and maintaining good interpersonal relationships with and among subordinates. But in Condition 1, when relationships are already good, and the other conditions are favourable, the leader may take subordinates for granted and start to pursue other, personal, objectives.

Condition 2.

- The task is unstructured.
- The leader's position power is low.
- Subordinates feel that their relationships with the boss are *moderately good.*

Relationship orientated leaders get better results in these moderately favourable circumstances where the maintenance of good relationships is important to both the ability of the leader to exert influence over subordinates and to get the work done. The task orientated leader ignores any deterioration in relationships and as the task lacks structure and the leader lacks position power the results are likely to be poor.

Condition 3.

- The task is unstructured.
- The leader's position power is low.
- Subordinates feel that their relationships with the boss are poor.

According to Fiedler, task orientated leaders get better results in these very unfavourable conditions. Why? The relationships orientated leader is unwilling to exert pressure on subordinates, avoids confrontations that might upset or anger them, gets involved in attempts to repair damaged relationships and ignores the task. The task orientated leader in this situation is impatient, attempts to structure the situation, ignores resistance from subordinates, reduces the uncertainty and ambiguity surrounding the work and achieves good performance.

Fiedler argues that the leader has first to diagnose or identify the main features of the organizational context and then adopt the appropriate style relevant to that context.

Fiedler's theory ignores the need for technical competence ...

The popular stereotype of the successful top manager is of a man who enjoys manipulating and controlling other people, who likes to make harsh decisions and who does not worry about what others think of him. David McClelland and Richard Boyatzis argue that this type of management style is effective only in some managerial jobs.

The research studied 235 male managers who had worked with the American Telephone and Telegraph company for over twenty years. Between 1956 and 1960, the managers were given a series of personality tests. They were asked to write creative stories about ambiguous pictures. The contents of their stories were then assessed for themes and images concerning the managers' needs for power and for friendship. The careers of the managers were followed up to 1978.

(The personality tests used in this research were similar to the projective Thematic Apperception Tests of personality explained in Chapter 6.)

Some of these managers had "technical" jobs and worked on the manufacture, installation and repair of telephone equipment. Others had "non-technical" jobs and were concerned with customer services, accounting, sales, administration and personnel management.

The non-technical managers who had a strong need for power and a weak need for friendship had been promoted faster. But the technical managers had been promoted for their technical, engineering abilities, not because of their personalities.

From David C. McClelland and Richard E. Boyatzis, "Leadership motive pattern and long-term success in management", *Journal of Applied Psychology*, 1982, vol. 67, no. 6, pp. 737-43.

The research to support this contingency theory is positive but weak, and Edgar Schein argues that it has three main problems. First, the three key variables, task structure, power and relationships, are very difficult to assess in practice. The leader who wants to rely on this framework to determine the most effective style for a given situation has to rely more on intuition than on systematic analysis. Second, the framework does not directly take into account the needs of subordinates. Third, the need for a leader to have technical competence relevant to the task is ignored.

This theory however has at least two merits. First, it helps to demonstrate the importance of contextual factors in determining leader behaviour and effectiveness. It reinforces the view that there is no one best style or one ideal personality that a leader must have to be successful. Second, it provides a systematic framework for developing the self-awareness of managers.

The framework can be used to increase the sensitivity of organizational leaders to their own personalities, to their relationships with their subordinates, and to the nature of the context in which they manage. This increased self-awareness is fundamental to the leader's ability to change style. We will examine in the following section whether or not managers can adapt their style in the way that theory prescribes.

CAN LEADERS CHANGE THEIR STYLES?

Contemporary theories of leadership are mainly contingency theories which argue that the most effective style for the leader to adopt depends on the context. Organizations, the abilities of their managers, the characteristics of their employees, the nature of their tasks and their structures are unique. No particular style of leadership can be said to be better than any other.

There is however a good deal of research that indicates that a participative style of leadership in organizations is generally (if not always) more effective. There are two main reasons for this.

First, the development of participative management is part of a wider social and political movement which has encouraged increased public participation in all spheres of social life. Participation thus reflects changing social and political values.

Rising levels of affluence and educational standards in western industrial countries have developed expectations about personal freedom and the quality of working life. Education may also be expected to raise ability to participate in the first place. There is a widespread recognition of the rights of the individual to develop intellectual and emotional maturity. These values encourage resistance to manipulation by mindless, impersonal bureaucracies and challenge the legitimacy of management decisions. This trend has affected local and national government as well as private industry and is well established. The trend appears to be a universal one, and is not restricted to Britain or America. European and Scandinavian countries have legislated on the rights of employees to information about and participation in the activities of their employers.

Second, participative management has been encouraged by research which has demonstrated that this style is generally more effective, although an autocratic style can be more effective in some circumstances.

A participative management style can improve organizational effectiveness by tapping the ideas of people with knowledge and experience, and by involving them in a decision making process to which they then become committed. This style can thus lead to better quality decisions which are then more effectively implemented.

Autocratic management may stifle creativity, not use available expertise, and fail to establish motivation and commitment to the task. Autocratic management may however be more effective when time is short, when the leader really is the most knowledgeable person, and where those who might participate could never reach a decision on which they could all agree.

People who are involved in setting standards or establishing methods are thus more likely to:

- Accept the legitimacy of decisions reached with their help;
- Accept change based on those decisions;
- Trust managers who actually make and implement decisions;
- Volunteer new and creative ideas and solutions.

Research and theory have thus indicated that organizational leaders should adopt a contingency approach and choose the most appropriate style for each occasion. There are however three reasons why an organizational leader may not be able to change style and still be effective.

Participative management leads to better decisions . . .

Many managers reject the concept of participative management because they do not want to lose control over "management" decisions. Participation thus depends on the attitudes of managers towards this aspect of their job. There is a lot of research that demonstrates the advantages of such an attitude change.

William Pasmore and Frank Friedlander were asked to study work injuries which were reducing productivity in an American electronics company. About a third of the company's 335 employees had complained about pains in their wrists, arms and shoulders, some had undergone surgery to relieve their symptoms, and one woman had permanently lost the use of her right hand. A series of medical and technical investigations had failed to find the cause of the injuries.

But the company management had never thought of asking the employees themselves about the possible causes of their injuries. So the researchers suggested that a "Studies and Communications Group" be set up drawing workers' representatives from each area of the factory. The group members discussed their own work experiences and injuries, designed a questionnaire, surveyed over 300 other employees and produced sixty recommendations for solving the injury problem.

Management at first rejected the Group's recommendations because management practices were identified as the main cause of the problem. The Group had found that injuries were related to:

- Inadequate training;
- Rapid, repetitive arm movements;
- Badly adjusted machines;
- Frustration at machine breakdowns;
- Stress from some supervisors' behaviour (such as favouritism);
- Pressure from management for more output.

The first attempts by management to solve the problem had in fact made it worse. When workers were injured, production fell, management increased the pressure for more output, which increased workers' stress, which in turn led to more injuries.

The researchers conclude that a permanent change in the relationships between workers and management is necessary to create a climate of effective participation. The managers in this company felt that they had lost control over the situation. But as the workers' recommendations were gradually implemented the number of injuries fell and the overall performance of the factory rose.

From William Pasmore and Frank Friedlander, "An action research programme to increase employee involvement in problem solving", *Administrative Science Quarterly*, 1982, vol. 27. no. 3, pp. 343-362.

First, personality may not be flexible enough. One of the theories of personality examined in Chapter 6 argues that personality is inherited and fairly static. This would create problems for the manager who wished to be participative in some circumstances and dictatorial in others. The manager who is motivated by affiliation and who values the friendship of others may find it hard to treat subordinates in a harsh and autocratic way.

Second, the demands of the task and of other managers constrain what is acceptable for an individual manager to do. If a manager's own superior believes in the effectiveness of an autocratic leadership style then it may be hard for subordinate managers to behave in a way that could block their own promotion chances.

Organizational demands constrain what the individual manager can do . . .

"On the shop floor it's said, about a couple of Riverside managers in particular, that 'They aren't bad blokes. Given that they're managers, that is. They'd do anything for you *personally.*' 'Personally' means letting a bloke borrow your car spraying equipment, or talking to him about what it would be like for his son to do O-level chemistry, or, providing things aren't too tight, helping him to get time off. It also means not driving it home unnecessarily that you are a manager. But 'personally' or not, these men *are* still managers. The theories of psycho-sociology notwithstanding, they've had to learn the hard way about 'man-management' and how to defend their 'right to manage'. And this means that 'in this game you can either be a bastard or a bad bastard'. ('Bad bastards' are managers who behave like bastards because they *are* bastards. Common or garden 'bastards' are men who find that, as managers, there are unpleasant things they have to do.)"

From Theo Nichols and Huw Beynon, *Living With Capitalism: Class Relations and the Modern Factory*, Routledge and Kegan Paul, London, 1977, p. 34.

Third, there may be advantages in honesty and consistency. Subordinates may not accept the fickle behaviour of the participative manager who adopts an autocratic style when that appears to be necessary. Subordinates may see through the act of the autocrat who tries to act in a participative way. The leader who changes style from one situation to another may not inspire confidence and trust in subordinates.

There are on the other hand three reasons why an organizational leader should be able to change style to suit the circumstances in order to be more effective.

First, theorists disagree about the rigidity of human personality. Many theorists have argued that it is possible for individuals to alter their personality and to incorporate new behaviours as a result of their experiences. So the autocrat who finds that a task orientated style does not always work well could adopt a participative approach at least in some circumstances.

Second, organizations themselves are not rigid social arrangements with fixed tasks and structures. The tasks of an organization and the people who perform them are constantly changing. Organizational leaders thus need to be able to change as organizational circumstances change. As demands for improved quality of working life and more worker participation develop, managers who fail to respond appropriately will find themselves in difficulty.

Third, the manager who is able to adapt in a flexible way to changes in circumstances may be seen as more competent than one who sticks rigidly to traditional routines that have become outmoded.

Participative management increases trust . . .

Should employees be allowed to participate in decisions about pay? This suggestion sounds like heresy to most managers. But Douglas Jenkins and Edward Lawler managed to convince the president of a small engineering company in Ohio that this could have advantages.

The company's fifty-eight male employees were mostly skilled machinists, married and in their mid-thirties. The researchers worked as advisors to a committee of employees and managers which designed a new payment system.

The workers called the old payment scheme "the bitch system". Each individual's pay was secret, wage rises were awarded without any explanation, and the workers felt that the basic rates were unfair.

The new system paid individuals according to their job performance and seniority. The wage of each employee was determined by a committee of two fellow workers and a supervisor. The new system was completely open and the secrecy was removed. But the old rates were still not revealed because the president was afraid of what the workers would do if they ever found out how unfair the old system really was.

Average wages rose by only 50 cents an hour. The total factory wage bill for a year increased by 5 per cent. The pay under the new scheme was around the average for that paid by other local companies.

Employee attitudes were surveyed before and after the new payment system was introduced. The survey results showed that the participative approach had increased employees' trust in management and their satisfaction with pay and their jobs. The workers also felt that the new system was fairer and easier to understand than the old one.

The researchers conclude that worker participation in decisions about pay is both possible and beneficial. They admit, however, that participation in designing payment *systems* may be a less sensitive topic that the traditional union activity of negotiating pay *rates*.

Most managers are likely to argue that this sort of participation can only work where workers and management have a high degree of trust in one another. But the researchers in this case argue that participation should be used to establish that trust in the first place.

From G. Douglas Jenkins and Edward E. Lawler, "Impact of employee participation in pay plan development", *Organizational Behaviour and Human Performance*, 1982, vol. 28, no. 1, pp. 111-28.

Leadership style is not a problem that an organization manager can approach in a mechanical way. The factors that have to be taken into account are many and complex and include:

- The manager's own personality;
- The needs of subordinates;
- The demands of the task;
- Organizational constraints;
- Social values.

There is therefore no simple recipe which the individual manager can use to decide which style to adopt to be most effective. Management style probably can be changed, but only if management values can be changed. Any attempt to change deep rooted cultural values is ambitious, but this may be necessary in the interests of organizational effectiveness. It is not enough to present managers with research findings and to try to convince them with logical argument that change is necessary. People become attached emotionally to their values and do not give them up easily.

Participative management saves money . . .

British and American managers, jealous of Japanese commercial success, are always on the lookout for oriental techniques that they can borrow to boost their own businesses. One Japanese technique that became popular in the late 1970s is the *quality control (QC) circle.*

QC circles are small groups of workers who meet regularly to discuss and solve work problems. Stephen Bryant and Joseph Kearns evaluated the use of the technique in an American naval dockyard.

The dockyard employed 11,000 people on submarine maintenance and had to compete with other similar yards for work. To improve productivity, management set up a QC circle programme in 1979, supported by the slogan, "It makes sense to reap from workers' brains as well as their bodies".

Volunteers were invited to set up nine circles whose members were trained in group problem solving and decision making techniques. Each circle included workers and a supervisor who led their discussions. Top managers sometimes joined in also. The circles met during working hours and were responsible for identifying problems, recommending solutions, and for taking the necessary action with the approval of management. The circles even gave themselves names like "Wild Bunch", "Sparkers", "Red Eye Express" and "Supply Storm Troopers".

The researchers calculated that the circles saved the yard over $200,000 a year through their recommendations for:

- Better tools and equipment;
- More effective waste disposal;
- Savings in workers' time and effort.

Quality control circles are a management technique for encouraging worker participation. The authors conclude that two conditions are necessary for the technique to operate successfully:

- Workers who are willing to participate;
- Managers who are willing to let them.

From Stephen Bryant and Joseph Kearns, "'Workers' brains as well as their bodies': quality circles in a federal facility", *Public Administration Review*, 1982, vol. 42, no. 2, pp. 144-50.

SOURCES

Bryant, S. and Kearns, J., 1982, "'Workers' brains as well as their bodies': quality circles in a federal facility", *Public Administration Review*, vol. 42, no. 2, pp. 144-50.

Cherniss, C., 1980, *Staff Burnout*, Sage Studies in Community Mental Health, no. 2.

Cromie, S., 1981, "Women as managers in Northern Ireland", *Journal of Occupational Psychology*, vol. 54, no. 2, pp. 87-91.

Dixon, N. F., 1976, *On The Psychology of Military Incompetence*, Futura Publications, London.

Drucker, P., 1955, *The Practice of Management*, Heinemann, London.

Fiedler, F. E., 1967, *A Theory of Leadership Effectiveness*, McGraw-Hill, New York.

Fiedler, F. E. and Chemers, M., 1974, *Leadership and Effective Management*, Scott, Foresman, Glenview, Illinois.

Fleishman, E. A., 1953a, "The description of supervisory behaviour", *Journal of Applied Psychology*, vol. 37. no. 1, pp. 1-6.

Fleishman, E. A., 1953b, "The measurement of leadership attitudes in industry", *Journal of Applied Psychology*, vol. 37, no. 3, pp. 153-8.

Fleishman, E. A. and Harris, E. F., 1962, "Patterns of leadership behaviour related to employee grievances and turnover", *Personnel Psychology*, vol. 15, pp. 43-56.

French, J. and Raven, B., 1958, "The bases of social power", in D. Cartwright (ed.), *Studies in Social Power*, Institute for Social Research, Ann Arbor, Michigan.

Jenkins, G. D. and Lawler, E. E., 1982, "Impact of employee participation in pay plan development", *Organizational Behaviour and Human Performance*, vol. 28, no. 1, pp. 111-28.

Kaplan, E. M. and Cowen, E. L., 1981, "Interpersonal helping behaviour of industrial foremen", *Journal of Applied Psychology*, vol. 66, no. 5, pp. 633-38.

Likert, R., 1961, *New Patterns of Management*, McGraw-Hill, New York.

McClelland, D. C. and Boyatzis, R. E., 1982, "Leadership motive pattern and long-term success in management", *Journal of Applied Psychology*, vol. 67, no. 6, pp. 737-43.

Popp, G. E. and Muhs, W. F., 1982, "Fear of success and women employees", *Human Relations*, vol. 35, no. 7, pp. 511-19.

Nichols, T. and Beynon, H., 1977, *Living With Capitalism: Class Relations and the Modern Factory*, Routledge and Kegan Paul, London.

Pasmore, W. and Friedlander, F., 1982, "An action research programme to increase employee involvement in problem solving", *Administrative Science Quarterly*, vol. 27, no. 3, pp. 343-62.

Schein, E., 1982, *Occupational Psychology*, Prentice Hall, New York (third edition).

Stewart, R., 1963, *The Reality of Management*, Pan/Heinemann Books, London.

Steinberg, R. and Shapiro, S., 1982, "Sex differences in personality traits of female and male Masters of Business Administration students", *Journal of Applied Psychology*, vol. 67, no. 3, pp. 306-10.

Chapter 20

Managing change

The problems of studying organizational change
The triggers of organizational change
Resistance to organizational change
Managing organizational change

A new concept of the future . . .

"We are constantly amazed at the speed with which our images
and attitudes absorb new ideas and new technologies. Novelty
appears to have a rapid decay rate in the modern western world.
Once television was made cheap enough for mass distribution, it
quickly became part of people's everyday lives. Within a year
after Sputnik was launched, space shots scarcely seemed
remarkable any more, even though the recent satellites' experiment packages are surely far more sophisticated achievements
than the vehicles that orbit them. Then, when satellite transmission of television broadcasts became work-a-day, we readily
accepted simultaneous worldwide visual communication as just
another clever technological novelty. By next year, heart-
transplants will scarcely warrant notice by the news media. And
so it has gone, step by step, each dramatic achievement — even
the unanticipated big leap — has a way of becoming commonplace after the fact."

From Melvin M. Webber, "Planning in an environment of change", *Town Planning
Review,* 1969, vol. 39, no. 3, pp. 179-81.

Key concepts:

Once you have fully understood this chapter, you should be able to define the following concepts in your own words:

Levels of change   The entrepreneurial spirit
Ad-hocracy   Self-fulfilling prophecy
Future shock   Self-defeating prophecy
Internal triggers of change   Alternative futures
External triggers of change   Resistance to change
Proactive change   The British disease

Objectives:

On completing this chapter, you should be able:

1. To understand the main problems of studying organizational change.
2. To identify the main triggers of organizational change.
3. To identify the main consequences of organizational change.
4. To understand the nature of resistance to change.
5. To understand techniques for overcoming resistance to change.

THE PROBLEMS OF STUDYING
ORGANIZATIONAL CHANGE

Change is a theme that has run throughout this book, although we have not dealt with it before as a separate topic.

In Part 1, we explored the possibilities of changing human motivation and personality. We examined the nature of learning, which also involves changes in human behaviour. In Part 2, we looked at how individual behaviour can be altered by group membership and at how group functioning can be changed to increase effectiveness. In Part 3, we devoted considerable space to the human implications of technical change. In Part 4, we examined the argument that different forms of organization structure may be required to cope with changing environments. And in the first chapter in Part 5, we explored how leaders change their subordinates' behaviour and whether or not leaders themselves can change their styles.

Sociologists who have studied change have been concerned with society as a whole across the sweep of history. They have been concerned with a range of issues such as social integration, the development of class structure and conflict, and social mobility (topics beyond the scope of this book).

The major changes that have affected western societies are usually described under the label "industrialization". Our society has developed over the past 200 years from an agricultural society in which most people lived and worked in rural communities, to a modern industrial society where most of us live in cities and work in factories and offices.

Industrialization, or "modernization" as these developments are also called, has involved changes that most of us take for granted, such as:

- The factory system of manufacturing;
- Large, complex industrial and commercial organizations;
- Increased life expectancy;
- Control of death and disease;
- Population growth;
- Mobility, affluence, individual freedom;
- "Consumer society";
- The small "nuclear" as opposed to the large "extended" family;
- State responsibility for education, transport, energy and health.

These changes have been encouraged and welcomed by most people. They are part of our normal, taken for granted experience. It is however common to hear the complaint that change is taking place too slowly. British industry in particular has been criticized for adopting new computing technologies more slowly than other industrialized countries. It is also common to hear the complaint that change is taking place too fast and that we are simply unable to cope with too much of it.

STOP!

List the main social and economic changes that have affected you personally over the past year.

How have you been affected?

Do you feel that change is happening too fast or too slow, and why?

Change is taking place too slowly . . .

"The rate of technological innovation in United Kingdom industry will need to increase if its products and manufacturing processes are to match those of our major competitors. This is a necessary condition of our future survival as a trading nation."

"We have no option but to attempt to match the productivity and product quality of our overseas competitors, to concentrate our efforts on those industries where we have most chance of success, and to adopt as fast as possible technical innovations from abroad, as well as those developed at home, which will enable us to do this."

From the Advisory Council for Applied Research and Development, *Technological Change: Threats and Opportunities for the United Kingdom*, HMSO, London, 1980. pp. 7 and 12.

Change is taking place too fast . . .

"Most of us have a vague 'feeling' that things are moving faster. Doctors and executives alike complain that they cannot keep up with the latest developments in their fields. Hardly a meeting or conference takes place today without some ritualistic oratory about 'the challenge of change'. Among many there is an uneasy mood — a suspicion that change is out of control."

From Alvin Toffler, *Future Shock*, The Bodley Head/Pan Books, London, 1970, p. 27.

Rapid change is commonplace. Complexity, disorganization and frustration are all natural aspects of our daily lives and normal features of organizational life. We would probably be more surprised by their absence.

Change is difficult to study. It is pervasive and hard to escape. It is difficult to stand back from a routine process in which one is constantly involved and look at it objectively. Change takes time to study and this may have discouraged some researchers. And the process of studying a change can itself influence the course of events by making participants more sensitive to their roles and how these are likely to be affected.

Change can be studied on several *levels*. We can examine its effect on individuals, groups, organizations, society, or the world. Here we are interested in the implications of change at the individual, group and organizational levels. Such changes must however be seen in the context of wider social, national and international developments.

Organizational change affects conditions of work, occupational divisions, the training and experience of workers, and hierarchical divisions. These developments in turn shape the structure of our society as a whole. So the different levels on which change can be studied are intimately interrelated and this makes it difficult to disentangle cause and effect.

The death of bureaucracy . . . the birth of ad-hocracy . . .

"The social structure of organizations of the future will have some unique characteristics. The by word will be 'temporary'. There will be adaptive, rapidly changing, *temporary* systems. These will be task forces organized around problems to be solved by groups of relative strangers with diverse professional skills. The group will be arranged on an organic rather than mechanical model; it will evolve in response to a problem rather than to programmed role expectations. The executive thus becomes coordinator or 'linking pin' between various task forces. . . . People will be evaluated not according to rank but according to skill and professional training. . . .

"Adaptive, problem-solving, temporary systems of diverse specialists, linked together by coordinating and task-evaluating executive specialists in an organic flux — this is the organizational form that will gradually replace bureaucracy as we know it. As no catchy phrase comes to mind, I call these new style organizations *adaptive structures*."

From Warren G. Bennis, *Organization Development: Its Nature, Origins and Prospects*, Addison-Wesley, Reading, Massachusetts, 1969, p. 34.

We can also examine the effects of change over different *time scales*, from weeks to centuries. Here we are interested in the implications of organizational change over comparatively short periods of time — weeks, months or years. It may be difficult to identify when a particular change began to take effect, when other changes started also to exert complementary influences, and to identify just when the implications have "worn off". Again it must be remembered that short term changes must be seen in their long term historical context.

At the individual, group and organization levels of change, interest has concentrated mainly on local and short run pressures and consequences. The main concern has been with organizational effectiveness. The practical, day-to-day concerns of managing organizations have led to the development of a number of techniques for introducing organizational change rapidly and without resistance. This preoccupation with the immediate demands of organizational performance may however have led to the current lack of theory concerning the social, psychological and structural processes involved in organizational change.

Organizations are in a constant state of change. Organizations that are not able to adjust to change have difficulty in surviving. This is why the management of change has become such a serious managerial problem. The problem is to create organizational forms that are stable enough to persist, but flexible enough to adapt to pressures for change.

It also seems that the rate of change in society, and thus in organizations, is increasing. Warren Bennis has argued that this increase in the rate of change makes traditional forms of organization obsolete. He predicts the "death of bureaucracy", because this type of organization simply cannot cope with:

- Rapid and unpredictable change;
- The increasing size and complexity of modern organizations;
- The diversity of specialized skills required;
- The acceptance of humanistic, participative management styles.

Bureaucracy *may* be a suitable form of organization to deal with:

- Stability and routine;
- Orderly and simple organization structures;
- Standardized jobs and skills;
- Impersonal, autocratic styles of management;

Bennis called the new flexible, "organic" organizations required to deal with rapid change *adaptive structures.* Alvin Toffler called these new organizations *ad-hocracies.*

Rapid change may be "normal", but it can also have severe psychological consequences. Alvin Toffler has argued that the rate of change is now out of control and that our modern society is potentially "doomed to a massive adaptational breakdown". Toffler believes that there is a limit to the amount of change that we humans can handle. He argues that "the shattering stress and disorientation that we induce in individuals by subjecting them to too much change in too short a time" is unhealthy. He calls this stress and disorientation *future shock,* or "the disease of change".

Future shock, the disease of change . . .

"I think that the future I describe is not necessarily a 'happy' one. Coping with rapid change, living in temporary work systems, developing meaningful relations and then breaking them, all augur social strains and psychological tensions. Teaching how to live with ambiguity, to identify with the adaptive process, to make a virtue out of contingency, and to be self directing — these will be the tasks of education, the goals of maturity, and the achievement of the successful individual."

From Warren G. Bennis, *Organization Development: Its Nature, Origins and Prospects*, Addison-Wesley, Reading, Massachusetts, 1969, p. 35.

STOP!

Do you feel that you are suffering from future shock?

What are your symptoms?

THE TRIGGERS OF ORGANIZATIONAL CHANGE

There are four basic features that we can expect of organizational change:

Triggers
Change is initiated by some kind of "disorganizing pressure" or *trigger* arising either within or outside the organization. Change may thus be triggered by the discovery that one of the company's machines is so old that it is beyond repair, or by changes in legislation that affect the ways in which employees have to be treated.

Interdependencies
The various facets of an organization are interdependent. Change in one aspect of an organization creates pressures for adjustments in other aspects. The introduction of word processing in the typing pool may require authors to alter the style in which they write and present reports and letters for typing.

Conflicts and frustrations
The technical and economic objectives of managers may often conflict with the needs and aspirations of employees and this leads to conflicts which in turn create pressures for and resistances to change. The new machine that management want to buy may lead to demands for a new payment system from the people who will have to operate it.

Time lags
Change rarely takes place smoothly. Instead it happens in an "untidy" way. Some parts of the organization change more rapidly than others. People and groups may need time to "catch up" with everyone else. The maintenance staff may still be learning new skills months after that new machine has been installed.

Organizational change may in fact be triggered by a multitude of factors. There are three obvious reasons for most changes.

First, there is the need to introduce internal changes to cope with developments occuring outside the organization such as changes in:

- Technology;
- Customers' tastes;
- Competitors' activities;
- Materials;
- Legislation;
- Social or cultural values;
- Changing economic circumstances.

Because these triggers for change arise outside the organization, they are called *external triggers of change*.

STOP!

What at the moment are the major external changes — social, economic, technological — affecting organizations?

Second, there is the desire to modify the attitudes, motives, behaviour, knowledge, skills and relationships of the organization's members in the interests of performance. This may be achieved through changes in:

- Job design and skills requirements;
- Product design;
- Office and factory layouts;
- Allocation of responsibilities;
- Technology.

Because these triggers for change arise within the organization, they are called *internal triggers of change*.

Third, there is the desire to anticipate future developments and to find in advance ways of coping with them. The organization may know that overseas competitors are introducing technical refinements that will eventually make their own products obsolete. This is called *proactive change*.

STOP!

Collect all the copies the "Business Page" from a quality national daily paper over five consecutive days.
From the articles, make a list of the issues to which you think organizations should be responding proactively.
Compile a master list along with your colleagues.

Harold J. Leavitt developed a simple scheme for organizing thinking, and practice, with regard to organizational change. He argues that organizations comprise four main interacting variables:

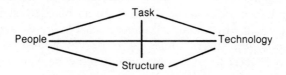

The *people* of an organization are its managers and its workforce — its members or its employees. We explored aspects of people's perception, motivation, learning and personality in Part 1, and aspects of people's behaviour in groups in Part 2.

The *technology* of the organization is the tools and techniques that the organization uses in the pursuit of its task. The technology may be a style of cutting hair, machine tools and lathes, or computers. We explored the nature of technology and technical change in Part 3.

The *structure* of the organization is the pattern of authority, responsibility, communications and workflow. We looked at the features of organization structure in Part 4.

The *task* of the organization is the reason for the organization's existence. This may be to make biscuits or to build ships or to cure patients or to provide a legal advice service. A university has two tasks — to generate and to disseminate knowledge. The task of an organization may be comparatively difficult to change. Universities would have considerable difficulty in switching to biscuit manufacture.

Leavitt argues simply that change can affect, or be directed at, any one of these variables. He calls them "entry points" for efforts to bring about change. In practice the various triggers of change are interdependent and their effects can be difficult to disentangle. Change in one variable usually results in change in the others. This has two consequences:

1.   One variable can be changed deliberately in order to bring about desired changes in the other variables;
2.   Changes to one variable may lead to unanticipated and undesirable changes in the other variables.

There is a tendency to "blame" technology as the main source of change in both organizations and in society as a whole. But to blame change and its organizational consequences on technology alone is to fall back into the trap of "technological determinism" which we discussed in Part 3.

A new technology will only create change if people in an organization see its potential and if others are ready to accept it and make it work effectively. The proposed change must therefore coincide with some perceived needs of at least some organizational members. This is why technology is regarded as a trigger, not a cause, of organizational change.

A second main trigger of change is therefore the perceived needs and goals of key individuals — who pursue their ends within the framework of opportunities that an organization offers. These individuals have been described as "champions" or "promoters" of change and as "entrepreneurs".

Social and organizational change has been attributed by many commentators, and in particular by the American economist Joseph Schumpeter, to *the entrepreneurial spirit.* This is similar to the concept of *need for achievement* introduced in Chapter 6. An entrepreneur is someone who introduces new technical and organizational solutions to old problems, an innovator who introduces new products, new production processes, new organizational arrangements. This may involve promoting change in the face of resistance from others and at risk to the time and money involved. Schumpeter argued that the subversive role of the entrepreneur is redundant in modern organization which strive to change in *planned* ways through group decision making, not in response to individual whims.

STOP!

From your Business Page collection, can you identify any individuals who might be described as entrepreneurs?

What characteristics do they have that would make you place them in this category?

Entrepreneurs trigger change . . .

"If there is one thing that all this research has taught me, it is that men can shape their own destiny, that external difficulties and pressures are not nearly so important in shaping history as some people have argued. It is how people respond to those challenges that matters, and how they respond depends on how strong their concern for achievement is. So the question of what happens to our civilization or to our business community depends quite literally on how much time tens of thousands or even millions of us spend thinking about achievement, about setting moderate achievable goals, taking calculated risks, assuming personal responsibility, and finding out how well we have done our job. The answer is up to us."

From David C. McClelland, 'Business drive and national achievement', *Harvard Business Review*, 1962 vol. 40, no. 4, p. 112.

A person with the entrepreneurial spirit has what is also called "executive drive", a need to do a good job and a need for recognition. Such individuals face the problem that they need organizations in which their entrepreneurial behaviour is accepted. Once again, they may trigger but not cause change.

Managers who wish to introduce organizational change in a planned way thus have a choice of strategies. The manager may:

Modify the task
This is a comparatively difficult change strategy. It involves altering the survival objective of the organization and the changes required to achieve this may be fundamental and take considerable time to put into effect. The conventional computer manufacturer who wishes to start making small personal computers may need a new factory with new sources of raw materials, new customers and staff with completely different skills.

Modify the technology
This is a popular strategy and the difficulty depends on the scope of the changes involved. Many organizations today are introducing the new forms of computing and information technology dealt with in Part 4. The change may involve the installation of one new word processor, or the complete redesign of a process plant's control system. These changes usually affect the knowledge and skill demands made on the users of the technology and can lead to changes in organization structure and the roles of managers associated with the new devices.

Modify the structure
This is also a popular change strategy. There are several ways in which organization structure can be used as an entry point for change. Management can alter job definitions and role relationships, areas of responsibility and spans of control. The whole pattern of organization decision making can be altered, for example by decentralizing decisions and giving more autonomy to lower levels of management and to subsections within the organization. Structural alterations change individuals' jobs and responsibilities, their experience with the organization and their relationships with other members.

Modify the people
This is probably the most popular organizational change strategy in use today. There are various techniques that claim to be able to change people's attitudes, values, motives, interpersonal skills and behaviour. This approach is probably the most popular because it is considered by many managers to be the easiest and most straightforward. This is not necessarily the case. There is a variety of approaches, which can be combined in various different ways, to bring about required changes. The "people" approach may not always be the most appropriate.

It is tempting to point to Leavitt's variables as "levers" that have to be pulled to bring about the desired organizational responses. Change has no single cause and no single set of outcomes can be associated in any straightforward way with any particular lever pulling. Change, its triggers, its consequences and its directions are a complex blend of human, social, cultural, political, economic and technical processes that we have yet to understand in a systematic way.

It is also tempting to believe that if one could understand change one could identify trends and predict the future. The complexity and uncertainty of change makes forecasting in this field a very risky business indeed. It may be possible to make realistic guesses that relate to local events in the short run. But the broader the area and time scale of such a forecast, the higher the probability of serious error.

But if we reject technological determinism, and any other form of determinism in the direction of change, then we are left in an awkward position. If human destiny does indeed lie in human hands, then we must be aware of the notion of *alternative futures*. Organizations are social arrangements designed by people and which can be changed by people's decisions. We therefore want to be able to make some predictions about the future, either to make sure that what we want indeed comes to pass, and that what we want to avoid is prevented.

Here we leave the field of scientific endeavour because such predictions involve speculation and moral judgements. Who is to say what type of social or organizational arrangements are better than any other? Our predictions may outline the consequences of a particular organizational change to enable others to evaluate its desirability. Social science may be able to indicate areas for evaluation and suggest criteria, although the selection of criteria is still a moral and political choice.

Social science forecasts are different from natural science ones as they have the following unusual properties:

1. Our predictions may be *self-fulfilling*. To suggest that something will happen can often make it happen.
2. Our predictions may be *self-defeating*. To prophecy something un-desirable may often trigger action to prevent it happening.

STOP!

Think of at least three examples of self-fulfilling prophecies and three examples of self-defeating prophecies that apply in organizations.

Social science itself is a thus a trigger of change. We study people and then feed back our findings to those we have studied. Those people may or may not like what we have found and may or may not disagree with what has been said about them. But whatever the outcome, the act of being studied makes people more aware and sensitive to those aspects of themselves that have been the subject of scrutiny. Increased self-awareness can lead to changes in values, attitudes and behaviour.

We can design alternative futures . . .

"This is to say, in effect, that among the consequences of the knowledge explosion is the emergence of a new way of thinking about the future. That conception is the derivative of our new capacities for prediction, our new images of our powers for controlling future events and, hence, a new outlook suggesting that, to a considerable degree, maybe we can invent the future."

From Melvin M. Webber, "Planning in an environment of change", *Town Planning Review*, 1969, vol. 39. no. 3, pp. 179-81.

Change is thus a difficult topic to investigate. In practice change is potentially within human control. Organizations invest heavily in forecasting and planning for the future. Organizational survival depends in part on the willingness to predict. We can perhaps predict and design the future more effectively if we reject false determinisms and plan deliberately and consciously.

RESISTANCE TO ORGANIZATIONAL CHANGE

Change has positive and negative attributes. On the one hand, change means experiment and the creation of something new. On the other hand, it means discontinuity and the destruction of familiar social structures and relationships. Despite the positive attributes, change may be resisted because it involves both confrontation with the unknown and loss of the familiar. Managers however often seem to regard change as intrinsically good and see resistance as undesirable.

It is widely assumed that *resistance to change* is a common and a natural phenomenon. All organizational change takes place because individuals change their attitudes, values, self-images and behaviour. This can be threatening. Change presents those caught up in it with new situations, new problems, ambiguity and uncertainty. Many people find change, or the thought of change, painful and frustrating. Arthur Bedeian cites four common *causes* of resistance to change in organizations:

Parochial self interest.
Individuals understandably seek to protect a status quo with which they are content and which they see as advantageous to them in some way.

Individuals develop vested interests in the perpetuation of particular organization structures and accompanying technologies. Organizational changes may mean the loss of power, prestige, respect, approval, status and security. Change may also be personally inconvenient for a variety of reasons. It may disturb relationships and arrangements that have taken much time and effort to establish. It may force an unwanted geographical move. It may alter social opportunities. Perceived as well as actual threats to the interests and values of individuals are thus likely to generate resistance to change.

People invest time, effort and commitment in programmes, systems, procedures and technologies to make them work. Individuals may identify themselves more closely with their specific function or role rather than with the organization as a whole. They then have a personal stake in their specialized knowledge and skills and in their creations, and may not be willing readily to see them made redundant.

Misunderstanding and lack of trust.

People resist change when they do not understand the reasons for the change or its nature and likely consequences.

If managers have little trust in their employees, information about impending changes may be withheld or distorted. Incomplete and incorrect information creates uncertainties and inaccurate rumours. This has the unfortunate result of increasing people's perceptions of threat, increasing defensiveness, and reducing further effective communication about the change. Thus *the way in which change is introduced* can be resisted rather than the change itself.

Contradictory assessments.

Individuals differ in the ways in which they evaluate the costs and benefits of change.

Ultimately, it is human values, not technology, that determine which organizational changes are promoted, which persist and succeed and which fail. Individuals differ in their perceptions of what a particular change will mean for them and for the organization as a whole. This is more likely to happen when information about the change is not adequate, and where all the right people do not have all the relevant information.

Bedian points out, however, that contradictory analyses of change can lead to constructive criticisms and improved proposals. Resistance to change is not necessarily disruptive. Resistance may lead to more effective forms of change.

Low tolerance of change.

Individuals differ in their ability to cope with change, to face the unknown, to deal with uncertainty.

Change that requires people to think and behave in different ways can challenge the individual's self-concept. We each have ideas about our abilities and our competence. One response to change may therefore be self-doubt and self-questioning in the form, "will I be able to handle it?". We may be afraid that we will not be able to develop the new skills and behaviours that new organizational arrangements will demand.

Some individuals have a very low tolerance of ambiguity and uncertainty.

The anxiety and apprehension that they suffer may lead them to oppose changes that they know to be beneficial.

Bedeian argues that these are the main common causes of resistance to change. There may be many other reasons and those which apply differ from one situation to another. The causes of resistance to change may thus be many and inter-related and may be difficult to uncover.

There are a number of common *responses* which may be identified with resistance to change:

1. *Resentment* at the manner in which change is introduced — perhaps without warning, without consultation or without the participation of those affected;
2. *Frustration* at the perceived loss or curtailment of promotion and career opportunities;
3. *Anxiety* at perceived threats to job security and income;
4. *Dissatisfaction* at reorganization which leads to loss of skill, meaning, discretion and status in work;
5. *Fear* of appearing incompetent, perhaps on encountering a new technology such as a computer for the first time;
6. *Insecurity* at the loss of order and certainty that accompanied the familiar routine.

The more rapid the change is, the more extreme these responses are likely to be.

Earlier in the chapter we indicated that the rate at which British industry changes may be too slow. There appear to be cultural, as well as psychological, reasons for this. So far we have looked at the nature of resistance to change at the individual level only.

The slow rate of change in British industry is part of what is commonly called *the British disease*.

Definition

The *British disease* is a " . . . general sense of strain and conflict at the place of work, and the withholding of effort by workers from managers to whom they are inherently opposed by differences of class".

From Hugh Phelps-Brown, "What is the British predicament?", *Three Banks Review*, 1977, no. 116, p. 13.

Resistance to change in British industry is thus partly a consequence of the class structure of British society. Managers and workers still see themselves in "them and us" terms — as belonging to different classes with different social status. These class distinctions in practice are based on differences of outlook, manner and speech.

Phelps-Brown argues that American visitors to British workplaces discover:

"...a general tendency to sense where a newcomer ranks in the social pecking order and treat him with deference or condescention accordingly, that stands in distasteful contrast with the democratic manners of his own country." (p. 16)

Britain has developed these "class conscious" attitudes, Brown argues, because we have never suffered defeat in war or occupation this century. We have had no revolutions or any similar events that could have changed our social structures and attitudes. "Our industrial relations", Brown points out, "remain the prisoners of their history." We have had no opportunity to make a "fresh start" as many European countries have had, along with America and Japan.

British education may discourage people from choosing managerial and engineering careers by emphasizing the higher social value of areas of knowledge and pursuits that are not concerned with actually making things:

The philosophy of liberal education not only denied the manufacturer and manager of their true status in society, but put the arts before science, and drew a firm line between 'higher education' and applied or vocational courses. The fresh start was inhibited by cultural values and social attitudes that had come down, little affected meanwhile by the industrial revolution, from a society dominated by the leisured landowner. (p. 26)

Meanwhile, however, the rest of the world has changed. Other countries now sell the goods for which Britain was once famous, such as motor bikes and ships and clothing. We have an inflexibility in both our attitudes and our organizations that is preventing us from adapting in appropriate ways to new trading and manufacturing requirements. Brown concludes that there is a "misfit between our traditional values and the way of life by which we can get a living in the world", and that Britain is in need of "a new Age of Reform". The long term remedy to resistance to change is therefore to change British culture. This argument presumes that economic growth and affluence are desirable social values and denies the possibility that we could pursue aims other than economic success in the world.

Why is Britain a class conscious society? The answer . . .

" . . . is to be found in the features of British society furthest removed from pecuniary matters. They lie in such things as emphasis on the social pecking order, concern with subtle differences of speech and manner, and the educational segregation from an early age of a so-called elite in fee-paying and often unpleasant residential institutions, strangely known as public schools.

"The important feature of this type of class division is that it cuts right across the higher echelons of society. Most British managers have not had the traditional upper-class education; and a captain of industry can feel socially inferior over a glass of sherry with a country parson or a retired army major. The old school conservative and the socialist reformer come together in a common dislike of merely commercial values. In all societies people care about their status in the eyes of their fellow men. In Britain, however, social status has less to do with merely making money than in almost any other Western society."

From S. Brittan, "How British is the British sickness ?", *Journal of Law and Economics*, 1978, vol. 21, pp. 262-3.

MANAGING ORGANIZATIONAL CHANGE

Because of the many sources of resistance to change, and of the pressing need for organizations to adapt to changing market and technological conditions, the management of change has become a central managerial problem. The problem is usually seen as concerning ways of overcoming resistance to make sure that change is accepted and introduced rapidly and effectively. The human aspects of change thus have to be managed as carefully as the technical and organization structural aspects.

Lester Coch and John French conducted one of the most famous experiments in overcoming resistance to change in an organization in the 1940s. The organization they studied was the Harwood Manufacturing Corporation in Marion, Virginia in America. The company made pyjamas and faced resistance from employees to the frequent changes to jobs and work methods that developments in the product and the production methods forced on them.

The employees showed their resistance through:

* Making lots of complaints about the pay rates;
* Absenteeism and simply leaving the company;
* Low standards of efficiency (although their pay depended on output);
* Deliberate restriction of output below what they could achieve;
* "Marked aggression against management".

The company management were sensitive to the human relations and welfare needs of their employees and they had used financial incentives to encourage employees to transfer to new jobs and methods. But the problem remained and Coch and French set out to find out why resistance was so strong and what might be done to overcome it.

The company employed about 500 women and 100 men with an average age of 23, and most of them had no previous industrial experience. The company's time study experts set output standards for all the jobs in the factory. Each employee's output was calculated daily and everyone's performance was made public in a daily list with the best producers at the top and the poorest at the bottom.

High output thus led to more money and to status in the factory. Most of the employees' grievances concerned the fact that as soon as they learned a particular job, and started to earn the bonus payments that came with high output, they were transferred to another task — so they lost money and had to start learning all over again.

The employees thus experienced resentment against management for making the frequent transfers. They were constantly frustrated by their loss of earnings, and potential inability to regain their former levels of production on a new task. This led to a reduction in individual aspiration levels, and to an acceptance of the output norms of the work groups.

Coch and French designed an experiment with three production groups in the factory. The changes that affected these groups were minor ones, but the groups each had different levels of participation in introducing the changes.

The non-participation group

Procedure:
A group of eighteen "hand pressers" changed the way in which they stacked their finished work. The production department announced the change and the time study department announced the new standard work rate. The changes were explained to the pressers but they were not allowed to participate in any of the decisions surrounding the change.

Results:
The group showed no improvement in their efficiency ratings. There was immediate resistance to the change. They argued with the time study engineer and were hostile and unco-operative with the supervisor. The group deliberately restricted their output level and some left the company. They were eventually split up and allocated to various different tasks around the factory.

The representation group

Procedure:
A group of thirteen pyjama folders had to fold trousers *and* jackets (having only done one before). The whole group were given a demonstration of the need to reduce costs. The purpose of the meeting at which the demonstration was given was to get general approval for a plan to improve work methods. Three representatives from the group were then given the appropriate training in the new methods, and they subsequently trained all the other folders. The representatives were reported to have been interested and co-operative and offered several useful suggestions for further improvements.

Results:
The group adopted a co-operative, permissive attitude and their efficiency ratings rose rapidly. Nobody argued with the time study engineer or the supervisor and nobody left the group.

The total participation group

Procedure:
Two groups of fifteen pyjama examiners altered their inspection routine. (One

group had eight examiners and the other had seven.) They had a preliminary meeting like that for the representation group, but everyone took part in the design of the new job and the calculation of the new time standard. Coch and French remark that, "It is interesting to observe that in the meetings with these two groups suggestions were immediately made in such quantity that the stenographer had great difficulty recording them".

Results:
The group recovered its efficiency rating very rapidly to a level much better than before the change. Again there was no conflict and no resignations.

Two and a half months later, the remaining thirteen members of the non-participation group were brought together again for a new pressing job. They followed the total participation procedure, and produced the same results as the previous total participation group — rapid increase in efficiency, no aggression and no resignations. This result confirmed the argument of Coch and French that it was not the people themselves or personality factors, but the way in which they were treated that created or overcame resistance to change.

Employee participation in change has since this study been one of the standard prescriptions for managers looking for a technique to overcome resistance. Participation in the Harwood pyjama factory led to faster relearning of the new methods, higher efficiency, and reduced hostility. The employees in the representation and total participation groups knew what was happening — indeed the changes were within their control — and they did not lose hope as they had previously done about regaining their efficiency, pay levels and status.

J. Kotter and L. Schlesinger have developed the general prescription of Coch and French and suggest six specific methods for overcoming resistance to change:

Education and communication
Managers should share their knowledge, perceptions and objectives with those to be affected by change. This may involve a major training programme, face to face counselling, reports, memos, and group meetings and discussions.

People may need to be trained to recognize the existence of problems that necessitate change (the pyjama folders were given information about the company's costs and the need to reduce them). Resistance as noted earlier may be based on misunderstanding and inaccurate information. It is therefore necessary to get the facts straight and to discuss and reconcile opposing points of view.

Managers can only use this approach if they trust their employees, and if in return management appear credible to the employees.

Participation and involvement
Those who might resist change should be involved in planning and imple-menting it. Collaboration can have the effect of reducing opposition and encouraging commitment. It helps to reduce fears that individuals may have

about the impact of changes on them and makes use of individuals' skills and knowledge.

Managers can only use this approach where participants have the knowledge and ability to contribute effectively and are willing to do so.

Facilitation and support
Employees may need to be given counselling and therapy to help overcome fears and anxieties about change. It may be necessary to develop individual awareness of the need for change, as well as the individual's self-awareness of feelings toward change and how these feelings could be altered.

Effective change depends on communication and consultation . . .

"Within the firm, the willingness to adapt to change is facilitated by the extent to which employees are involved in the planning and development of the business, enabling better understanding and informed decision-making. In the past, UK companies in general have adopted a fairly restrictive approach to the provision of relevant information to employees and many companies have relied on employees' representatives being self-informed. Information about aspects of the business operation and how this relates to the company's financial position needs to be made more readily available to employees and their representatives.

"A number of firms have nevertheless established fairly structured arrangements for handling information or consulting with employees about company plans and progress. These arrangements have included joint union/management production committees to discuss the introduction of new machinery and plant layout; new technology agreements covering these areas; committees designed to co-ordinate the views of participating unions; and company newsletters providing fairly comprehensive information about company plans and finances. No single model or structure exists which is necessarily the most appropriate, given the wide range of sizes and types of firm within the industry, although some organization and routine with the minimum number of restrictions on disclosure is a prerequisite for success. The degree of formalized structure is perhaps less important than the requirement that the method of communication devised allows an early and full discussion of the information which is provided."

From *Policy for the Electronics Industry*, National Economic Development Office, Report of the Electronics Economic Development Committee, NEDO, London, 1982, p. 19.

Negotiation and agreement
It may be necessary to reach a mutually agreeable compromise, through trading and exchange. The nature of a particular change may have to be adjusted to meet

the needs and interests of potential resistors.

Management may have to negotiate, rather than impose, change where there are individuals or groups who are going to be affected and who have enough power to resist. The problem for managers is that this creates a precedent for future changes — which may also have to be negotiated although the circumstances surrounding them may be quite different.

Manipulation and co-optation

This involves covert attempts to sidestep potential resistance. Management puts forward proposals that deliberately appeal to the specific interests, sensitivities and emotions of key groups involved in the change. The information that management disseminates is selective and distorted to emphasize the benefits of change to particular groups and ignores the disadvantages. Co-optation involves giving key resistors access to the decision making process, such as giving individuals managerial positions.

These techniques may work in the short run but create other problems. Managerial manipulation will eventually be discovered and will discredit the reputations of those involved. And trouble makers who are co-opted tend to stay co-opted and may continue to create difficulties from their new position of power.

Explicit and implicit coercion

Management here abandons any attempt at consensus. This may happen where there is a profound disagreement between those concerned with a change, and where there is little or no chance of anyone altering their views. The result is the use of force or threats. This need not involve violence. It may be sufficient to offer to fire, transfer or demote individuals or to stifle their promotion and career prospects.

These six techniques may be used in combination. The choice in any given situation must clearly depend on the likely reactions of those involved and on the long term implications of solving the immediate problem.

It has been found in many studies that successful change depends on a redistribution of power in organizations. Managers who attempt to impose change unilaterally, or autocratically, on others, without participation, are usually responsible for ineffective or less effective changes. This is similar to the conclusion that was reached in the previous chapter about the effectiveness of different leadership styles.

Change can be *planned* and not left to chance or introduced in a careless way. It should be possible to anticipate:

- The alternative forms of work organization available;
- All the individuals and groups likely to be affected;
- The likely reactions and sources of resistance;
- The shifts in influence and authority that are involved;
- The time scale of the change – which is usually slow.

It should therefore be possible to find ways to reduce the disadvantages and thus overcome resistance before the changes start to have their effect.

Twelve rules for overcoming resistance to change . . .

Who brings the change?

1. Resistance will be less if administrators, teachers, board members and community leaders feel that the project is their own —not one devised and operated by outsiders.
2. Resistance will be less if the project clearly has the wholehearted support from top officials of the system.

What kind of change?

3. Resistance will be less if participants see the change as reducing rather than increasing their present burdens.
4. Resistance will be less if the project accords with values and ideals which have long been acknowledged by participants.
5. Resistance will be less if the programme offers the kind of new experience which interests participants.
6. Resistance will be less if participants feel that their autonomy and their security is not threatened.

Procedures in instituting change

7. Resistance will be less if participants have joined in diagnostic efforts leading them to agree on what the basic problem is and to feel its importance.
8. Resistance will be less if the project is adopted by consensual group decision.
9. Resistance will be reduced if proponents are able to empathize with opponents; to recognize valid objections; and to take steps to relieve unnecessary fears.
10. Resistance will be reduced if it is recognized that innovations are likely to be misunderstood and misinterpreted, and if provision is made for feedback of perceptions of the project and for further clarification as needed.
11. Resistance will be reduced if participants experience acceptance, support, trust and confidence in their relations with one another.
12. Resistance will be reduced if the project is kept open to revision and reconsideration if experience indicates that changes would be desirable.

From Goodwin Watson, *Resistance to Change*, 1966, National Training Laboratories, Washington DC.

SOURCES

Advisory Council for Applied Research and Development, 1980, *Technological Change: Threats and Opportunities for the United Kingdom*, HMSO, London.

Bedeian, A. G., 1980, *Organizations: Theory and Analysis*, The Dryden Press, Illinois.

Bennis, W., 1969, *Organization Development: Its Nature, Origins and Prospects*, Addison Wesley, Reading, Massachusetts.

Brittan, S., 1978, "How British is the British sickness?", *Journal of Law and Economics*, vol. 21, October, pp. 245-68.

Brown, H. P., 1977, "What is the British predicament?", *Three Banks Review*, no. 116, December, pp. 3-29.

Coch, L. and French, J. R. P., 1948, "Overcoming resistance to change", *Human Relations*, vol. 1, pp. 512-32.

Etzioni, A. and Etzioni, E. (eds), 1964, *Social Change: Sources, Patterns, and Consequences*, Basic Books, London.

Greiner, L. E., 1967, "Patterns of organizational change", *Harvard Business Review*, vol. 45, no. 3, pp. 119-30.

otter, J. P. and Schlesinger, L. A., 1979, "Choosing strategies for change", *Harvard Business Review*, vol. 57, no.2, pp. 106-14.

Leavitt, H. J., 1965, "Applied organizational change in industry: structural, technological and humanistic approaches", in J. G. March (ed), *Handbook of Organizations*, Rand McNally, Chicago, pp. 1144-70.

McClelland, D. C., 1962, "Business drive and national achievement", *Harvard Business Review*, vol. 40, no. 4, pp. 99-112.

National Economic Development Committee, 1982, *Policy for the UK Electronics Industry: Report of the Electronics EDC*, NEDC, London.

Toffler, A., 1970, *Future Shock*, The Bodley Head/Pan Books, London.

Watson, G., 1966, *Resistance to Change*, National Training Laboratories, Washington D.C.

Webber, M., 1969, "Planning in an environment of change", *Town Planning Review*, vol. 39. no. 3, pp. 179-277.

Chapter 21

Managing conflict

What is organizational conflict?
Ideologies of conflict
Argument, competition and conflict
Management strategies for dealing with conflict
Conclusion

"Conflict is not necessarily good or bad, but must be evaluated in terms of its individual and organizational functions and dysfunctions. In general, conflict generates pressure to reduce conflict, but chronic conflict persists and is endured under certain conditions, and consciously created and managed by the politically astute administrator".

From Louis Pondy, 'Organizational Conflict: Concepts and Models', *Administrative Science Quarterly*, June, 1967, p. 320.

Key concepts:

Once you have fully understood this chapter, you should be able to define the following concepts in your own words:

Unitary ideology of conflict	Argument
Pluralistic ideology of conflict	Competition
Radical ideology of conflict	

Objectives:

On completing this chapter, you should be able to:

1. Distinguish between consensus and conflict perpectives of the study of organizations.
2. Differentiate between the different types of conflict to be found in organizations.
3. List the different ways in which conflict can be resolved.

WHAT IS ORGANIZATIONAL CONFLICT?

Managerial texts on conflict focus on how conflict might be handled and resolved. But Karl Weick writes:

> "Organizational theory has often been stifled because it has worked on problems that managers thought were problems and has studied them using managerial concepts rather than psychological or sociological ones. The only way in which understanding can be advanced is if the symbols used by practitioners are removed, and the phenomena recast into language that has psychological or sociological meaning."
>
> From Karl Weick, *The Social Psychology of Organizing*, Addison Wesley, Reading, Massachusetts, 1969, p. 22.

This is an important point since a consideration of organizational conflict is a political minefield. For managers conflict may be a "problem to be solved" and a consultant might be paid to find a "solution". For the researcher, conflict may appear to be the natural state of organizations and it may be more interesting to study why "peace has broken out". John Eldridge (1968) argues that it is as important to study co-operation, order and stability as it is to investigate the sources of conflict.

Differences in views of conflict are also found between trade unionists and managers, between members of the same and different unions within a company, and not least between managers at different levels within the same organization. It is therefore not surprising that there has been a great deal of controversy in conflict research about what should be studied, how it should be studied, how the results should be presented and what they mean. It is both impossible and undesirable to sidestep these issues since they constitute a central aspect of organizational life. The intention is therefore to present a number of different perspectives on conflict to help readers understand some of the key issues in the study of the topic.

This chapter looks at conflict in organizations, and this means *social* conflict that occurs between individuals and groups. The label "conflict" is sometimes used loosely to refer to stress and frustration which can be regarded as the consequence of conflict between individuals and the environment in which they find themselves. Since the conflict in which we are interested involves more than one person, it is a social process. Groups and individuals in organizations have collective and personal goals. It is inevitable that there will be some competition for scarce resources to help achieve those goals. Such competition may result in conflict.

It is important first to distinguish the different meanings attributed to organizational conflict since these meanings determine the ways in which conflicting parties respond to their situation.

Graeme Salaman (1978) has argued that in the managerial literature, organizations tend to be presented as:

- Harmonious, co-operative structures;
- Where no systematic conflict of interest exists;
- Where conflicts which do arise are seen as exceptional; and
- Where conflicts are seen to arise from misunderstandings and confusions, personality factors, from extra-organizational factors over which the company has no control, and from the expectations of stubborn and inflexible employees.

Conflict can take many different forms:

"Industrial conflict has more than one aspect; for the manifestation of hostility is confined to no single outlet. Its means of expression are as unlimited as the ingenuity of man. The strike is the most common and visible expression. But conflict with the employer may also take the form of peaceful bargaining and grievance handling, of boycotts, of political action, of restriction of output, of sabotage, of absenteeism, or of personnel turnover. Several of these forms, such as sabotage, restriction of output, absenteeism and turnover, may take place on an individual as well as an organized basis and constitute alternatives to collective action. Even the strike itself is of many varieties. It may involve all the workers or only key men. It may take the form of refusal to work overtime or to perform a certain process. It may even involve such rigid adherence to rules that output is stifled."

From Clark Kerr, *Labour and Management in Industrial Society*, Doubleday, New York, 1964, pp. 170-1.

For Salaman, this "happy family" view of organizations is reflected in the personnel and development policies of companies. Organizations are seen as teams that are organized to achieve an agreed common objective. Peter Drucker supports this view when he says that:

"Any business must build a true team and weld individual efforts into a common effort. Each member of the enterprise contributes something different, but they must all contribute towards a common goal. Their efforts must all pull in the same direction, without friction. without unnecessary duplication of effort."

From Peter Drucker, *The Practice of Management*, Pan Books, London, 1968, p. 150.

The view of a conflict-free enterprise organized around teams finds its way into management development and staff appraisal procedures. These often involve goal-setting in which tasks are allocated and performance standards set in agreement with individuals and groups. This perspective views the organization as a system which is there to achieve certain known and agreed goals. The problems and conflicts which arise can be dealt with in this view through appropriate training and motivational techniques.

To maintain the idea of a conflict-free organization, the conflict that does occur has to be explained away. The easiest way to explain the existence of something that should not be there is to point to mismanagement, bad communication or "bloody-minded" workers. Staff appraisal schemes very often ignore the fact that employees are more than organizational members. Because they work in the organization they are necessarily involved in relationships with other people.

The happy family picture of organizations can be contrasted with the view that conflict is an inherent feature of organizations. Salaman (1978) points out that our Drucker quotation contains four "musts" and is not a true reflection of reality. For Salaman, organizations are arenas for individual and group conflict. Combatants fight for professional values, limited resources, career progress, privileges and other rewards.

In this view organizational goals are ambiguous. Goals do not determine behaviour, but are used rather as means for justifying or legitimating actions. Choices of organizational structure and type of technology are considered to be part of the struggle for control by one individual or group over another. The assumption made in the most extreme version of this perspective, is that individual and organizational interests will rarely coincide. This Marxist view sees organizations as one of several "theatres of war" on which the class struggle is fought. The opponents of the working class are the bourgeoisie and are to be found in the political party, the school, the church and in the organization. Organizational conflict is thus part of the inevitable struggle between those who own and control the means of production and those who do not:

> "The history of all hitherto society is the history of class struggles. Freeman and slave, patrician and plebeian, lord and serf, guildmaster and journeyman, in a word, oppressor and oppressed, stood in constant opposition to one another, carried on an uninterrupted, now hidden, now open fight, a fight that each time ended, either in a revolutionary reconstitution of society at large, or in the common ruin of the contending parties."

> From Karl Marx and Friedrich Engels (1888), *The Communist Manifesto*, Penguin Books, Harmondsworth, p. 1.

This conflict view of organizational life, in one form or another, continues to exist as a potent force. Much modern commentary on trade union matters continue to depict management, workers and "the public" in class-based, stereotyped ways.

Those who see organizations as one of the "theatres of war" in society, where the class struggle is waged, also see them containing a number of different "fronts". Within a company, such fronts may include wage negotiation, equal opportunities, industrial democracy and health and safety at work.

Some common current stereotypes . . .

From: Alan Cambell and John McIlroy, *Getting Organized*, Pan Books, London, 1981, p. 35.

What about your workplace?

Think about your own workplace. Who designed it? Who decided what equipment you would use? Who tells you what job to do and how fast you must do it? Obviously, it's your employer or his representative, like a foreman or a supervisor. It's your employer who decides what's in the workplace, what machines and chemicals are used, what is produced and who, therefore determines whether your work is safe or not. That's where your problems begin. Like most people your main interest is in keeping healthy so you are in a fit state to enjoy your wages. It is your employers or manager or supervisor's job to keep costs to the minimum and production at the maximum. Money spent on safety is often regarded as 'non-productive'. Often employers try to cut corners or ignore safety altogether. As a manager of a Sheffield company told a reporter:

"I am not in the business to kill or maim employees, but I am in the business to make steel. If it comes to the final choice between production and safety, often production must come first."

From Dave Eva and Ron Oswald, *Health and Safety at Work*, Pan Books, London, 1981, pp. 19-20.

Groups and individuals thus have different views of organizations and their place in them. From the social science point of view, it is not a question of the conflict perspective being right or wrong, better or worse. What is important in order to understand organizational behaviour is that people hold different views of conflict. Thus entreatments by managers (with a consensus view) to workers (with a conflict view) to be "reasonable" and suspend industrial action are unlikely to be effective. Understanding conflict is the first step in managing it.

Two different views of conflict in organizations have been identified. The "happy family" view considers conflict to be disruptive and thus should be avoided or eradicated if it erupts. Traditional sociology and management practice have started from a position which the former would call "social order" and the latter would call "industrial peace". Both groups then treat all threats to these forms of stability as problems which are to be eliminated. A second perspective is the Marxist tradition. It starts with stability and lack of conflict as the problem. It considers that existing social and organizational arrangements ought to be eliminated. Conflict is seen here as a way of instituting revolutionary change.

A third tradition we shall consider views expressions of conflict as a means of reinforcing the status quo. Here, conflict within limits is held to assist evolutionary and not revolutionary change. Acting as a safety valve, it keeps organizations flexible to internal and external changes while retaining intact their essential characteristics such as the power distribution and the organization hierarchy. Lewis Coser wrote that:

> ". . . conflict, rather than being disruptive and dissociating, may indeed be a means of balancing and hence maintaining a society as a going concern. . . . A flexible society benefits from conflict because such behaviour, by helping to create and modify norms, assures its continuance under changed conditions."
>
> From Lewis A. Coser, *The Functions of Conflict*, Routledge and Kegan Paul, London, 1956, pp. 137 and 154.

STOP!

Why do you think we still have a "them and us" barrier between management and workers in modern organizations? Is this:

1. A misunderstanding of the team spirit in which organizations should function?
2. A symptom of the wider class struggle in which rich and powerful managers exploit poor and powerless employees?
3. A characteristic of the legitimate pursuit of competing interests by different occupational and organizational groups?

IDEOLOGIES OF CONFLICT

One's view about the causes of conflict will depend on the particular perspective one takes on the nature of society and of the organizations in it. To understand organizational conflict, it is necessary to consider the framework presented by Alan Fox (1975) who outlined three different ideologies in the study of industrial relations which he labelled unitary, pluralist and radical (Marxist), and which are related to the perspectives that have already been introduced.

Unitary ideology

This frame of reference sees all members of the organization, managers, workers and shareholders, as having common objectives and values which unite them. Managerial prerogative is accepted with unified authority and there is strong company loyalty. Unions are tolerated but are no longer seen as serving any useful purpose, other than perhaps as a channel of communication. However, they do offer a vehicle for "troublemakers" and, while they cannot be suppressed, they need to be controlled. The organization is seen as team or a family with the "father" manager having the right to impose his will for the long-term interest of all.

Management's strike problem . . .

"Strikes appear as a problem to employers for three main reasons. The least important . . . is that they disrupt the process of production — though this is the reason most frequently cited. What is far more important is the fact that through their actual or potential use of the strike weapon, workers can impose limits to management's control over them. And thirdly, the occurrence of strikes is a persistent practical contradiction of the ideology of harmony of interests which assigns legitimacy to managerial power."

From Richard Hyman, *Strikes*, Penguin Books, Harmondsworth, Middlesex, 1972 p. 161.

Pluralist ideology

Here organizations are seen as coalitions of individuals and groups each with their own interests and objectives. The task of management is to make decisions which take account of the different constituents such as workers, managers, government, suppliers, the law and so on. The manager's job is to manage the differences between interest groups. Management has to achieve a compromise in order to create a viable collaborative structure within which all the stakeholders can, with varying degrees of success, pursue their aspirations. There is an underlying belief that conflict can be resolved through compromise which is acceptable and workable for all. This implies that all parties limit their claims to a level which is at least tolerable to the others and which allows further collaboration to continue. A mutual survival strategy is agreed.

Organizations as conflicting cliques . . .

Melville Dalton described organizational structure as consisting of conflicting cliques which engaged in struggles in order to increase their power and thus obtain a greater share of the rewards which the organization had to offer. He found that individuals and groups were primarily interested in the pursuit of their own narrow interests. They tried to consolidate and improve their own position of power, even if this was at the expense of the organization as a whole. He described how such political activity was skilfully and scrupulously camouflaged. As a result of this, the policies pursued appeared to be in harmony with the official ideology and the organizational handbook. His view of organizational life is one of swiftly changing and conflicting cliques cutting across departmental and other boundaries.

Based on Melville Dalton, *Men Who Manage*, Wiley, New York, 1959.

Radical (Marxist) ideology

This view argues that there is a disparity of power between the owners and controllers of economic resources (shareholders and managers) and those who depend on access to those resources for their livelihood (wage earners). The "ruling strata" maintain their position by preventing any genuine power sharing taking place. This conflict between the "proletariat" and the "bourgeoisie" does *not* presume mutual survival. Those in power perpetuate the exploitation of others by making their own rights as property-holders appear legitimate. They indoctrinate the "have-nots" into accepting the system as it exists.

The unequal nature of organizational life . . .

"The political dimension of organizational employment is revealed in another obvious feature of organizations: the unequal nature of organizational life and the constant possibility of subordinates resisting or avoiding the effects of their seniors (however mediated or obscured) to control them. Within employing organizations a number of highly valued resources and highly depriving — possibly dangerous — experiences are unequally distributed. The majority of members not only receive significantly lower wages than middle and senior management, their conditions of work and employment are far inferior, and their work experiences are vastly more damaging and depriving. It is precisely these least advantaged members of the organization who find themselves controlled by senior (and more privileged) members. Workers who experience the reality of insecurity, deprivation, dehumanized work

and subordination are likely to demonstrate resistance to the oppressive controls to which they are subject."

From Graeme Salaman, *Class and Corporation*, Pan Books, 1981 p. 44.

ARGUMENT, COMPETITION AND CONFLICT

From a pluralist perspective, Charles Handy (1983) provides a useful way of
thinking about the management of conflict in organizations. He describes
organizations as political systems in which individuals compete for resources
and influence. Differences between people are both natural and to be expected.
He suggests that the job of senior company personnel is to manage such
differences in order to achieve the overall organizational task. Handy's basic
concept is *difference*. He distinguishes three kinds of differences which he calls
argument, competition and *conflict*. Handy thus uses the term conflict in a more
precise way than other writers. The main points of his framework are presented
in Figure 21.1.

From this figure it can be seen that both argument and competition are
seen as potentially fruitful and beneficial, whereas conflict is, from the outset,
considered to be harmful. The figure also highlights the fact that both argument
and competition can degenerate into conflict if badly managed. The implication
of this, in Handy's view, is that managers ought to strive to have argument and
competition without conflict in their organizations. Alternatively, when conflict
occurs, they should seek to turn it into argument or competition. In using the
terms beneficial, harmful and fruitful, Handy meant to identify situations where
more than one person benefited from the outcomes of conflict.

Argument is the resolution of differences by discussion. The value of
argument as a way of resolving differences stems from the fact that the
contributions of a number of different viewpoints aid the production of a better
solution. There are two prerequisites for effective argument. One concerns the
characteristics of the group doing the discussing and the second concerns the
logic of the argument.

Handy argues that leadership in a group needs to be shared by the group
members. Additionally, they should have confidence in and trust one another.
The tasks on which the group are engaged ought to be challenging and should
make full use of the abilities and the knowledge of members.

Handy also argues that different people are often found to be arguing about
different things. Moreover, the arguing members often lack the necessary
information with which to reach a resolution of the matter. He suggests that the
issues first be clarified, and that the discussion focus on the facts available, the
goals sought and the methods to be pursued. He also suggests that the values of
group members also have to be considered because they play a part in
assessment of the facts and the selection of methods. Finally, there is a need for

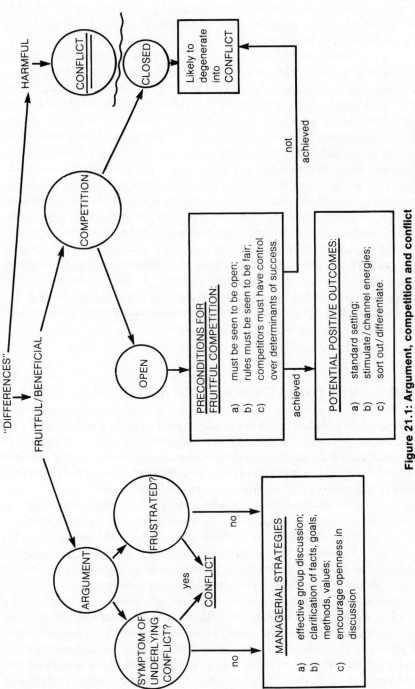

Figure 21.1: Argument, competition and conflict

Based on Charles B. Handy, *Understanding Organizations*, Penguin Books, Harmondsworth, 1983, Chapter 8.

the open expression of feelings by participants. This can be a problem since in many organizations the expression of such feelings is unacceptable. The figure shows that where argument is either frustrated or is the outcome of some underlying conflict, then it will degenerate into harmful conflict.

Handy offers *competition* as a second form of fruitful difference. He suggests that it can set standards by establishing, through comparison, what is best performance. Competition can also motivate individuals to produce higher performance as well as sorting out the better from the worse ones. The beneficial nature of competition depends on whether it is operated in an open or a closed manner. If it is closed, as in the case where one party's gain will be another's loss, then destructive conflict can be the consequence. This win-lose situation (also sometimes referred to as "zero-sum" game) is illustrated in a case where an increased pay settlement means lower dividends to shareholders. In contrast, when competition is open, that is, when all the participants can increase their gains, then the beneficial aspects of competition are gained. The idea of productivity bargaining when workers receive increased wages as a result of increased output is an example of open competition. The managers and shareholders also gain since higher productivity can lead to increased profits and dividends. What is crucial in Handy's view is not whether the competition is closed or open in practice, but how it is *perceived* by the parties involved. Where the preconditions for open competition are not met, then even open competition can, in the end lead to conflict.

MANAGEMENT STRATEGIES FOR DEALING WITH CONFLICT

Handy defines conflicts as harmful differences. Figure 21.2 summarizes what Handy sees as the fundamental causes, symptoms and tactics of conflict. Of particular interest are the two broad types of strategies used by managers to deal with it. The aim of the strategy is to turn the conflict into one of the two fruitful forms of difference, or failing this, to manage it in some way.

The *environmental ("ecological") strategy* or "control by ecology" as Handy calls it, involves trying to create a work environment in which individuals can interact with each other in a collaborative manner. The design of such a work environment has to pay attention to the way in which goals are set, decisions made, how information is handled, how groups can move towards their goals and the development of positive trusting attitudes. This is likely to be time consuming and research shows that it is rarely achieved. In practice what usually happens is that management has to employ *regulation strategies* to control conflict. This involves the use of various formal procedures which, while they may control it, also tend to recognize legitimate conflict and perpetuate it. Inter-level conflict, for example, is more capable of being structured and arbitration procedures can be instituted. Companies such as IBM give employees a right of appeal via an upward channel of communication. Nancy

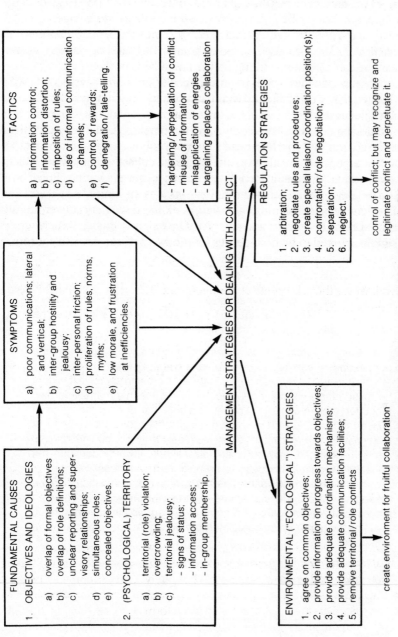

Figure 21.2: Causes, symptoms and tactics of conflict

Based on Charles B. Handy, *Understanding Organizations*, Penguin Books, Harmondsworth, 1983, Chapter 8.

Foy (1974) described the IBM "Open Door" policy where the employee goes to his boss with his complaint; if his own boss cannot right the wrong (or is the grievance) the employee has the right (and sometimes the duty) to go directly up the line, to whoever he chooses, whether it be the next manager, the top local man, or the country general manager. The employee usually chooses the level that fits his idea of the seriousness of the conflict. Unless he started with the chairman, he can continue working up the line if he is not satisfied.

Commenting on these types of conflict resolution approaches, Scott (1965, p. 124) noted that, "The difficulty with many formal programmes of redress is that their values and the values of the organization . . . are not perceived by the participants to be different. This is why a grin is often provoked when a person is told he can go over his superior's head if he has a problem." Management-union conflict has largely been institutionalized through collective bargaining which is a social device for bringing conflict to a successful resolution. Rules and procedures operate here. American unions, such as the United Auto Workers negotiate fiercely before signing a detailed, book-like document concerning all aspects of working conditions and payment. Once signed, this agreement tends to be rigidly adhered to by both parties for the two or three years that it runs.

The Glacier Metal Company in Britain is well known for its appeal procedures. A subordinate has a right of appeal against some order or command made by a manager to him if he objects to it or feels that the order may be in some way unjust or improper.

"The *Company Policy Document* specifies that any individual has the right to appeal against the decision of a manager which he considers affects him adversely in an unjust manner. In order to exercise this right he must inform his manager-once-removed (i.e. his manager's own manager) that he wishes to appeal. The manager-once-removed must then arrange a date and time as soon as possible to hear the appeal. If at this hearing the appellant is not successful in getting the original decision changed, and he is still dissatisfied, he may continue the appeal by requiring his case to be reviewed by successively higher levels of manager in the same line of command up to and including the managing director. In presenting his case he may ask an elected representative from within the company to act as his advisor, and in practice the advisor may completely conduct the case on behalf of the appellant."

From Ron Barnes, "Appeals procedure at the Glacier Metal Company", *Industrial and Commercial Training*, vol. 8, no. 10, 1976 p. 385.

STOP!

Identify an industrial dispute that is reported in the media during your organizational behaviour course.

Collect copies of as many newspaper reports of the dispute as you can, using different newspapers.

Can you identify the views of management, workers, unions and journalists as either unitary, pluralist or radical?

Are the differences at issue in the dispute seen by the participants as beneficial or harmful?

CONCLUSION

Since the 1960s, the managerial literature has, however reluctantly, began to acknowledge the existence of conflict, but has sought to redefine it.

Old View	*New View*
Conflict is avoidable	Conflict is inevitable and is linked to change
Conflict is caused by "troublemakers"	Conflict is determined by structural factors, e.g., class system, design of career structure
Conflict is detrimental to task achievement	A small level of conflict is useful particulary if it is used constructively

---

Differences can be fruitful . . .

Conflict can improve rather than impede organizational decision making. When those who have opposing ideas try to agree, they develop a better understanding of each other's positions, bring their differences to the forefront, and reach a decision with which everyone is satisfied. This conclusion was reached by Dean Tjosvold and Deborah Deerner from the results of an experiment which they designed.

They asked sixty-six student volunteers to take the roles of foremen and workers at an assembly plant. Conflict had arisen over the workers' job rotation schemes. The "student workers" were first given inform-ation about the benefits of the scheme (it gave more job satisfaction) and were asked to defend it. The "student foremen" were told about its disadvantages (workers did not remain in their jobs long enough to develop expertise) and were asked to argue for its abolition. A third group of students was told that the company had a good industrial relations record and that the company tried, where possible, to *avoid controversy*. Another group was told that the company had a history of open, frank discussion of differences and that the norm was *co-operative controversy*, and that groups tried to win any arguments that arose. The students were offered lottery tickets for complying with these norms in the experiment. Workers and foremen then met in pairs for fifteen minutes to discuss and resolve the issue. They then noted their decision and answered questions about their attitudes to their discussions.

It was found that where controversy was avoided, the decisions were dominated by the views of the foremen. Where controversy was competitive, the students were generally not able to reach any agreement and experienced feelings of hostility and suspicion towards their adversary. Under the co-operative controversy conditions, decisions were reached that integrated the views of workers and foremen. Feelings of curiosity, trust and openness were also found to be induced. Co-operative controversy may therefore be good for decision making. But how does one get real foremen and real workers to comply with this apparently useful social or organizational norm?

From Dean Tjosvold and Deborah Deerner, "Effects of controversy within a co-operative or competitive context on organizational decision making", *Journal of Applied Psychology*, vol. 65, no.5, 1980, pp. 590-5.

The notion of "constructive conflict" has been increasingly used in the managerial literature. Conflict is welcomed, and indeed encouraged, provided that it is likely to make minor incremental adjustments to the existing organizational order and arrangements. Chris Argyris (1970), for example, saw conflict as aiding the decision-making process and claimed that one of the requirements of an effective organization was that, "conflict is identified and managed in such a way that the destructive win/lose stance with its accompanying polarisation of views is minimized".

The win/lose perspective refers to Alan Fox's radical (Marxist) ideology described earlier. Argyris argues for the constructive, unemotional appraisal and evaluation of alternative options. This involves the active challenging of assumptions and perceptions which may have been applied to individual group matters. Schelling (1960) also wrote that conflict can only be of positive value if its potential value can be realized. This depends on how it is managed and resolved. In his view this requires the careful appraisal of potential conflict areas. It would also depend on one's perspective regarding the nature of organizational life, that is, whether one held a unitary, pluralist or radical perspective.

The Abilene Paradox . . .

This phenomenon is based on the experience of Jerry Harvey and his family on a miserable trip to Abilene in Texas. It was an appallingly hot day, the round trip was 104 miles through desert, and the food in the restaurant was terrible. During the argument that followed the trip, each member of the family blamed the others for the mistake, and they discovered that none of them had ever really wanted to go in the first place. Each assumed that the others had wanted to go. But they had all been unwilling to voice their misgivings about the trip because, ironically, each wanted to "keep the peace in the family". Individually, none of them wanted to go to Abilene, but the family went anyway.

The Abilene Paradox can be stated in the following terms: "Organizations frequently take actions in contradiction to what they really want to do and therefore defeat the very purposes that they are trying to achieve". A corollary of the paradox is that the inability to manage *agreement* is a major source of organizational dysfunction.

Harvey quotes a number of case studies to support his view. The best known of these is the Watergate scandal. How was it, he asks, that so many prominent men in public office, including the President of the United States, instigated, colluded or tried to cover up behaviour which was reprehensible and foolish. Analysing the testimonies of the Senate investigation committee into "The Watergate Affair", Harvey points to White House staff who said how they "drifted along" and "feared group pressure". The key individuals involved all agreed that the plan was inappropriate, but implemented it in contradiction to their shared agreement. The plan increased their problems rather than reduced them. Each of them then proceeded to blame the other. Harvey argues that because of their inability to cope with the fact that they agreed, the organization took a trip to Abilene.

Those caught in the web of the Abeline Paradox suffer not from the inability to manage conflict but from failure to manage agreement. Six symptoms are identified by Harvey:

1.   Members agree individually what the organization's problem is.
2.   They individually decide what steps to take to solve the problem.
3.   They fail accurately to communicate their views to other members and lead the others to misperceiving the collective reality.
4.   Using this inaccurate information, a collective decision is made contrary to what they want to do, and produces results counterproductive to the organization's aims.
5.   A consequence of these actions is a feeling of frustration, irritation and anger with the organization. Subgroups form which proceed to blame other subgroups.
6.   Failure to deal with the inability to manage agreement leads to the cycle repeating itself.

From Jerry Harvey, "The Abilene Paradox: The Management of Agreement", *Organizational Dynamics*, vol. 3., no. 1, 1974, pp. 63-80.

Conflict can be regarded as a symptom of a much wider issue. What is really at stake here is the extent to which we regard existing social and organizational arrangements as legitimate. Those who hold unitary and pluralist perspectives tend to regard inequalities of power and wealth in society and organizations as natural and on the whole uncontentious. Those who hold a radical Marxist perspective see these inequalities as the result of inhuman exploitation which can only be overcome through the destruction of capitalism. The behaviour of the parties in conflict may be expected to reflect their respective stances on this wider issue of legitimacy. A large proportion of strikes in Britain for example are "unconstitutional" in that they involve trade union members breaking agreements that they have previously entered into with management. Where these agreements are seen to have been made forcibly, they are regarded as illegitimate, and trade unions feel that it is legitimate to break them.

Management literature now admits to the existence of conflict as a feature of organizational life. But it still tends to:

- Treat conflict at the interpersonal level - the objective is to obtain consensus from fellow organizational members;
- Assume that organizational goals are agreed and that it is the means which are being argued about — a unitary perspective;
- Reinforce the group nature of organizational life — "they must consider themselves as part of the team".

This redefinition presents conflict as a challenge to the means by which organizational goals are to be pursued, rather than to the goals themselves. The bases on which conflict and consensus are founded in an organization can be identified by looking within it and not by looking at the wider social structures in which it is set. Organizations have structures which direct the behaviour of employees in certain directions, usually towards the organization's goals rather than towards their own personal goals. These control mechanisms exist within a context of differing power, status and resources. The success of these controls is thus dependent on the extent to which those subjected to them see them as legitimate.

SOURCES

Argyris, C., 1970, *Intervention Theory and Method: A Behavioural Science View*, Addison Wesley, Reading, Massachusetts.

Barnes, R., 1976, "Appeals Procedure at the Glacier Metal Company", *Industrial and Commercial Training*, vol. 8, no. 10, pp. 383-86.

Cambell, A. and McIlroy, J., 1981, *Getting Organized*, Pan Books, London.

Coser, L. A., 1956, *The Functions of Conflict*, Routledge and Kegan Paul, London.

Dalton, M., 1950, "Conflict Between Staff and Line Managerial Officers", *American Sociological Review*, June, pp. 342-51.

Dalton, M., 1959, *Men Who Manage*, Wiley, New York.

Drucker, P. F., 1968, *The Practice of Management*, Pan Books, London.

Eldridge, J. E. T., 1968, *Industrial Disputes*, Routledge and Kegan Paul, London.

Eva D. and Oswald, R., 1981, *Health and Safety at Work*, Pan Books, London.

Foy, N., 1974, *The IBM World*, Eyre Methuen, London.

Fox, A., 1971, *A Sociology of Work in Industry*, Collier Macmillan, London.

Fox, A., 1975, "Industrial relations: a social critique of pluralist ideology", in B. Barrett, E. Rhodes and J. Beishon, (eds.) *Industrial Relations and the Wider Society: Aspects of Interaction*, Collier Macmillan, London.

Handy, C., 1983, *Understanding Organizations* Penguin Books, Harmondsworth, Middlesex.

Harvey, J., 1974, "The Abilene paradox: the management of agreement", *Organizational Dynamics*, vol. 3, no. 1, pp. 63-80.

Hyman, R., 1972, *Strikes*, Penguin Books, Harmondsworth, Middlesex.

Kerr, C., 1964, *Labour and Management in Industrial Society*, Doubleday, New York.

Pondy, L., 1967, "Organizational conflict: concepts and models", *Administrative Science Quarterly*, June, pp. 342-51.

Salaman, G., 1978, "Management development and organizational theory", *Journal of European Industrial Training*, vol. 2, no. 7, pp. 7-11.

Salaman, G., 1981, *Class and Corporation*, Fontana, London.

Schelling, T. C., 1960, *The Strategy of Conflict*, Harvard University Press, Boston, Massachusetts.

Scott, W. G., 1965, *The Management of Conflict: Appeals Systems in Organizations*, Irwin Dorsey, Homewood, Illinois.

Tjosvold, D. and Deerer, B. K., 1980, "Effects of controversy within a cooperative or competitive context on organizational decision making", *Journal of Applied Psychology*, vol. 65, no. 5, pp. 590-5.

Weick, K., 1969, *The Social Psychology of Organizing*, Addison-Wesley, Reading, Massachusetts.

Chapter 22

Management control

"Like a rider who uses reigns, bridle, spurs, carrot, whip and training from birth to impose his will, the capitalist strives, through management to *control*. And control is indeed the central concept of all management systems . . ."

From Harry Braverman, *Labour and Monopoly Capital: The Degradation of Work in the Twentieth Century,* Monthly Review Press, New York, 1974, p. 68.

451

Key concepts:

Once you have fully understood this chapter, you should be able
to define the following concepts in your own words:

Management control   Social control
Rigid bureaucratic behaviour   Insidious control
Authoritarian personality

Objectives:

On completing this chapter you should be able:

1. To distinguish between the different uses of the concept of control.
2. To appreciate the economic and psychological need for control in organizations.
3. To understand the political nature of management control.
4. To identify the different ways in which control is exercised in organizations.
5. To understand the importance to management of the legitimacy of control.

CONFLICTING VIEWS OF CONTROL

"The inherent preferences of organizations are clarity, certainty, and perfection. The inherent nature of human relationships involves ambiguity, uncertainty, and imperfection. How one honours, balances, and integrates the needs of both is the real trick of management."

From Richard T. Pascale and Anthony G. Athos, *The Art of Japanese Management*, Penguin Books, Harmondsworth, 1982, p. 105.

The concept of control has a number of positive meanings. It stands for predictability, order, reliability, and stability. The absence of control from this point of view means anarchy, chaos, disorder and uncertainty.

Control in an organization means that people know what they have to do and when. Suppliers know what they have to deliver and when. Customers know when they are going to get their goods or services. Employees know how much they are going to get paid. Control from this point of view appears to be a necessary aspect of organizational life. Most individuals require some degree of order, predictability and certainty in their lives. Control thus also appears to be psychologically desirable.

But the concept of control also means coercion, domination, exploitation and manipulation. The absence of control from this point of view means freedom, individuality, discretion, responsibility and autonomy.

Control in an organization can mean stifling the personality and intellect of the individual. This notion of control runs counter to our democratic political ideal which suggests that individuals should have a say in matters that concern them. Most individuals dislike being told what to do all or most of the time. Managers who attempt to manipulate and dominate their subordinates invariably meet with resistance, hostility and poor performance. Control from this point of view appears to be an undesirable aspect of organizational life. Ability to exercise freedom of choice and expression appears to be necessary to the development of the mature personality. Control thus also appears to be psychologically undesirable.

Organizational control can have three main connotations:

1. It is an *economically* necessary activity. If control breaks down, then operations get out of hand, resources are wasted, money is spent unnecessarily. Control is therefore a means of securing efficiency by achieving the continuing best use of resources.

2. It is *psychologically* necessary to create stable and predictable conditions within which people can work effectively. Control is thus a means of establishing predictability as psychological well being and work performance can be disrupted by uncertainty, ambiguity and disorder.

3. It is a *political* process in which certain powerful individuals and groups dominate others. Decisions in the control process are taken by managers

who resist attempts to let others, particularly subordinates, interfere. Control is thus a means of perpetuating inequalities of power and other resources in organizations (and in society as a whole).

THE NATURE OF MANAGEMENT CONTROL

"Control, then, is neutral; it is demanded by the task in hand, which in turn is for the benefit of society at large, indeed for the workers themselves as citizens and consumers, and is achieved through the application of science and technology."

From Graeme Salaman, *Class and the Corporation*, Fontana, London, 1981, p. 152.

Social science has had difficulty in defining just what constitutes an organization. It is not clear what aspects of what we call organizations distinguish them from other forms of social arrangements. Most people would agree that IBM and Shell Oil are organizations. But what about the local sports club? What criteria should be used to make the distinction?

We suggested in Chapter 1 that it is the *preoccupation with controlled performance* that sets organizations apart from other forms of social arrangement. If the managers and players of the local football team have such a preoccupation then we have to call the team an organization. The performance of an organization as a whole determines whether or not it survives. The performance of a department or section within an organization determines the amounts of resources allocated to it. The performance of individuals determines their pay and promotion prospects.

Organizations are concerned with the *adequacy* of group and individual performances. Not just any level of performance will do. We live in a world in which the resources available to us are not sufficient to meet all of our conceivable needs. We have to make effective use of the resources that we have. The performances of individuals, departments and organizations are therefore tied closely to standards which stipulate what counts as adequate, satisfactory or good performance. Such a specific concern with what constitutes adequacy in terms of performance is not a feature of other social arrangements such as families. So we do not feel happy about putting "family" into the category of "organization".

It is economically necessary to control performance in an organization to ensure that it is good enough, and to ensure that some action is taken when it is not good enough. The production of most modern goods and services is a complex process. The varied work activities of large groups of people have to be organized and co-ordinated to achieve the controlled performances required to mass produce toothpaste or build custom made computers.

Definition

Management control is the process through which plans are implemented and objectives are achieved by:
Setting standards;
Measuring performance;
Comparing actual performance with standards;
Deciding necessary corrective action and feedback.

STOP!

Consider the course in organizational behaviour that you are now studying. In collaboration with your fellow students, analyse the process through which your performance on the course is controlled in the following terms:

What standards of performance are you expected to achieve?

Who sets the standards?
Do you know what the standards are?
Are the standards clearly defined or ambiguous?
Do you think the standards are too high or too low?

How is your performance measured?

Is your performance measured on one or on many criteria?
Do you know what the criteria are?
How often is your performance measured?

Who compares your performance with the standard?

Is this done publicly or in secret?
Is this done by one person or by several?
Are students involved as well as teaching staff?
Is the comparison objective and straightforward or subjective?

What happens if your performance is not up to standard?

What kind of feedback do you get?
Is the feedback useful in telling you how to improve?
Is the feedback provided frequently or only on rare occasions?
Is the feedback accurate?

Now prepare a report based on your analysis and submit it with a series of recommendations for improvement of the control process to the teaching staff involved with the course.

Note their reactions to your proposals.

Management control thus involves a recurring sequence of activities. Objectives and standards provide guidelines for performance and set the norms for activities and procedures. They specify what performance levels are required, or what levels of performance are going to be regarded as satisfactory, unsatisfactory and superlative. It is sometimes difficult to decide on the level at which standards should be set. If they are set too high they are usually ignored. If they are set too low, then performance may be artificially lowered. It is also sometimes hard to decide on the number and complexity of standards to set. A large number of standards that are difficult to understand may produce a cumbersome and ineffective organization.

The performance objectives for most students are expressed in terms such as, "get at least 50 per cent in assignments and exams". This can however in practice be an ambiguous standard as many students are not clear what they have to do to achieve it. Examination answers tend to be assessed on several criteria, such as style, content, structure, quality of critical evaluation, comparison of arguments and theories, synthesis of material and so on. But it is hard to specify what these criteria mean in practice in clear terms. The performance objectives for a typist on the other hand may be expressed as "50 words a minute" and "no errors". These are comparatively unambiguous standards and it is usually quite clear when they have been achieved.

Actual performance clearly has to be measured in some way to see if it is consistent with the standards that have been set. Measurement can involve personal observation by the superior, oral and written reports from subordinates, the collection of statistics, and the measurement of performance indicators by mechanical or electronic mechanisms.

The measurement of student performance is usually achieved through the student's written work, and sometimes through the teacher's observation of the student's oral presentations. For most social science subjects this form of measurement can be very subjective. The measurement of factory work can be expressed in terms of saleable units of output, say packets of biscuits over an hour or a day. This is a comparatively objective measurement which may be made by personal observation or through reports.

The timing of measurement is also important. Students' performance is traditionally measured at the end of each university session — about every ten weeks. The performance of a biscuit making line and its operators is measured constantly throughout each shift. If performance is measured too early, or too late, the value of the feedback in correcting any problems will be reduced.

Corrective action or feedback involves a control decision to put things right, or the provision of information to enable those involved to take appropriate action. This step is itself sometimes identified as the control task, but it is important to see this as only one stage of a logical process of control. The control process can be used to identify performance trends that should be defeated or encouraged, as well as simply to ensure that predefined targets are being achieved.

Students are told whether or not their understanding of course material is adequate. Lecturers usually just provide this information and leave decisions about corrective action to the student. Lecturers vary in their willingness and ability to give helpful feedback information to students. The comment, "not bad, but could do much better", is informative but not particularly helpful. A supervisor in a biscuit factory who discovers that something is going wrong with the baking process may tell operators about the problem and expect them to solve it themselves. The supervisor may on the other hand decide to take action and, say, replace a faulty piece of machinery or shut the process down until a repair team arrives.

STRATEGIES AND PROBLEMS OF MANAGEMENT CONTROL

The problem is to establish control processes that are effective in that they lead to the achievement of the desired levels of performance. Control has traditionally been regarded as one of the main functions of management. Fayol for example regarded control as one of five main management responsibilities. Some commentators have argued that control is the single most important management function. Others have suggested that management in all its aspects is a control function.

Design your own control process

You are a manager responsible for a typing pool with twelve typists and one senior typist who acts as a supervisor. Other managers in the company have been complaining that the quantity and quality of their typing work is not good enough. They have asked you to find ways of controlling the work of the typists to improve matters.

What action would you consider under the headings:

- Setting standards for typing quality and quantity?
- Measuring the typists' performance?
- Comparing their performance with the standards?
- Giving feedback and taking corrective action?

You could write a book of rules and regulations to make the standards clear. You could ask the typists to fill in work record sheets to measure their typing output. You could appoint a second supervisor to share the monitoring load. You could consider involving the typists and perhaps even the authors in the control process in some way.

Compare your suggestions with those of your colleagues.

Evaluate the impact of your suggestions taking into account the arguments of:

- Richard Hackman and Greg Oldham on job design (Chapter 4);
- Chris Argyris on personality development (Chapter 16);
- Norman Macrae on intrapreneurial groups (Chapter 17).

The control process has to ensure that the members of the organization are behaving as they are required to behave as well as ensuring that their activities are achieving the desired results. Performance has to be standardized to some extent to achieve consistent output quantity and quality. Organizations have to reduce waste, theft, sabotage and fraud in the interests of economic survival.

The main mechanism through which management control is achieved is organization structure. Organization members have to carry out the tasks of the control process as well as the operating tasks required to fulfil the organization's objectives. The need for controlled performance leads to a deliberate and ordered allocation of functions, or division of labour, between the organization's members, and to the establishment of hierarchical authority relationships. The activities and interactions of staff and workers are intentionally programmed and structured. Admission to membership of organizations is also controlled. The price of failure to perform to standard is invariably loss of membership.

The steps in the management control process are achieved in a number of ways less obvious than those we have identified so far. Don Hellriegel and John Slocum identify six common management control strategies:

Control through the organization structure

Most large organizations give their employees written job descriptions which set out the individual's tasks and responsibilities. These job descriptions can be more or less narrow, detailed, specific and ambiguous or broad, general, vague and ill defined. They also establish communication flows and the location of decision making responsibility.

Job descriptions constrain the behaviour of the individual by identifying what things can and cannot be done, and by placing the individual in the organization hierarchy. The standards that have to be achieved are thus part of the description of the job that the individual holds.

Control through recruitment and training

Organizations preoccupied with controlled performance cannot afford to be staffed with people who behave in unstable, variable, spontaneous, random and "individual" ways. Organizations require stability and predictability in the behaviour of their members. This is achieved through the selection of stable people and through the emphasis on consistency and reliability in training.

Managers can exercise a great deal of discretion in the criteria that are used in selection and in the content of training programmes. Managers usually select people who "fit" the organization in terms of their attitudes and values as well as their skills. (Management can discriminate against employees in several dimensions other than sex and race.) Training can cover attitudes and values relevant to the company culture or climate as well as traditional skill and knowledge training. These processes try to ensure that the standards that have to be achieved are part of (or through training become part of) the individual's personal value system.

Controllers sometimes give inaccurate feedback . . .

The research of Daniel Ilgen and William Knowlton suggests that supervisors do not always tell their subordinates the truth about how good their performance is.

The researchers asked forty students each to supervise a group of three workers who were coding questionnaires for two hours. The "workers" were collaborators of the researchers and had been specially trained for the experiment.

The student supervisors were first shown the results of a "personnel test" which they were told had measured the abilities of their subordinates for the coding job. Each work group had one "discrepant" worker who worked much better, or much worse, than the other two. The discrepant worker behaved enthusiastically in some groups and apathetically in others. The supervisors were thus led to attribute the performance of the discrepant worker to either high or low ability or to high or low motivation.

After the work session, the supervisors rated the ability and motivation of all their subordinates on scales which ranged from "unsatisfactory" to "outstanding". They then completed a separate "feedback report form" using the same scales, in the belief that they would then have to convey the contents in person to one of their subordinates who would be chosen "at random". In fact the discrepant worker was always chosen.

For the purposes of the feedback, the supervisors had to select one of twelve statements that best described their evaluation of the subordinate, such as "You have done very well. I believe I would try to do even better next time if I were you", or "Your performance is not good at all. You really need to put more into it." In addition, the supervisors had to make recommendations for the subordinate, such as "attend a special training session", "concentrate more on the task", or "try harder". When they had done this, the supervisors were told that there would be no feedback session and the deception was explained to them.

As expected, the ratings of ability and motivation of the subordinates were higher when the supervisors believed that they would have to give personal feedback. Where low performance was attributed to motivation, the feedback reflected this accurately. But where low performance was attributed to ability, the supervisors recommended an inappropriate mix of feedback, directed at both motivation and skill.

The researchers argue that if supervisors in organizations systematically distort their assessments in this way, many employees will have inflated views of their abilities.

From Daniel R. Ilgen and William A. Knowlton, "Performance attributional effects on feedback from superiors", *Organizational Behavior and Human Performance*, 1980, vol. 25, no. 3, pp. 441-56.

Control through rewards and punishments

Organizations provide their members with a number of extrinsic and intrinsic rewards. Extrinsic rewards are material, monetary incentives and associated fringe benefits such as cheap loans, company car, free meals and so on. Intrinsic rewards include satisfying work, personal responsibility and autonomy.

The behaviour of employees can be controlled by offers to provide and to withdraw these rewards in return for compliance or defiance with respect to management directions. Although psychology has shown that punishment (or the threat of punishment) is not an effective means for controlling behaviour, the withdrawal of rewards is still a common organizational control mechanism. Individuals whose performance is up to standard are thus rewarded while those who do not comply find that their rewards are diminished or withheld.

Control through policies and rules

Written policies and rules guide employees' actions, structure their relationships and try to establish consistency. Some typical organizational rules were examined in Chapter 15. Rules establish acceptable behaviour and levels of performance and are another attempt to lay down standards.

Control through budgets

Individuals and sections in an organization can be given financial targets to guide their performance. These targets may concern the level of expenditure that the section has, the level of costs incurred, or the level of sales volume to be achieved in a month. Production budgets may involve non financial standards such as labour hours used, machine downtime, materials used, waste material and so on.

Control through machinery

This form of control has been most popular in process industries where chemicals are manufactured automatically with very little human intervention. Computer sensors capture process performance information, compare it with preprogrammed standard performance criteria, and decide automatically on corrective action when necessary. Developments in electronics and computing are likely to increase the extent to which machinery takes over all the steps of the control process in manufacturing operations. Machines can even control other machines and the need for human controllers is reduced.

People subjected to organizational control systems do not always behave in required and expected ways. Edward Lawler has argued that management control strategies create three major human problems for organizations.

First, management controls lead to what Lawler describes as *rigid bureaucratic behaviour*. Most people want to behave in ways that make them look good. The standards in the control process tell people what they have to do to perform well and maybe to get promoted. People then behave in ways required by the control process and this is not necessarily in the interests of the organization as a whole.

Lawler cites research in a department store which used a pay incentive scheme to reward employees according to the volume of sales they achieved. Sales increased when the scheme was introduced. But employees were busy "tying up the trade" and "sales grabbing" to sell as much as they could and other essential tasks such as display work and stock checking were ignored. The control system did not set any standards for stock and display work, only for sales volume.

STOP!

Can you identify examples of rigid bureaucratic behaviour in your education institution?

The control process cannot measure everything. It is therefore difficult to establish just what should be measured. The problem is that controls focus attention on whatever criteria are chosen. Rigidity arises from the desire of individuals to defend their actions by pointing to their satisfactory performance on the measure — such as the level of sales.

Second, *inaccurate information* can be fed into the control process. Several studies have suggested that the more important the measure, the more likely is the information in the process to get distorted. Subordinates are prone to provide incorrect information both on what has been done and on what can be done. Lawler cites the following examples:

"In one case, a group, who worked together in assembling a complicated and large sized steel framework, worked out a system to be used only when the rate setter was present. They found that by tightening certain bolts first, the frame would be slightly sprung and all the other bolts would bind and be very difficult to tighten. When the rate setter was not present, they followed a different sequence and the work went much faster.

"The budget bargaining process managers go through with their superiors is not too dissimilar from the one that goes on between the time study man and the worker who is on a piece rate plan or work standard plan. The time study man and the superior both try to get valid data about what is possible in the future, and the employees who are subject to the control system often give invalid data and try to get as favourable a standard, or budget, as they can."

From Edward E. Lawler, "Control systems in organizations", in H. D. Dunnette (ed), *Handbook of Industrial and Organizational Psychology*, Rand McNally Publishing Co., Chicago, 1976, p. 1260.

Some subordinates give inaccurate information . . .

Do subordinates always tell their bosses the truth about how well they are performing at work? An experiment conducted by Janet Gaines suggests that some subordinates distort the information they feed into the management control process in systematic ways.

Gaines gave forty employees in an American aluminium company a description of an "organizational situation". Half of the subjects were given a story about "troublesome communications", such as getting bad news through the grapevine or not getting clear instructions. The others were given a story about "routine communications". When the employees had finished reading their story they were asked to rate the chance that they would tell their superior about it, compose a memo (assuming that they decided to tell), and to rate their trust in their superior and their own personal ambition.

Their memos were classed as either "withholding", "puffing" (exaggerating), or "sieving" (selecting) information.

Withholding was the most popular form of information distortion. Ambitious subordinates who trusted their bosses were less likely to tell them about routine matters. They perhaps felt competent to deal with these issues themselves and would have shown weakness by asking for the boss's help.

But ambitious and trusting subordinates were more likely to pass on information about problems, perhaps because they felt that their superior needed to know and would find out anyway.

The results suggested that, contrary to popular belief, ambitious people do not exaggerate and do not try to deceive others to achieve their personal aims. Managers have most to worry about where their subordinates are unambitious and do not trust them.

From Janet H. Gaines, "Upward communication in industry: an experiment", *Human Relations*, 1980, vol. 33, no. 12, pp. 929-42.

Information may be distorted or withheld where employees want to look good and where mistakes and poor performance can be hidden in some way. Information may also be distorted where employees feel that the standards imposed on them are unfair. If standards are felt to be unreasonable, it may be seen as legitimate to cheat. Information that is used for assessment and reward is therefore more likely to get distorted than information supplied for "neutral" purposes.

STOP!

Can you identify examples of information distortion in your educational institution?

Information used for reward purposes may be distorted . . .

"In the United States many so-called commercial blood banks in large cities pay donors for the blood they give. In large cities there is a high incidence of patients coming down with hepatitis after they have received transfusions. The research shows that the incidence of hepatitis is much higher among patients receiving commercial blood than among those receiving free blood. Apparently the blood of paid donors is more likely to contain hepatitis than the blood of voluntary donors. The reason for this is that blood banks have to rely on their donors to give accurate medical histories in order to prevent harmful blood from being collected."

From Edward E. Lawler, "Control systems in organizations", in H. D. Dunnette (ed), *Handbook of Industrial and Organizational Psychology*, Rand McNally College Publishing Co., Chicago, 1976, p. 1263.

Third, controls may be resisted when they threaten the satisfaction of human needs and create hostility and lack of co-operation. Controls may:

- Automate human skill and expertise. Skill is a source of identity and self-esteem and its loss may be hard to bear.
- Create new experts with new sources of power and autonomy. Those who used to have the expertise and power may resist this.
- Measure individual performance more accurately and comprehensively than before. It may be to the advantage of the individual for everyone to know how hard they work. But some people will fear exposure from all embracing controls on their behaviour.
- Change the social structure of an organization and disrupt social groupings, and interaction and friendship opportunities. This can also mean the creation of competing and conflicting groups.
- Reduce opportunities for intrinsic need satisfaction by reducing individual autonomy.

STOP!

Can you identify examples of resistance to controls in your educational institution?

These three reactions to management controls are sometimes described as *dysfunctional* because they create human behaviours that run counter to the behaviours that the controls are seeking to establish. This is the dilemma of management control system design.

THE PSYCHOLOGICAL NEED FOR CONTROL

The previous section emphasized the need for management control to achieve satisfactory organizational performance. The following section presents a contrasting critical perspective on management control. Before we proceed with that it is useful first to consider the positive psychological advantages of control in organizations.

Why would anyone want to be controlled at all? This notion is inconsistent with our social values of democratic decision making and individual freedom of expression. Edward Lawler suggests that control has three psychological functions.

First, control processes give people feedback on their performance. This feedback constitutes information which the individual can use to improve performance. Without feedback, learning is difficult or impossible and feedback is generally sought for this reason. Feedback can also have a motivating effect by providing recognition for past achievement which in turn provides incentive to sustain and to improve performance levels.

STOP!

Consider what your reaction would be if your lecturers stopped telling you how well you had performed in term assignments and examinations (with the exception of telling you at the end of the course whether you had got your degree or diploma or not).

Is there evidence in your reaction and that of your colleagues that you have a psychological need for control?

In other words, people naturally want to know how well they have done on a particular task and welcome the feedback information from the control process which tells them just that. Supervisors in organizations however often lack the skill to provide the quantity and quality of feedback that employees require for the development of their skills and motivation.

Second, control processes give people structure, define methods and indicate how their performances will be measured. Most of us require some degree of structure and definition in what we do. Some of us need a lot, and prefer rigid, tightly specified jobs where the rules and limits are clear. It is reassuring to know precisely what one is required to do and how the outcome will be evaluated.

Third, controls encourage dependency. Some people seem to enjoy submitting themselves to authority. This enjoyment goes beyond the reassurance of knowing the rules of the control process and appears to be part of the *authoritarian personality*. This personality type was first identified by American researchers during and after the Second World War.

Definition

The *authoritarian personality* is a personality type which includes a cluster of personality traits concerned with conservative attitudes, submission to and preoccupation with authority, fatalistic and rigid thinking and hostility to humanistic values.

Employees need helpful feedback . . .

It is difficult to maintain or improve work performance in the absence of feedback on how well one is doing. Many companies have schemes in which supervisors annually appraise the performance of their subordinates and give them feedback. But these schemes are often ineffective.

Daniel Ilgen, Richard Paterson, Beth Martin and Daniel Boeschen studied the performance appraisal process in an American wood products company with 7,000 employees. The supervisors were supposed to meet each of their subordinates regularly to discuss their performance. At the end of each year the supervisors held special sessions with each subordinate to rate their performance and to decide on standards for the coming year. The supervisor's rating determined the size of the subordinate's salary increase.

Sixty separate pairs of supervisors and subordinates were chosen at random for the study. Their attitudes to the company's appraisal procedures were assessed by two questionnaires, issued two weeks before and then one month after the annual review sessions.

Supervisors and subordinates had different perceptions of the appraisal scheme. The supervisors overestimated their knowledge of their subordinates' jobs and the quality of the feedback they gave them. The subordinates felt that their supervisors' ratings of their performance were too low and that the feedback they got was vague. The subordinates who were most satisfied with the scheme were those who got frequent, detailed and considerate feedback.

The authors conclude that feedback should be regular, not annual, and that supervisors should improve their knowledge of their subordinates' perceptions. Feedback works if it is understood and regarded favourably by the recipient. But supervisors may try to maintain a friendly atmosphere by avoiding criticism and unpleasant feedback.

From Daniel Ilgen, Richard Paterson, Beth Martin and Daniel Boeschen, "Supervisor and subordinate reactions to performance appraisal sessions", *Organizational Behaviour and Human Performance*, 1981, vol. 28, no. 3, pp. 311-30.

This is an extreme form of personality type with complex causes related mainly to early socialization. Individuals with authoritarian personalities need and like tight organizational control processes. But Norman Dixon has argued that large bureaucratic organizations like the military attract individuals with this cluster of personality traits because they offer a structured, ordered, controlled environment that is consistent with authoritarian needs.

Authoritarian individuals fit the military organization so well that they get promoted to responsible positions. The problem however is that the rigid thinking of the authoritarian personality produces disastrous decisions. Dixon provides numerous illustrations of this phenomenon from military history. The same may be true of large non military bureaucratic organizations.

The traits of the authoritarian personality . . .

"1. *Conventionalism*, i.e., rigid adherence to conventional middle-class values.
2. *Authoritarian submission*, i.e. a submissive, uncritical attitude towards the idealized moral authorities of the group with which he identifies himself.
3. *Authoritarian aggression*, i.e., a tendency to be on the look-out for and to condemn, reject and punish people who violate conventional values.
4. *Anti-intraception*, i.e., opposition to the subjective, the imaginative and the tender-minded.
5. *Superstition and stereotypy*, i.e. a belief in magical determinants of the individual's fate, and the disposition to think in rigid categories.
6. *Power and 'toughness'*, i.e. a preoccupation with the dominance-submission, strong-weak, leader-follower dimension, identification with power-figures, overemphasis upon the conventionalized attributes of the ego, exaggerated assertion of strength and toughness.
7. *Destructiveness and cynicism*, i.e. generalized hostility, vilification of the human.
8. *Projectivity*, i.e., the belief that wild and dangerous things go on in the world; the projection outwards of unconscious emotional impulses.
9. *'Puritanical' prurience*, i.e., an exaggerated concern with sexual 'goings-on'."

From Norman F. Dixon, *On the Psychology of Military Incompetence*, Futura Publications, London, 1976, p. 258.

The work of Tom Burns and George Stalker in the Scottish electronics industry in the 1950s is often used to illustrate the effectiveness of "organismic management systems" in dealing with change and of "mechanistic management systems" in dealing with routine.

Mechanistic management systems use rigid job descriptions, clear hierarchical lines of authority and responsibility, and rely on position power when decisions have to be taken. Such organizations can also be described as bureaucratic in Max Weber's sense of that term. Organismic management systems on the other hand use loose and flexible job descriptions, have vaguely defined lines of authority and responsibility, and rely on expert power to take decisions, regardless of where in the organization the expert happens to be.

At first glance, the organismic management system with its absence of hierarchical controls on behaviour sounds like a more pleasant place in which to work. The individual has considerable autonomy in the absence of oppressive hierarchical authority. But Burns and Stalker present evidence to suggest that some individuals do not like working within organismic systems because of the insecurity that the apparent freedom can create.

Lack of control creates insecurity . . .

" . . . when individuals are frustrated in their attempts to get their own work successfully completed, when they are worried by the successful rivalry of others, when they feel insecure or under attack — these situations provoke an urge for the clarity, the no-nonsense atmosphere, of a mechanistic organization. It promises so many other dividends too. It is not only quicker to divide tasks into parcels, label them 'responsibilities': and post them to subordinates or other parts of the structure; this kind of procedure has the connotations of visibly controlling others, and the appearance of knowing one's own mind, which are valued aspects of executive authority. Conversely, one has the security of unquestioned power through orders to subordinates, the security of knowing the limits of one's responsibility and of the demands and orders of superiors, which the existence of something like Queen's Regulations can give."

From Tom Burns and G. M. Stalker, *The Management of Innovation*, Tavistock Publications, London, 1961, p. 132.

Burns and Stalker argue that the "penumbra of indeterminacy" that surrounds roles in an organismic organization has three major implications. First, the lack of job specifications leads to feelings of insecurity because individuals do not know where they stand in relation to others. Second, although anxious about the insecurity, people in these kinds of circumstances do not want their positions clarified. The advantages of freedom of manoeuvre are too great. Third, the uncertainty surrounding individual jobs is a source of flexibility and efficiency in dealing with rapid technical change.

Organizations that have to cope with rapid change benefit from organismic flexibility. But their members have to suffer insecurity and anxiety.

Insecurity is good for the organization, bad for the individual . . .

" . . . the insecurity attached to ill-defined functions and responsibilities and status, by increasing the emotional charge of anxiety attached to the holding of a position, increases also the feeling of commitment and dependency on others. By this means the detachment and depletion of concern usual when people are at, or closely approaching the top of their occupational ladder, the tendency to develop stable commitments, to become a nine-to-fiver, was counteracted. All this happened at the cost of personal satisfactions and adjustment — the difference in the personal tension of people in the top management positions and those of the same age who had reached a settled position was fairly marked."

From Tom Burns and George M. Stalker, *The Management of Innovation*, Tavistock Publications, London, 1961, p. 135.

Before we argue that control is an undesirable feature of organizational life, therefore, it is necessary to recognize the positive features of the control process and the relationships between control and psychological needs. There are clearly instances where the absence of control will have adverse consequences for the psychological well being of the individual.

SOCIAL CONTROL

Graeme Salaman claims that "organizations are structures of control":

"... if (the worker) chooses not to do what management tells him (which he may be 'told' either directly and personally by managers, or through their impersonal rules and regulations about working practices, or indirectly through the technology which mediates the imperative to produce for profit) — if and when he chooses not to comply with these dictates, he will make explicit what otherwise can lie dormant, namely the question of control."

From T. Nicols and P. Armstrong, *Workers Divided*, Fontana, 1976, p. 5.

To control in the social sense means to dominate, to give orders, to exercise power, authority or influence over others, and to obtain compliance. Management control is not simply an administrative process designed to achieve economic goals. Control of employee behaviour and attitudes is an essential component of organizational functioning and survival, but clearly has undesirable connotations.

The inequality of power in our organizations, and in society as a whole, is not regarded by everyone as legitimate. Management control is a social process with political and moral components. In organizations, some individuals are controlled by others. Managers control the allocation and withdrawal of rewards and penalties such as money, career chances, conditions, status, approval and other benefits of organizational membership. This control can be regarded as a form of exploitation of those in weak subordinate positions. Control is not simply a logical process for the achievement of economic efficiency.

Definition

Social control is the process through which obedience, compliance and conformity to predetermined standards of behaviour are achieved through interpersonal and group processes.

Control is thus a property of the *relationship* between controller and controlled. Social control is a pervasive aspect of our social and organizational lives. Our behaviour is influenced in numerous ways, more or less obvious and subtle, through our relationships with others.

STOP!

In what ways is your behaviour controlled through your relationships and interactions with others?

" . . . to *manage* is to *control*. When managers lay claim to the 'right to manage' they lay claim to the right to control 'their' workers . . . "

From T. Nichols and P. Armstrong, *Workers Divided*, Fontana, 1976, p. 9.

Frederick Winslow Taylor argued that manual and managerial work should be clearly separated in the interests of efficiency. This division of labour relies on the assumption that experts are necessary to handle the complex tasks of achieving effective organizational control. This argument makes the management control function a legitimate one and explains the higher financial rewards that controllers get compared with mere workers.

But Karl Marx and his followers argue that management control is necessary for another reason. Capitalism as an economic system creates two broad classes of people. The capitalist class includes those who own and control the means of production. The working class includes those who do not own and control the means of production and who have to sell their labour power to capitalists in order to make a living.

The capitalist and working classes need each other — they are interdependent. But their interests are different. The aim of the capitalist is to make profits which can be used to accumulate more capital and make still more profits. The aim of the workers is to earn higher wages to improve their standards of living. These interests are in direct conflict and cannot be reconciled within the capitalist system. Marx regarded this as one reason why capitalism would eventually be overthrown (a prediction that has so far not come true).

The manager in a capitalist organization cannot rely on the willing co-operation, commitment and loyalty of the workforce. The relationship between capitalist and worker is not merely one of interdependence and conflict of interest. It is also an exploitative one due to the inequalities of power between the classes. The capitalist controls the resources and is in a position to refuse employment to those who question the way in which those resources are used.

The apparent compliance of workers with management directions is thus superficial. Compliance appears to be remunerative but is in reality coercive. This in part explains the organizational preoccupation with controlled performance. Employees cannot be expected to produce adequate levels of performance if left to their own devices.

Managers cannot rely on a willing workforce . . .

"The political dimension of organization employment is revealed in another obvious feature of organizations: the unequal nature of organizational life and the constant possibility of subordinates resisting or avoiding the efforts of their seniors (however mediated and obscured) to control them."

From Graeme Salaman, *Class and the Corporation*, Fontana, London, 1981, p. 144.

Harry Braverman, an American Marxist sociologist, has stimulated a great deal of interest in contemporary forms of management control and their implications for the experience of work. Braverman was not just an academic. He was a skilled coppersmith who enjoyed the practice of his craft and understood most other crafts in the shipbuilding industry. He practised pipefitting, sheet metal work, worked in a naval shipyard and a railroad repair shop, sheetmetal shops and in the manufacture of steel plate and structural steel.

Braverman argued that the need for management control to cope with uncommitted workers led to the degradation of work skills and workers. He claimed that although science and technology were demanding more education, training and exercise of mental effort, work was increasingly subdivided into routine and easy to learn fragments as Taylor had suggested. Braverman claimed that:

"... my views about work are governed by nostalgia for an age that has not yet come into being, in which, for the worker, the craft satisfaction that arises from conscious and purposeful mastery of the labour process will be combined with the marvels of science and the ingenuity of engineering, an age in which everyone will be able to benefit, in some degree, from this combination."

From Harry Braverman, *Labour and Monopoly Capital: The Degradation of Work in the Twentieth Century*, Monthly Review Press, New York, 1974, p. 7.

Braverman argued that this new age was prevented by the class relationships formed by the capitalist mode of production of goods and services. The need for managers to maintain a disciplined workforce led them into a continuing process in which approaches to control were perpetually refined and intensified.

Control of work and workers is a central theme of scientific management practice. This involves gathering workers together in one place, setting performance standards, dictating work times, using personal supervision to ensure diligence, and the enforcement of rules against distractions (such as talking and smoking). Management control is made much easier through the simplification and standardization of work activities into well defined and simple to measure tasks in which workers have no discretion. And workers who exercise less skill get paid less than skilled craftsmen.

These extensions of management control erode craft skill, reduce the worker's independence, and reduce the importance of the worker's knowledge of the craft. Workers are excluded from decisions about methods and the pace of work. Braverman on the other hand wanted to see workers:

> " ... become masters of industry in the true sense, which is to say when the antagonisms in the labour process between controllers and workers, conception and execution, mental and manual labour are overthrown, and when the labour process is united in the collective body which conducts it."

> From Harry Braverman, *Labour and Monopoly Capital: The Degradation of Work in the Twentieth Century*, Monthly Review Press, New York, 1974, p. 445.

But Braverman saw technology being used to reduce worker skill and discretion, to fragment tasks as Taylor recommended, to stifle individual development, to reduce wages and to enhance management status. The research in Scotland by David Buchanan and David Boddy also suggests that management apply new information and computing technologies in ways that:

- Reduce human intervention in work;
- Replace people with machines;
- Reduce dependence on human control of equipment and processes;
- Increase the amount of performance information available.

Control is a central theme of scientific management . . .

" ... Taylor raised the concept of control to an entirely new plane when he asserted as an *absolute necessity for adequate management the dictation to the worker of the precise manner in which work is to be performed*. Management, he insisted, could be only a limited and frustrated undertaking so long as it left to the worker any decision about the work. His 'system' was simply a means for management to achieve control of the actual mode of performance of every labour activity, from the simplest to the most complicated."

From Harry Braverman, *Labour and Monopoly Capital: The Degradation of Work in the Twentieth Century*, Monthly Review Press, New York, 1974, p. 90.

Braverman regards this as an undesirable development, a consequence of the capitalist organization of production. Attempts to improve the quality of working life through job enrichment schemes leave the inequalities of capitalism intact and are superficial. They do not alter the exploitative nature of management control in capitalist organizations.

Employees cannot be trusted . . .

"Capitalism, being based upon the *exploitation* of those who sell their labour, necessarily sets the capitalist, or his agents, problems of control, direction and legitimacy. Employees cannot be 'trusted' to identify with the goals of management, or to adhere to the spirit — or the letter — of their work instructions, for the goals of their organization, and the procedures and specifications which follow from them, are quite antithetical to their interests. The structure of the organization, and everything within it, reflects the employer's pursuit of profit at the expense of his employees, and the constant possibility and occasional reality, of their apprehending this over-riding fact, either as a source of personal withdrawal, 'instrumentality' or bloody-mindedness or as a cause for group, organized resistance."

From Graeme Salaman, *Class and the Corporation*, Fontana, London, 1981, p. 164.

Inequalities of power in organizations lead to inequalities in the distribution of other resources. These inequalities can be seen in the conditions of work of those at the bottom of the organizational hierarchy. They generally have lower wages, poorer working conditions, sometimes have to perform duties that are psychologically and physically damaging, have limited promotion and career opportunities and less job security. Those further up the hierarchy have better working conditions, financial rewards, fringe benefits and opportunities. These obvious inequalities should increase the chances of resistance to management controls.

There does however appear to be a widespread acceptance or at least tolerance in modern organizations of the need for management control. Why should this be the case when management controls highlight inequalities and adversely affect the quality of working life? The answer lies in the ways in which managers attempt to legitimate their role.

Most managers are of course today not capitalists and few actually own the organizations in which they work. Most managers are employees like their subordinates. The picture that Marx described of two principal classes is in fact oversimplified and the modern reality is much more complex. But the positions that managers hold lead them to behave as "agents of capitalism": they are paid to do their work and take their decisions as if they were owners of their employing organizations.

Managers are thus concerned with the legitimacy of their controlling role. In order to fulfil the responsibilities with which they have been charged, they need agreement from those being controlled that the management function is indeed necessary and desirable. Managers thus argue that the complexity of modern technology, the scale of manufacturing and commercial operations, and the need for efficiency all make control through hierarchy and rules necessary. These aspects of modern organizational life make the management function, and management control, appear legitimate.

Managers rely on popular acceptance of the values associated with capitalism and efficiency. The extent of compliance with management directives is a measure of the extent to which those values are accepted. One way in which legitimacy has been achieved has been through the use of control processes that *appear to be neutral* — through bureaucratic hierarchy, formality, impersonality and rules. These can be seen as necessary attributes of a modern efficient organization rather than as attempts by a managerial elite to retain their dominant position.

Managers want to retain their dominance, but do not wish to be seen as domineering because that could potentially threaten their perceived legitimacy. Managers design control systems that have the appearance of impartiality, that appear to reflect some kind of "bureaucratic logic", and that are determined by the interplay of markets, technology, and administrative necessity.

Peter Blau and Richard Schoenherr argue that management achieve legitimacy for their controls by designing them in ways that make them unobtrusive as well as apparently neutral. They call these *insidious controls:*

Management control has to appear "neutral" . . .

"Organizational control is required by capitalism and the search for profit through exploitation, not by the task, or technology, except inasmuch as these themselves are designed in terms of the search for profit. It is therefore capitalism, not industrialism, which establishes the need for control. Furthermore, all aspects of the organization reflect, in one way or another, this constant and necessary preoccupation: profit and control. The achievement of control, however, depends as much on extra-organizational factors as on internal ones. It is only in the light of external preparation and experience that internal arrangements can appear 'normal' or rational, or succeed in their purpose of employee control and direction. Finally, the centrality and primacy of control within capitalist employing organizations requires, if it is to succeed, that it appear neutral, a requirement of neutrally-designed tasks, or a reflection of some natural ordering of individual qualities and achievements. Successful organizational control is regarded as legitimate and necessary. Hence the significance attached to such legitimacy."

From G. Salaman, *Class and the Corporation*, Fontana, London, 1981, p. 167.

Definition

Insidious controls affect human behaviour and attitudes in ways that do not involve the experience of being controlled or manipulated.

Blau and Schoenherr argue that bureaucratic hierarchy of authority, explicit rules and regulations, traditional incentives and machine pacing are more or less obvious forms of control. The chain of command in an organization enforces discipline through orders and sanctions passed down a fixed hierarchy. Obedience to rules ensures discipline and predictability in behaviour and decisions. Incentives are dependent on compliance instructions and adequate performance levels. Machinery constrains the worker's behaviour and determines the pace of work in a variety of ways. These overt forms of control leave their recipients with the feeling that they have been controlled.

But Blau and Schoenherr argue that three forms of insidious control have become more important in modern organizations. These include:

Control through expert power

Educated and qualified employees can be controlled by appealing to their professional commitment to their work. Physical force, threats and mere money are not necessary. They will behave as required and achieve the required performance level because they feel that this is the "right" thing to do and value competence in their fields.

This form of insidious control creates problems. It is often difficult to identify the real decision makers in an organization. When decision makers are located, they resort to expert, technical arguments about efficiency. It is difficult to challenge or blame experts who take decisions on technical grounds in the interests of efficiency for the human, social or political consequences of their decisions.

Control through selective recruitment

Management can either recruit whoever applies for work and manage them autocratically, or recruit only those individuals with the technical competence and professional interest to perform on their own the necessary tasks to the required performance levels.

This is how universities and research institutes are run. Staff have discretion on how to perform their duties within broad policy constraints. Lecturers are rarely told what to do or how to do it. But control over lecturing activities is achieved in the long run through selective recruitment.

Control through the allocation of resources

In universities, administrators cannot significantly interfere with teaching and research work. Staffing decisions are made by individual departments and faculties. But administrators control the direction of the organization's work in the long run by the way in which resources are allocated which determines which fields can expand and which contract:

> "The allocation of personnel and other resources is the ultimate mechanism of organizational control, not only in the sense that it is fundamental and nearly always complements other mechanisms, but also in the sense that reliance primarily on it is the polar opposite of Weberian bureaucratic control through a chain of command backed with coercive sanctions."
>
> From Peter M. Blau and Richard A. Schoenherr, *The Structure of Organizations*, Basic Books, New York, 1971.

Appeal to professional commitment . . .

"Slave drivers have gone out of fashion not because they were so cruel but because they were so inefficient. Men can be controlled much more effectively by tying their economic needs and interests to their performances on behalf of employers. . . . The efforts of men can be controlled still far more efficiently than through wages alone by mobilizing their professional commitments to the work they can do best and like to do most and by putting these highly motivated energies and skills at the disposal of the organization."

From Peter Blau and Richard Schoenherr, *The Structure of Organizations*, Basic Books, New York, 1971.

Blau and Schoenherr argue that insidious controls are:

Deceptive	Because they leave those who are controlled with the feeling that they are simply conforming with the "logic of the situation", in terms of the requirements of the task in hand, or of conforming with widely agreed social values such as the need for efficiency and competence;
Elusive	Because nobody can be held accountable for harmful decisions;
Unresponsive	Because they are not recognized as forms of control and are thus immune to democratic constraints.

The experience of insidious control is quite different from the experience of overt manipulation and direction by superior authority figures. This is not a question of individuals misusing their positions. The problem lies in organization structures which create opportunities which individuals may exploit. Insidious controls appear to be neutral and appear also to be consistent with democratic values because they do not rely on direct commands from superior authority figures. So insidious controls attract little resistance and are more effective than overt uses of authority.

Many organizational employees may thus not challenge the management controls which reduce their discretion and erode their skills because the controls are not visible as such. Many facets of organizational life which are regarded as normal, taken for granted, necessary attributes of effective performance can still have a significant influence on members' behaviour. These attributes are unchallenged because they may never be regarded as management controls at all.

CONCLUSIONS

Managers are responsible for the success of the organizations which employ them. The management function incorporates several tasks that have to be carried out if the organization is to survive. These functions are however carried out mainly by an occupational group — some would say an elite — who have a vested interest in maintaining their status.

Managers are preoccupied with the control of their subordinates for two reasons. First, the goals of individual employees may not be consistent with the goals of the organization as a whole. Second, wider social class conflict creates antagonisms that lead managers to place little trust in the loyalty and commitment of their subordinates.

Managers are thus also preoccupied with the legitimacy of their organizational roles. A lot of management behaviour can be interpreted as attempts to reaffirm that legitimacy. It is clear from this why some commentators have emphasized that control is the single most important management function —that to manage is to control. Most of the chapters of this book have in fact concerned control in some form or other.

Managers are thus reluctant to engage in participation schemes which potentially represent an erosion of the "right to manage" and of management control. To lose control is to lose occupational status. Managers as an occupational group defend their controlling role because their legitimacy and social status are perceived to depend on it. Many management techniques for increasing organizational effectiveness appear to erode management control. These techniques include job enrichment, autonomous work groups, intrapreneurial groups, organismic management systems and democratic leadership style.

But we have already suggested, in Chapter 19, that managers do not necessarily lose power by delegating control. By allowing subordinates to take decisions on matters where they in fact know better — that is where they have more expert power — the manager may strengthen subordinates' beliefs in the manager's own expert power. To delegate in an appropriate way and show warranted trust and confidence in others is hardly a sign of incompetence or weakness. But many managers disagree with this analysis.

Why do managers seem more concerned with the struggle to legitimate their position power than with developing their expert power? The former is a much more complex and difficult task than the latter.

The problem for most managers here is that they too are controlled, in two distinct ways. First, managers also have superiors whose directions they must follow and to whom they must answer for their actions. The range of choices of action for the individual manager may thus be narrowly constrained. Second, managers are constrained in their behaviour by the social and organizational contexts in which they work. In the organizations that we have been discussing here, that context is a capitalist one with inherent conflicts and antagonisms. Position power is more useful than expert power in circumstances where groups are destined perpetually to disagree with each other.

SOURCES

Braverman, H., 1974, *Labour and Monopoly Capital: The Degradation of Work in the Twentieth Century*, Monthly Review Press, New York.

Blau, P. M. and Schoenherr, R. A., 1971, *The Structure of Organizations*, Basic Books, New York.

Burns, T. and Stalker, G. M., 1961, *The Management of Innovation*, Tavistock Publications, London.

Dixon, N. F., 1976, *On The Psychology of Military Incompetence*, Futura Publications, London.

Gaines, J. H., 1980, "Upward communication in industry: an experiment", *Human Relations*, vol. 33, no. 12, pp. 929-42.

Hellriegel, D. and Slocum, J. W., 1978, *Management: Contingency Approaches*, Addison-Wesley Publishing Company, Reading Massachusetts.

Ilgen, D. R. and Knowlton, W. A., 1980, "Performance attributional effects on feedback from superiors", *Organizational Behaviour and Human Performance*, vol. 25, no. 3, pp. 441-56.

Ilgen, D. R., Paterson, R., Martin, B. and Boeschen, D., 1981, "Supervisor and subordinate reactions to performance appraisal sessions", *Organizational Behaviour and Human Performance*, vol. 28, no. 3, pp. 311-30.

Lawler, E. E., 1976, "Control systems in organizations", in H. D. Dunnette (ed), *Handbook of Industrial and Organizational Psychology*, Rand McNally College Publishing Co., Chicago.

Nichols, T. and Armstrong, P., 1976, *Workers Divided*, Fontana, London.

Pascale, R. T. and Athos, A. G., 1982, *The Art of Japanese Management*, Penguin Books, Harmondsworth.

Salaman, G., 1981, *Class and the Corporation*, Fontana, London.

Storey, J., 1983, "After Japan/after Braverman: a consideration of management control, management science and social science", *Trent Business School Occasional Paper Series*, no. 3, Trent Polytechnic, Nottingham.

AUTHOR INDEX

SUBJECT INDEX